INTERNATIONAL CENTRE FOR MECHANICAL SCIENCES

COURSES AND LECTURES - No. 258

ALGEBRAIC CODING THEORY AND APPLICATIONS

EDITED BY

G. LONGO
UNIVERSITA' DI TRIESTE

WITH A PREFACE BY

CARLOS R.P. HARTMANN
SYRACUSE UNIVERSITY

Springer-Verlag Wien GmbH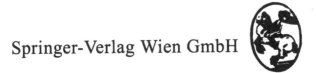

ISBN 978-3-662-38752-8   ISBN 978-3-662-39641-4 (eBook)
DOI 10.1007/978-3-662-39641-4

FOREWORD

Ten years have elapsed now from the foundation of the International Centre for Mechanical Sciences and while collecting and editing the various contributions which appear in this book, I was planning to devote it to professor Luigi Sobrero, the founder of the Centre.

But on March 11, 1979, Luigi Sobrero died from a heart attack, and I can only devote this volume to him in memoriam.

May this be a small sign of my gratitude for his associating me to the last enterprise of his life.

Giuseppe Longo

Udine, April 1979

PREFACE

The last twenty-five years have witnessed the growth of one of the most elegant and esoteric branches of applied mathematics: Algebraic Coding Theory. *Areas of mathematics which were previously considered to be of the utmost purity have been applied to the problem of constructing error-correcting codes and their decoding algorithms. In spite of the impressive theoretical accomplishments of these twenty-five years, however, only recently has algebraic coding been put into practice.*

To present some of the latest results on the theory and applications of algebraic coding, a number of scholars who have been active in the various areas of coding research were invited to lecture at the summer school on "Algebraic Coding: Theory and Applications", organized by Giuseppe Longo at the Centre International des Sciences Mécaniques (CISM) in Udine, a picturesque city in northern Italy, for a period of two weeks in July, 1978.

The first contribution, "A Survey of Error-Control Codes", by P.G. Farrell (the University of Kent, Great Britain) is an excellent compilation and condensation of numerous results on error-correcting codes. This contribution consists of four main sections. The first introduces the reader to the basic facts about error-correcting codes, the second describes various decoding methods, the third lists some classes of error-control codes which have found practical application, and the last is devoted to the performance of such codes.

The second contribution, "The Bounds of Delsarte and Lovász, and Their Applications to Coding Theory", is by R.J. McEliece (University of Illinois, U.S.A.). In 1972, P. Delsarte developed a new powerful technique for obtaining upper bounds on the largest possible number of codewords in a code of fixed length and minimum Hamming distance. This technique is nowadays usually called the linear programming approach. In 1977, L. Lovász produced an astonishingly simpl solution to a long-standing problem in information theory which was posed by C. Shannon in 1956, namely the problem of computing the zero-error capacity of a certain discrete memoryless channel having five inputs and outputs. Lovász's technique can be applied to any graph (or discrete memoryless channel), although in general it gives only an upper bound for the "Shannon capacity", rather than the true value. In his paper, McEliece offers a unified treatment of these two techniques using standard methods of linear algebra. The result is an extremely powerful and general technique for studying combinatorial packing problems. This technique is used to obtain, as special cases, the McEliece-Rodemich-Rumsey-Welch bound for binary codes and Lovász's bound on the "Shannon capacity" of many graphs.

The third contribution, "An Introduction to Anticodes", again by P.G. Farrell, is an introduction to the construction of linear anticodes and codes derived from anticodes. The study of anticodes is important in the construction of shortened codes derived from maximum-length-sequence codes. For example, Solomon and Stiffler showed that optimum binary linear codes can be constructed by deleting certain columns of a maximum-length-sequence code array. If m columns are to be deleted, it is desirable that the maximum weight, δ , of the rows of the array of deleted columns be as small as possible, since this maximum value of row weight will determine the minimum distance of the resulting code. The array of deleted columns should yield the minimum value of δ for a given m; alternatively, for a given value of δ , the maximum value of m is sought. These properties are exactly the opposite of the properties we want for a code, thus the array of deleted columns is called a linear "anti-code".

The fourth contribution, "Array Codes", by the same author, is concerned with codes formed by generalizing or iterating one or more component codes into arrays in two or more dimensions. Both known and new array codes and decoding techniques are described. The performance of such codes is also investigated.

The next contribution, "Association Schemes", by J.-M. Goethals (MBLE Research Laboratories, Brussels, Belgium) presents a survey of the algebraic theory of association schemes as developed by P. Delsarte. The material is divided into three main sections. The first section serves as a general introduction to association schemes. The eigenmatrices P and Q which play a fundamental role in the theory are introduced. The emphasis is then on a subset Y of the point set X of an association scheme. The second section deals with the important case in which the point set X of an association scheme can be given the structure of an Abelian group. In this case a dual association scheme can be defined for which the eigenmatrices are obtained by interchanging the roles of the matrices P and Q of the original scheme. For subsets Y which are subgroups of X, the above duality has a nice interpretation in terms of dual subgroups and their inner distributions. Examples of this duality are given. The third section introduces the concept of a polynomial scheme. A scheme is P-polynomial if and only if it is a metric. In this case, Y is a code for which the concept of minimum distance and external distance are well defined. A generalization of Lloyd's theorem for perfect codes is also given.

The sixth contribution, "Generalized Quadratic-Residue Codes", is by J.H. van Lint (Eindhoven University of Technology, The Netherlands). At the 1975 CISM Summer School on *Information Theory*, P. Camion introduced a generalization of *quadratic-residue* codes (*QR-codes*), and another generalization of QR-codes had been introduced one year earlier by H.N. Ward. Essentially these codes (at least in the binary case) were introduced by P. Delsarte in 1971. Recently J.H. van Lint and F.J. McWilliams showed that the methods that are used to deal with QR-codes can easily be generalized to give a completely analogous treatment of the generalized *quadratic-residue* codes (*GQR-codes*). In this paper, after a brief survey of the theory of classical QR-codes, GQR-codes are described in this way.

The seventh contribution, "*Soft-Decision Detection Techniques*", by P.G. Farrell, is a thorough survey of the existing soft-decision decoding techniques and contains more than fifty references. As J. Massey has pointed out, the use of hard-decision demodulation can, in overall system performance terms, cancel out most or all of the gain provided by the coding scheme. Hence soft-decision decoding should be adopted whenever possible.

The eigth contribution, "*Soft-Decision Decoding*", is by this writer, and presents an algebraic soft-decision decoding technique whose complexity varies inversely with the code rate. It is shown that using all of the p^{n-k} parity-checks of an (n, k) linear block code it is possible to obtain a soft-decision decoding rule which minimizes the probability of symbol error. The asymptotic performance of this decoding rule for the additive white Gaussian-noise channel is presented. A simplified soft-decision decoder for L-step orthogonalizable codes is also described. The complexity of such a decoder is comparable to that of a conventional hard-decision majority decoder. For codes in which the number of orthogonal parity checks is exactly $d_H\text{-}1$, where d_H is the minimum Hamming distance of the code, the performance of the soft-decision decoder is asymptotically optimum for the Gaussian channel. An iterative decoding technique is also discussed.

The ninth contribution, by R.M.F. Goodman (University of Hull, Great Britain), is divided into three main sections. The first section is entitled "*Towards the maximum-likelihood Decoding of Long Convolutional Codes*", and presents a new minimum-distance decoding algorithm for convolutional codes which uses a sequential decoding approach to avoid an exponential growth in complexity with increasing constraint-length. It also utilizes the distance and structural properties of convolutional codes to reduce considerably the amount of tree searching needed to find the minimum-distance path, hence making it require less computation than sequential decoding. This makes the algorithm attractive for both long and short constraint-length convolutional codes. In the second section, entitled "*On the Design of Practical Minimum Distance Convolutional Decoders*", the author assesses quantitatively the decoding effort required by his algorithm and shows that this is indeed much less than that required by sequential decoding. He also proposes modifications to the algorithm to further reduce the computational efforts. The last section is entitled "*Soft-Decision Threshold Decoders*". Coding system designers are interested in threshold decoding for convolutional codes because of the hardware simplicity of the decoder. Unfortunately, majority-decision threshold decoding is a sub-optimum scheme and this causes a loss in the coding gain. In this section, the author introduces a new method for implementing soft-decision threshold decoding which enables some of the loss to be recovered without too great a sacrifice in hardware simplicity.

The last contribution, "Algebraic Codes in the Frequency Domain", is by R.E. Blahut (I.B.M., Owego, U.S.A.). Analysis and synthesis problems in communication theory and signal processing depend heavily on reasoning in the frequency domain. In particular, in the study of real-valued or complex-valued signals, the Fourier transform plays a basic role. Likewise, when the time variable is discrete, the discrete Fourier transform plays a parallel role. Hence these transforms are among the major tools of engineers. It is also possible to define Fourier transforms for functions of a discrete index that take values in a Galois field. Finite field transforms have recently been introduced into the subject of error-control codes as a vehicle for reducing decoder complexity. However, these transforms can be made to play a much more central role in the subject. Known ideas of coding theory can be described in a frequency domain setting. For example, cyclic codes can be defined as codes whose codewords have certain specified spectral components equal to zero. Also, the decoding of many codes (including BCH, RS and Goppa codes) can be described spectrally. This paper casts much of the subject of error-control codes in a transform setting. In this way, the author hopes to stimulate interest in, and to accelerate the development of, a spectral point of view of coding. It is his belief that the spectral formulation brings the subject much closer to the subject of signal processing and makes error-control coding more accessible to the nonspecialist in coding theory.

Carlos R.P. Hartmann

Syracuse, N.Y., April 1979.

CONTENTS

Contents

NOTICE

It is unfortunate that a contribution to the summer school by professor Rom Varshamov of the Armenian Academy of Sciences, Erevan, Soviet Union, was not included in this volume, as the author could not provide the text timely.

A SURVEY OF ERROR-CONTROL CODES

P.G. Farrell
Electronics Laboratories
The University of Kent at Canterbury
Canterbury, Kent, CT2 7NT
England

4:    Practical Error-Control Codes

5:    Performance of Error-Control Codes

References

Figures

1:   Introduction

In order to introduce error-control coding, it is convenient initially to consider coding in a wider context. In general, coding is a form of mapping; that is, the conversion of a given sequence, stream or set of digits or symbols into another sequence or set of digits. Conceptually, this digital mapping process, or encoding process, may be thought of as taking place in an encoder, which operates on the input sequence of digits so as to produce an output sequence of digits with properties in some way more desirable than those of the input sequence:-

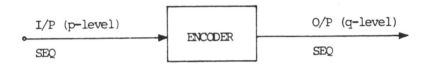

The encoder may operate in a serial or parallel mode, or in any convenient combination. The input sequence may be visualised as coming from a data source, which emits a sequence of p-level (p-ary) digits. The encoder processes these into a sequence of q-level (q-nary) digits, where $p \neq q$, in general. It is useful to define the rate (or efficiency) of the coding process performed by the encoder, as follows:

$$R_e = \frac{L_{in} \ \log_2 p}{L_o \ \log_2 q}$$

where L_{in} and L_o are the statistical average lengths of all the possible distinct input and output sequences, respectively, of the decoder.

R_e is the ratio of the maximum amount of information (in the information theory sense[1]) that can potentially be input to the encoder, over the maximum amount of information that can potentially be output from the encoder. Of course, the actual amount of information deriving from the data source can only be unaltered or decreased by passage through the encoder. Thus the transinformation[1] , and the rate or efficiency, of the overall source-encoder system are

$$I_{SYST} \leq H(X) \cdot R_e$$

and

$$R_{SYST} = \frac{H(X)}{L_{in} \log_2 p} \cdot R_e = \frac{H(X)}{L_o \log_2 q}$$

where $H(X)$ is the source entropy, and

$$R_s = \frac{H(X)}{L_{in} \log_2 p}$$

is the source relative entropy[1] or efficiency. Unless information is lost in the encoder, in which case the mapping process is not entirely one-to-one but partially many-to-one, then $R_{SYST} \leq 1$ always. Since information is not generated in the encoder,

$$R_{SYST} \leq R_s R_e$$

equality holding where there is no loss of information in the encoder. R_e may be greater than, equal to, or less than unity; it is also called the compression ratio of the encoder, when $R_e > 1$; if $R_e < 1$, then $1/R_e$ is called the expansion ratio.

When $R_c > 1$, redundancy in the encoder input sequence is reduced or removed; this is <u>source coding</u> or <u>data compression</u>[2-6]. For example, the following set of six binary 4-tuples of <u>weight</u> 2 (the weight of an n-tuple is the number of non-zero digits it contains) may be encoded into a set of six binary 3-tuples:-

I/P	O/P
1 1 0 0	0 0 0
1 0 1 0	0 0 1
1 0 0 1	0 1 0
0 1 1 0	0 1 1
0 1 0 1	1 0 0
0 0 1 1	1 0 1
$L_{in} = 4$	$L_o = 3$

Assuming the 4-tuples occur equiprobably and with statistical independence, then $H(X) = \log_2 6$, and $R_s = \log_2 6/4 \log_2 2 = 0.646$. Now $R_e = 4 \log_2 2/ 3 \log_2 2 = 1.333$, and therefore $R_s R_e = 0.862$. The aim of source coding is to make the product $R_s R_e$ approximate to unity as closely as possible.

When $R_e = 1$, the proportion of redundancy in the encoder input sequence is unchanged by the coding process, though it may be altered into a more useful form. This is <u>translation</u>, and it may be a form of <u>line</u> or <u>transmission coding</u>[7]. A simple example is conversion from multi-level (say, quaternary) digits to binary digits, to facilitate transmission of multi-level data over a binary channel:-

I/P	O/P
O	O O
1	O 1
2	1 O
3	1 1

$$L_{in} = 1 \qquad L_o = 2$$

$$R_s = 1 = R_e$$

Another example is differential encoding[8,9], which is used in PSK carrier transmission systems to facilitate demodulation. It is interesting to note that $R_e = 1$ may also result from joint[10] source and channel coding (see below).

When $R_e < 1$, redundancy is increased by the coding process. The increase may arise from a need to alter spectral or other properties of a sequence, so as to make it easier to transmit and/or receive. Methods of achieving this are additional forms of line or transmission or synchronisation coding[7,38]; and the coding process may involve partial one-to-many mapping. An example is the alternate-mark-inversion (AMI) technique used in PCM systems[11]:-

> ENCODER I/P SEQ.   ...... 1 0 1 1 0 1 0 1 1 1 0 .....
>
> "   O/P "   ...... 1 0 -1 1 0 -1 0 1 -1 1 0 ....

If the zeros and ones in input sequence are equiprobable and statistically independent (ESI), then $L_{in} = L_o$, $R_s = 1$, and $R_e = 0.631$. Another important reason for increasing the redundancy of a sequence or set of sequences is to be able to detect and possibly correct any errors that may occur during transmission over a noisy channel. This is error-control coding, or channel coding, or error-detection-and-correction (EDC) coding.[9,12-17] For example, a 6-level source may be encoded into the six weight 2 4-tuples mentioned above:-

	I/P	O/P
	0	1 1 0 0
	1	1 0 1 0
	2	1 0 0 1
	3	0 1 1 0
	4	0 1 0 1
	5	0 0 1 1
	$L_{in} = 1$	$L_o = 4$

This permits detection of all single, all triple and some double errors, in any 4-tuple. If the data source is ESI, $R_s = 1$, and

$$R_e = \log_2 6/4 \log_2 2 = 0.646.$$

The aim of channel coding is to achieve a high degree of error-control with R_e as large as possible. This aim is, unfortunately, often incompatible with the realisation of a practical coding system. The problems occur mainly in the decoder: if a high-rate powerful code is to be implemented, a decoder is often impossibly complex, whereas the encoder is relatively simple, to implement. The complexity of the decoder arises because the decoding process is a many-to-one mapping. Errors occuring during transmission or storage change or mutilate digits in the coded sequence; these errors have to be identified and correctly mapped back into the original source data sequence digits. In contrast, encoding is normally a simple one-to-one mapping process.

Interest in error-control codes and methods of coding grew out of Shannon's early work[32] on the mathematical theory of communication; the first non-trivial EDC codes were devised by Colay[33,34] and Hamming[23], and the first systematic presentation of linear binary codes was by Slepian[24]. Most work on the theory and practice of coding circuits stems from the original studies of linear sequential digital networks by Huffman[35,36] and Elspas[37].

The types of coding mentioned in this introduction are summarised in Fig. 1. Error-control codes are classified in Section 2. Methods of decoding are discussed in Section 3. Section 4 is a survey of practical error-control codes and systems. Finally, the performance of channel coding systems is reviewed in Section 5. Sufficient information is given, it is hoped, to enable definitions, descriptions and comparisons to be understood and appreciated; further details of codes and coding systems will be found in the extensive list of references.

2:   Classification of Error-Control Codes

An error-control code is a mapping of one set of sequences into another set, by means of the controlled addition of redundancy in such a way that the additional redundancy can be used to detect and/or correct any errors which may occur during storage or transmission of the sequences. Conceptually, the coding process may be visualised as taking place in an encoder, with its associated coding rate or efficiency, as defined in the Introduction above. The aim of error-control coding (or channel coding or EDC coding) is to protect the information contained in the original sequences as much as possible, with as high as possible

a value of rate R (the subscript e can be omitted without causing

confusion, as it is usual, when discussing channel codes, to assume

one-to-one mapping of ESI source (data) symbols or sequences, so that

normally $R_s = 1$).

2.1 Binary and Multi-Level Codes

If q, the number of output levels of the encoder (i.e., the output

alphabet or symbol size) is 2, then the code is <u>binary</u>; it is <u>multi-</u>

<u>level</u>, or <u>q-nary</u>, if q > 2. Most practical codes are binary, for ease

of processing, storage and transmission, and because of the availability

of relatively cheap and simple coding hardware.

2.2 Block and Non-Block (Convolutional) Codes

The encoder adds redundancy to the input or <u>data</u> sequence in one of

two basic ways

(i) The encoder may process digits in blocks, so that a block of

n consecutive coded (output) q-nary digits is related only to a

particular block of k consecutive p-ary data (input) digits. This is

<u>block coding</u>, with block length n, and rate $R = k \log_2 p / n \log_2 q =$

$\log_2 N / n$ if q = 2. N is the number of possible distinct data blocks,

which map into N possible distinct coded blocks; this complete set of

coded blocks is called the <u>code book</u> (or sometimes the <u>code</u>), and each

block is called a <u>code word</u>. The error-control code example in the

Introduction is a block code. Another simple example is the following single-parity-check (SPC) code with n = 3, p = q = 2, k = 2 and R = 2/3:-

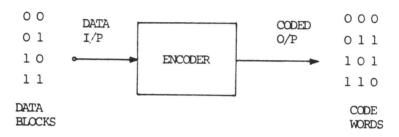

A possible encoder realisation (omitting timing arrangements, etc.) is:-

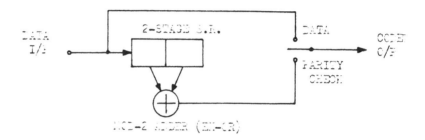

Blocks of data digits are input to the register two at a time, and are simultaneously output. A parity check (modulo-2 sum) of the two data digits in the register is computed, and output after the data digits. Successive code words may be transmitted in any convenient serial or parallel format, but are decoded independently at the receiver. All single, and triple, errors in a block may be detected.

(ii) Alternatively, an encoder may process the data digits in such a way that output blocks, or segments are associated with more than one input block. Thus the redundancy is in relationships extending across several successive coded segments. The fixed block structure of a block code is lost - it is replaced by a "sliding" block structure, and encoding becomes a quasi-continuous process. This is non-block coding, or tree coding, since the output of the encoder may be represented by a tree with branches corresponding to possible coded segments. Possible paths through the tree are code sequences, and correspond to the code words of a block code. The encoder accepts k_o input digits at a time, and stores h of these input segments. It outputs n_o $(n_o \geq k_o)$ coded digits (a code segment) between acceptance of each input or data segment, and discards the "oldest" stored data segment. Each n_o length code segment is computed from all the $h.k_o$ digits stored in the encoder. The quantity hk_o is called the encoding constraint length of the code; $n = hn_o$ is the decoding constraint length, or just the constraint length, of the code. The constraint length represents the maximum spread of digits over which the redundancy relationships hold. The rate is $R = k_o \log_2 p / n_o \log_2 q = \log_2 N_c / n_o$ if $q = 2$ and N_o is the number of distinct data input segments. Also, since $k_o/n_o = hk_o/hn_o = hk_o/n$, then $R = h \log_2 N_o/n$. It is conceivable that the encoder could modify its mapping process each time a fresh k_o length data segment is input; this is the most general form of non-block or tree encoder. In practice, however, most useful non-block encoders process each fresh data segment alike; this is convolutional, or recurrent, coding[30,52,53]. An example of a convolutional code, with $k_o = 1$, $n_o = 2$, $h = 2$, $n = 4$, and $R = \log_2 2/2 = 1/2$ is:-

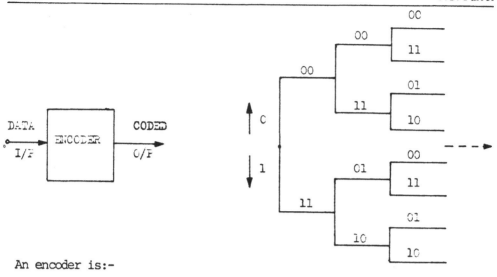

An encoder is:-

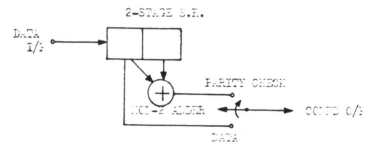

Data and check digits are output alternately. Again, transmission of
the coded digits may be in any convenient format, but to decode a
non-block code many successive received segments are processed. In
theory, the whole received sequence should be processed, but this is in
practice impossible; provided a certain minimum number of segments
are processed (about 5h), the loss of performance is negligible. This
code is capable or correcting any single error in a constraint length
(4 digits).

    The quantity $v = hk_o - 1$ is often called the degree of a con-
volutional code; v+1 represents the length of the encoding shift
register (SR). Note that if h = 1, a block code results; thus block

codes are a sub-class of the class of non-block codes.

2.3 Linear and Non-Linear Codes

If the encoder determines the coded digits by combining the relevant
data digits in sums modulo-q (generalised parity checks), and q is a
power of a prime, then a <u>linear code</u> results. This is equivalent to
saying that a code with block or constaint length n is linear if and
only if it is a subspace of the vector space of all n-tuples[12,54]; a
code is <u>non-linear</u> otherwise. The codes given as examples in section
2.2 above are linear codes - the error-control code mentioned in the
Introduction is non-linear. Codes may be non-linear either because the
redundant digits are not parity checks (i.e. are some non-linear
function of the data digits, e.g. NAND), or because there is no data-
digit/redundant-digit structure in the code word or segment (e.g.,
the constant weight block code given in the Introduction).

Because a linear code is a subspace of the vector space of all
n-tuples, it is possible to generate all the code words of a linear
code from a set of k basis code words, or hk_o basis sequences,
corresponding to the basis vectors of the subspace[12-17]. The k x n
or hk_o x n array of basis words or sequences is called the <u>generator</u>
<u>matrix</u> of the code. All the code words or sequences may be generated
by taking all the q^k (or $q^{hk}o$) linear combinations of the basis words
(or sequences); ie.e.:-

$$[x] = [k] . [G]$$

where $[x]$ is the desired code word or sequence and $[k]$ is the data (information) digits to be encoded. $[G]$ may, by row (or column)

interchange, or by linear combinations or rows, be expressed in

standard echelon form (SEF), or canonical echelon form. In the case of

a block code:

$$[G]_{SEF} = [I : g]$$

where $[I]$ is a k x k unit matrix, and $[g]$ is a k x c matrix of columns of

which specify the data digits involved in each check digit sum (parity

check equation). In the case of a lienar convolutional code;

$$[G]_{SEF} = \begin{bmatrix} I & g_1 & 0 & g_2 & & 0 & g_h \\ & & I & g_1 & & 0 & g_{h-1} \\ & & & & & & \\ 0 & & & & & & \\ & & & & & 0 & g_2 \\ & & & & & I & g_1 \end{bmatrix}$$

where the $[I]$ are k_o x k_o unit matrices, the $[0]$ are k_o x k_o null

matrices and the $[g_i]$ are k_o x (n_o-k_o) matrices. In the case of a

general tree code (i.e., a non-convolutional code) the rows of the

partitions below the top partition would not be truncated shifts of the

contents of the top partition; instead all the possible g_i could be

different. Codes with generator matrices which reduce to the same

matrix in SEF are equivalent; that is, they have the same error-

control properties.

The genrator matrices of the codes used as examples in section 2.2
are respectively:-

$$
\left[G \right]_{SPC} = \left[\begin{array}{cc|c} 1 & 0 & 1 \\ 0 & 1 & 1 \end{array} \right]
$$

and
$$
\left[G \right]_{CONV} = \left[\begin{array}{cc|cc} 1 & 1 & 0 & 1 \\ \hline 0 & 0 & 1 & 1 \end{array} \right]
$$

Because of the continuous nature of convolutional encoding, the generator
matrix of a convolutional code is potentially semi-infinite in both
dimensions.

The parity-check equations of a linear code also describe the code.
They may be written in the form

$$
[H] \ \{x\} = \{0\}
$$

where $[H]$ is a $c \times n$ (or $h(n_o - k_o) \times n$) matrix specifying the check
equations, $\{x\}$ is a code word (or sequence (now in column vector
notation) and $\{0\}$ is the null column vector. The above equation states
that any code word or sequence satisfies the parity check equations.
$[H]$, in the case of a block code, may also be expressed in SEF:-

$$
[H] = [h \ \vdots \ I]
$$

where $[I]$ is a $c \times c$ unit matrix. It can then be shown that

$$
[G] \cdot [H]^t = [0]
$$

and $\therefore$ $[g] = [h]^t$

where subscript t indicates matrix transpose.

For convolutional codes:-

$$
[H] = \begin{bmatrix} h_1 & I & & & & & & & & \\ h_2 & 0 & h_1 & I & & & & O & & \\ h_3 & 0 & h_2 & 0 & h_1 & I & & & & \\ & & & & & & \searrow & & & \\ h_h & 0 & & h_3 & 0 & h_2 & 0 & h_1 & I \end{bmatrix}
$$

where the $[I]$ are $(n_o-k_o) \times (n_o-k_o)$ matrices, the $[0]$ are $(n_o-k_o) \times k_o$ matrices, and $[g_1] = [h_1]^t$.

For the codes used as examples above:-

$$[H]_{SPC} = \begin{bmatrix} 11 & \vdots & 1 \end{bmatrix}$$

i.e. $[h] = \begin{bmatrix} 1 & 1 \end{bmatrix}$ and $[h]^t = \begin{bmatrix} 1 \\ 1 \end{bmatrix}$

and $[H]_{CONV} = \begin{bmatrix} 1 & 1 & \vdots & 0 & 0 \\ 1 & 0 & \vdots & 1 & 1 \end{bmatrix}$

i.e. $[g_1] = [g_2] = [1] = [h_1]^t = [h_2]^t$.

Again, $[H]_{CONV}$ is potentially semi-infinite.

Since $N = q^k$ and $N_o = q^{k_o}$, the rate of a linear code is simply $R = k/n$ or $R = k_o/n_o = hk_o/n$. It is convenient to specify a linear block code by means of the numbers (n,k) and a convolutional code by (n,hk_o).

Strictly, convolutional codes may be linear or non-linear, just as tree codes, of which convolutional codes are a sub-class, may be linear or non-linear. Because linear codes are always used in practice, however, the term "convolutional code" has come to always mean "linear convolutional code". This also accords with the fact that convolutional encoding is equivalent to convolving the information stream with the generator sequence of the encoder[53].

2.4 Group Codes

Another consequence of the subspace property of a linear code is that the set of all code words or sequences with block or constraint length n forms a group under digit-by-digit modulo-q addition. Thus the sum of two or more code words (or sequences) is another code word (or sequence). This may be verified for the above linear code examples. Thus all linear codes are group codes, but the reverse is not necessarily true: some group codes are non-linear. For example, the q = 4, n = 3, N = 16 block code, having code words constructed with the symbols 0, 1, 2, 3 and generated from all the lienar (mod-4) combinations of the two words 1 0 1 and 0 1 1, is a group code, but is non-linear. It is a group code because the code words satisfy the axioms for a group (closure, association, identity and inverse[12]), under digit-by-digit modulo-4 addition. It is not a linear code because the symbols 0, 1, 2 and 3 do not form a field; i.e., 2 does not have a multiplicative inverse. Thus the code is not a sub-space. One consequence of this is that the above code is not equivalent to the code generated from all linear (mod.-4) combinations of the words 2 0 2 and 0 2 2. The first code, which has the generator matrix

$$\begin{bmatrix} 1 & 0 & 1 \\ 0 & 1 & 1 \end{bmatrix}$$

can be used for detection of all single errors, (i.e. has Hamming distance 2, see section 2.7 below), whereas the second code, which has generator matrix

$$\begin{bmatrix} 2 & 0 & 2 \\ 0 & 2 & 2 \end{bmatrix}$$

is not capable of detecting all single errors (i.e. has Hamming distance 0 see section 2.7 below). Reducing the generator matrix of this code to SEF is not possible, because it leads to the generator matrix of the first code, to which it is not equivalent; this is another consequence of 0, 1, 2 and 3 not forming a field. These two group but non-linear codes appear to have all the other properties of linear codes. Petersen and Weldon[12] state that "linear" codes may be defined with symbols which form a ring, thus putting no constraint on the value of q. Certainly, group codes may be found for all values of q, as in the case of binoid codes[27], for example. In order to define a strictly linear code constructed from 4-level digits, it is necessary to use the symbols 0, 1, A, B, with addition and multiplication tables appropriately constructed so that these symbols form a field. This is necessary for all values of q which are not prime, but are a power of a prime[18]. When q is a prime p, then the integers may be used as symbols. Thus codes constructed from integer symbols are both group and linear when q is a prime. Because binary codes with symbols 0 and 1 may be both group and linear, and since binary codes are also by far the most used type of codes, the term "group code" is often used in the literature[19,20] to mean "linear binary code". A more general class of multi-level codes with group properties is the class of Group Codes for the Gaussian Channel[16,28]; Permutation Modulation Codes[26] are a sub-class of this class.

2.5 Systematic and Non-Systematic Codes

The code words of a systematic code may be partitioned into data or information digits, and redundant digits. Thus the data or information digits to be encoded appear unchanged (except possibly for translation, see Introduction) in the code word of a block code or the code sequence of a non-block code. In the case of block codes, the definition of systematic sometimes includes the restriction that the information digits must appear consecutively in the left-most positions of the code word; e.g. $k_1 k_2 k_3 k_4 c_1 c_2 c_3$ is systematic, but $c_1 c_2 k_1 c_3 k_2 k_3 k_4$ is not (using k_i and c_j to represent information and redundant digits, respectively). No such restriction is applied to non-block codes. Systematic codes may be linear or non-linear, since redundant digits may be calculated using a linear (i.e. parity check) or non-linear rule. The linear codes used as examples in section 2.2 are both systematic; the non-linear code in the Introduction is non-systematic. In the linear code case, the distinction between systematic and non-systematic is trivial, because if the information digits do not appear explicitly in a code word, then they can be made to do so by conversion of the generator matrix of the code into SEF. In the linear convolutional code case, the distinction is not trivial. On the one hand, systematic linear convolutional codes are free from the catastrophic[21] behaviour which can occur if a

potentially infinite weight input data sequence can give rise to a
finite weight code sequence. On the other hand, the error control
performance of non-systematic linear convolutional codes is often
superior[22] to that of systematic codes with the same rate and constraint
length.

In the early literature on block codes[23,24], "systematic" was used
to mean "linear and binary".

2.6 Cyclic Codes

Cyclic codes are an important practical sub-class of block codes.
A code is cyclic if all the cyclic translates of every code word are also
code words in the code. A cyclic translate of a code word is the new
sequence formed by cyclically shifting all the digits in the code used by
one or more digits. The simple SPC code introduced in Section 1 is a
cyclic code:

0 0 0 → has not distinct cyclic translates

0 1 1 → has translates 1 0 1 and 1 1 0   which are other

1 0 1 → has translates 0 1 1 and 1 1 0   code words in

1 1 0 → has translates 0 1 1 and 1 0 1   each case.

A cyclic code may be non-linear, but almost all practical cyclic
codes are linear.

A linear cyclic code may be defined in terms of a Generator Polynomial.
In the binary case, any polynomial in a dummy variable x, say, with
coefficients over GF(2), can be a generator polynomial, $G(x)$. The degree
of the polynomial is the number of check digits, c. If the polynomial

belongs to the exponent p then full cyclic codes exist with block length

n = i.p, i = 1, 2, ... (i.e., the shortest full cyclic code will have

n = p). Thus k = n - c = ip - c. The exponent to which a polynomial

belongs is the least value of p for which the polynomial exactly divides

x^p + 1, in GF(2). The generator matrix of the code may be constructed

by taking G(x) (in its binary form) as the bottom row of $[G]$, xG(x)

as the second row, and so on, with $x^{n-c-1}G(x)$ as the top row. The

cyclic nature of this matrix guarantees the cyclic nature of the code,

because the code is linear (i.e., the code words are linear combinations

of the rows of $[G]$). $\ulcorner G \urcorner$ will not be in SEF, but by row interchange

and combination, it can be made so (column interchange is not possible,

as this destroys the cyclic properties of the code). $[H]$ can be found

from $[G]$ in the usual way. As an example, consider the polynomial:

$$G(x) = x^3 + x + 1 \equiv 1 0 1 1$$

which belongs to 7. Thus c = 3, n = i.7 = 7, say, k = 7 -3 = 4, and

$$[G] \equiv \begin{bmatrix} x^3G(x) \\ x^2G(x) \\ xG(x) \\ G(x) \end{bmatrix} = \overset{\longleftarrow 7 \longrightarrow}{\begin{bmatrix} 1 & 0 & 1 & 1 & 0 & 0 & 0 \\ 0 & 1 & 0 & 1 & 1 & 0 & 0 \\ 0 & 0 & 1 & 0 & 1 & 1 & 0 \\ 0 & 0 & 0 & 1 & 0 & 1 & 1 \end{bmatrix}} 4 \quad \begin{matrix} d \\ \\ c \\ \\ b \\ \\ a \end{matrix}$$

$$x^3 + x + 1 \longleftarrow G(x)$$

Converting to SEF:

$$[G]_{SEF} = \begin{bmatrix} 1 0 0 0 & 1 0 1 \\ 0 1 0 0 & 1 1 1 \\ 0 0 1 0 & 1 1 0 \\ 0 0 0 1 & 0 1 1 \end{bmatrix} \begin{matrix} a + b + d \\ a + c \\ b \\ a \end{matrix}$$

$$1 + x + x^2 + x^4 \longleftarrow \quad H(x)$$

$$\text{Hence } [H] = \begin{bmatrix} 1 1 1 0 & 1 0 0 \\ 0 1 1 1 & 0 1 0 \\ 1 1 0 1 & 0 0 1 \end{bmatrix}$$

In this case there are four sets of cyclic translates. This is a single-error-correcting (SEC) code.

The rows of $[G]$ are multiples of $G(x)$, so that all the code words of a cyclic code are multiples of $G(x)$. To encode, check digits must be associated with the information digits in such a way that the resulting code word is a multiple of $G(x)$. This is done as follows:

Let the information digits, followed by c consecutive zeros (i.e. a code word with the check digits all identically equal to zero) be represented by a polynomial $F(x)$. Then

$$F(x) = Q(x) G(x) + R(x)$$

where $R(x)$ is the remainder when $F(x)$ is divided by $G(x)$.

Thus $F(x) + R(x) = X(x) = Q(x) G(x)$

is the desired code word, since $X(x)$ is a multiple of $G(x)$. Therefore encoding for a cyclic code consists of dividing $F(x)$ by $G(x)$ to find $R(x)$, so that $F(x) + R(x)$ can be transmitted. Since $F(x) = x^c.K(x)$, this can be conviently be done by simultaneously multiplying

$K(x)$ by x^c and dividing by $G(x)$. An encoder for the
above example is thus:

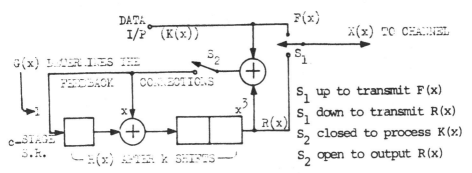

S_1 up to transmit $F(x)$
S_1 down to transmit $R(x)$
S_2 closed to process $K(x)$
S_2 open to output $R(x)$

Since $G(x)$ divides $x^p + 1$ exactly, there is a polynomial $H(x)$ such
that

$$G(x)\ H(x) = x^p + 1$$

$H(x)$ is the parity check polynomial of the cyclic code (compare the
above equation with the previously quoted equation for a general linear
code $[G].[H]^t = [O]$). $H(x)$ is the top row of the $[H]$ matrix of a cyclic
code (see, e.g., the $[H]$ matrix above). $[H]$ may be constructed from
$H(x)$ in a way similar to the construction of $[G]$ from $G(x)$: that is, by
taking $H(x)$, $xH(x)$, $x^2H(x)$, $\ldots x^{c-1}H(x)$ as the rows of $[H]$, and then
converting to SEF. This corresponds to the fact that the parity check
equations of a cyclic code are also cyclic. Thus it is also possible,
by implementing the cyclic parity checks, to encode a cyclic code with a
k-stage shift register[12].

2.7 Codes for Random Errors and for Burst Errors

Information (data) protected by encoding into code words or
sequences is usually transmitted (or stored) by means of an analogue base-
band or modulated carrier signal. This signal may be perturbed by a

variety of noise or interference effects, such as thermal noise, impulses,
fading, intersymbol interference, adjacent-channel interference, etc.
All these perturbations can lead to the generation of errors in the digits
of the code words or sequences after demodulation. Thus it is convenient,
in the context of error-control coding, to represent the noisy analogue
transmission channel by means of a simple digital model consisting of a
modulo-q adder and error generator:-

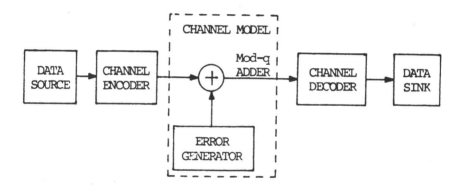

If x is a transmitted code word (or sequence), and e in an error sequence
representing the errors which occur during transmission of x, then y,
the received word (or sequence) is given by y = x + e, where the
addition is mod-q.

When the transmission channel is perturbed by predominantly white
Gaussian noise, and demodulation is symmetric, favouring no particular
symbol, then errors occur at random (i.e., with a binomial probability
distribution), so the equivalent error generator in the model is a
random error generator. In the binary case, the error generator produces
binomially distributed ONES to represent errors, with a given error
probability, P_e, and ZEROS to represent no error. This random error

model is called the binary symmetric channel[1,12] (BSC);   the error

probability P_e is the cross-over probability or error rate of the BSC.

Most error-control codes are designed to correct the random errors

generated by this model.

In order to be able to detect and correct an error pattern e, it is

necessary that the received sequence y = x + e be different from any

other code word (or sequence) in the code.   Thus, to detect single

errors, all the sequences resulting from an error occurring in any one

digit of a code word must not be another code word;   that is, some

sequences must be made redundant.   In the case of the simple SPC code,

for example, the sequences that result when a single error occurs are

not any of the code words.   Notice that the distance between each pair of

code words (i.e. the number of digit positions in which they differ)

is 2, whereas the distance of a non-redundant set of words is unity.

To correct a single error, the "opening up" process must continue

still further.   This may be illustrated with the following SED code

(see section 4.):-

$$(k_1 \ k_2 \ c_1 \ c_2 \ c_3)$$

0	0	0	0	0	
1	0	1	1	0	code words
0	1	1	0	1	
1	1	0	1	1	

k = 2, c = 3

n = 5, N = 4

All the other 28 5-tuples are redundant sequences.   The minimum distance

between each pair of code words is now 3.   All redundant sequences

resulting from a single error in a given code word will be "closer" to

that code word than any other code word, so correction can unambiguously be done. A geometrical analogy may now be invoked: to ensure t-error correction (of random errors), each code word, represented by a point in n-dimensional space, must be surrounded by a "sphere" of "radius" at least t, each point in the sphere representing a redundant (non-code-word) sequence.

Thus, if d = Hamming[23] distance of the code,

then   d = minimum value of the distances between any pair

                 of code words,

$$x_i, x_j \ (i \neq j),$$

$$= \min_{i,j} \{w(x_i \oplus x_j)\}$$

                 where $\oplus \equiv$ modulo-2 addition, and

                 $w(x)$ = weight of x;

$$= \min_i \{w(x_i)\}, \text{ if the code is linear, since the}$$

                                mod-2 sum of any two code words

                                is another code word.

The random error control power of the code is then:

$t = \left\lfloor \dfrac{d-1}{2} \right\rfloor$, the number of errors the code can correct;

$e = d-1$, the number of errors the code can detect (the

                 spheres may overlap but must not include a code

                 word); and in general

$d = t+e+1$, the spheres overlapping to a certain extent, but

                 $t \leq e$ (since correction implies detection first);

                 this is partial error correction combined with

                 error detection.

The above analysis was oriented towards block codes, but the same considerations apply to convolutional codes. The minimum distance measure in this case is called the free distance, d_{free}, and n is the decoding constraint length. For the simple convolutional code introduced in section 2.2, d_{free} = 3, which makes the code single-error-correcting.

If the transmission channel is perturbed by impulse noise or by fading, for example, then errors will occur in bursts; that is, the channel will be characterised by periods (which may be quite short) when the incidence of errors is high (the burst) separated by hopefully longer periods during which errors do not occur (or are very infrequent). The error generator in the model is then a burst error generator, and this model is called the classic bursty channel[28] (CBC). Of interest is the distribution of burst lengths (the burst length is defined as the total number of consecutive digits spanning the period of the burst, including the first and last digit in error in the burst), the distribution of the relative number of errors in the burst (i.e. the distribution of burst error density), and the distribution of error-free gap-length between bursts. In practice, since the occurrence, length and density of a burst are all random variables, it is difficult to be precise about the minimum, average and maximum values of these parameters (e.g., two adjacent short bursts can also be interpreted as one longer burst). The synthesis of codes capable of detecting and correcting bursts of errors, subject to a minimum error-free guard-space between bursts, is well understood, however; particularly in the case of block codes. A burst-error-control code[12,13] with burst length b and guard space g is capable of detecting and/or correcting any error pattern involving b or fewer consecutive digits, provided the next burst does not occur until g or more error-free digits have been received. The same general considerations that applied to random-error-control codes apply also to burst-error-control codes. The "burst distance" between the code words (or sequences) must be such that no burst of length $\leq$ b can change one code word into another, for burst-error detection; in addition, for burst-error correction, the received sequence must be "nearest" to the code word that was actually transmitted. These may seem to be more stringent conditions than those imposed on random-error-control codes; but a code capable of controlling bursts of length b is potentially more efficient than a code capable of controlling b random errors, because of the fact that in the burst case the errors are known to fall within a span of up to b digits.

Burst-error-control convolutional codes were originally called recurrent codes[29]; later recurrent was used to mean both random and burst error-control convolutional codes[30], but recently it seems to have fallen out of use.

Most practical channels cannot be modelled with either the BSC or the CBC, because they exhibit longer or shorter periods during which errors are few and approximately randomly distributed, interspersed with periods of higher error-rate or bursts of errors. These so-called compound or diffuse channels (or channels with memory) are difficult to model accurately[31], and present a severe coding problem. There exist, however, block and convolutional codes capable of correcting both random and burst errors (see Section 4).

2.8 Methods of Achieving Error Correction

Correction is the ultimate purpose of error control. It can be achieved by using an error correcting code: this is forward error control (FEC). It can also be achieved if an error detection code is used in conjunction with an auxiliary feedback channel which can initiate the re-transmission of any data received in error; this is re-transmission error control (REC). Label the data source A, and the data sink B. If a feed-back or return link is available from B to A, then it can be used in one of two basic ways:-

(i) Data is simultaneously stored at A and transmitted to B without coding. It is then transmitted back to A via the feedback link, where it is compared with the stored data. Any digit found to be in error (in practice the blocks containing the errors) are then re-transmitted to B, and the process is repeated as many times as required. This is information feedback; the feedback link must have the same capacity as the forward link.

(ii) Data is transmitted with coding for error detection from A to B. At B, a request for the re-transmission of any blocks found to contain errors is sent to A via the feedback link. The capacity of the feedback link can now be much less than that of the forward link. This is decision feedback, or ARQ (Automatic request for a repeat[39,40]). If each block is acknowledged by B before transmission of the next block from A begins, operation is revertive. Non-revertive operation, which can take many forms[41,42] is more efficient, though also more complex: A transmits

blocks continuously, without pausing for B to acknowledge, and
interruption for re-transmission does not take place until after the
end of the block currently being transmitted.

The use of a feedback link does not increase the capacity of the
forward link, but error control can be achieved more efficiently, and
with less complexity, if one is available, because of the existence of
powerful yet simple error detection codes. Hybrid FED-ARQ systems[45,46]
combine forward error correction with error detection and re-transmission
via a decision feedback link; such systems overcome some of the problems
(e.g. low rate at high error rates) of pure ARQ systems. A feedback
channel can also be used to optimise the operation of the forward link
demodulator-detector or of the decoder. The former adaptive detection
type of system is sometimes called sequential decision detection[43,44].
The latter adaptive decoding type has been called Adaptive Incremental
Redundancy[47] and REC with Memory[48]. Adaptive coding REC systems with
variable block length[49] (i.e. variable rate); with fixed block length
but variable redundancy[50]; and combining block and convolutional
codes[59], have also been studied. With the rapid development of data
communication networks and packet switching, REC coding procedures are
often embedded in the data handling protocols of these networks[51].
REC and hybrid systems normally involve block codes, but can also
incorporate convolutional codes[60].

2.9 Summary

The various major types of EDC code introduced in this section are summarised in Figs. 2 - 4.

- Codes may be <u>binary</u> or <u>multi-level</u> (q-nary); most practical codes are binary, though applications for multi-level codes are opening up because of the increasing use of m-ary signalling, and the advent of CCD multi-level processors.

- Codes may be <u>block</u> (independent code words) or <u>non-block</u> (a sequence of inter-related segments); the theory and practice of block codes is better understood and developed, but the performance of non-block codes is often superior. Block codes may be desirable, however, in certain situations; such as for the transmission of short messages, when system synchronisation has to be achieved very rapidly, or when very simple codes are required. The most important practical class of non-block codes is the <u>convolutional</u> codes.

- Codes may be <u>linear</u> (parity check) or <u>non-linear</u>. Linear codes have a high degree of mathematical structure, which makes them relatively easy to synthesise, encode and decode. The performance of non-linear codes is potentially superior, however.

- All linear codes are <u>group</u> codes; this additional mathematical structure is a useful further property of linear codes. Certain non-linear group codes are also of interest.

- <u>Cyclic</u> codes (code words are cyclic shifts of each other) are a large practical class of block codes; though cyclic codes may be linear or non-linear, most useful cyclic codes are linear.

- Codes may be <u>systematic</u> (explicit data digits) or <u>non-systematic</u>; the distinction is trivial for block codes, but is vital for convolutional

codes, because though non-systematic convolutional codes have potentially
superior performance, they also are liable to catastrophic behaviour.

- Codes may be used to control random or burst errors; and may be
used to detect or correct errors.

- Error correction may be achieved by means of forward error control
using an error-correcting code; or by means of re-transmission error
control, using an error-detecting code, and a feedback channel. The
advantages of FEC are that no feedback channel is required, and that data
flow is constant without the need for buffer storage. The disadvantages
are that relatively high complexity is required for efficient (high rate)
powerful codes, and that never more than about half the possible error
patterns can be corrected (i.e., where N = Z). The advantages of REC
are that redundancy is used when it is required (i.e., when errors occur),
that almost all error patterns can be detected and corrected (by making c
c or n_o-k_o large enough), and that adaptive or variable redundancy methods
are easily added on. The disadvantages are the need for a feedback channel,
and the variable data flow possibly necessitating transmitter and receiver
buffers.

3.   Methods of Decoding Error-Control Codes

3.1   General Comments

Conceptually, there is only one optimum way to decode an error-
control code: the received sequence is "compared" with all the possible
code words or sequences in the code, and the code word or sequence
"nearest" to the received sequence, according to some suitable measure

(or metric), is selected as the one most likely to have been transmitted. A suitable measure is Hamming minimum distance in the case of random errors, and some other distance measure (burst distance) in the case of burst errors. Now in practice this complete decoding is often either too complex or too time-consuming to do. Thus there are a variety of practical decoding methods which seek to reduce the complexity of the basic method; some of these methods are optimum, and some are not (incomplete decoding or bounded distance decoding).

It is often convenient to think of the decoding process as being in two stages: error detection followed by error correction. The initial detection stage determines whether or not the received sequence contains detectable errors; i.e., is it a possible code word (or sequence) or not? If it is not a code word or sequence, then the subsequent correction stage consists of finding the code word (or sequence) nearest to the received sequence. This splitting of the decoding process emphasises that any error pattern that converts one code word into another is undetectable, and is therefore by definition not correctable. Furthermore, the complexity of decoding is found to occur mainly in the correction stage; as will be shown below, error detection is quite simple to implement. Finally, the correction process may itself be incorrect; if there are more errors than the code has power to cope with, then a wrong correction will be made, thus adding further errors to the original ones.

If re-transmission error control (REC) is possible, then only the initial, or error detection, stage of decoding is required. This greatly simplifies decoding, but a feedback channel is required. A simple partial-error-correction decoding algorithm (incomplete decoding) can also be used to advantage with REC. Most of what follows is concerned with FEC, unless otherwise stated.

3.2 Minimum Distance Decoding

This is the basic decoding algorithm introduced at the beginning of section 2.1: comparison of the received sequence with all possible code words or sequences, and selection of the nearest. It is quite a simple algorithm conceptually, but is impossibly complex to implement if the number of code words (for a block code), or the number of input sequences (2^{hk_o}, for a convolutional code) exceeds about 1000. Thus, if the block or constraint length of the code is long, then the rate must be low. It is, however, the only optimum decoding algorithm applicable to non-linear block codes. It is an optimum (i.e. maximum likelihood) decoding algorithm. It is not often considered for use with burst-error-correcting codes. Computation with this algorithm may be halved if the code is transparent; that is, when the logical complement (inverse) of every code word (or sequence) is also in the code. Further simplification will be described below. Some of the simplified versions are fully equivalent to the basic algorithm, in the sense of still being optimum, and so are sometimes also called minimum distance decoding algorithms. To distinguish the basic algorithm from the simplified versions, it may be called full minimum distance decoding.

3.3 Syndrome Decoding

If the code is linear, then minimum distance decoding can be considerably simplified. Consider

$$[y] \cdot [H]^t = [S]$$

where $[y]$ is the received sequence, $[H]^t$ the parity check matrix of the code, and $[S]$ is a c-digit (or an $h(n_o-k_o)$-digit) row matrix called the syndrome. Now

$$[y] = [x] + [e]$$

where $[x]$ is a code word or sequence, and $[e]$ is an error sequence. Also, from linear code theory (section 2.2)

$$[x] \cdot [H]^t = [0]$$

Therefore, $\quad [y] \cdot [H]^t = [e] \cdot [H]^t = [S]$

Thus the syndrome pattern is independent of the particular code word or sequence transmitted, and is dependent only on the error pattern. Thus there is a correspondence between error patterns and syndromes; since many error patterns can give rise to the same syndrome, and there are q^c (or $q^{h(n_o-k_o)}$) syndromes, only q^c (or $q^{h(n_o-k_o)}$) distinct error patterns may be corrected. There is then a one-to-one correspondence between correctable error patterns and syndromes. Every error pattern, except those patterns which are non-zero-weight code words (by the group property of linear codes, these are the patterns which convert one code word into another), will result in a non-zero syndrome. Thus error detection is very simple in the case of a linear code. The operation of multiplying $[y]$ by $[H]^t$ is, because of the structure of $[H]$, identical with re-calculation of parity checks from the received information digits, and comparison with the received parity checks;   that is:

$[S]$ = [re-calculated parity checks] + [received parity checks].

This operation may be simpler to implement than matrix multiplication; it is almost identical with the encoding operation, and is hardly more complex.   It is particularly simple in the case of a cyclic linear code.

Thus complete decoding can be implemented in two stages: (a) syndrome calculation, followed by (b) determination of the error pattern corresponding to the syndrome.   Step (b) can be implemented in a number of ways:-

(i)   By storing a <u>list</u> of syndromes and their corresponding error patterns;   this, again, is complex if the number of syndromes exceeds about 1000.

(ii)   By systematically searching through all the correctable error patterns, calculating the syndrome for each, until the syndromes agree;   the decoding delay of this <u>systematic search</u> algorithm may be unacceptably large if the number of correctable patterns is very large.   This method becomes a form of bounded distance (incomplete) decoding if the set of error patterns searched through is restricted (e.g., if a t-error-correcting code, to just the error patterns of weight $\leq$ t).

(iii)   By implementing a combinatorial logic circuit to convert the syndrome into its error pattern.   This method (normally bounded distance) is impractical for t > 3, but is applicable to both block and convolutional codes. It is considerably simplified if the code is a cylcic block code, because the partial syndrome which determines whether a particular digit is in error or not is the same for all cyclic shifts of the received sequence (Meggitt[56] decoding).

(iv) The considerable mathematical structure of cyclic codes makes it possible to find simplifying algorithms for converting the syndrome into the corresponding error pattern. Such algorithms are called algebraic decoding algorithms[15]. They make the decoding of quite complex and efficient codes (e.g. at t = 2, n = 511, c = 18, k = 493 BCH code, see below) possible, but a disadvantage of their use is that the full error control properties of the code cannot be achieved. This, however, is not normally a consideration, since full minimum distance decoding would be too complex to implement.

(v) If the weight of the error pattern corresponding to a syndrome can relatively easily be determined (i.e., with less complexity than that implied by the list decoding method), then step-by-step decoding[12] can be used. One by one, each digit in the received sequence is replaced by all the other q-1 symbol values, in turn. For each value, the syndrome is re-calculated, and the error sequence weight is re-determined. The digit is altered to the symbol value giving the lowest error sequence weight, unless replacement does not reduce the error sequence weight, in which case the digit is left unaltered. If a

correctable error pattern has occurred, then after all the
digits of the received sequence have been so processed, the
error sequence weight will be zero, i.e. a code word will have
resulted. This method is optimum; that is, it is equivalent
to full minimum distance decoding. Meggitt decoding, mentioned
above, is a form of step-by-step decoding, since the partial
syndrome (and hence the partial error weight) is reduced to
zero at each step.

(vi) Error trapping is a linear cyclic code decoding algorithm[12,57]
of particular use for burst errors. It relies on the following
facts:-

(a) a burst-error-correcting code has $c \geq b$, where b is the
burst length, and c the number of parity checks;

(b) if the number of errors in the burst is $\leq t$, then the
syndrome has weight $\leq t$ only if the errors are confined
to the parity check section of the code word (a simple
example is the code at the beginning of section 3.3, see
also the cyclic code in section 2.6);

(c) the syndrome pattern is the same as the error pattern if
(b) holds;

(d) cyclically shifting the received sequence will eventually
shift an error burst of length $b \leq c$ containing t errors
into the parity check section of the code word; this
condition can be detected by simultaneously calculating
the syndrome for each shift, and noting its weight;

(e)   if the syndrome weight becomes $\leq$ t, the correction can
take place by adding the syndrome register contents
(suitably shifted) to the received sequence;   if the
syndrome weight never falls to t or less, then an
uncorrectable burst has occurred.

This method can be used for efficient random error correction
provided n/k > t;   thus it is best applied only to low rate
and/or small t codes.   A great deal of the error-correcting
ability of more powerful codes is wasted if error trap
decoding is used.   In practice it is not necessary to
cyclically shift the received sequence, but only the contents
of the syndrome register[12,13].

(vii)   Error trapping succeeds because cyclic shifting is a code-
preserving permutation of the received digits, so that the
same decoder can be used after shifting.   If non-cyclic
code-preserving permutations of the received digits can be
found, then these can also be used to trap errors, thus
extending the range of error patterns for which trapping is
effective.   This is permutation decoding[58].

(viii)   Error trapping can also be extended slightly if a trial-and-
error technique[12] is used.   Suppose that a cyclic code can
correct up to t errors, but it cannot be guaranteed that more
than t-1 errors can be trapped (i.e., the syndrome weight
threshold is t-1).   Say t errors have occurred (t-1 or less
can be trapped in the usual way).   Then, one at a time, invert

each digit of the received sequence, attempting each time
to error trap. At some stage, an error digit will be
inverted, thus reducing the number of errors to t-1, which
can successfully be trapped. This can be extended, of course,
to 2 or more "extra" errors, but the decoding delay grows
expondentially.

3.4 Majority Logic Decoding

Majority logic decoding is a method of decoding which can be used
with any linear code (block or convolutional), provided the parity check
equations of the code are self-orthogonal, or can be orthogonalised. A
set of parity check equations is orthogonal if one information digit
appears in all the equations, and all the other (information and check)
digits appear only once anywhere in the set of equations. A trivial
example is the repetition code:-

$$k_1 \quad c_1 \quad c_2 \qquad c_1 = k_1 \qquad \text{i.e.} \quad [H] = \begin{bmatrix} 1 & \vdots & 1 & 0 \\ 1 & \vdots & 0 & 1 \end{bmatrix}$$

$$0 \quad 0 \quad 0 \qquad c_2 = k_1$$

$$1 \quad 1 \quad 1$$

The two equations are orthogonal on k_1. Because of the orthogonality
property, error in k_1 causes both checks to fail, whereas a single error
elsewhere (i.e., in c_1 or c_2) causes only one check to fail. Thus
failure of both parity checks unambiguously indicates an error in k_1.
Another example is the simple convolutional code introduced in section
2.2. Each information digit is involved in two parity checks, one with
the information digit preceding it, one with the information digit

following it. An orthogonal set of equations exists, therefore:-

$$c_i = k_i + k_{i-1}$$

$$c_{i+1} = k_{i+1} + k_i$$

Thus an error in k_i is unambiguously indicated by both the associated

checks failing, whereas a single error elsewhere within the constraint

length causes only one check to fail. Hence the decoder:-

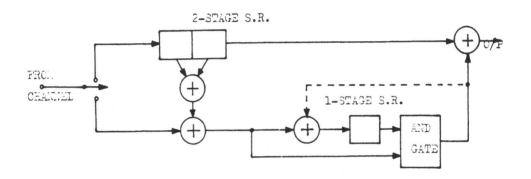

If a code is not self-orthogonal then a set of orthogonal check sums is

required. The definition is as above, with "parity check equation"

replaced by "parity check sum". A parity check sum is a linear

combination of one or more parity check equations, or rows of the parity

check matrix; that is, a set of parity check sums is a set of code words

from the <u>dual code</u> (the code formed by taking $[H]$ as a generator matrix).

For example, the cyclic code with n = 7, k = 4, c = 3, and d = 4 has[61]:-

$$[H] = \begin{array}{c} \begin{array}{ccccccc} k_1 & k_2 & k_3 & c_1 & c_2 & c_3 & c_4 \end{array} \\ \left[\begin{array}{ccc|cccc} 1 & 0 & 1 & 1 & 1 & 0 & 0 \\ 1 & 1 & 1 & 0 & 1 & 0 & 0 \\ 1 & 1 & 0 & 0 & 0 & 1 & 0 \\ 0 & 1 & 1 & 0 & 0 & 0 & 1 \end{array} \right] \begin{array}{c} c_1 \\ c_2 \\ c_3 \\ c_4 \end{array} \end{array}$$

The three check sums

$$c_1 \qquad 1\,0\,1\,1\,0\,0\,0$$

$$c_3 \qquad 1\,1\,0\,0\,0\,1\,0$$

$$c_2 + c_4 \qquad 1\,0\,0\,0\,1\,0\,1$$

are orthogonal on k_1. Thus a single error can only cause all three check sums to fail if it is in k_1. Because the code is cyclic, there is no need to find check sums orthogonal on k_2 and k_3, since errors in these positions can be corrected by using the same procedure, after cyclically shifting the received sequence or the contents of the syndrome register. Thus majority logic decoding is particularly useful for cyclic codes, and for convolutional codes with $k_o = 1$. Since the syndrome digits are themselves parity check sums, two types of majority logic decoder can be used: Type I, which processes the syndrome digits (in the example let $[s] = [s_1 \ s_2 \ s_3 \ s_4]$, then s_1, s_3 and $s_2 \oplus s_4$ must be combined in a majority gate); and Type II, which implements the check sums directly, as described above. Thus majority logic decoding in one sense is a simplified syndrome decoding method; in another sense it is a simplified full minimum distance decoding method. Hence two decoders for the cylcic code used in the above example:-

TYPE I MAJORITY LOGIC DECODER

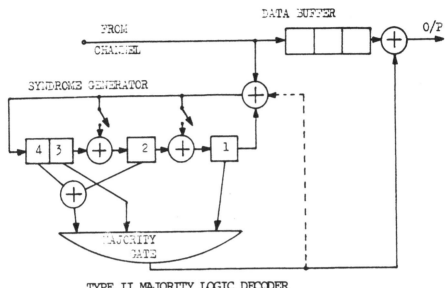

TYPE II MAJORITY LOGIC DECODER

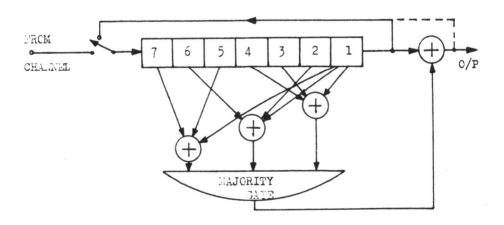

The majority gate has output ONE when more than half its inputs are ONE, and ZERO otherwise. The Type II circuit can be simplified by using a k-stage shift register. In general, if J orthogonal parity check sums can be found, then $\left\lfloor \frac{J}{2} \right\rfloor$ errors may be corrected. Thus only two orthogonal

check sums are required for single-error-correction with the above (7,3)

code example, and the code is self-orthogonal for SEC. The example is

useful, however, because it illustrates the general rule that if d-1

orthogonal check sums, on all the information digits, can be found, then

the minimum distance of the code is at least d. If d is in fact the

minimum distance of the code, and d-1 orthogonal check sums can be found,

then the code is said to be completely orthogonalisable.

Dotted feedback connections are shown on the majority logic decoder

given above. This enables prior corrections to modify the decoding process.

Without the dotted connections, the circuits are definite decoders[12,61];

with the dotted connections, the circuits are feedback decoders.

Correction of patterns of weight > $\left\lfloor \frac{J}{2} \right\rfloor$ is enhanced by the feedback

connection; the performance is better than that of a definite decoder

at high error rates, whereas, because of the possibility of error

propagation effects, it may be no better or worse at low error rates.

The decoding algorithm described above quite often cannot be used

to correct up to the number of errors predicted by the minimum distance.

This is the same as saying that it is not possible to find d-1 orthogonal

check sums. The maximum number of errors that can be corrected is given

by:-

$$t_1 \leq \frac{n-1}{2(\bar{d}-1)}$$

where $\bar{d}$ is the minimum distance of the dual code. If a sufficient number

of orthogonal parity check sums on each information digit cannot be

found, then perhaps a set of check sums orthogonal on more than one digit can be found. By using several levels of majority gates, these can then be combined to give a final sum orthogonal on one digit. This is called L-step majority logic decoding[12,61]. In this case, the maximum number of errors that can be corrected is

$$t_L < \frac{n - \left\lfloor \frac{d}{2} \right\rfloor}{2 \left(\bar{d} - \left\lfloor \frac{\bar{d}}{2} \right\rfloor \right)}$$

The number of majority gates required for L-step can be reduced, at the expense of a linear increase in decoding dealy, if some or all of the check sums are cyclic snifts of another check sum. Then sequential circuit techniques can be used to store the sums for eventual majority voting. This is sequential code reduction[14,63]. An alternative to L-step decoding, particularly in the case of finite geometry codes (see section 4 is to use non-orthogonal check sums[12,102]. This is about as complex to implement as L-step decoding, but does not correct as many errors. Again, in the case of finite geometry codes (particularly projective geometry codes), the decoders can be considerably simplified, because of the mathematical structure of these codes[64].

The performance of majority logic decoding can be improved, at the expense of greater complexity and decoding delay, by using variable threshold majority gates. Decoding is initiated with the threshold set at d-1, after which it is progressively lowered to $\frac{d-1}{2}$[62].

Finally, it can be shown that any binary linear code can be decoded using weighted majority, or threshold gates, in a one-step algorithm. This is threshold decoding[14,65,66]. It is potentially

useful for cyclic codes in particular, and for convolutional codes;
unfortunately, the threshold function may in general involve all the
2^c parity check sums, though in some cases of practical interest this
number can be reduced[65]. The term "threshold decoding" is also often
used to mean just majority logic decoding[66].

3.5   Sequential Decoding

The complexity of a minimum distance decoder grows exponentially
with block or constraint length. Sequential decoding[72] was developed to
overcome this problem; it is most effective when used with a convolutional
code. A minimum distance decoder correlates the received coded sequence
with all possible code words or sequences over the entire code length,
and then selects the code word "nearest" to the received sequence as the
one that was transmitted. A sequential decoder, on the other hand, does
not complete every correlation, if it is able to decide that a code
word is so "far away" from the received sequence that it is unlikely to
be the code word ultimately chosen. In this way, much unnecessary
computation can be avoided, and the reduced complexity of the decoder
effectively compensates for the possible slight increase in the probability
of error. If the code is convolutional, there are two further advantages:-

(i)   To decode each segment, the decoder can correlate (if necessary)
over more than the constraint length of the code, limited
only by the available storage and speed of operation. This
means that the error control performance of sequential
decoding is better than that of majority logic decoding,

since in effect it makes use of a longer portion of the

semi-infinite syndrome of a convolutional code.

(ii)   the tree-like structure of convolutional codes with respect

to the segments enables the decoder to reject unlikely

sequences more rapidly.

A disadvantage of using sequential decoding is the error

propagation effect: if a segment is decoded in error, then the probability

of subsequent decoding errors increases. This effect is not peculiar to

sequential decoding only; majority logic decoders are also prone to it,

as has been noted above. Another problem with sequential decoding is that

the amount of computation required to decode each segment is a Pareto

distributed variable, so that there is a finite (and non-trivial)

probability of decoder storage over-flow, with consequent failure to

decode[67,68]. This problem can be overcome by using a feedback channel

to request re-transmission if overflow occurs[60,69]. With sequential

decoding, it is possible to achieve efficient transmission of data at

very low error rates, with a complexity that grows algebraically,

instead of exponentially, with the code constraint length (i.e.

proportional to n^2 instead of 2^n) provided the code rate is less than a

rate R_{comp}, which in turn is less than the channel capacity[12].

A basic problem with sequential decoding algorithms, such as the

Fano algorithm[70], is that if the distance threshold between the received

sequence and the paths being searched from a given node in the tree is

exceeded, then the decoder must return to the previous node, and search

branches from that node. If this also fails, the process of "backing up"

and searching is repeated as many times as required. This occasionally

leads to excessive computation and overload, as indicated above. Various
schemes have been proposed for alleviating this problem. One approach
in particular, which makes use of the group and linear properties of
convolutional codes, has been developed[71]. In essence, the scheme is
able to indicate which node the search should back up to, if paths from
the current node exceed the threshold. This results in an enormous
saving in complexity and decoding delay, and makes minimum distance
sequential decoding practical for relatively long and powerful
convolutional codes (e.g. n > 50 segments, $R = \frac{1}{2}$).

Sequential decoding is optimum for random error control, but can
be modified for use with burst errors, either by means of interleaving
(see section 4), or by means of burst-tracking methods[73]. Sequential
decoding is also called probabilistic decoding in the literature[70].

3.6   Trellis Decoding

The output tree of a convolutional code grows exponentially
without limit, of course, so it is a rather cumbersome way of depicting
the output sequence. After a number of steps, however, the tree
begins to repeat itself; in the case of the example of section 2.2,
nodes a and c lead to identical branches, as do nodes b and d. Thus,
a and c, and b and d, can be joined, and a compact trellis diagram
results:

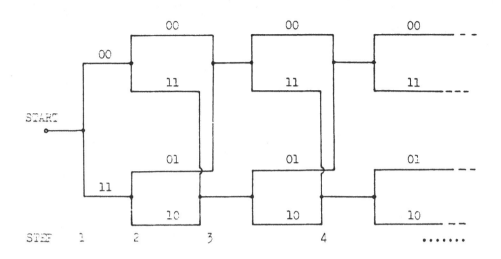

or, more neatly, and once the initial stage is completed:

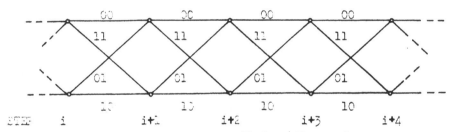

Thus, convolutional codes are often called <u>trellis codes</u>.

The aim of a convolutional decoder is to retrace the path of the
encoder through the trellis. A minimum distance decoder seeks to select
the path nearest in Hamming distance to the received path. The decoder
must compare all possible paths with the received path. This is, in
general, (as noted above under sequential decoding) a lengthy and complex
process, but the structure of convolutional codes and use of the
Viterbi decoding algorithm[74] permits a considerable simplification. The
Viterbi algorithm (VA) works as follows:

(i) Encoding is initiated with all registers, etc., set to zero, i.e. as if a very long sequence of zeros had been received.

(ii)   Compute the distances (incremental scores) between the
first received segment of n_o digits and the segment
associated with each path between two adjacent nodes on the
trellis.

(iii) Select the lowest score path arriving at each node (state),
and store the score and its corresponding path. If there are
two or more equal lowest values, select one arbitrarily. Thus
for each node there is a running score and an associated
survivor sequence.

(iv)   Repeat (ii) for the next n_o received digits (moving one step
along the trellis), and add the new incremental scores to
the appropriate previous running scores, to obtain new
running scores for each possible path in the trellis.

(v)   Repeat the selection process if (iii), storing the new
running scores and the associated survivor sequences for
each node.

(vi)   Continue the process until all digits have been received.

(vii) Output either the survivor sequence which has most digits
in common with all the other survivor sequences, or which
has the lowest running score. Normally, unless excessive
errors have occurred, the two indicators will agree.

For the example

(a)   NO ERROR CASE

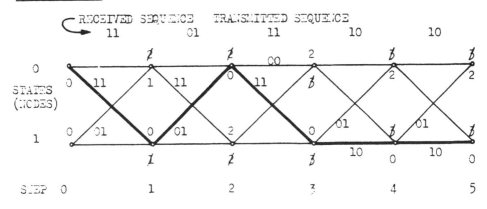

NOTE: When scores equal, upper path selected

It is convenient to list in a table the running scores and survivor

sequences at each step.

Step	State 0		State 1	
	Score	Survivor Sequence	Score	Survivor Sequence
1	1	01	0	11
2	0	11 01	2	01 11
3	2	11 01 00	0	11 01 11
4	2	11 01 11 01	0	11 01 11 10
5	2	11 01 11 10 01	0	11 01 11 10 10

lowest   *correct*
score   *seq.*

The correct sequence is easily determined.

(b)   ONE ERROR CASE

Transmitted sequence   11 01 11 10 10

Error   "   00 10 00 00 00

Received   "   11 11 11 10 10

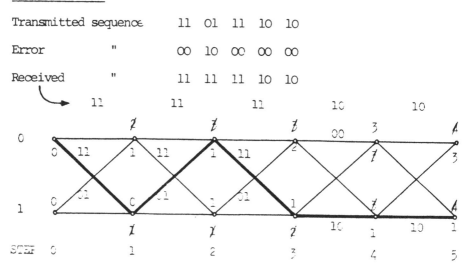

N.B.   Again, upper path selected when scores agree.

Calculating:

Step	State 0		State 1	
	Score	Survivor Sequence	Score	Survivor Sequence
1	1	01	0	11
2	1	11 01	1	01 11
3	2	01 11 01	1	11 01 11
4	3	01 11 01 00	1	11 01 11 10
5	3	11 01 11 10 01	1	11 01 11 10 10

lowest   *correct*
score   *seq.*

Again, the correct sequence can be selected, even at the third

step.   In practice, there are a number of further simplifications:

(1)   Only the information digits in (or corresponding to) the

survivor sequences need to be stored, thus reducing the

amount of storage required.

(2)   If the input sequence is long, then the survivor sequence
      stores will overload. Before this occurs, the "oldest" k_o
      digits on which the survivor sequences agree, or the ones
      corresponding to the survivor sequence with the lowest score,
      are output from the decoder. A store length (search length)
      of approximately 5 hk_o (6 x input constraint length) is
      found to be adequate, for the code error rate performance
      hardly increases if it is made any longer. Thus, the
      decoding delay is also approximately 5 hk_o.

(3)   Overload of the running score counters may be avoided by
      always nor...lising the scores so that the lowest running
      score is zero; it is only the differences between the
      running scores that matter, so the lowest score may be
      subtracted from all at each step.

Viterbi algorithm decoding is practical for encoding constraint lengths
of up to about 12. For longer and more powerful codes, sequential
decoding or majority logic decoding is appropriate. The algorithm can
be used on certain types of burst-error channel[75], but it is most
effective on random-error channels. The algorithm can be simplified in
various ways[76,77], without serious loss of performance. The so-called
stack algorithms[78,79,80] are mid-way, as it were, between sequential
and trellis decoding, combining features of both in an attempt to
efficiently decode longer codes with acceptable complexity.

An optimum syndrome decoding method for convolutional codes has
been proposed and recently developed[81,82]. After derivation of the
syndrome, a recursive algorithm like the Viterbi algorithm is used to

estimate the error sequence. Of considerable interest is the fact that
implementation of the algorithm is much simplified by making use of the
algebraic structure of the code.

Finally, trellis decoding can also be effectively applied to linear
block codes[83]. In the case of a cyclic code, the trellis is periodic.
The trellis has, in general, 2^c states, but in some cases, particularly
for product codes (see section 4.4) this number can be considerably reduced.

3.7   Soft-Decision Decoding

An optimum method of detection (demodulation and decoding), for a
data transmission system with channel (error correction) coding, is
coherent correlation detection (or matched filtering) of the sequence of
signal elements corresponding to the block length in the case of a block
code, or to the decoder search length, in the case of a convolutional
code. In practice, unless the block or search length (and therefore
the constraint length) is very short, this ideal detector is too complex
to realise, because of the difficulty of generating, storing and
correlating the large number of analogue signal elements required. Thus
most practical detectors consist of an analogue demodulator, possibly
coherent, operating on individual signal elements, followed by a purely
digital decoder operating on blocks of the digits produced by the "hard"
decisions of the demodulator. However, some of the information which
would be lost by only correlating over a singal element can be used to
assist and improve the decoding process, and vice-versa. Additional
information can be fed forward from the demodulator to improve operation
of the decoder, or fed back from the decoder to improve operation of the

demodulator. The advantage of these forms of partially combined demodulation and decoding (or inter-active demodulation and decoding) is that they are much less complex to implement than fully combined forms of demodulation and decoding such as coherent correlation detection or matched filter detection. In addition, under certain circumstances the performance of some interactive demodulation and decoding methods (or probabilistic decoding methods[84], as they were collectively called) is asymptotically close to that of ideal detection.

Null-zone, or forced erasure detection, or failure correction decoding are all ways of implementing feedforward between the demodulator and the decoder: processed signal elements with values lying near the threshold level of the demodulator, and thus of doubtful worth, are passed forward to the demodulator labelled as erasures. The decoder now has some knowledge of where errors are likely to be in the block, and can decode accordingly[85]. In this way the error-correcting power of a code can be approximately doubled (a code with Hamming distance d can correct d-1 errors in a block transmitted over a binary erasure channel, but only $\lfloor (d-1)/2 \rfloor$ on a BSC, where $\lfloor x \rfloor$ is the largest integer $\leq$ x).

Null-zone detection can be extended to double-null-zone detection with an improvement in performance[86], and can be generalised to more than two "null-zones", though with gradually diminishing rise in peformance as the number of zones (16 or 32 zones is quite adequate) is increased. This general form of null-zone detection is called <u>soft-decision decoding</u>. Thus, strictly speaking, soft-decision decoding is a type of probabilistic decoding. Because of its importance, however, the term "soft-decision" has come to replace the word "probabilistic", which has fallen into disuse. Thus soft-decision decoding not only refers to the

particular method, but also has come to mean the whole field of decoding

with confidence (reliability) information[87]. The improvement due to

soft-decision demodulation depends on the particular code and channel

error statistics, but one or two orders of magnitude or more decrease

in output error rate, for white Gaussian noise channels with error rates

in the range 10^{-2} to 10^{-4}, is typical. This corresponds to 1.5 to 2 dB

improvement in signal-to-noise ratio. In non-Gaussian noise the improvement

is considerably greater.

Soft-decision decoding became of practical importance with the

discovery of the Viterbi algorithm[74] (VA) for maximum likelihood

(minimum distance) decoding of convolutional codes. Use of soft-decision

demodulation does not significantly increase the complexity of a VA

decoder, which is a function of the rate and constraint length of the code.

Soft-decision sequential decoding[71,88] and threshold decoding[89] of

convolutional codes is also possible.

Soft-decision techniques were less generally applicable to block

codes until comparatively recently. Hamming single-error-correcting

codes with soft-decision decoding have been studied[90,91]. Work on

generalised minimum distance decoding[92] led to the application of soft-

decision techniques to iterated and concatenated codes[93], to algebraic

decoders[94], and to error-trapping decoders based on successive erasure

decoding[95]. Weighted erasure (multiple syndrome) decoding[96], is a soft-

decision decoding technique applicable in principle to any block code

for which a decoding procedure is known. Work on threshold decoding

led to the combination of soft-declision techniques with majority logic decoding[97]. A quite different approach, which may be called soft-decision dual-code-domain decoding[98], is an optimum decoding method in a symbol-by-symbol sense in that it minimises the symbol error probability, rather than the code-word error probability. It is important because it applies to codes of high rate, unlike most of the methods mentioned previously. More general application of soft-decision decoding to block codes is possible if full decoding is used, particularly if the code used has some internal structure which can simplify decoding; for example, if the code is a product or concatenated code[99,100,101]. Also Wolf has shown that any linear block code can be soft-decision decoded using the Viterbi algorithm[83].

3.8   Summary

The types of decoding mentioned in this section are listed in figure 5. There is one basic method: full minimum distance decoding. This, except for relatively short, or low rate, codes, is too complex to implement. Among the various methods of decoding which are practical, four categories emerge: syndrome, sequential, trellis and majority logic (threshold) decoding. Soft-decision techniques can be appplied to decoders in all of these categories, though not to all cases within a category. Roughly speaking, optimum (i.e., equivalent to full minimum distance decoding) methods can be used with codes having k, c, hk_o or $h(n_o - k_o)$ less than about 12. Sub-optimum methods are required for the more powerful and longer codes. Use of soft-decision in these cases often partially or wholly compensates for the loss of optimality.

4.   Practical Error-Control Codes

In this section are listed those classes of error-control codes which have found some practical application; that is, have been implemented and tested on real channels. The list is not exhaustive; it was not intended to be, and probably could not be, complete. Many classes of codes, mainly of theoretical rather than practical interest, are not included; these and all the codes listed in this section, will be found in references previously mentioned[12-17]. All the codes mentioned are binary unless otherwise stated.

4.1   Repetition Codes

- Block, linear, systematic.

- Each information digit is transmitted m times.

- Optimum decoding possible with hard or soft decision minimum distance decoding (correlation), or by majority logic decoding.

- $d = m$; $R = 1/m$; $k = 1, N = 2$.

- These codes are powerful but inefficient. Perhaps the most widely used and ancient form of coding. It is often implemented implicitly; for example, all forms of diversity are repetition codes[103], as are direct sequence spread-spectrum systems[87,100,101,104,105,141]. Repetition codes can very successfully be used, in cascade or concatenation with other codes, to combat very high error rates[101,107].

4.2   Constant Weight Codes

- Block, non-linear, systematic or non-systematic.

- Code words are all (or a subset of) the sequences of length n and weight w. May also generate from any other block code by replacing

each ZERO by a sequence (say 0 1) and every ONE by the inverse of the

sequence (1 0), with the restriction that the weight of the sequence

and its inverse must be the same[108]. Other constructions are also

given in the same reference[108].

    - If all words of weight w are taken, d = 2;

     $n = n!/(n-w)!w!$;

$$R = \frac{\log_2 \left[n!/(n-w)!w! \right]}{n}$$

Using the alternative construction, d = twice the distance of the

original code; N = number of words in the original code; R = half the

original code rate, since n has doubled.

    - For error correction, full minimum distance (maximum likelihood)

decoding is the only feasible method,; for error detection, weight

violation can be used.

    - These codes are also called <u>fixed-ratio</u>, <u>constant-ratio</u>[109]

or <u>m-out-of-n</u> codes. A 4-out-of-7 code was the first code to be

explicitly used in an EDC system[110,111,112,113,114]. They are useful

for asymmetric channels.

4.3   Single-Parity-Check Codes

    - Block, linear, systematic, trivially cyclic.

    - The modulo-2 sum of k information digits forms the single

parity check.

    - $d = 2$; $R = k/(k+1)$; $N = 2^k$; $n = k+1$

- Syndrome error detection.

- This is the most widely used code[112,115,125]. If error correction
is required, then an ARQ system is necessary, or soft-decision detection
may be used[85,112].

It is surprisingly efficient as an ED code, as it detects half of
all possible error patterns in a block length n. Very simple to implement,
and has optimum parameters for SED. Can be generalised to q-nary
residue or modulus codes[115,122].

4.4   Array Codes

- Block, linear, systematic.

- Simplest class is generalisation of the single-parity-check
code to two dimensions: row and column checks (product, two-coordinate,
or matrix code). In general, any code formed by generalising (or
iterating) one or more component codes into arrays in (conceptually) two
or more dimensions (not necessarily orthogonal[116]).

- $d = d_1 \times d_2 \times d_3 \times \ldots$; $R = R_1 \times R_2 \times R_3 \times \ldots$;

  $n = n_1 \times n_2 \times n_3 \times \ldots$; $k = k_1 \times k_2 \times k_3 \times \ldots$;

- Majority logic decoding is most appropriate;   algebraic syndrome
techniques can also be used[117];   and adaptive minimum distance decoding,
with soft decision, is also possible[101].

- Can be used for random error detection[118] or correction;   or for
burst error detection or correction[116]. Has very good random ED
properties;   and has optimum parameters for burst ED. Can also be used
to correct "patches" of errors in arrays. Very useful for data presented

in a rectangular format, i.e. punched card or magnetic tape[119,120,121].

Array codes are used on the SITA airline ticket reservation network.

4.5   Hamming Single-Error-Correcting Codes

- Block, linear, systematic.

- The parity check matrix of these codes (not in SEF) is:

$$
[H] \quad = \quad \overset{\xleftarrow{\hspace{2cm} n \hspace{2cm}}}{\underset{c}{\left[
\begin{array}{ccccccccc}
c_1 & c_2 & k_1 & c_3 & k_2 & k_3 & k_4 & c_4 & k_5 \cdots \\
1 & 0 & 1 & 0 & 1 & 0 & 1 & 0 & 1 \\
0 & 1 & 1 & 0 & 0 & 1 & 1 & 0 & 0 \quad \cdots \\
  &   & 1 & 1 & 1 & 1 & 0 & 0 & \\
  & O &   &   &   &   & 1 & 1 &
\end{array}
\right]}}
$$

where n = k + c may be truncated at any required length.

- Syndrome and majority logic decoding possible, using cyclic code techniques, since these codes are equivalent to a class of cyclic codes.

- This famous[23] class of single-error-correcting codes is the only example of a class of t-error-correcting codes optimum for all values of n. When $n = 2^c$, the code has exactly the required number of syndrome patterns for single-error-correction. For these values of n, the code is said to be perfect[123]. In general, a code is perfect if the sphere-packing bound[23] is exactly met:-

$$
2^c = 1 + \binom{n}{1} + \binom{n}{2} + \cdots \binom{n}{t}
$$

where $\binom{n}{x} = \frac{n!}{x!\,(n-x)!}$. The Hamming SEC codes, and the Golay code

(see below), are the only non-trivial examples of binary perfect codes[123].

Because of their simplicity, optimality and high rate, these codes have

been used, either as described above, or <u>extended</u> to d = 4 (SEC-DED) by

the addition of an overall parity check, in a wide variety of applications

to communications systems[112,124,125,126,127,128], and to computer memory

protection[115,129,130]. These codes may also be generalised to provide

b-adjacent-error-correction[132], and single-burst-error-correction[133].

4.6   <u>Single and Double-Adjacent Error-Correcting Codes (SEC-DAEC Codes)</u>

        - Block, linear, systematic, cyclic.

        - Equivalent to the extended Hamming codes, arranged as 2-adjacent

error correcting codes[132,134].

        - b = 2, n $\leq$ $(2^C-1)/2$

        - Any cyclic decoding procedure.

        - These are simple burst-error-correcting cyclic codes, particularly

suitable for correcting errors arising in Differential Phase-Shift-Keying

carrier systems[9,135]. Many types of double-random EC code may be converted

to SEC-DAEC operation[136].

4.7   <u>Reed-Muller Codes</u>

        - Block, linear, systematic, in some cases cyclic.

        - A large class of codes with rather less error-control power

than equivalent rate BCH (see below) codes[137,138]. Their importance

lies in two facts:

(i)   they can be easily decoded using majority logic
      decoding (they are the archetypal class of majority
      logic decodable codes); and

(ii) they are a sub-class of a much broader class of
      majority logic decodable geometrical codes; which
      includes projective geometry and Euclidean geometry
      codes, many of which are cyclic[14,64].

- An early EDC code implementation used an RM code[139]; RM codes
have also been used in computer store address decoders[115], and for space
systems[17].

4.8   Other Linear Block Codes

- A variety of simple linear block codes have been implemented
including a (10, 5) code[106], also extended by interleaving[113]; and an
interleaved (24,12) code[140] (probably the Golay code, see section 4.11).

4.9   Sequence Codes

- Block, non-linear (in general), non-systematic (in general), cyclic.

- Constructed by taking as code words all the n cyclic shifts of
a sequence of length n.

- If the normalised periodic auto-correlation function (ACF) of
the sequence is $\phi(\tau)$, and max $\phi(\tau \neq 0)$ is the maximum value of $\phi(\tau)$ for
any shift other than no shift, then

$$d = \frac{n}{2} \{1 - \max \phi(\tau \neq 0)\}.$$

- These codes are useful for spread-spectrum systems[141], and correlation detection schemes[142].

- They may be extended by taking also, as appropriate, the all-ZERO word or the all-ONE word, and the inverses of the cyclic shifts of the sequence[9]. A particular class of sequence codes which is linear and optimum is the m-sequence codes[12], for which $n = 2^k - 1$ and $d = 2^{k-1}$; these codes are derived from maximum-length pseudo-random sequences, and are simplex (see next section).

4.10 Orthogonal, Bi-Orthogonal and Simplex Codes

- Block, non-linear (in general), non-systematic (in general).

- A code is orthogonal if the normalised cross-correlation between any pair of code-words is always zero; i.e. $\rho(x_i, x_j) = 0$, all $i \neq j$.

- A bi-orthogonal code consists of the code words of an orthogonal code, together with all their complements (first order Reed-Muller codes, section 4.7, are bi-orthogonal codes).

- A code is trans-orthogonal if $\rho(x_i, x_j) < 0$, all $i \neq j$, and simplex if $\rho(x_i, x_j) = -1/(N-1)$, N even; or $\rho(x_i, x_j) = -1/N$, N odd; all $i \neq j$.

Simplex codes are the most efficient in this class, followed by bi-orthogonal codes.

- The existence of these codes depends on the existence of Hadamard matrices[9,131]. Hadamard matrices are T x T matrices which have mutually orthogonal rows or columns; they exist for $T = 2^k$, k integer, and for all $T = 4t$, t integer, to $T \leq 200$, except $T = 116$, 156 & 188.

Thus any Hadamard matrix is an orthogonal code with $n = T$, $N = T$ and

$d = T/2$; the matrix plus its logical complement is a bi-orthogonal code

with $n = T$, $N = 2T$, $d = T/2$; and there are simplex codes with $n = T - 1$,

$T - 1$, $T - 2$, $T - 2$; $N = T$, $T - 1$, $T/2$, $(T/2) - 1$, and $d = T/2$ in all

cases, respectively.

- Decoding, if the code is non-linear, can only be done by a hard-
or soft-decision full minimum distance method.

- Practical applications are mentioned in references 131, 139, 142,
143 and 144.

4.11   The Golay Code

- Block, linear, systematic, cyclic, perfect[12,14,33,123].

- $d = 7$ (i.e. $t = 3$), $n = 23$, $k = 12$, $R \simeq 0.5$, $b = 5$. Can be

extended to $(n, k, d) = (24, 12, 8)$, $R = 0.5$.

- Can be decoded optimally using syndrome techniques, or non-optimally

using majority-logic methods.

- EDC systems incorporating this code have been implemented for

HF[128,145], satellite[143,146], troposcatter[146], and telephone channels[147].

4.12   BCH Codes

- Block, linear, systematic, cyclic, random error correcting[148,149].

- $d \geq 2t + 1$; $n = 2^m - 1$, m integer; $k \geq 2^m - 1 - mt$; i.e. $c < mt$.

These are _primitive BCH codes_; i.e. their generator polynomials (section

2.6) are primitive. More generally, the _BCH bound_[148,149] states that the

distance of any cyclic code is greater than the number of consecutive

roots of its generator polynomial[12,61].

- Many of these codes are optimum or near-optimum in efficiency, they cover a wide range of error-control properties, and they are relatively easy to encode, and decode using algebraic techniques[12,15]. BCH codes have been used on voice channels[150,151,152], satellite channels[153], HF and other fading channels[113,128,142,154,155], and VHF channels[155].

4.13 Fire Codes

- Block, linear, systematic, cyclic, burst-error-detecting and correcting[156].

- For single-burst-correction: $G(x) = (x^{2b-1} + 1)P(x)$, where $P(x)$ has degree $m \geq b$, is primitive (i.e. belongs to $p = 2^m - 1$), and $n = $ LCM of $2b - 1$ and p. For double-burst-detection: $G(x) = (x^c + 1)P(x)$, where $c + 1 = b_1 + b_2$, $P(x)$ is irreducible with degree $m \geq b_2$, and belongs to p, and $n < $ LCM of c and p.

- Decodable using syndrome techniques.

- Have been used on voice-grade data communication systems[151].

4.14 Other Cyclic Codes

- A half-rate random- or burst-error-correcting cyclic coding system, with very long block length and adaptive decoding (DACOR), has been implemented[157,158].

- Cyclic product codes (see section 4.4), with soft-decision minimum distance adaptive decoding, have also been implemented[101].

- Computer-generated cyclic codes for burst-error-correction[61].

- Cyclic codes are very widely used in data networks for error detection, as part of RED schemes (see also section 4.20); for example,

in the ARPA network and the British Post Office EPSS network; and in a
variable redundancy scheme for HF channels[50]. In this context they are
often called polynomial codes, but see next section.

4.15 Reed-Solomon Codes

- Block, linear, systematic, multi-level, cyclic[159].

- t-multi-level-error-correcting; or t-binary-burst-error-
correcting. A multi-level generalisation of certain BCH codes (those for
which m = 1).

- Reed-Solomon codes are a sub-class of the broad class of cyclic
codes called polynomial codes[12], which also includes BCH codes, Hamming
codes, Reed-Muller codes, and finite geometry codes.

- Reed Solomon codes are possibly the only multi-level codes to have
been implemented. They have been used for deep-space network teletype
circuits[160], in computer systems[132], and in concatenated coding systems[154,161].

4.16 Convolutional Codes

- Non-block, linear, systematic or non-systematic.

- Wide variety of parameters; good codes mostly found by
computer search.

- Decodable by syndrome, threshold (majority-logic), sequential and
trellis methods.

- Suitable for random errors, with trellis, sequential or syndrome
decoding; or for burst errors, either by interleaving random convolutional
codes, or directly with sequential or threshold decoding (see also below).

- Systematic codes guarantee non-catastrophic behaviour, but as n is increased, their d_{free} is asymptotically half that of a non-systematic code.

- Convolutional codes with Viterbi algorithm decoding have been used on satellite links[143,162,163,169,177,] for fading channels[164], on microwave links[107], and for space links[168]; with sequential decoding, on satellite links[163,165], and on space links[166,167]. Simple syndrome decoding applications include a digital video application[170]; and threshold decoding applications include satellite channels[162,171], and radio systems[145,172].

4.17   Hagelbarger Codes

- Non-block, linear, systematic, convolutional burst-error-correcting[29].

- For burst length b, n = 2b + 2, R = 1/2;   there are also R = 3/4 codes.

- Majority logic decoding.

- These codes (also called recurrent codes) have been used for a telephone line data transmission system[173].

4.18   Diffuse Codes

- Non-block, linear, convolutional, systematic, burst-and-random-error-correcting[2,174].

- These codes are "self-interleaved" convolutional codes (this technique can also be used effectively with cyclic codes[13]), normally half-rate and threshold (majority-logic) decodable.

- They have been applied to HF channels[146,154,175], to tropo-scatter links[146,175], satellite circuits[146,210], and to telephone lines[175].

4.19 Burst-Trapping Codes

- Convolutional/block, linear, systematic, burst-and/or-random-error-correcting.

- These codes are a form of time diversity or repetition codes, with certain convolutional code properties. They first emerged as codes capable of either correcting bursts or random errors[147], and were later generalised into burst-and-random error-correcting codes[176].

4.20 ARQ Coding Systems

The use of various (often unspecified) error detecting codes and sum checks (modulus systems) for data and computer networks is reported in a large number of references (178-188).

4.21 Summary

The codes mentioned in Section 4 are listed in Fig. 6. This survey confirms that the overwhelming majority of practical codes are linear and binary. There are no practical non-linear or multi-level convolutional (non-block) codes. There is only one practical multi-level code class, the Reed-Solomon codes. All practical REC (ARQ) systems use block ED codes, of which most are cyclic. The relatively short list of non-block codes disguises the fact that a wide range of practical convolutional codes exists, and reflects the fact that there are relatively few distinct classes of convolutional codes, since many have been found by try-and-see techniques and computer searches.

5.   Performance of Error-Control Codes

5.1   Calculation of Decoder Output Error Rate

        In order to be able to choose a suitable error-correcting code, it
is necessary to measure or estimate the decoder output error rate. The
result of the measurement or estimate calculation will depend not only on
the parameters of the code, but also on the error statistics of the
channel (or channel model) and on the decoding method. The actual decoder
implementation or algorithm is important, because this determines the error
multiplication or propagation effects which in turn determine the exact
output bit (or digit) error rate. Thus calculation of output error rate
is in general a complex procedure, particularly for high channel error
rates. Often decoder simulation is used to determine high error-rate
performance. The output bit-error-rate, P_o, of a block code may be
estimated from

$$P_o = \sum_{i=t+1}^{n} \frac{i+t}{n} \binom{n}{i} P_e^i (1-P_e)^{n-i}$$

where t is the number of errors the code can correct, assuming bounded
distance decoding; n is the block length; and P_e is the channel error
rate, assuming a BSC. This estimation assumes forward error control;
for retransmission systems, t+1 is replaced by d, the minimum distance of
the code. The results of a simulation of this formula for various
approximately half-rate linear (n,k) t-error-correcting codes is given
in Fig. 7[189]. Note that though the longer block length codes do best for

output error rates $P_o \ll P_e$, they do worse than shorter codes when

$P_o \geq P_e$; that is, when the channel error rate is relatively high. Low

rate codes perform better than high rate codes, in general. The above

formula also assumes that the decoder outputs t additional errors whenever

it decodes incorrectly; more exact calculations or simulations can also

be found (refs. 190,191,192,193,200). Calculations can also be performed

for various types of channel, particularly the white Gaussian noise

channel[194] and fading channels[201]; this in turn enables estimations

to be done for soft-decision decoding[87]. The effective rate of re-

transmission EC methods is also of interest[57,198,199], because it enables

the performance of FEC and ARQ systems to be compared.

The output error-rate of a linear convolutional code is rather

more difficult to estimate than that of a block code. It is possible,

however, by using signal-flow diagram techniques[74], to find an expression

of the form

$$f(y,z) = \sum_k a_k \, y^l z^m$$

where a_k is the number of paths in the trellis which diverge from, and

later rejoin, the all-zero path, with weight, l, generated from an input

sequence of weight m (thus d_{free} is the degree of y in the first term of

$f(y,z)$, and erroneous selection of a path of weight l will result in the

corruption of m information digits). Then

$$P_o \leq \left. \frac{\partial f(y,z)}{\partial z} \right|_{\substack{z=1 \\ y=2\sqrt{P_e(1-P_e)}}}$$

This overbound on P_o assumes minimum distance decoding, and a BSC. More exact formulae have been computed[195,196], but simulation is often used, particularly at high channel error rates where the various estimation formulae are less exact. The output error rate of 1/2, 1/4 and 1/8 rate convolutional codes with input constraint length 5 (i.e., degree 4) is given in Fig. 8[197]. Note that low rate codes perform better than high rate codes; higher constraint length codes would also perform better.

5.2   Coding Gain

The overall performance of a code, or coding system, depends not only on the decoder output error rate, but also on the rate of the code. As seen above, rate (or efficiency) and output error-rate may be exchanged; high rate implying poor (high) error rate, and low rate implying good (low) error-rate. It is not appropriate, however, to evaluate the error-rate performance of a code purely on the basis of the question "is $P_o > P_e$ for the P_e range of interest?" Because of the redundancy required by the code, information digits may be transmitted with more energy per bit when the channel is uncoded. Thus the P_e of the uncoded channel will in general be lower than that of the coded channel, and it is this uncoded P_e with which P_o must be compared. So the appropriate question becomes "is P_o less than the error rate of the channel when all the "space" used for coding redundancy is used to transmit the same number of information digits only?" This uncoded error rate is in general very difficult to estimate, because it depends on the signal and noise statistics and the frequency response of the channel, and on the demodulator used. If it is assumed, however, that the channel is perturbed by white Gaussian noise, then the uncoded, and coded, P_e can be calculated for a number of modulation/ demodulation methods, so that plots of error rate versus the ratio of energy per information bit over the noise spectral density (noise power per cycle of bandwidth), E_b/N_o, may be constructed. If the curve for the system with coding lies to the left of the curve for no coding, then the coded system is said to exhibit coding gain. Fig. 9 shows curves for convolutional and BCH codes, operating on a PSK channel perturbed by white Gaussian noise[197]. Note that (i) the convolutional codes are superior in performance to the considerably more complex BCH codes; and (ii) the 1/2 rate codes of both types perform better than the 1/4 or 1/8 rate codes, seemingly reversing the results of Fig. 8 which did not take rate into account. The performance of a long constraint length convolutional code with sequential decoding is also shown, together with the ultimate coding gain curve calculated from Shannon's theorem[197]. All the codes are assumed to be decoded using hard decision minimum distance methods (Viterbi and bounded distance algebraic). Soft-decision methods (see Fig. 10) add 1.5 - 2.0 db to the coding gain[87,202]. Multi-level codes, because of their superior efficiency, offer higher coding gains than comparable complexity binary codes, when the comparison is with binary or multi-level uncoded transmission, respectively. If multi-level codes are used to protect binary data, however, they appear to offer little advantage over binary codes[18].

These curves all involve theoretical calculations and assumptions. In practice, the performance of a coding system is degraded by a number of factors. Even when the channel model and the decoder error rate calculations are good approximations to actual behaviour, there is normally an implementation loss of 1-2 db. If the channel model is not appropriate (e.g. when the channel fades or exhibits multipath effects) then the theoretical curves can be quite misleadingly inaccurate. Finally, most calculations and models assume perfect block, digit and carrier synchronisation, whereas all practical systems suffer from synchronisation problems at the start of, and during transmission. This all adds to the implementation loss; see, for example, Fig. 10, where curves for a satellite QPSK system with 1/2 rate convolutional codes with Viterbi hard and soft decision decoding are plotted.[162] Thus, the performance of many real channels (e.g. telephone and HF channels) and coding systems, for which appropriate calculations and estimations are too complex to be worthwhile[31], can only be obtained by actual implementation and testing. It is perhaps surprising to note how robust in performance a well-designed coding system can be in practice (refs. 101, 203, 207).

It is worth pointing out that coding gain is not always a suitable criterion upon which to judge the usefulness, or not, of an EDC coding system. This is partly because of the unreliability of coding gain, mentioned above, when the channel is non-Gaussian. It is also due to the fact that in certain situations it is necessary to use inefficient codes in order to obtain a desired output error rate, because of the lack of any alternative way of reducing the error rate. For example, it is inappropriate to reject codes with low, or even negative, coding gain, if the implied alternative, an increase in transmitter power, is impossible (e.g. on a satellite or space link), or has a negligible effect on the channel error rate (e.g. on certain HF channels). Thus it may be necessary to use a code, or a combination of codes, regardless of their coding gain; and in these cases it is, of course, desirable to design an EDC system with as much coding gain as possible. If the channel error rate is high, however ($> 10^{-2}$, say) then an efficient code will be impossibly complex to instrument, because of the very long block or constraint lengths implied[101,107]. A similar complexity constraint arises even when the required longer code can be implemented, but only using a non-optimum decoding algorithm, such as majority logic decoding. In this case cascaded, interleaved, or concatenated simpler codes, with optimal decoding, may outperform the longer code[101,204].

5.3   Conclusion

This paper ends with a number of comments, by way of conclusion, about the material presented in it. No attempt will be made, even if it were possible, to further summarise the field of error-control coding; the comments are offered, rather, for interest and as pointers towards ways of designing effective error control systems now and in the future.

5.3.1 System Constraints

In practice the channel offered to a coding system designer can place severe limitation on any error-control scheme he may wish to use. For example, the redundancy is often required to be 75%, 50%, 25%, 12.5%, etc; ie, the rate must be 3/4, 1/2, 1/4, 1/8, etc. Half-rate may even be the only rate offered: two parallel channels. Only a few codes have such "nice" rates; thus they have to be shortened, or padded out, by a number of digits, which may reduce their EDC effectiveness. Another example concerns the choice between FEC and REC (ARQ) systems. There is normally no choice! Either a feedback channel is available, or it is not. Even

if a feedback channel can be used, the loop delay and/or the variable
data flow of the system may make REC impossible; eg, for digital voice
on satellite links. Format, or message length, constraints may further
restrict the choice of code. Short messages preclude the effective use
of either convolutional codes, or high degrees of interleaving. Perhaps
most important of all, the coding designer has often to work without a
detailed knowledge of the channel error statistics. Since most practical
channels exhibit bursty tendencies, it is difficult to match the coding
to the channel if the burst statistics are not known. The designer is
forced to overkill, and fall back on a powerful random-error-correcting
code combined with a high degree of interleaving. Finally, a designer
may be faced with having to provide error control whilst still maintaining
the same effective data rate, and still using the same bandwidth, as the
uncoded system. This is one situation where multi-level signalling and/or
coding may have to be used; there are encouraging suggestions that this
may also be an effective way of applying error control[205,206].

5.3.2 The Successes

Error control has been successfully and usefully applied in a number
of areas. Space channels, which exhibit "almost-random" error character-
istics, have been well protected by means of block and convolutional codes
with soft-decision full minimum distance, and sequential and soft-decision
Viterbi decoding, respectively. Error detection and ARQ retransmission
methods have been universally implemented for digital transmission systems
on telephone networks, and for dedicated high-speed digital data networks
using co-axial cables and microwave links. It is also interesting to note

that relative success of what might be called "hybrid" coding sytems: combinations of relatively short codes, simple to decode optimally, in schemes such as interleaving, concatenation, cascading, product and other arrays, hybrid FEC-ARQ[208], etc, particularly when combined with soft-decision techniques. A recent notable development has been the emergence of soft-decision methods; these may now be applied to almost all methods of decoding, and in particular can make the performance of non-optimum decoding (eg, majority logic) approximate to that of optimum decoding, at much less cost in complexity.

5.3.3 The Failures (so far)

Coding theory has developed a comprehensive set of burst-error-control codes, with relatively simple implementation complexities. In practice, however, these are little used, mainly because of the lack of adequate channel error statistic characterisation. It is not always feasible to use interleaving to randomise bursts, because of synchron-isation and framing problems. Application of burst codes is therefore of potential interest. Or are they doomed to remain interesting but useless?

Low rate codes appear to decrease in "coding effectiveness" as rate decreases. Thus the coding gain decreases as rate decreases, and it seems almost impossible, even using all the tricks of the trade, to achieve channel capacity with low rate codes[209]. Perhaps it is necessary to pay more attention to the frequency domain properties of error-control codes, or to combine source and channel coding techniques, in an attempt to improve the effective rate of low rate error-control codes.

It is interesting to note that the large and seemingly effective class of cyclic finite geometry codes (projective geometry and Euclidean geometry codes) are not, apparently, worth implementing in practice. It seems strange that these codes, which are relatively easy to decode, are not used at all in practical coding systems. Or has the present reviewer missed reports in the literature of such applications?

True threshold decoding[65] tantalisingly offers good performance, at the expense of some complexity, but with the promise of significant simplification. This promise never seems to have been investigated. Or has soft-decision decoding overtaken true threshold decoding, making it redundant?

Finally, the potential high performance of multi-level codes requires further, and more systematic, development. Perhaps the advent of CCD devices and soft-decision decoding will open the way for further advances in this aspect of error-control coding.

Coding theorists, bounders, algebraists, engineers and designers should not despair, however. The subject, it is worth pointing out, is relatively new! It is only 28 years since Hamming's important paper[23]. This combination of newness and unsolved problems is what makes coding so interesting and demanding a field to work in!

REFERENCES

1.   F.M. Reza, *An introduction to information theory*, McGraw-Hill, 1961.

2.   R.G. Gallager, *Information theory and reliable communication*, Wiley, 1968.

3.   T. Berger, *Rate distortion theory - A mathematical basis for data compression*, Prentice-Hall, 1971.

4.   D.A. Huffman, A method for the construction of minimum redundancy codes, *Proc. IRE*, 40, 1098, Sept. 1952.

5.   G. Longo, Source coding theory, Lecture notes, CISM, Udine, 1970.

6.   B.P. Tunstall, Synthesis of Noiseless compression codes, Ph.D. Dissertation, Georgia Inst. Tech., Atlanta, 1968.

7.   D.W. Davies & D.L.A. Barber, *Communication networks for computers*, Wiley, 1973.

8.   J. Salz & B.R. Saltzberg, Double error rates in differentially coherent phase systems, *IEEE Trans*, COM-12, 202, June, 1964.

9.   P.G. Farrell, Coding for noisy data links, Ph.D. Dissertation, Universtiy of Cambridge, 1969.

10.   J.L. Massey, Joint source and channel coding, *Proc. NATO ASI on Comm. Systs and Random Process Theory*, North-Holland, 1978.

11.   K.W. Cattermole, *Principles of pulse code modulation*, Iliffe, 1969.

12.   W.W. Peterson & E.J. Weldon, *Error-correcting codes*, MIT Press, 1972.

13.   Shu Lin, *An introduction to error-correcting codes*, Prentice-Hall, 1970.

14.   F.J. Macwilliams & N.J.A. Sloane, *The theory of error-correcting codes*, Vols. I & II, North-Holland, 1977.

15.   E.R. Berlekamp, *Algebraic coding theory*, McGraw-Hill, 1968.

16.   I.F. Blake & R.C. Mullin, *The mathematic theory of coding*, Academic Press, 1975.

17.   H.B. Mann (Ed.), *Error correcting codes*, Wiley, 1968.

18. E.G. Search, Performance of Multilevel error control codes,
     M.Sc. Dissertation, University of Kent at Canterbury, 1977.

19. D. Slepian, Some further theory of group codes, *BSTJ*, 39, 5, 1219,
     Sept. 1960.

20. N. Tokura et al., A search procedure for finding optimum group
     codes for the binary symmetric channel, *IEEE Trans*, IT-13, 4,
     587, Oct. 1967.

21. J.L. Massey & M.K. Sain, Inverses of linear sequential machines,
     IEEE Trans, C-17, 330, April 1968.

22. D.J. Costello, A strong lower bound on free distance for periodic
     convolutional codes, *Proc. IEEE Int. Symp. on Info. Theory*,
     Noordwijk, 1970.

23. R.W. Hamming, Error detecting and error correcting codes, *BSTJ*, 26,
     2, 147, April 1950.

24. D. Slepian, A class of binary signalling alphabets, *BSTJ*, 35,
     203, Jan. 1956.

25. D. Slepian, Group codes for the Gaussian channel, *BSTJ*, 47, 575, 1968.

26. D. Slepian, Permutation modulation, *Proc. IEEE*, 53, 3, 228, March 1965.

27. S.I. Samoylenko, Binoid error-correcting codes, *IEEE Trans*, IT-19,
     95, Jan. 1973.

28. G.D. Forney, Burst-correcting codes for the classic bursty channel,
     IEEE Trans, COM-19, 5, 772, Oct. 1971, Part II.

29. D.W. Hagelbarger, Recurrent codes - easily mechanised burst-
     correcting, binary codes, *BSTJ*, 38, 4, 969, July 1959.

30. A.D. Wyner & R.B. Ash, Analysis of Recurrent Codes, *IEEE Trans*,
     IT-9, 3, 143, July 1963.

31. A. Kohlenberg & G.D. Forney, Convolutional coding for channels
    with memory, *IEEE Trans*, IT-14, 5, 618, Sept. 1968.

32. C.E. Shannon, A Mathematical Theory of Communication, *BSTJ*, 27,
    July p 379, Oct. p 623, 1948 (also Univ. of Illinois Press, 1963).

33. M.J.E. Golay, Notes on Digital Coding, *Proc IRE*, 37, 6, 657, Jan.1949.

34. M.J.E. Golay, Binary coding, *IRE Trans*, IT-4, 23, Sept. 1954.

35. D.A. Huffman, The synthesis of linear sequential coding networks,
    3rd London Symp. on Info. Theory, Sept. 1955; Ed. Cherry, 1956.

36. D.A. Huffman, A linear circuit viewpoint on error-correcting codes,
    IRE Trans, IT-2, 3, 20, Dec. 1956.

37. B. Elspas, The theory of Autonomous linear networks, *IRE Trans*,
    CT-6, 1, 45, March 1959.

38. J.J. Stiffler, *Theory of synchronous communications*, Prentice-Hall,
    1971.

39. H.C.A. VanDurren, Typendruktelegraphie over Radioverbindigen,
    Tydschrift van het Netherlands Radio Genootschap, 16, 53,
    March 1951.

40. H.C.A. Van Durren, Error probability and transmission speed on
    circuits using error detection and automatic repetition of
    signals, *IRE Trans*, CS-9, 1, 38, March 1961.

41. R.J. Benice & A.H. Frey, Improvements in the Design of Retransmission
    Systems, *IEEE Trans*, COM-15, 3, 463, June 1967.

42. A.R.J. Sastry, Improving ARQ performance on satellite channels
    under high error rate conditions, *IEEE Trans*, COM-23, 4,
    436, April 1975.

43. J.P.M. Schalkwijk & T. Kailath, A coding scheme for additive noise channels with feedback - Part i: No bandwidth constraint, *IEEE Trans*, IT-12, 2, 172, April 1966; Part II: Band-limited signals, 183.

44. A.J. Kramer, Use of Orthogonal signalling in sequential decision feedback, *Info. & Control*, 10, 509, May 1967.

45. K. Brayer, ARQ and Hybrid FEC-ARQ system design to meet tight performance constraints, *Proc. NTC DAllas*, II, 24.6-1/6-5, Nov.-Dec. 1976.

46. E.Y. Rocher & R.L. Pickholtz, An analysis of the effectiveness of hybrid transmission schemes, *IBM Jour Res Dev*, 426, July 1970.

47. D.M. Mandelbaum, An adaptive feedback coding scheme using incremented redundancy, *IEEE Trans*, IT-20, 3, 388, May 1974.

48. P.S. Sindhu, Retransmission error control with memory, *IEEE Trans*, COM-25, 5, 473, May 1977.

49. R.L. Kirlin, Variable Block length and transmission efficiency, *IEEE Trans*, COM-17, 3, 350, June 1969.

50. R.M.F. Goodman & P.G. Farrell, Data transmission with variable redundancy error control over a high-frequency channel, *Proc. IEE*, 122, 2, 113, Feb. 1975.

51. G. Neri, et al., A reliable protocol for high-speed packet transmission, *IEEE Trans*, COM-25, 10, 1203, Oct. 1977.

52. P. Elias, Error-free coding, *IRE Trans*, IT-4, 29, Sept. 1954.

53. J.M. Wozencraft, Sequential decoding for reliable communication, *IRE Nat. Conv. Rec.*, Pt 2, p 11, 1957.

54. Z. Kiyasu, Res. and Dev. Data No 4, Elec. Comm. Lab., Nippon Tele.

Corp., Tokyo.

55. G. Forney & E.K. Bower, A high-speed sequential decoder, *IEEE Trans*, COM-19, 5, Pt. II, 821, Oct. 1971.

56. J.E. Meggitt, Error correcting codes and their implementation for data transmission systems, *IEEE Trans*, IT-7, 4, 234, Oct. 1960.

57. V.C. Rocha, Versatile error-control coding systems, Ph.D. Dissertation, Univ. of Kent at Canterbury, 1976.

58. F.J. Macwilliams, Permutation decoding of systematic codes, *BSTJ*, 43, 485.

59. J.J. Metzner, VAriable-length block codes with internal sequential decoding and retransmission strategies, *Proc. NTC Dallas*, II, 24.2-1/3-5, Dec. 1976.

60. J.L. Katz, A feedback communication system using convolutional codes, Ph.D. Dissertation, Purdue Univ. 1971.

61. R.W. Lucky, J. Salz & E.J. Weldon, *Principles of aatu commmunication*, McGraw-Hill, 1968.

62. R.L. Townsend & E.J. Weldon, Self-orthogonal quasi-cyclic codes, *IEEE Trans*, IT-13, 2, 183, April 1967.

63. L.D. Rudolph & C.R.P. Hartmann, Decoding by sequential code reduction, *IEEE Trans*, IT-19, 4, 549, July 1973.

64. L.E. Wright & L.F. Turner, Simplified decoders for projective-geometry codes, *Proc IEE*, 125, 5, 365, May 1978.

65. L.D. Rudolph, Threshold decoding of cyclic codes, *IEEE Trans*, IT-15, 3, 414, May 1969.

66. J.L. Massey, *Threshold decoding*, MIT Press, 1963.

67. I.M. Jacobs & E.R. Berlekamp, A lower bound to the distribution
     of computation for sequential decoding, *IEEE Trans*, IT-13, 2,
     167, April 1967.

68. J.E. Savage, The distribution of sequential decoding computation
     time, *IEEE Trans*, IT-12, 143.

69. J.M. Wozencraft & M. Horstein, Coding for two-way channels, *Proc.*
     4th London Symp. on Info. Theory, Ed. C. Cherry, p 11, 1961.

70. R.M. Fano, A heuristic discussion of probabilistic decoding,
     IEEE Trans, IT-9, 2, 64, April 1963.

71. W.H. Ng & R.M.F. Goodman, An efficient minimum-distance decoding
     algorithm for convolutional error-correcting codes, *Proc IEE*,
     125, 2, 97, Feb. 1978.

72. See 53.

73. J. Hagenauer, Sequential decoding for burst-error-channels,
     Proc. NATO ASI on Comm. Systems and Random Processes,
     North-Holland, 1978.

74. A.J. Viterbi, Error bounds for convolutional codes and an
     Asymptotically optimum decoding algorithm, *IEEE Trans*, IT-13,
     2, 260, April 1967.

75. J.G. Proakis, Performance capabilities of the Viterbi Algorithm
     for combatting intersymbol interference on fading multipath
     channels, *Proc. NATO ASI on Comm. Systs and Random Processes*,
     North-Holland, 1978.

76. F. Hemmati & D.J. Costello, Truncation error probability in Viterbi
     decoding, *IEEE Trans*, COM-25, 5, 530, May 1977.

77. P.S. Moharir, Totally selective convolutional decoding, *Elec. Letters*, 12, 7, 161, 1st April 1976.

78. F. Jelinek, A fast sequential decoding algorithm using a stack, *IBM Jour. Res. Dev.*, 13, 675, Nov. 1969.

79. D. Haccoun & M.J. Ferguson, Genralised stack algorithms for decoding convolutional codes, *IEEE Trans*, IT-21, 6, 638, Nov. 1975.

80. P.R. Chevillat & D.J. Costello, A multiple stack algorithm for erasure free decoding of convolutional codes, *IEEE Trans*, COM-25, 12, 1460, Dec. 1977.

81. J.P.M. Schalkwijk & A.J. Vinck, Syndrome decoding of convolutional codes, *IEEE Trans*, COM-23, 789, July 1975.

82. J.P.M. Schalkwijk, On the performance of a maximum likelihood decoder for convolutional codes, AGARD Symp. on Dig. Comms in Avionics, Munich, June 1978, pp 13-1/13-6 (AGARD Conf. Preprint No. 239).

83. J.K. Wolf, Efficient maximum likelihood decoding of linear block codes using a trellis, *IEEE Trans*, IT-24, 1, 76, Jan. 1978.

84. J.M. Wozencraft & R.S. Kennedy, Modulation and demodulation for probabilistic decoding, *IEEE Trans*, IT-12, 4, 291, July 1966.

85. M. BAlser & R.A. Silverman, Coding for constant-data-rate systems, Part I, *Proc IRE*, 42, 9, 1428, Sept. 1954; Part II, *Proc IRE*, 43, 6, 728, June 1955.

86. C.R. Cahn, Binary decoding extended to Nonbinary demodulation of phase shift keying, *IEE Trans*, COM-17, 5, 583, Oct. 1969.

87. P.G. Farrell, E. Munday & N. Kalligeros, Digital communications

using soft-decision detection techniques, AGARD Symp. on Dig.
Comms in Avionics, Munich, June 1978, p 14.1/9.

88.   K.L. Jordan, The performance of sequential decoding in conjunction
      with efficient modulation, *IEEE Trans*, COM-14, 3, 283, June 1966.

89.   R.M.F. Goodman & W.H. Ng, Soft-decision threshold decoding of
      convolutional codes, *Proc IERE on Digital processing of signals
      in communications,* 37, 535, Loughborough, England, 1977.

90.   C.E. Sundberg, Asymptotically optimum soft-decision decoding
      algorithms for Hamming codes, *Elec Letters*, 13, 2, 38, 20th Jan.
      1977.

91.   C.N. Harrison, Application of soft decision techniques to block
      codes, *Proc IERE Conf. on Digital processing of signals in
      communications*, 37, 331, Loughborough, England, 1977.

92.   G. Forney, Genralised minimum distance decoding, *IEEE Trans*, IT-12,
      2 (April), 125, and in "Concatenated codes", MIT Res. Memo.
      37, 1966.

93.   S.M. Reddy & J.P. Robinson, Random error and burst correction by
      iterated codes, *IEEE Trans*, IT-18, 182, 1972.

94.   G. Einarsson & C.E. Sundberg, A note on soft-decision decoding
      with successive erasures, *IEEE Trans*, IT-22, 1 (Jan.), 88, 1976.

95.   R.M.F. Goodman & A.D. Green, Microprocessor controlled soft-decision
      decoding of error-correcting block codes. *Proc. IERE Conf. on
      Digital processing of signals in communications*, 37, 37,
      Loughborough, England, 1977.

96.   E.J. Weldon, Decoding binary block codes on Q-ary output channels,
      IEEE Trans, IT-17, 6 (Nov.), 713, 1971.

97. C.E. Sundberg, One-step majority logic decoidng with symbol reliability information, *IEE Trans*, IT-21, 2 (March), 236, 1975.

98. C.R.P. Hartmann & L.D. Rudolph, An optimum symbol-by-symbol decoding rule for linear codes, *IEEE Trans*, IT-22, 5 (Sept), 514, 1976.

99. B. Dorsch, A decoding algorithm for binary block codes and J-ary Output channels, *IEE Trans*, IT-20, 3 (May), 391, 1974.

100. P.G. Farrell, Soft-decision minimum-distance decoding, *Proc NATO ASI on Communications systems and random process theory*, Darlington, England, Aug. 1977; North-Holland, 1978.

101. P.G. Farrell & E. Munday, Variable-redundancy HF digital communications with adaptive soft-decision minimum-distance decoding, Final Rep. Res. Study Contract AT/2099/05/ASWE MOD, May 1978.

102. D. McQuilton & M.E. Woodward, Pseudostep orthogonalisation - an algorithm for improving Reed-Massey threshold codes, *Elec Letters*, 14, 12, 355, 8th June 1978.

103. Barry Research Corp, Time-diversity modem, Palo Alto, Calif. USA, 1974.

104. G. Andjargholi, Spread-spectrum data transmission at HF, Ph.D. Thesis, University of Kent at Canterbury, 1976.

105. P.G.Farrell & G. Andjargholi, A spread-spectrum digital transmission system for reliable communication in the HF band, *Proc IEE Colloq. on HF Communication systems*, London, Feb. 1976.

106. P.R. Keller, An automatic error correction system for uniderectional HF teleprinter circuits, *Point-to-Point Telecoms*, 7, 3, 1, June 1963.

107. M. Tomlinson & B. H. Davies, Low error rate correction coding for channels with pahse jitter, Report No.77004, RSRE, Feb. 1977.

108. J. Pieper, et al., The use of constant weight block codes for the underwater channel, *Proc IEEE EASCON*.Sept. 1977, Arlington, U.S.A., p 36.

109. J.B. Moore, US Patent 2,183,147, 1934.

110. See 40.

111. The Netherlands, Contribution to data transmission over isochronous systems and to error control, CCITT Blue Book 1964, Supp.17, 169.

112. H.B. Voelcker, Simple codes for fading circuits, *IRE Trans*, CS-6, 47, Dec. 1958.

113. R. Treciokas, Application of FEC to a Raleigh fading HF communication channel, *Proc IEE*, 125, 3, 173, March 1978.

114. Marconi Ltd., SPECTOR, A new telegraph error correcting system.

115. M.-Y. Hsiao & J.T. Tou, Application of error-correcting codes in computer reliability studies, *IEEE Trans*, R-18, 3, 108, Aug.1969.

116. G. Riley, Error control for data multiplex systems, Ph.D. thesis, Univ. of Kent at Canterbury, 1975.

117. M. Goldberg, Easily decoded error-correcting codes and tehcniques for their generation, Ph.D. thesis, Univ. of London, 1971.

118. N.E. Head, A high-speed data transmission system, *GEC Jour*, 30, 3, 129, 1963.

119. N.J.A. Sloane, A simple description of an error-correcting code for high-density magnetic tape, *BSTJ*, 55, 2, 157, Feb. 1976.

120. D.T. Brown & F.F. Sellers, Error correction for IBM 800-bit-per-inch magnetic tape, *IBM Jour. Res. Dev.*, 384, July 1970.

121. C.D. Mathers, Digital video recording - some experiments in error protection, BBC Res. Dept. Rep. 1976/1, Jan. 1976.

122. M.E. Kanter, A check digit technology for data preparation (off-line) equipment, M.Sc. dissertation, Univ. of Kent at Canterbury, 1971.

123. J.H. Van Lint, *Coding theory*, Springer-Verlag, 1971.

124. Scientific Control Systems Ltd, SPARQ of life for HF.

125. P. Darrington, Wireless World Teletext Decoder, *Wireless World*, 498, Nov. 1975.

126. R.W. Levell, The application of a Hamming error correcting codes to a standard teletype equipment, *Jour. Brit. IRE*, 371, Nov. 1961.

127. A.H. Cribbens, et al., An experimental application of microprocessors to railway signalling, *Electronics & Power*, 209, March 1978.

128. B. Hillam & G.F. Gott, An experimental evaluation of interleaved block coding in aeronautical HF channels, AGARD Symp on Dig. Comms in Avionics, Munich, June 1978.

129. J. Brooks, Error correcting stores for a small computer, *New Elec*, 30, October 5th, 1976.

130. M.Y. Hsiao, A class of optimal minimum odd-weight-column SEC-DED codes, *IBM Jour. Res. Dev.*, 395, July 1970.

131. S.W. Golomb (Ed.), *Digital communications with space applications*, Prentice-Hall, 1964.

132. D.C. Bossen, b-Adjacent error correction, *IBM Jour. Res. Dev.*, 402, July 1970.

133. G. Benelli, et al., Generalised Hamming codes for burst-error-correction, *Alta Frequenza*, 44, Nov. 1975.

134. N.M. Abramson, A class of systematic codes for non-independent errors, *IRE Trans*, IT-5, 4, 150, Dec. 1959.

135. C. Badran, Double adjacent error correction, M.Sc. Dissertation, Univ. of Kent at Canterbury, March 1976.

136. C.R. Telfer, The generation of codes for DPSK channels, Proc. Conf. on Dig. Proc. of Signals in Comms, Loughborough, p 403, Sept. 1977.

137. I.S. Reed, A class of multiple-error-correcting codes and the decoding scheme, *IEEE Trans*, Vol IT-4, 38, 1954.

138. D.E. Muller, Application of Boolean algebra to switching circuit design and to error detection, *IEEE Trans*, V-3, 6, 1954.

139. J.H. Green & R.L. San Soucie, An error-correcting encoder and decoder of high efficiency, *Proc IRE*, 46, 7, 1741, Oct. 1958.

140. H.J. Crowley, A field test of error control systems, *IEEE Trans*. COM-17, 5, 569, Oct.1969.

141. R.C. Dixon, *Spread-spectrum systems*, Wiley, 1976.

142. E.D. Gibson, Exceptionally cost-effective error control, *IEEE Int. Comms. Conf. Digest*, June 1976.

143. Linkabit Corp., *Error control products*.

144. B.E. Sinclair, An error reducing coding system for digital satellite communication systems, IEE Conf. Pub. No.39, April 1968.

145. P. McNanamon, R. Janc & S. Tsai, HF communications performance: Coding and diversity, *Telecoms*, 27, August 1970.

146. K. Brayer, Error-correction code performance on HF, troposcatter and satellite channels, *IEEE Trans*, COM-19, 5, 781, Oct. 1971.

147. S.-Y. Tong, Burst trapping techniques for a compound channel, *IEEE Trans*, IT-15, 6, 710, Nov. 1969.

148. R.C. Bose & D.K. Ray-chaudhuri, On a class of error correcting binary group codes, *Info & Control*, 3, 68, March 1960 and 279 1960.

149. A.A. Hocquenghem, Codes correcteurs d'erreurs, *Chiffres*, 2, 147, 1959.

150. R.L. Townsend & R.N. Watts, Effectiveness of error control in data communication over the switched telephone network, *BSTJ*, 43, 6, 2611, Nov. 1964.

151. R.F. Steen, Error correction for voice grade data communication using a communication processor, *IEEE Trans*, COM-22, 10, 1595, Oct. 1974.

152. F. Schreiber, et al., An error-correcting data transmission system with block-by-block synchronous operation over telephone channels, *IEEE Int. Conv. Rec.*, pt 5, 73, 1964.

153. British Post Office, Error correction for digital transmission of broadcast quality TV signals, June 1977.

154. D.L. Cohn, Performance of selected block and convolutional codes on a fading HF channel, *IEEE Trans*, IT-14, 5, 627, Sept. 1970.

155. J.R. Juroshek, Interleaved block coding tests over VHF and HF channels, *IEEE Trans*, COM-19, 5, 709, Oct. 1971.

156. P. Fire, A class of multiple-error-correcting binary codes for non-independent errors, Sylvania Elec. Products Inc., Rpt No. RSL-E12, March 1959.

157. A.H. Frey & R.E. Kavanaugh, Every data bit counts in transmission cleanup, *Electronics*, 77, Jan. 22nd 1968.

158. A.H. Frey, Adaptive decoding without feedback, *IBM Tech*. TR 48-67-001, 1967.

159. I.S. Reed & G. Solomon, Polynomial codes over certain finite fields, *Jour. Soc. Ind. Applic. Maths*, 8, 300.

160. H. Fredricksen, Error correction for deep space network teletype circuits, NASA Jet Prop. Lab, Rep 32-1275, June 1968.

161. G.D. Forney, Concatenated codes, MIT Res. Memo no. 37, 1966.

162. A.M. Walker, High data rate PSK modems for satellite communications, *Mic. Jour*, p27, July 1976.

163. B.H. Batson & G.K. Huth, Convolutional coding at 50 MBPS for the shuttle KU-band return link, Proc. Int. Telecoms. Conf., L.A. Calif. USA, 175, Sept. 1976.

164. J.W. Modestino & S.Y. Mui, Performance of convolutionally encoded noncoherent MFSK modem in fading channels, Proc Int. Telecoms Cont. L.A. Calif. USA, 433, Sept. 1976.

165. G.D. Forney & E.K. Bower, A high-speed sequential decoder, *IEEE Trans*, COM-19, 5, 821, Oct. 1971.

166. J.L. Massey & D.J. Costello, Nonsystematic convolutional codes for sequential decoding in space applications, *IEEE Trans*, COM-19, 5, 806, Oct. 1971.

167. J.W. Layland & W.A. Lushbaugh, A flexible high-speed sequential decoder for deep space channels, *IEEE Trans*, COM-19, 5, 813, Oct.1971.

168. J.A. Heller & I.M. Jacobs, Viterbi decoding for satellite and space communication, *IEEE Trans*, COM-19, 5, 835, Oct. 1971.

169. G.C. Clark & R.C. Davis, Two recent applications of error-correction coding to communications systems design, *IEEE Trans*, COM-19, 5, 856, Oct. 1971.

170. J.H. Stott, et al., Digital video-error-correcting codes and a practical study of a Wyner-Ash error correctior, BBC Res. Dept. Rep. RD 1974/40, Dec. 1974.

171. SPC/PSK and SCPC/PCM/PSK System Specification, Oct. 1976.

172. R.T. Chien, et al., Error correction in a radio-based data
     communications system, *IEEE Trans*, COM-23, 4, 458, April 1975.

173. W.R. Bennett & F.E. Froehlich, Some results on the effectiveness
     of error-control procedures in digital data transmission, *IRE Trans*,
     CS-9, 1, 58, March 1961.

174. M.J. Ferguson, "Diffuse" threshold decodable rate ½ convolutional
     codes, *IEEE Trans*, IT-17, 2, 171, March 1971.

175. See 31.

176. W.K. Pehlert, Design and evaluation of a generalised burst-trapping
     error control system, *IEEE Trans*, COM-19, 5, 863, Oct. 1971.

177. B.H. Davies & G. Foley, The implementation of Viterbi decoding on
     satellite communication circuits, Proc Conf on Dig. Proc. of Sigs
     in Comms, Loughborough, IERE Conf. Pub. No. 37, 159, 1977.

178. Codex Corp, 6000 Series intelligent network processor.

179. Hewlett-Packard Ltd., On line/on location data collection,
     Computer Advances 2, 6, 1977.

180. Int. Data Sciences, Inc., Automatic data error corrector.

181. R. Metcalfe & D.R. Boggs, Ethernet-distributed packet switching for
     local computer networks, *Comm. ACM*, 19, 7, 395, July 1976.

182. J.R. Nielsen & D.S. Kaplan, Data entry and communication systems have
     network capabilities, *Hewlett Packard Jour*, 21, March 1978.

183. T.D. Wells, et al., Implementation of an efficient inter-computer
     network for the distribution of multidestination messages, *Elec.
     Letters*, 14, 6, 189, 16th March 1978.

184. Cambridge Consultants Ltd., High speed inter-computer highway, *Elec. & Power*, 337, May 1978.

185. Ocitt Special Study Group A, Report on methods of error control, Blue Book 1964, Suppl. 61, 535.

186. Ocitt Special Study Group A, Error control systems for use on the International Telex Network, Blue Book 1964, Suppl. 12, 145.

187. H.O. Burton & D.D. Sullivan, Error and error control, *Proc. IEEE*, 60, 11, 1293, Nov. 1972.

188. E.R. Aylott & E.S. Simmonds, Error correction in data transmission systems, *Jour. Brit IRE*, 141, Aug. 1962.

189. F. Mirshekari, An error control simulator, M.Sc. Dissertation, Univ. of Kent at Canterbury, Dec. 1977.

190. O.O. Olaniyan & L.F. Turner, On the error-correcting capability of optimum linear block codes, *Proc. IEE*, 123, 1, 26, Jan. 1976.

191. A.M. Michelson, The calculation of post-decoding bit-error probabilities for binary block codes, Nat. Telecoms Conf., Dallas, II, 24.3-1, Nov.-Dec. 1976.

192. A.B. Fontaine & W.W. Peterson, Group code equivalence and optimum codes, *Special Supp. IEEE Trans*, CT-6, 60, May 1959.

193. C.F. Hobbs, Approximating the performance of a binary goup code, *IEEE Trans*, IT-11, 142, Jan. 1965.

194. C.R.R. Hartmann, et al., Asymptotic performance of optimum bit-by-fit decoding for the white Gaussian channel, *IEEE Trans*, IT-23, 4, 520, July 1977.

195. K.A. Post, Explicit evaluation of Viterbi's union bounds on con-volutional code performance for the BSC, *IEEE Trans*, IT-23, 3, 403, May 1977.

196. See 82.

197. J.A. Gordon, Some aspects of adaptive multiplexing, Ph.D. Thesis, Hatfield Polytechnic, England, June 1977.

198. J.M. Morris, Throughput performance of data - communication systems using ARQ error-control schemes, US Naval Res. Lab. Re.8140, Sept.1977.

199. See 46.

200. S.H. Lebowitz, High-rate error correction codes, the correlation decoding approach, Nat. Telecoms Conf, Dallas, I, 13.1-1, 1976.

201. A.H. Levesque, Block-error distributions and error control code performance in slow Rayleigh fading, Nat. Telecoms Conf., II, 24.4-1, 1976.

202. See 168.

203. J.P. Odenwalder, Carrier tracking, bit synchronization and coding for S-band communications links, Proc. Int. Telem. Conf, Los Angeles, 467, Oct. 1974.

204. T.H. Abdel-Nabi et al., On interleaving certain block codes, Canadian Comms & Power Conf, 209, 1976.

205. G. Ungeroeck, Channel coding with multilevel/phase signals, IBM Zurich Res. Rep. May 1977.

206. J.B. Anderson & R. De Buda, Better phase-modulation error performance using trellis phase codes, *Elec Letters*, 12, 22, 587, 28th Oct. 1976.

207. I.M. Jacobs, Practical applications of coding, *IEEE Trans*, IT-20, 3, 305, May 1974.

208. J. Conan et al., Performance of ARQ, FEC and Hybrid ARQ/FEC error control schemes for high speed data transmission on satellite channels, Canadian Conf. on Comms & Power, 216, 1976.

209. B.G. Dorsch & F. Dolainsky, Tehoretical limits on channel coding under various constraints, AGARD Symp. on Dig. Comms in Avionics, Munich, June 1978.

210. A. Sewards, et al., FEC for the aeronautical satellite communications channel, AGARD Symp. on Dig. Comms in Avionics, Munich, 9.1, June 1978.

Figure 1 : Coding

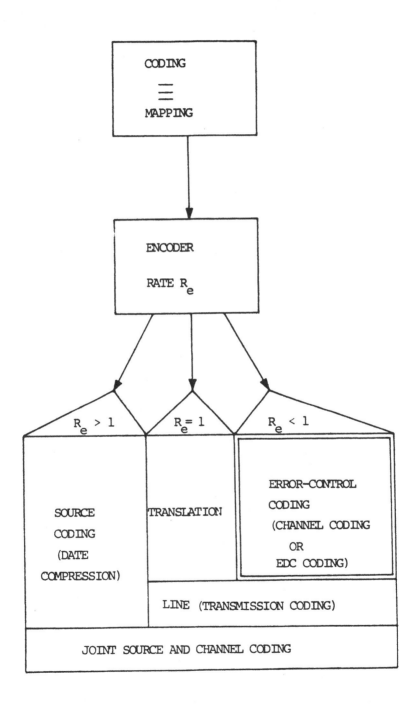

Figure 2 : Classification of Codes

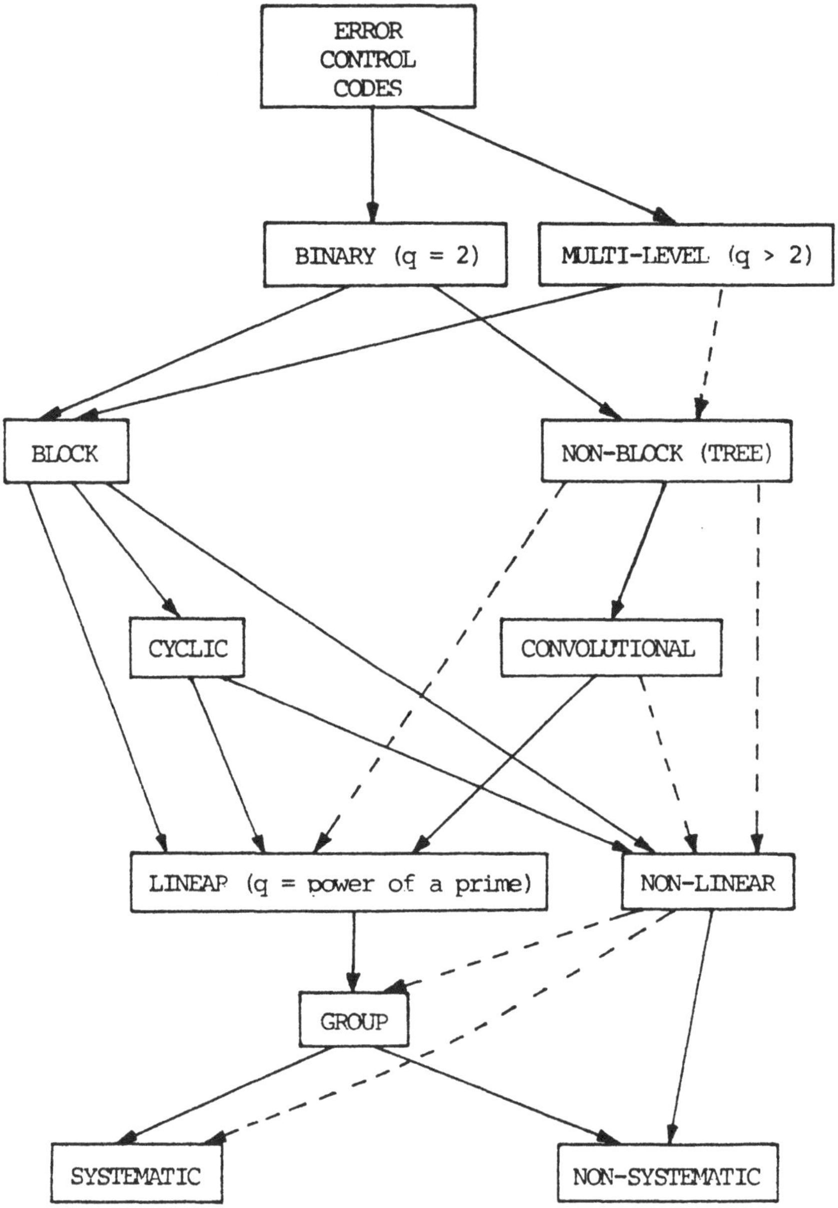

<u>Figure 3 : Classification of codes</u>

(continued)

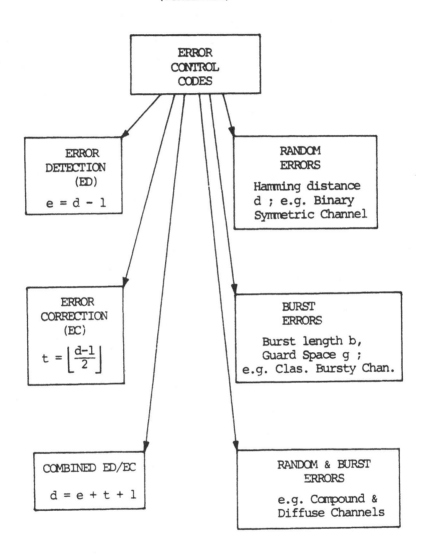

Figure 4 : Error Correction

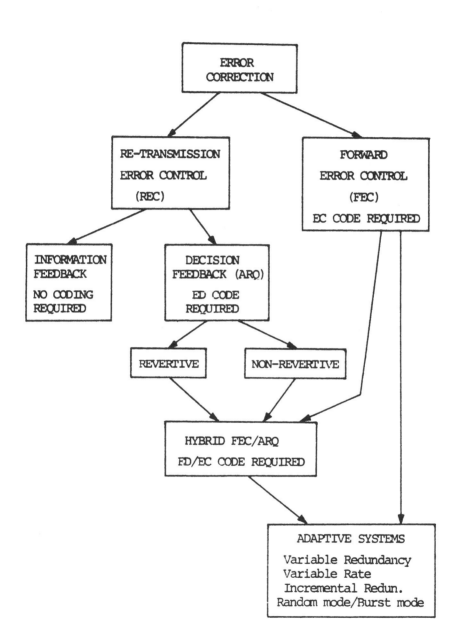

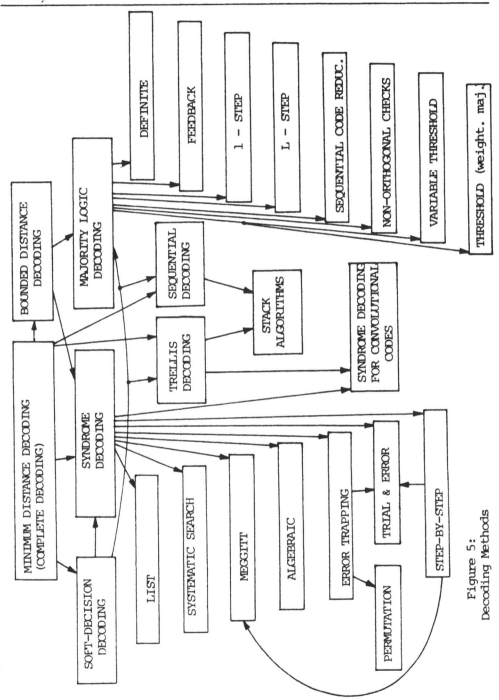

Figure 5:
Decoding Methods

Figure 6 : Classes of Codes

BLOCK			NON-BLOCK
NON-LINEAR	LINEAR		
NON-CYCLIC			WYNER-ASH (Recurrent) CONVOLUTIONAL (General) HAGELBARGER DIFFUSE
CONSTANT WEIGHT ORTHOGONAL	REPETITION SINGLE PARITY CHECK ARRAY HAMMING SEC REED-MULLER		
CYCLIC			
SEQUENCE SIMPLEX	SINGLE PARITY CHECK GOLAY SEC-DAEC BCH FIRE COMPUTER GENERATED FOR BURST EC REED-SOLOMON (Multi-level) ERROR DETECTION (for ARQ)		
	BURST TRAPPING		

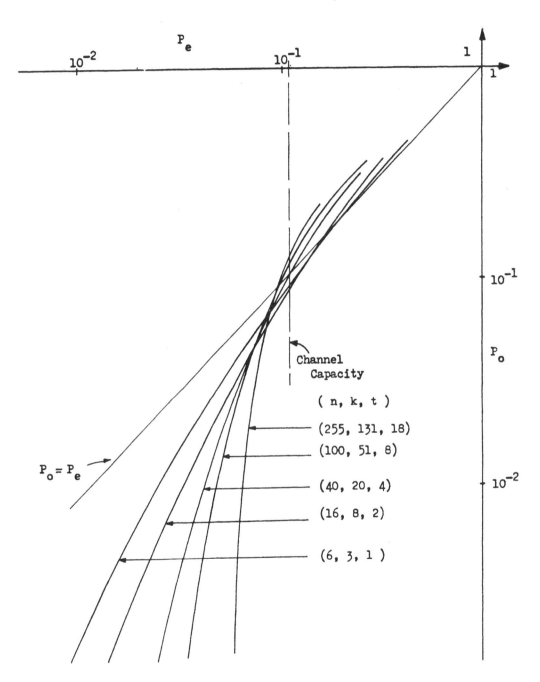

Figure 7 : Performance of half-rate block codes - random errors
Hard-Decision Decoding

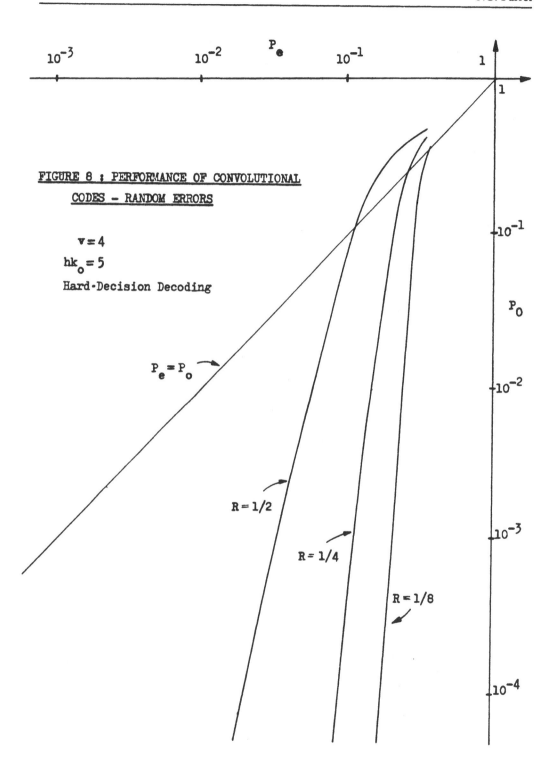

FIGURE 8 : PERFORMANCE OF CONVOLUTIONAL
CODES - RANDOM ERRORS

$v = 4$
$hk_o = 5$
Hard-Decision Decoding

$P_e = P_o$

$R = 1/2$

$R = 1/4$

$R = 1/8$

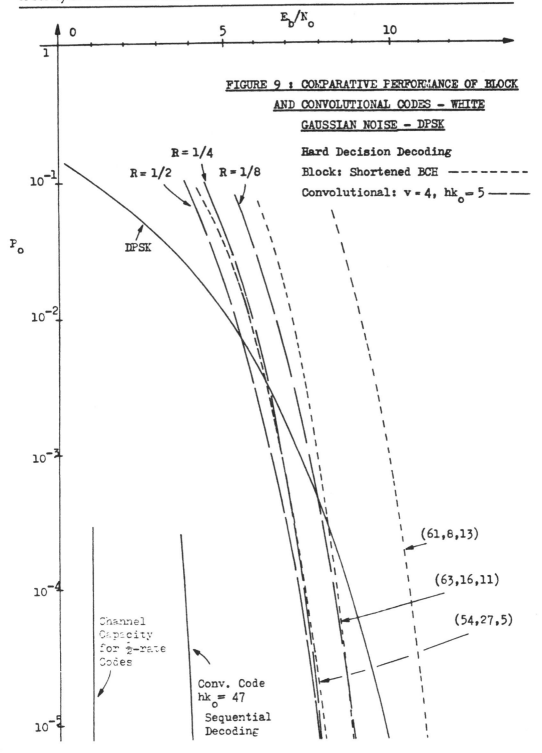

FIGURE 9 : COMPARATIVE PERFORMANCE OF BLOCK
AND CONVOLUTIONAL CODES — WHITE
GAUSSIAN NOISE — DPSK

Hard Decision Decoding
Block: Shortened BCH — — — — — —
Convolutional: $v = 4$, $hk_o = 5$ — — —

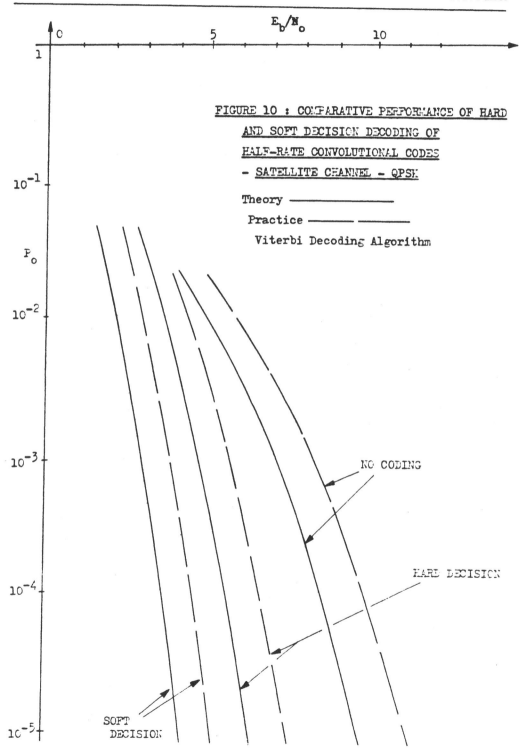

FIGURE 10 : COMPARATIVE PERFORMANCE OF HARD
AND SOFT DECISION DECODING OF
HALF-RATE CONVOLUTIONAL CODES
- SATELLITE CHANNEL - QPSK

Theory ————————
Practice ——— —— ———
Viterbi Decoding Algorithm

THE BOUNDS OF DELSARTE AND LOVÁSZ,

AND THEIR APPLICATIONS TO CODING THEORY

Robert J. McEliece[*]
Department of Mathematics
University of Illinois
Urbana, Illinois   61801, U.S.A.

1. INTRODUCTION

1.1 Preliminary Remarks

Our object in this article is to introduce the reader to two important topics in coding theory, and to a recently developed mathematical tool
that can be used to derive some extremely important results about them.

The coding theory topics are <u>sphere-packing in the Hamming metric</u>,
and the <u>zero error capacity of discrete memoryless channels</u>. The mathematical tool has no commonly agreed-upon name, but we will refer to it as
the <u>Delsarte-Lovász bound</u> after its two principal contributors.

[*]Much of this manuscript was prepared while the author was employed by
the Jet Propulsion Laboratory, California Institute of Technology, under
Contract No. NAS7-100, sponsored by the National Aeronautics and Space
Administration.

1.2 Sphere-Packing in the Hamming Metric

Let V_n denote the set of all 2^n binary n-tuples, a typical element
of V_n being $\underline{x} = (x_1, x_2,\ldots,x_n)$, with each $x_i = 0$ or 1. For
$\underline{x}, \underline{y} \in V_n$, denote by $\| \underline{x}-\underline{y} \|$ the __Hamming distance__ between $\underline{x}$ and $\underline{y}$,
i.e., the number of components in which $\underline{x}$ and $\underline{y}$ differ. A subset
$C = \{\underline{x}_1,\ldots,\underline{x}_M\} \subseteq V_n$ is called a binary __code of length n__; the $\underline{x}_i$ are
called __codewords__.

The __minimum distance__ of C is defined by

$$d_{min}(C) = \min\{ \| \underline{x}_i-\underline{x}_j \| : i \neq j\} \tag{1.1}$$

The significance of the minimum distance is this. Suppose person A
transmits one of the codewords from C, say $\underline{x}$, over a noisy binary channel to person B, and that B receives a garbled version of $\underline{x}$, denoted
by $\underline{y}$. B then tries to guess which codeword gave rise to $\underline{y}$ by compar-
ing $\underline{y}$ to each codeword $\underline{x}_i$; B's guess is that $\underline{x}_i$ for which $\| \underline{x}_i-\underline{y} \|$
is smallest. Of course B could make a mistake using this procedure,
but if $\| \underline{x}-\underline{y} \| < d_{min}(C)/2$, one can easily see that B will correctly
interpret $\underline{y}$. The integer $\| \underline{x}-\underline{y} \|$ is the number of errors caused by the
channel, and so $d_{min}(C)$ measures the code's ability to correct channel
errors.

Clearly the larger the code's minimum distance, the fewer codewords
it can contain, and so we define

A(n,d) = the largest integer M such that there exists M codewords
$\{\underline{x}_1, \ldots,\underline{x}_M\}$ from V_n such that $\| \underline{x}_i-\underline{x}_j \| \geq d$ if $i \neq j$.
Alternately,

A(n,d) = the largest number of codewords possible in a code of length n and minimum distance d.

The study of the numbers A(n,d) is regarded by many as the central problem of combinatorial coding theory. Although A(n,d) is rarely known exactly unless n and d are relatively small, or 2d $\geq$ n, a great deal of first-rate research has gone into the problem of finding good upper and lower bounds for A(n,d). The reader interested in what is known about this problem is urged to consult the recent book by MacWilliams and Sloane[1]. Here we will be content to describe what is currently the most powerful technique for obtaining <u>upper bounds</u> on A(n,d); it is called the <u>linear programming</u> approach.

The linchpin of the linear programming approach is a fascinating set of real numbers, which we denote by $K_j^{(n)}(i)$, where i and j lie in the range {0,1,...,n}. By definition

$$K_j^{(n)}(i) = \text{coefficient of } y^j \text{ in } (1-y)^i (1+y)^{n-i} \tag{1.2}$$

$$= \sum_{k=0}^{j} (-1)^k \binom{i}{k} \binom{n-i}{j-k}.$$

We will have much more to say about these numbers in Sec. 4. For now, we content ourselves with the statement of the following theorem.

Theorem 1.1

Let $(\lambda_0, \lambda_1, \ldots, \lambda_n)$ be n+1 real numbers satisfying

$$\lambda_0 > 0, \lambda_j \geq 0, \qquad j = 1, 2, \ldots, n \tag{1.3}$$

$$\sum_{j=0}^{n} \lambda_j K_j^{(n)}(i) \leq 0, \qquad i = d, d+1, \ldots, n. \tag{1.4}$$

Then,

$$A(n,d) \leq \frac{1}{\lambda_0} \sum_{j=0}^{n} \lambda_j K_j^{(n)}(0). \tag{1.5}$$

(The proof of Theorem 1.1 will be given in Sec. 4.2, using the general results derived in Sec. 2.)

Theorem 1.1 (or any of several variants of it) leads immediately to the <u>linear programming bound</u> for $A(n,d)$. This is because if we normalize the parameters λ_j so that $\lambda_0 = 1$, Theorem 1.1 implies that

$$A(n,d) \leq 1 + \sum_{j=1}^{n} \lambda_j K_j^{(n)}(0), \tag{1.5'}$$

provided that

$$\lambda_j \geq 0, \quad j = 1, 2, \ldots, n \tag{1.3'}$$

$$\sum_{j=1}^{n} \lambda_j K_j^{(n)}(i) \leq 0, \quad i = d, d+1, \ldots, n. \tag{1.4'}$$

Thus if we define $A_{LP}(n,d)$ as the minimum possible value of the linear function on the right side of (1.5'), subject to the linear constraints (1.3') and (1.4'), it follows that $A(n,d) \leq A_{LP}(n,d)$. The value $A_{LP}(n,d)$ is called the linear programming bound.

The values of $A_{LP}(n,d)$ can be computed exactly via the simplex method[2] with a computer for $n \leq \sim 200$. For larger values of n, at present no one knows how to compute $A_{LP}(n,d)$ exactly, but it can be estimated from above using the theory of orthogonal polynomials. We will describe this estimation in Sec. 4.3.

At present, the best known upper bounds on $A(n,d)$ for almost every pair (n,d) come from the linear programming bound or a modification of it[3]. Here we shall focus our attention only on the __asymptotic form__ of the A(n,d) problem, which we now describe.

The __rate__ of the code $\{\underline{x}_1, \ldots, \underline{x}_M\}$ is defined as $R = \log_2(M)/n$. It is a number between 0 and 1 and is a kind of measure of the density with which the codewords are packed into V_n. (In information - theoretic terms R measures the number of bits of information carried by each transmitted bit.) The rate of the best code of length n and minimum distance d is thus

$$R(n,d) = \frac{1}{n} \log_2 A(n,d).$$

The asymptotic problem is: how does R(n,d) behave for large n if we fix the ratio d/n? More formally, we define, for each $0 \le \delta \le 1$,

$$\bar{R}(\delta) = \sup \overline{\lim_{n \to \infty}} R(n,d_n)$$

$$\underline{R}(\delta) = \inf \underline{\lim_{n \to \infty}} R(n,d_n), \tag{1.6}$$

where the "sup" and "inf" are both taken over all sequences $(d_n)_{n=1}^{\infty}$ of positive integers satisfying $d_n/n \to \delta$. It is annoying that both an upper and a lower value of $R(\delta)$ must be defined, but unfortunately no one has ever succeeded in proving that the limits in (1.6) exist. For simplicity in what follows, however, we shall refer only to $R(\delta)$, it being understood that an upper bound on $R(\delta)$ is really an upper bound on $\bar{R}(\delta)$, and a lower bound is a lower bound on $\underline{R}(\delta)$.

It is known, and relatively easy to prove, that R(0) = 1 and $R(\delta) = 0$ for $\frac{1}{2} \le \delta \le 1$, but $R(\delta)$ is unknown for $0 < \delta < \frac{1}{2}$. The best known lower bound for $R(\delta)$ was obtained by Gilbert in 1952:

Gilbert: $R(\delta) \geq 1 - H_2(\delta)$,   (1.7)

where $H_2(\delta) = -\delta \log_2 \delta - (1-\delta)\log_2(1-\delta)$ is the binary entropy function.
There has been a whole series of steadily decreasing upper bounds on $R(\delta)$.
The earliest were due to Hamming (1950) and Plotkin (1951):

Hamming: $R(\delta) \leq 1-H_2(\delta/2)$

Plotkin: $R(\delta) \leq 1-2\delta$.

Neither of these bounds includes the other as a special case, and for about
10 years the Hamming and Plotkin bounds together were the best known.   Then
in 1960 Elias discovered a bound which was simultaneously better than both
the Hamming and Plotkin bonds:

Elias: $R(\delta) \leq 1-H_2(\frac{1-\sqrt{1-2\delta}}{2})$.

(Elias did not publish his bound; the first publication was Bassilygo's
1964 independent rediscovery of it.   The papers of Gilbert, Hamming, Plotkin, and Bassilygo are reprinted in Berlekamp's anthology[4].)

Then, after a lapse of another 10 years or so, in 1974 Sidelnikov[5]
and Levenshtein[6] found upper bounds on $R(\delta)$ that improved Elias' for
all $0 < \delta < \frac{1}{2}$.   (The actual form of these bounds is rather complicated,
and the numerical improvement over Elias' bond is rather small, so we will
not state them explicitly.)

Finally, in 1977 McEliece, Rodemich, Rumsey, and Welch, using the
linear programming appraoch discussed above, discovered a pair of upper
bounds that are at this writing the best known for all $0 \leq \delta \leq \frac{1}{2}$:

$R(\delta) \leq H_2(\frac{1}{2} - \sqrt{\delta(1-\delta)})$ (1.8)

$$R(\delta) \leq \min_{0 \leq u \leq 1-2\delta} \{1 + g(u^2) - g(u^2 + 2\delta u + 2\delta)\}, \tag{1.9}$$

where $g(x) = H_2((1 - \sqrt{1-x})/2)$. (Actually (1.9) includes (1.8) as a special case, since the expression in brackets in (1.9), when evaluated at $u = 1-2\delta$, equals $H_2(\frac{1}{2} - \sqrt{\delta(1-\delta)})$. But in fact, one can show that the bound of (1.8) actually equals (1.9) for $0.273 < \delta \leq \frac{1}{2}$.)

In summary (see (fig. 1.1), the true value of $R(\delta)$ must lie somewhere between the Gilbert lower bound (1.7) and the MRRW upper bound (1.9). Most researchers seem to believe that in fact $R(\delta) = 1-H_2(\delta)$, but there seems to be little hope of proving this any time soon. For the present we must be satisfied with the MRRW upper bound. And in Section 4 of this paper, we will show how this bound can be derived from the linear programming approach described above.

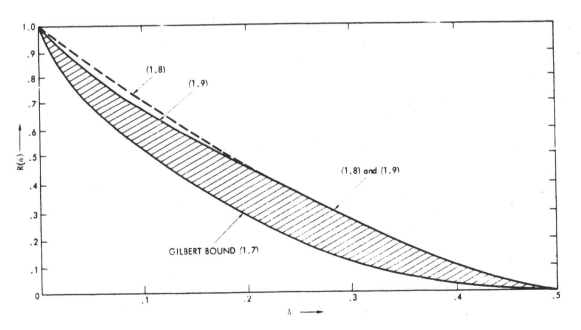

Figure 1.1.   Bounds on $R(\delta)$

1.3   The Zero Error Capacity of a Discrete Memoryless Channel

It is perhaps best to begin this section with a quotation from

Shannon's original paper[8] on the subject:

"The ordinary capacity   C   of a noisy channel may

be thought of as follows.   There exists a sequence of

codes for the channel of increasing block length such

that the input rate of transmission approaches   C   and

the probability of error in decoding at the receiving

point approaches zero.   Furthermore, this is not true

for any value higher than   C.   In some situations it

may be of interest to consider, rather than codes with

probability of error approaching zero, codes for which

the probability is zero and to investigate the highest

possible rate of transmission (or the least upper bound

of these rates for such codes).   This rate, C_0,...

would appear to be a simpler property of a channel than

C, [yet] it is in fact more difficult to calculate and

leads to a number of as yet unsolved problems."

We shall be concerned only with finite discrete memoryless channels.

Such a channel is described by its transition probabilities $\{p(y|x)\}$,

where $p(y|x)$ denotes the probability that the input letter   x   will be

received as the output letter   y.   Here   x   and   y   belong to finite sets

A_X and A_Y, called the input and output alphabets.   In Figure 1.2, we

give two examples, in which the letters in A_X and A_Y are represented

by nodes; the node corresponding to $x \in A_X$ and the node corresponding
to $y \in A_Y$ are connected by a straight line, provided $p(y|x) \neq 0$. (It
will soon become apparent that for purposes of computing the

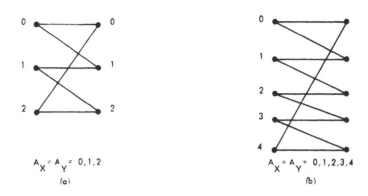

Figure 1.2. Two Discrete Memoryless Channels

zero-error capacity, one only needs to know which of the transition probabilities are equal to zero, and this information is contained in graphi-
cal representations such as those in Fig. 1.2.)

    Let us agree to call two input letters x, x' **adjacent** provided
there exists an output letter y such that $p(y|x)$ and $p(y|x')$ are
both non-zero. Note that if $\underline{x} = (x_1, x_2, \ldots, x_n)$ and $\underline{x}' = (x_1', \ldots, x_n')$
are two input sequences of length n, and if for each i, x_i and x_i' are
adjacent, $\underline{x}$ and $\underline{x}'$ can be confused with each other by the channel.
This is because if $\underline{y} = (y_1, y_2, \ldots, y_n)$ is a received sequence such
that $p(y_i|x_i)$ and $p(y_i|x_i')$ are both nonzero, for all i, then if $\underline{y}$
is received both $\underline{x}$ and $\underline{x}'$ are possible causes for $\underline{y}$. In particular,
this shows that if <u>all</u> input letters are adjacent to each other, any code
of any length with more than one codeword has a probability of error at

the receiver greater than zero.[*]

If, however, not all of the input letters are adjacent to each other,
then it is possible to transmit at a rate greater than zero with zero
probability of error. This can be seen as follows. Let $B = \{x_1, x_2, \ldots,$
$x_M\} \subseteq A_X$ be a set of mutually non-adjacent input letters; we assume
$M \geq 2$. If the receiver knows in advance that one of the letters from B
is going to be sent over the channel, then he will always be able to recover the transmitted letter from the received letter. This is because
our assumption of non-adjacency ensures that for each $y \in A_Y$ there is
at most one $x \in B$ such that $p(y|x) \neq 0$. If now B is regarded as a
code whose codewords are of length one, we see that we have achieved zero
error probability at rate $R = \log(M)$.

More generally, let $B_n = \{\underline{x}_1, \underline{x}_2, \ldots, \underline{x}_M\}$ be a zero error probability code of length n. That is, each $\underline{x}_k = (x_{k1}, x_{k2}, \ldots, x_{kn})$ is
an n-tuple of channel input letters, and the different $\underline{x}_k$'s are non-
adjacent. What this means is that if $\underline{x}_j = (x_{j1}, \ldots, x_{jn})$ and $\underline{x}_k =$
$(x_{k1}, \ldots, x_{kn})$ with $j \neq k$, there exists at least one index i such
that the letters x_{ji} and x_{ki} are non-adjacent. The rate of this code
is $R = \log(M)/n$, and the probability of error is zero.

We are thus led to define the <u>zero error capacity</u> of the channel as
follows. For each n, let M_n denote the largest possible number of
non-adjacent codewords of length n. The zero error capacity is then

---

[*] If P_e denotes this error probability, one can show that $P_e \geq \frac{M-1}{M} P_{min}^n$,
where M is the number of codewords, n is the length of the code,
and P_{min} = the least nonzero $p(y|x)$.

$$C_0 = \sup_n \frac{1}{n} \log(M_n) \qquad (1.10)$$

It is fairly obvious at this point that C_0 as defined by (1.10) is indeed the largest rate at which one can transmit information over the

channel with an error probability exactly equal to zero.

We should now like to state the definition (1.10) in terms of graph

theory. To this end let us define the <u>adjacency graph</u> corresponding to

a given discrete memoryless channel as the graph whose vertices correspond

to channel input letters; two such vertices are connected by an (undirect-

ed) edge if and only if the corresponding letters are adjacent. For

example, we give in Fig. 1.3 the adjacency graphs corresponding to the

channels of Fig. 1.2.

Let us agree to call two vertices x_1, x_2 of such a graph <u>adjacent</u>

if either $x_1 = x_2$ or if x_1 and x_2 are joined by an edge. Then

clearly $B = \{x_1, \ldots, x_M\}$ is a set of mutually non-adjacent input letters

if and only if the vertices corresponding to the elements of B are them-

selves non-adjacent. A set of non-adjacent vertices is commonly called

an <u>independent set</u> of vertices in a graph, and so we are led to define

$$\alpha(G) = \max \{|B| : B \text{ is an independent set of vertices in } G\}. \qquad (1.11)$$

Figure 1.3. The Adjacency Graphs Corresponding to the Channels of Fig. 1.2

To deal with codes of length ≥ 2, we must define the n-th direct

power of G, denoted G^n. The vertex set of G^n is the set $V^n = \{(v_1,$

$v_2, \ldots, v_n) : v_i$ a vertex of $G\}$; $\underline{v} = (v_1, \ldots, v_n)$ and $\underline{v}' = (v_1',$

$\ldots, v_n')$ are joined by an edge provided v_i and v_i' are adjacent for

each $i = 1, 2, \ldots, n$. With this definition, the cardinality of the

largest error-free code of length n is clearly $\alpha(G^n)$, and so a graph-

theoretic equivalent to (1.10) is

$$C_0 = \sup_n \frac{1}{n} \log \alpha(G^n). \tag{1.12}$$

Strictly speaking, C_0 as defined by (1.12) should be called the

capacity of the graph G, but since the significance of the logarithm is

not apparent to graph-theorists, frequently the quantity

$$\theta(G) = \sup_n \alpha(G^n)^{1/n} \tag{1.13}$$

is called the _capacity_ of the graph G. Note that this definition makes

sense for any undirected graph, whether or not it is given as the adjacen-

cy graph of a discrete memoryless channel.[*]

In his original paper, Shannon noted this close connection between

the zero error capacity of a discrete memoryless channel and the computa-

tion of $\alpha(G^n)$ for $n = 1, 2, \ldots$. He developed several techniques

which enabled him to compute the capacity of many, but not all graphs.

For example, Shannon showed that if there exists a mapping ϕ of the

---

[*] Also note that for any graph G, there exists a discrete memoryless channel which has G as its adjacency graph.

vertex set V into an independent set of vertices, such that if v and

v' are non-adjacent, so are $\phi(v)$ and $\phi(v')$, then $\alpha(G^n) = \alpha(G)^n$, and.

so $\theta(G) = \alpha(G)$.

He also gave an interesting probabilistic upper bound on $\theta(G)$: Let

P be a probability distribution on the set of vertices of G. We define

a <u>clique</u> in G as a set $\{x_1, \ldots, x_M\}$ such that x_i and x_j are ad-

jacent, for all (i, j). Shannon's bound is

$$\theta(G) \leq \lambda^{-1},$$

where

$$\lambda = \min_{P} \max \{P(X) : X \text{ a clique}\}, \tag{1.14}$$

the minimization in (1.14) being extended over all possible probability

assignments.

These two results enabled Shannon to calculate $\theta(G)$ for all graphs

with 5 or fewer vertices, with the single exception of the graph of Fig.

1.3(b). For this graph, which we shall denote by C_5, his results yielded

only .

$$\sqrt{5} \leq \theta(C_5) \leq 5/2. \tag{1.15}$$

Then, twenty-one years later, Lovász[9] devised a beautiful new tech-

nique for finding upper bounds on $\theta(G)$; his bound applied to C_5 gives

$\theta(C_5) \leq \sqrt{5}$, and hence establishes that $\theta(C_5) = \sqrt{5}$. We shall present

Lovász' technique for estimating graph capacities in Sections 2 and 3.

At present, Lovász' technique is the best way to estimate $\theta(G)$ for most,

(but not all; see Sec. 3.7) graphs G.

We have now introduced the reader to two classic coding theory prob-

lems: the computation of A(n,d) for various n and d, and the compu-

tation of the zero error capacity of an arbitrary discrete memoryless
channel. Let us conclude this section by observing that both problems
are special cases of the more general problem of estimating $\alpha(G)$ for an
arbitrary undirected graph G. We have already seen this in the case of
the zero-error capacity (see Eq. (1.13)). To cast the $A(n,d)$ problem
as an $\alpha(G)$ problem, define the graph $H_{n,d}$ for arbitrary positive integers $n \geq d$ as follows. The vertices in $H_{n,d}$ are the 2^n binary n-
tuples. Two vertices v and v' are connected by an edge if and only
if the Hamming distance between v and v' is $\leq d-1$. Then it is clear
that

$$A(n,d) = \alpha(H_{n,d}). \tag{1.16}$$

Having made this observation, we shall now devote our next section
to deriving techniques for estimating $\alpha(G)$, without further reference to
the underlying problems of coding theory. In Section 3 we shall apply
these techniques to the problem of computing graph (and hence zero-error)
capacities, and in Section 4, we will apply them to the $A(n,d)$ problem,
especially its asymptotic form.

2. THE BOUNDS OF DELSARTE AND LOVÁSZ

2.1 Introduction

In Sec. 1 we saw that two important coding theory problems can be
phrased in graph-theoretic terms. Because of this fact the present section - which contains the key results of this article - is wholly graph-

theoretic.

Let $V = \{v_1,\ldots,v_N\}$ be a finite set with N elements, and let E be a collection of two-element subsets of V. Then the set G consisting of the singletons $\{v_i\}$ from V and the elements of E is called a graph* on V. The elements of V are called the vertices, and those of E, the edges, of G. Using this definition the "pentagon" graph of Fig. 1.3b becomes

$$G = \{\{0\},\{1\},\{2\},\{3\},\{4\},\{0,1\},\{1,2\},\{2,3\},\{3,4\},\{4,0\}\}.$$

(For future reference, we will denote this graph C_5.)

A subset $Y = \{y_1,\ldots,y_M\}$ of V is called an independent set if none of the pairs $\{y_i,y_j\}$, $i \neq j$, are edges of G. The cardinality of the largest possible independent set in G is denoted by $\alpha(G)$:

$$\alpha(G) = \max \{|Y|: \ Y \text{ independent set in } G\}. \qquad (2.1)$$

For example, $\alpha(C_5) = 2$, and the set $Y = \{0,2\}$ is a maximal independent set for C_5.

For any integer $n \geq 2$, we now define the n-th direct power of G, denoted by G^n, as follows. The vertex set of G^n is the Cartesian power V^n, i.e., the set of all N^n n-tuples $\underline{v} = (v_1,\ldots,v_n)$ from V. The edge set of G^n consists of all pairs $\{\underline{v},\underline{v}'\}$ from V^n such that $\{v_i,v_i'\} \in G$ for all i. Let A be the incidence matrix of G, i.e. the following $N \times N$ matrix whose rows and column are indexed by elements of V:

---

*More accurately, an undirected graph.

$$A(v,v') = \begin{cases} 1 \text{ if } \{v,v'\} \in G \\ 0 \text{ if not.} \end{cases}$$

Then the incidence matrix of G^n is the n-th direct (Kronecker) power of A.

The <u>capacity</u> of G, denoted by $\theta(G)$, is now defined as follows:

$$\theta(G) = \sup_n \alpha(G^n)^{1/n} \qquad (2.2)$$

As we saw in Sec. 1, this notion was introduced by Shannon[8] in connection with the problem of finding the zero-error capacity of a discrete memory-less channel. In his original paper he developed techniques which enabled him to compute the capacity of many, but not all, graphs. The techniques developed later by Lovasz[9] are more powerful than Shannon's, though still not sufficient to determine $\theta(G)$ in all cases. Let us briefly sketch Lovasz' technique.

Lovász defines an <u>orthonormal representation</u> of G as a realization of G in which the vertex set V is a set of vectors in a Euclidean vector space, with the property that $\{v,v\} \in G$ iff. $v \cdot v' \neq 0$.

If G has such an orthonormal representation, and if b is any unit vector, Lovász' bound is as follows:

$$\theta(G) \leq (\min\{(v \cdot b)^2 : v \in V\})^{-1}. \qquad (2.3)$$

Lovász applied (2.3) to the graph C_5 by considering an "umbrella" with five ribs $\{v_1, v_2, \ldots, v_5\}$ of unit length. If the umbrella is opened to the point where the angle between alternate ribs is 90°, then $\{v_1, \ldots, v_5\}$ is an orthonormal representation of G in Euclidean 3-space. If the

handle b is also a unit vector then one easily shows that $b \cdot v_i = 5^{-1/4}$
for all i, and hence by (2.5), $\theta(C_5) \leq \sqrt{5}$. We shall give further applications of Lovász' technique to specific graphs in Sec. 3.

The derivation of the Lovász bounds in this section are due to
McEliece, Rodemich, and Rumsey[10], and in this derivation the concept of
orthonormal representation disappears. However, we felt it was important
to introduce the reader to Lovász' key idea as soon as possible; and, in
Sec. 2.4 we shall prove that the approach presented here is equivalent to
Lovasz' bound (2.5).

In Section 2.2 we give our derivation of the Lovasz bounds. It will
be seen that computing these bounds amounts to solving a certain nonlinear
programming problem.

In Section 2.3, we will demonstrate that if the graph G is sufficiently symmetric (in a sense to be made precise there), this nonlinear programming problem becomes a linear programming problem. This will lead us
naturally to the concept of an association scheme, and then to Delsarte's
linear programming bounds for cliques in association schemes.

In Sec. 2.4, we present a proof that the bound on $\theta(G)$ given in
Sec. 2.2 is equivalent to Lovász' bound (2.3).

2.2 The Lovász Upper Bounds

In this section and the next, G will denote a fixed graph. We will
continually be dealing with vectors and matrices whose components are
indexed by the vertex set V of G. If x is such a vector, and $v \in V$,
the v-th component of x will be denoted by x(v); if A is such a

matrix, its (v,v')-th component will be denoted by A(v,v').

We will also be working with the <u>quadratic forms</u> associated with

such vectors and matrices. If x is a (column) vector, and A a symme-

tric matrix, the quadratic form $x^T Ax$ is defined by

$$x^T Ax = \sum_{(v,v') \in V^2} x(v) \; x(v') \; A(v,v').$$

We will always view $x^T Ax$ as a function of the components of the vector

x.

The following will no doubt appear quite trivial, and yet it is our

main result. The remainder of this section will be devoted "merely" to

exploring its consequences.

Theorem 2.1:

Let A be a symmetric real matrix such that

$$A(v,v') = 1 \quad \text{if} \quad v = v'$$
$$\leq 0 \quad \text{if} \quad \{v,v'\} \notin G \tag{2.4}$$

Then if $u = (1,1,\ldots,1)$ denotes the all-ones vector,

$$\inf \{x^T Ax : x \cdot u = 1\} \leq \alpha(G)^{-1}. \tag{2.5}$$

Proof:

Let $Y \subseteq V$ be a maximal independent set in G, i.e., $|Y| = \alpha(G)$.
Define the vector y by

$$y(v) = \alpha(G)^{-1} \quad \text{if} \quad v \in Y$$
$$= 0 \qquad \text{if} \quad \text{not.}$$

Then clearly $y \cdot u = 1$, and by (2.4), $y^T Ay \leq \alpha(G)^{-1}$. This proves (2.5).■

Let us denote by $\lambda(A)$ the value of the left side of (2.5),

$$\lambda(A) = \inf \{x^T A x : x \cdot u = 1\} \tag{2.6}$$

Theorem 2.1 gives an upper bound on $\alpha(G)$, viz., $\alpha(G) \leq \lambda(A)^{-1}$, provided $\lambda(A) > 0$. Clearly in order to apply this bound we will need to know more about the function $\lambda(A)$. We shall now interrupt our development briefly in order to derive some of the more important properties of $\lambda(A)$. Throughout the following discussion we assume A is real and symmetric.

Lemma 1:

$\lambda(A) \geq 0$ iff A is positive semidefinite (hereafter abbreviated

p.s.d.).

Proof:

Since A is a real symmetric N x N matrix, according to the Principal Axis Theorem[11], there exists a set $\{\xi_1, \ldots, \xi_N\}$ of N orthogonal eigenvectors of A:

$$\xi_i \cdot \xi_j = 1 \quad \text{if} \quad i = j \tag{2.7}$$
$$= 0 \quad \text{if} \quad i \neq j;$$
$$A\xi_j = \lambda_j \xi_j, \quad j = 1, 2\ldots,N. \tag{2.8}$$

Thus, if $x = x_1 \xi_1 + \ldots + x_N \xi_N$ and $y = y_1 \xi_1 + \ldots + y_N \xi_N$, we have:

$$x \cdot y = \sum_{j=1}^{N} x_j y_j \tag{2.9}$$
$$x^T A y = \sum_{j=1}^{N} \lambda_j x_j y_j. \tag{2.10}$$

If one of the eigenvalues λ_j is negative, we can construct a vector x with $x \cdot u = 1$ and $x^T Ax < 0$, as follows. Let

$$u = u_1 \xi_1 + \ldots + u_N \xi_N \qquad (2.11)$$

be the expansion of u with respect to the basis $\{\xi_j\}$, and let $v = v_1 \xi_1 + \ldots + v_N \xi_N$ be a fixed vector with $v \cdot u = 1$. Assuming $\lambda_j < 0$, define for any real number β

$$x = \frac{\beta \xi_j + v}{\beta u_j + 1} . \qquad (2.12)$$

Clearly $x \cdot u = 1$, and from (2.10) we compute

$$x^T Ax = \frac{1}{(\beta u_j + 1)^2} \left\{ \lambda_j \beta^2 + 2\beta v_j + \sum_{i=1}^{N} \lambda_j v_j^2 \right\} .$$

Clearly this will be negative if β is large enough, since the expression in brackets is then dominated by the term $-|\lambda_j| \beta^2$. This proves Lemma 1.   ∎

In view of Lemma 1, we will get no information from A about $\alpha(G)$ from Theorem 2.1 unless A is p.s.d., and from now on we will assume A has this property. This means that the eigenvalues λ_j in (2.8) are all nonnegative. Let $u = u_1 \xi_1 + \ldots + u_N \xi_N$ be the expansion of u with respect to the basis $\{\xi_1, \ldots, \xi_N\}$. We can now give an explicit formula for $\lambda(A)$.

Lemma 2:

If A is p.s.d., then (cf. Eqs. (2.8), (2.11))

$$\lambda(A) = 0 \quad \text{if} \quad u_j \neq 0, \quad \lambda_j = 0 \quad \text{for some} \quad j \qquad (2.13)$$

$$= \left(\sum_j u_j^2 / \lambda_j \right)^{-1} \quad \text{otherwise,} \qquad (2.14)$$

where the summation in (2.14) is extended only over subscripts j with $\lambda_j > 0$. (Alternatively (2.14) includes (2.13) as a special case if we extend the summation over all j and make the appropriate conventions about infinity.)

Proof:

Since A is assumed p.s.d., the eigenvalues $\{\lambda_j\}$ in (2.8) are all non-negative. If for some index j we have $\lambda_j = 0$ but $u_j \neq 0$, and if we set $x = u_j^{-1} \xi_j$, then $x \cdot u = 1$, $x^T A x = 0$. This proves (2.13).

On the other hand if $u_j = 0$ whenever $\lambda_j = 0$, we get by Schwarz' inequality

$$\left(\sum x_j u_j \right)^2 \leq \left(\sum \lambda_j x_j^2 \right) \left(\sum \lambda_j^{-1} u_j^2 \right) , \qquad (2.15)$$

where the summation is extended only over indices for which $\lambda_j > 0$. Since by (2.9) and (2.10) $\sum x_j u_j = x \cdot u$, and $\sum \lambda_j x_j^2 = x^T A x$, (2.15) immediately implies that if $x \cdot u = 1$, then $x^T A x \geq \left(\sum \lambda_j^{-1} u_j^2 \right)^{-1} = \lambda$. On the other hand, by choosing $x_i = u_i \lambda_i^{-1} \lambda$ for all i, we get $x \cdot u = 1$ and $x^T A x = \lambda$. This proves (2.14). ∎

Lemma 3:

If A is p.s.d., and if u is an eigenvector of A with eigenvalue σ, then

$$\lambda(A) = \sigma/N. \qquad (2.16)$$

Proof:

Under the given hypothesis, in the expansion (2.11), u_j must be zero unless $\lambda_j = \sigma$. Hence from (2.16), $\lambda(A) = (\sigma^{-1} \sum u_j^2)^{-1} = \sigma/N$, since $\sum u_j^2 = u \cdot u = N$. This proves Lemma 3. ∎

Lemma 4:

If A is p.s.d., then

$$\lambda(A) = \max \{\lambda : A - \lambda J \text{ is p.s.d.}\}, \qquad (2.17)$$

where J denotes the matrix of all ones.

Proof:

Observe that

$$x^T(A - \lambda J)x = x^T A x - \lambda(x \cdot u)^2$$

$$= \left(\sum \lambda_j z_j^2\right) - \lambda(\Sigma x_j u_j)^2.$$

Comparing this to (2.15), we see that this expression will be nonnegative for all x if and only if $\lambda \leq \left(\sum \lambda_j^{-1} u_j^2\right)^{-1}$, i.e. $\lambda \leq \lambda(A)$. This proves Lemma 4. ∎

Lemma 5:

If A and B are p.s.d., then

$$\lambda(A \times B) = \lambda(A)\,\lambda(B).$$

Proof:

Suppose that $\xi_1, \ldots, \xi_N$ are principal axes for the matrix A, with corresponding eigenvalues $\{\xi_j\}$, and that $\eta_1, \ldots, \eta_M$ are principal axes for B, with eigenvalues $\{\mu_k\}$. Suppose further that $u^{(A)} = u_1^{(A)} \xi_1 + \ldots + u_N^{(A)} \xi_N$, $u^{(B)} = u_1^{(B)} \eta_1 + \ldots + u_M^{(B)} \eta_M$ are the expansions of the all ones vectors, with respect to these two bases.

It follows from known results[12] that the MN vectors $\xi_j \times \eta_k$ are principal axes for the matrix $A \times B$, with associated eigenvalues $\lambda_j \mu_k$. Furthermore the expansion of the MN - dimensional all-ones vector with respect to the basis $\{\xi_j \times \eta_k\}$ is clearly

$$u = \sum_{j,k} u_j^{(A)} u_k^{(B)} (\xi_j \times \eta_k).$$

Thus according to Lemma 2

$$\lambda(A \times B) = \left\{ \sum_{j,k} (\lambda_j \mu_k)^{-1} \left[u_j^{(A)} u_k^{(B)} \right]^2 \right\}^{-1}$$

$$= \lambda(A) \lambda(B),$$

establishing Lemma 5.   ∎

Having disposed of this background material on $\lambda(A)$, we now return to our main concern, the application of Theorem 2.1 to the problem of esti-mating $\alpha(G)$ and $\theta(G)$. According to Lemma 1, Theorem 2.1 will only give non-trivial information about $\alpha(G)$ if A is p.s.d. This leads us to define the following two sets of matrices.

Definition 1:

The set $\Omega(G)$ is defined as the set of all matrices $A = (A(v,v'))$

indexed by the vertices of G, satisfying

    A is p.s.d.   (2.18)

    $A(v,v) = 1$ for all $v \in V$ (2.19)

    $A(v,v') \leq 0$ if $\{v,v'\} \notin G$ (2.20)

Definition 2:

    Similarly $\Omega_0(G)$ is the set of matrices satisfying (2.18) and (2.19), with the condition (2.20) replaced with the stronger condition

    $A(v,v') = 0$ if $\{v,v'\} \notin G$ (2.20')

    The significance of the class $\Omega(G)$ is obvious, in view of Theorem 2.1 and Lemma 1.

Theorem 2.2:

    $\alpha(G) \leq \lambda(A)^{-1}$ for all $A \in \Omega(G)$.

    The significance of $\Omega_0(G)$ is given in the next theorem, which is essentially equivalent to the Lovasz bound (2.3). (For a proof of this equivalence, see Sec. 2.4.)

Theorem 2.3:

    $\theta(G) \leq \lambda(A)^{-1}$ for all $A \in \Omega_0(G)$.

Proof:

    The key to the proof is the fact that if $A \in \Omega_0(G)$, then the n-th direct power $A^{[n]} = A \times A \times \ldots \times A$ (n factors) will belong to $\Omega_0(G^n)$.

To see this, observe first that $A^{[n]}$ is p.s.d., being a direct pro-
duct of p.s.d. matrices. Next, if $\underline{v} = (v_1, \ldots, v_n)$ and $\underline{v}' = (v_1', \ldots, v_n')$ are vertices in G^n, then by definition of the direct product,

$$A^{[n]}(\underline{v},\underline{v}') = \prod_{j=1}^{n} A(v_j, v_j') \qquad (2.21)$$

It follows immediately that $A^{[n]}(\underline{v},\underline{v}) = 1$ for all $\underline{v} \in G^n$, since each of the factors on the right side of (2.21) will then be 1. If $\{v,v'\} \notin G^n$, there must exist at least one index j such that $\{v_j, v_j'\} \notin G$. Since $A \in \Omega_0(G)$, it follows from (2.20') that $A(v_j, j_j') = 0$ and hence that $A^{[n]}(\underline{v},\underline{v}') = 0$ as well. Hence $A^{[n]}$ satisfies (2.18), (2.19), and (2.20'), and thus lies in $\Omega_0(G^n)$.

Since $\Omega_0(G^n) \subseteq \Omega(G^n)$, we may apply Theorem 2.2 to the matrix $A^{[n]}$, and conclude that $\alpha(G^n) \leq \lambda(A^{[n]})^{-1}$. But from Lemma 5, $\lambda(A^{[n]}) = \lambda(A)^n$. Hence $\alpha(G^n) \leq \lambda(A)^{-n}$ for all n, and so from the definition (2.2) of $\theta(G)$, we get $\theta(G) \leq \lambda(A)^{-1}$.

We now define the <u>Lovász bounds</u> $\alpha_L(G)$ and $\theta_L(G)$:

$$\alpha_L(G) = \min \{\lambda(A)^{-1} : A \in \Omega(G)\} \qquad (2.22)$$

$$\theta_L(G) = \min \{\lambda(A)^{-1} : A \in \Omega_0(G)\} \qquad (2.23)$$

We have shown in Theorems 2.2 and 2.3 that $\alpha(G) \leq \alpha_L(G)$, $\theta(G) \leq \theta_L(G)$. Unfortunately we know of no efficient algorithm for computing $\alpha_L(G)$ and $\theta_L(G)$ for an arbitrary graph. However, we will now show that one can use the symmetries of G to simplify the calculations somewhat. In Section 2.3 we will extend these ideas and show that if G is highly symmetric, the bounds $\alpha_L(G)$ and $\theta_L(G)$ can be computed via linear programming. This result will lead to a generalization of Delsarte's linear programming bound for cliques to association schemes.

2.3 Computing the Lovász Bounds via Linear Programming

In this section we will show that if the graph G is sufficiently symmetric, the computation of the bounds $\alpha_L(G)$ and $\theta_L(G)$ can be greatly simplified. First, however, we must be precise about what is meant by symmetry.

A <u>symmetry</u> of the graph G is a permutation of the vertex set V that leaves the edge set E invariant. Thus if π is a permutation of V, it is a symmetry of G if and only if $\{\pi(v), \pi(v')\} \in E$ whenever $\{v,v'\} \in E$. Notice that a symmetry of G is also a symmetry of the <u>complementary graph</u> G', which has vertex set V and edge set E', the set of pairs not in E.

Let P be the group of symmetries of G, and let $E_1, \ldots, E_s$ be the orbits of E under the action of P. Similarly let $E_1', \ldots, E_t'$ be the orbits of E'. We shall call two edges lying in the same orbit <u>equivalent edges</u>.

Now suppose that $A \in \Omega(G)$ or $\Omega_o(G)$. Then it is easy to see that the matrix $\overline{A}$ defined by

$$\overline{A}(v,v') = \frac{1}{|P|} \sum_{\pi \in P} A(\pi(v), \pi(v')) \qquad (2.24)$$

also lies in the same set. Moreover, the matrix $\overline{A}$ has the property that if $\{v_1,v_1'\}$ and $\{v_2,v_2'\}$ are equivalent edges, then $\overline{A}(v_1,v_1') = \overline{A}(v_2,v_2')$. Additionally, we can show that $\lambda(\overline{A}) \geq \lambda(A)$. For if we denote by $\pi(A)$ the matrix with entries $A(\pi(v), \pi(v'))$, then for any value of λ,

$$\bar{A} - \lambda J = \frac{1}{|P|} \sum_{\pi \epsilon P} (\pi(A) - \lambda J)$$

$$= \frac{1}{|P|} \sum_{\pi \epsilon P} \pi(A - \lambda J).$$

If we let $\lambda = \lambda(A)$ then by Lemma 4, $A - \lambda J$ is p.s.d. and hence so is each $\pi(A - \lambda J)$. Thus $\bar{A} - \lambda J$ is p.s.d. and so by Lemma 4 $\lambda(\bar{A}) \geq \lambda(A)$.

Let us denote by B_j, $j = 1, 2, \ldots, s$ the edge incidence matrices for the edge orbits E_j:

$$B_j(v,v') = 1 \quad \text{if} \quad \{v,v'\} \epsilon E_j$$

$$= 0 \quad \text{if not.}$$

Similarly we define the matrices B'_k, $k = 1, 2, \ldots, t$ as the edge incidence matrices for the edge orbits E'_k. Then according to the preceding discussion, the matrix $\bar{A}$ can be expressed as a linear combination of these matrices, together with the $N \times N$ identity matrix I:

$$\bar{A} = I + \sum_{j=1}^{s} \mu_j B_j + \sum_{k=1}^{t} \mu'_k B'_k \qquad (2.25)$$

We have thus shown that starting with any matrix A in $\Omega(G)$ (resp. $\Omega_o(G)$), we can construct a matrix $\bar{A}$ of the form (2.25) lying in the same class such that $\lambda(\bar{A}) \geq \lambda(A)$. What this means is that in the computation of the bounds $\alpha_L(G)$ and $\theta_L(G)$, we can safely restrict ourselves to matrices of the form (2.25). More formally, we define

$\overline{\Omega}(G)$ = p.s.d. matrices of the form (2.25)

with $\mu_k' \le 0$ for $k = 1,2,\ldots,t$.

$\overline{\Omega}_0(G)$ = p.s.d. matrices of the form (2.25)

with $\mu_k' = 0$ for $k = 1,2,\ldots,t$.

We have then the following computationally simpler definition of the Lovasz bounds:

$$\alpha_L(G) = \min \{\lambda(A)^{-1} : A \in \overline{\Omega}(G)\} \qquad (2.26)$$

$$\Theta_L(G) = \min \{\lambda(A)^{-1} : A \in \overline{\Omega}_0(G)\}. \qquad (2.27)$$

The formulas (2.26) and (2.27) are considerably simpler than (2.22) and (2.23) if the graph G has a lot of symmetry. We have repeatedly alleged that the computation of these bounds can be done via linear programming, provided the graph is highly symmetric. We can now prove this allegation.

The degree of symmetry we require is that the <u>incidence matrices</u> $\{B_j\}$, $\{B_k'\}$ in (2.25) <u>commute with each other</u>. That this is in fact a statement about the symmetry group of G can be seen as follows.

Suppose P is the symmetry group of G. With each $\pi \in P$ we associate the corresponding permutation matrix π^*:

$\pi^*(v,v') = 1$ if $\pi(v) = v'$

$= 0$ if not.

Naturally the edge orbits $\{E_j\}$, $\{E_k'\}$ are left invariant by the symmetries $\pi \in P$; in terms of the corresponding incidence matrices, this can be expressed as

$$\pi^* B_j = B_j \pi^*, \text{ all } j = 1, 2, \ldots, s, \quad \pi \in P,$$

$$\pi^* B_k' = B_k' \pi^*, \text{ all } k = 1, 2, \ldots, t, \quad \pi \in P. \tag{2.28}$$

Now let P^* denote the group of all permutation matrices correspond-ing to the permutations in P, and let $Z(P^*)$ be the <u>centralizer ring</u> of P^*, i.e. the set of all matrices that commute with all $\pi^* \in P^*$. According to (2.28), the matrices $\{B_j\}$, $\{B_j'\}$ all belong to $Z(P^*)$.

If the ring $Z(P^*)$ were known to be commutative, then it would follow immediately that the matrices B_j, B_k' commute with each other. Fortunately, this frequently turns out to be the case. Indeed it can be shown[13] that if P is transitive, then $Z(P^*)$ is commutative if and only if the complex representation of P afforded by the matrix group P^* de-composes into a sum of inequivalent irreducible representations. In parti-cular if P contains a transitive abelian subgroup, or if for any pair (v, v') of distinct vertices there is an element of P which exchanges v and v', this condition will be satisfied.

Motivated by the preceding discussion, we now place our results in the following general setting.

Let V be a finite set containing N elements, and let $\{E_1, E_2, \ldots, E_n\}$ be a partition of the collection E of all two-element subsets of V. For each $j = 1, 2, \ldots, n$ let A_j be the incidence matrix for E_j:

$$A_j(v, v') = 1 \text{ if } \{v, v'\} \in E_j$$

$$= 0 \text{ if not.}$$

Let A_0 denote the $N \times N$ identity matrix. Assume that the matrices $\{A_j : j = 0, 1, \ldots, n\}$ commute with each other. In summary, the assumptions are that the A_j's are (0,1) matrices satisfying

$$A_0 = I, \quad \sum_{j=0}^{n} A_j = J \tag{2.29}$$

Each A_j is symmetric   (2.30)

$$A_j A_k = A_k A_j \quad \text{for all} \quad j,k = 0,1,\ldots,n. \tag{2.31}$$

If C is a fixed subset of $\{1,2,\ldots,n\}$, let G_C be the graph with vertex set V and edge set

$$E_C = \bigcup_{j \in C} E_j. \tag{2.32}$$

Our goal is to give "linear programming" upper bounds on $\alpha(G_C)$ and $\theta(G_C)$ (Theorems 2.4 and 2.5, below). To state these results, however, we need some preliminary discussion.

Notice that because of (2.29) and (2.31), each matrix A_j commutes with J, the all ones matrix, and hence the $n + 2$ matrices $J, A_0, \ldots, A_n$ all commute with each other. Since these matrices are moreover symmetric, and hence diagonalizable, it follows from a known theorem of linear algebra[14], that there exists a set $\{\xi_m\}_{m=1}^{N}$ of linearly independent <u>simultaneous eigenvectors</u> for these $n + 2$ matrices.

In particular the ξ_m's are eigenvectors for J:

$$J \xi_m = \lambda_m \xi_m, \quad m = 1,2,\ldots,N. \tag{2.33}$$

$\{\lambda_m\}$ being the set of eigenvalues for J. But J has only the eigenvalues $\{0,N\}$, and a simple calculation shows that if $J\xi = N\xi$, then ξ must be a scalar multiple of u, the all ones vector. Thus we may assume that $\xi_1 = u$.

Now for each j,m, define the eigenvalues $\lambda_{j,m}$ by

$$A_j \, \xi_m = \lambda_{j,m} \, \xi_m \qquad j = 0,1,\ldots,n \qquad (2.34)$$

$$m = 1,2,\ldots,N.$$

We come now to our "linear programming" bounds for $\alpha(G)$ and $\theta(G)$.

Theorem 2.4:

Let $\mu_1,\mu_2,\ldots,\mu_n$ be real numbers such that

$$\mu_j \leq 0 \quad \text{if} \quad j \notin C, \qquad (2.35)$$

and

$$1 + \sum_{j=1}^{n} \mu_j \, \lambda_{j,m} \geq 0, \quad m = 1,2,\ldots,N \qquad (2.36)$$

Then

$$\alpha(G_C) \leq N \Big/ \left(1 + \sum_{j=1}^{n} \mu_j \, \lambda_{j,1}\right).$$

Theorem 2.5:

Let $\mu_1,\ldots,\mu_n$ satisfy (2.36), and also

$$\mu_j = 0 \quad \text{if} \quad j \notin C. \qquad (2.35)$$

Then

$$\theta(G_C) \leq N \Big/ \left(1 + \sum_{j=1}^{n} \mu_j \, \lambda_{j,1}\right).$$

Proofs.

For the given constants $\{\mu_j\}$, define

$$A = I + \sum_{j=1}^{n} \mu_j \, A_j.$$

Clearly the vectors $\{\xi_m\}$ are eigenvectors for A, since

$$A \, \xi_m = \xi_m + \sum_{j=1}^{n} \mu_j \, A_j \, \xi_m$$

$$= \left(1 + \sum_{j=1}^{m} \mu_j \, \lambda_{j,m} \right) \xi_m$$

Furthermore, the hypothesis (2.36) ensures that the eigenvalues $\{1 + \Sigma \, \mu_j \, \lambda_{j,m}\}$ of A are nonnegative, and hence that A is p.s.d. The conditions (2.35), (2.35') now imply that the matrix A belongs to $\Omega(G_C)$ or $\Omega_0(G_C)$. Thus by Theorems 2.2 and 2.3, we get $\alpha(G_C) \le \lambda(A)^{-1}$, $\theta(G_C) \le \lambda(A)^{-1}$.

To compute $\lambda(A)$ observe that $\xi_1 = u$ is an eigenvector for A, with corresponding eigenvalue $1 + \sum_{j=1}^{n} \mu_j \, \lambda_{j,1}$, and so by Lemma 3, $\lambda(A) = (1 + \Sigma \, \mu_j \, \lambda_{j,1})/N$. Theorems 2.4 and 2.5 now follow.   ∎

In order to get the best possible bounds of the kind given in Theorems 2.4 and 2.5, we are essentially required to maximize the linear function $\sum_{1}^{n} \mu_j \, \lambda_{j,1}$ subject to the linear constraints (2.35) (or (2.35')), and (2.36). This is a linear programming problem (once the eigenvectors and eigenvalues of the matrices A_j are known); and hence we have succeeded in showing that <u>the Lovasz bounds $\alpha_L(G)$ and $\theta_L(G)$ can be computed via linear programming, provided the incidence matrices B_j, B'_k of the edge orbits E_j, E'_k commute.</u>

Prior to Lovász' work, Delsarte[15] obtained an upper bound on the maximum cardinality of a clique in an association scheme that can be computed using linear programming. We will now demonstrate that Delsarte's bound is subsumed under our Theorem 2.4.

Let V be a finite set, and let $R = \{R_0, R_1, \ldots, R_n\}$ be a family of n + 1 subsets of the Cartesian square V^2. The R_j are relations on V

and can be described by their incidence matrices

$A_j(v,v') = 1$ if $(v,v') \varepsilon R_j$

$= 0$ if not.

The pair (V,R) is called a (symmetric) <u>association scheme</u>* if the follow-

ing conditions are satisfied:

A1. R is a partition of V^2, and R_0 is the diagonal, i.e.,

$R_0 = \{(v,v) : v \varepsilon V\}$.

A2. The relations $\{R_j\}$ are symmetric, i.e., $(v,v') \varepsilon R_j$ implies

$(v',v) \varepsilon R_j$.

A3. There exist numbers $p_{i,j}^{(k)} = p_{j,i}^{(k)}$ such that for all

i,j = 0,1,...,n,

$$A_i A_j = \sum_{k=0}^{n} p_{i,j}^{(k)} A_k.$$

If M is a subset of $\{0,1,...,n\}$ with $0 \varepsilon M$, a nonempty subset

$Y \subseteq V$ is called an <u>M-clique with respect to R</u> if it satisfies

$R_j \cap Y^2 = \phi$ for all $j \notin M$

Delsarte gave an upper bound on the number of points in an M-clique which

is the value of a certain linear program.

But we can equally apply our Theorem 2.4 to the same problem, for the

matrices $\{A_j\}$ of the association scheme certainly satisfy conditions

---

*The reader is urged to consult Delsarte's original paper[15], or perhaps even
better, the article by Goethals[16] in this volume, to learn more about
association schemes.

(2.29) - (2.31) (note that since $p_{i,j}^{(k)} = p_{j,i}^{(k)}$, condition (A.3) is considerably stronger than (2.31)). If we let $C = \{j : j \notin M\}$, then an M-clique
as defined above is an independent set in G_C, and so the upper bound of
Theorem 2.4 is an upper bound on the cardinality of any M-clique in G_C.
One can in fact show that this is the same bound as Delsarte's[17]. Hence
Theorem 2.4 is more general than Delsarte's bound, since it applies to
many cases which are not association schemes.

2.4 Equivalence of Theorem 2.3 with Lovász' Bound (2.3).

Given an orthonormal representation of the graph G, define the
matrix A by

$A(v,v') = v \cdot v'$.

Clearly $A \in \Omega_0(G)$. If b is a unit vector and if $\lambda = \min\{(v \cdot b)^2 :$
$v \in V\}$, then $A - \lambda J$ is p.s.d. This is because we can write $A - \lambda J =$
$B + C$, where the matrices B and C are defined by

$B(v,v') = (v-(v \cdot b)b) \cdot (v'-(v' \cdot b)b)$

$C(v,v') = (v b) \cdot (v' \cdot b) - \lambda$.

B is p.s.d., since it is the matrix of inner products of a set of vectors.
C is also p.s.d., since if $\{x(v) : v \in V\}$ is any set of real numbers,

$x^T C x = (\Sigma_v x(b) (v \cdot b))^2 - \lambda(\Sigma(x(v))^2$

≥ 0,

since $(v \cdot b) \geq \sqrt{\lambda}$ for all v. Thus $A - \lambda J$, being the sum of two p.s.d.
matrices, is also p.s.d.

Since $A \in \Omega_0(G)$ and $A - \lambda J$ is p.s.d., it now follows from Lemma
4 that $\lambda(A) \geq \lambda$ and hence from Theorem 2.3 that $\theta(G) \leq \lambda^{-1} =$

$(\min\{(v \cdot b)^2 : v \in V\})^{-1}$. Thus Theorem 2.3 implies the Lovász bound (2.5).

Conversely, if $A \in \Omega_0(G)$, let $\lambda = \lambda(A)$. Then $A - \lambda J$ is p.s.d., and from a known theorem[11], there exists a matrix B such that $B^T B = A - \lambda J$. Letting $\{w(v) : v \in V\}$ denote the column vectors of B, we have

$$w(v) \cdot w(v') = A(v,v') - \lambda$$
$$= 1 - \lambda \text{ if } v = v'$$
$$= -\lambda \text{ if } \{v,v'\} \notin G.$$

Now, let t be a vector orthogonal to all the $w(v)$'s with $|t|^2 = \lambda$ (increase the dimension of the underlying space, if necessary), and define

$$x(v) = w(v) + t.$$

The $x(v)$'s are unit vectors, since

$$x(v) \cdot x(v') = A(v,v')$$

The orthogonality graph defined by the x's is thus a subgraph (same vertex set, a subset of edges) G' of G.

Furthermore if we define the unit vector b:

$$b = \frac{t}{|t|} ,$$

we have $x(v) \cdot b = |t| = \sqrt{\lambda}$ for all $v \in V$. Hence by Lovász' bound (2.3) $\theta(G') \leq \lambda^{-1} = \lambda(A)^{-1}$. But clearly $\theta(G) \leq \theta(G')$, and so Lovász' result implies our Theorem 2.3.

2.5 Concluding Remarks.

In this section we have derived algebraic upper bounds $\alpha_L(G)$ and $\theta_L(G)$ on the quantities $\alpha(G)$ and $\theta(G)$ associated with an arbitrary undirected graph G. We have called them both Lovasz bounds, although the bound $\alpha_L(G)$ was derived by McEliece, Rodemich, and Rumsey[10] after those authors read Lovász' original paper[9].

The remainder of this article will be devoted to applying the Lovász bounds to the coding theory problems cited in Section 1.

3. Applications to the Zero-Error Capacity Problem

3.1 Introduction

In this section we shall return to the problem of computing the zero-error capacity of an arbitrary discrete memoryless channel. In view of our discussion in Section 1.3, we will not need to mention the underlying channel, and will instead focus our attention on the capacity of the channel's adjacency graph G (see the definition, Eq. (1.13)). It is well to bear in mind, however, that the zero-error capacity of the channel is the logarithm of the capacity of its adjacency graph.

In general terms, the object of this section is to apply the results of Section 2 to certain specific graphs, or families of graphs. Our main tools will be Theorems 2.3 and 2.5. In Section 3.2, we give a theorem (Theorem 3.1) which can be applied to any regular graph, but which gives a bound which is in general larger than $\Theta_L(G)$ unless G has an edge-transitive symmetry group. In Section 3.3 and 3.4, we consider two infinite families of graphs, the cyclic graphs and the quadratic residue graphs. Both of these families can be thought of as generalizations of the "pentagon" graph of Figure 1.3b. In Section 3.5 we consider three interesting graphs, the Peterson graph, the Dodecahedron graph, and the

Icosahedron graph.   In Section 3.6 we consider a special graph on 7 ver-

tices that gives a nice illustration of the power of Theorem 2.5.

Finally in Section 3.7 we discuss some of the difficult problems which

remain to be solved in this area.   In particular we shall cite one graph

(the incidence graph for the 27 lines on a cubic surface) for which

$\theta(G) < \theta_L(G)$.

3.2   Regular Graphs

A graph G is said to be **regular** if the number of edges incident to

a given vertex v is a constant r, independent of v, called the **valence**

of G.

Recall that the incidence matrix for G is defined by

$B(v,v') = 1$ if $\{v,v'\} \in E$

$= 0$ otherwise.

Theorem 3.1:

If G is a regular graph of valence r, and if the least eigenvalue

of the incidence matrix is λ_{min}, then

$$\theta(G) \leq \frac{N}{1 + r/|\lambda_{min}|}$$

Note: λ_{min} will be negative, unless the edge set E is empty, in which

case $\lambda_{min} = 0$. This can be seen as follows: Suppose $\{v_1,v_2\} \in E$. De-

fine the vector $x(v)$ as follows:

$x(v_1) = +1$

$x(v_2) = -1$

$x(v) = 0$, otherwise.

Then, $x^T Bx = -2$, and hence B is not positive semidefinite. This shows that B has at least one negative eigenvalue. (Of course, if $E = \emptyset$, the matrix B is zero, and all of its eigenvalues will be zero.)

Proof of Theorem 3.1:

The idea is to show that the matrix $A = I + \mu B$ belongs to the class $\Omega_0(G)$ defined in Section 2.2, provided μ is small enough. Clearly A satisfies (2.19) and (2.20') for any value of μ, so we need only verify that A is p.s.d. However, if $\{\lambda_j\}$ is the set of eigenvalues for B, then $\{1 + \mu\lambda_j\}$ is the set of eigenvalues for A, and so A will be p.s.d., provided $\mu \geq |\lambda_{min}|^{-1}$.

Thus, if $A = I + |\lambda_{min}|^{-1} B$, then by Theorem 2.3, $\theta(G) \leq \lambda(A)^{-1}$. But since G is regular, $Bu = ru$, where $u = (1, 1, \ldots, 1)$. It follows that $Au = (1 + r|\lambda_{min}|^{-1}) u$, and hence by Lemma 3 in Section 2.2, $\lambda(A)^{-1} = N/(1 + r|\lambda_{min}|^{-1})$. Theorem 2.1 follows. ∎

Corollary:

If, in addition, the group of symmetries of G permutes the edges transitively,

$$\theta_L(G) = \frac{N}{1 + r/|\lambda_{min}|}$$

Proof:

This follows from the results of Section 2.3, since under the given

hypothesis Eq. (2.25) shows that the extremal matrix in $\overline{\Omega}_0(G)$ has the

form $A = I + \mu B$.

3.3 The Cyclic Graphs C_N

Denote by C_N the cyclic graph on N vertices, i.e., $V = \{0,1,\ldots,$

$N-1\}$, $E = \{\{i,i+1\} : i = 0,1,\ldots,N-1\}$, with indices taken mod. N. These

graphs are all regular, and indeed the cyclic group of order N permutes

the edges transitively, so we may compute $\theta_L(C_N)$ by the Corollary to

Theorem 3.1.

To find the eigenvalues of the incidence matrix B in this case, ob-

serve that the vectors $x(\zeta) = (1,\zeta,\ldots,\zeta^{N-1})$, where ζ is any complex

N-th root of unity, form an independent set of eigenvectors for B, and

indeed

$$Bx(\zeta) = (\zeta + \zeta^{-1}) \; x \; (\zeta)$$

Hence the eigenvalues of B are $\{(\zeta + \zeta^{-1})\} = \{2 \cos (2\pi k/N) : k = 0,1,$

$\ldots,[N/2]\}/$ The least member of this set is clearly -2 if N is even,

and $2 \cos (\pi - \pi/N) = -2 \cos(\pi/N)$ if N is odd and ≥ 3. Thus by

Theorem 3.1

$$\theta(C_N) \leq N/2, \quad N \quad \text{even}$$

$$\leq N/(1 + (\cos \pi/N)^{-1}), \quad N \quad \text{odd}, \quad \geq 3. \tag{3.1}$$

For N even, or $N = 3$, this bound is sharp; but these results are quite

elementary and were already known to Shannon.

For odd $N \geq 5$, however, the bounds are non-trivial. With $N = 5$, for example, we have $\theta(C_5) \le \sqrt{5}$, the celebrated result of Lovász.

For odd $N \ge 7$, the upper and lower bounds on $\theta(C_N)$ do not agree. Here is a table of the upper bound (3.1) versus the best known lower bounds[18] for odd $7 \le N \le 19$:

$$7^{3/5} = 3.21410 \le \theta(C_7) \le 3.31767$$

$$81^{1/3} = 4.32675 \le \theta(C_9) \le 4.36009$$

$$148^{1/3} = 5.28957 \le \theta(C_{11}) \le 5.38630$$

$$247^{1/3} = 6.27431 \le \theta(C_{13}) \le 6.40417$$

$$380^{1/3} = 7.24316 \le \theta(C_{15}) \le 7.41715$$

$$4913^{1/4} = 8.37214 \le \theta(C_{17}) \le 8.42701$$

$$7666^{1/4} = 9.35712 \le \theta(C_{19}) \le 9.43477$$

Thus the problem of computing $\theta(C_N)$ remains open for odd $N \ge 7$.

3.4   The Quadratic Residue Graphs

Let $p \equiv 1 \pmod 4$ be a prime. The graph Q_p has vertex set $V = \{0, 1, \ldots, p-1\}$, and edge set $E = \{\{v, v'\} : v - v'$ is a quadratic residue (q.r.) mod $p\}$. (Note that Q_5 is isomorphic to the pentagonal graph C_5.) Q_p is regular with valence $(p-1)/2$. The edge-incidence matrix is given by

$$B_p(v - v') = 1 \quad \text{if} \quad v - v' \quad \text{is a q.r. (mod } p\text{)}$$

$$= 0 \quad \text{if not.}$$

One easily verifies that the p vectors $x(\xi) = (1, \xi, \ldots, \xi^{p-1})$, where ξ is any complex p-th root of unity, are eigenvectors for B_p, and that the eigenvalue associated with $x(\xi)$ is $\Sigma\{\xi^a$: a is a q.r.$\}$. It is well known[19] that these sums assume only the three distinct values $(p-1)/2$, $(-1 \pm \sqrt{p})/2$. Hence the least eigenvalue of B_p is $(-1 - \sqrt{p})/2$, and Theorem 3.1 yields $\theta(Q_p) \le \sqrt{p}$. On the other hand, if b is a fixed quadratic nonresidue (mod p), the p ordered pairs (v,bv), $v \in V$ form an independent set in Q_p^2, and hence $\alpha(Q_p^2) \ge p$. These two inequalities establish the fact that $\theta(Q_p) = \sqrt{p}$, for all $p \equiv 1 \pmod 4$. Because of this result, it appears that the graphs Q_p form a more satisfactory generalization of the pentagon of Figure 1.3b than the graphs C_N.

3.5 Some Miscellaneous Edge-Transitive Graphs

In this section we will apply Theorem 3.1 to three interesting regular graphs. In each case there is only one equivalence class of edges, so that the bounds obtained are all equal to $\theta_L(G)$. In each case $\theta_L(G)$ is strictly less than any bound that could be obtained by Shannon's techniques.

The Peterson Graph. This is a regular graph with $N = 10$, $r = 3$:

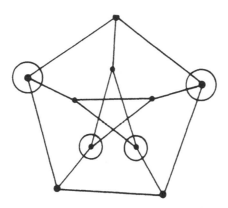

Figure 3-1. The Peterson Graph

The minimum eigenvalue here turns out to be -2, so Theorem 3.1 yields $\theta(G) \leq 4$. On the other hand $\alpha(G) = 4$ (note the four circled vertices in Figure 3.1), and so $\theta(G) = 4$.

• The Icosahedron Graph. This graph has $N = 12$, $r = 5$; its vertices and edges are formed from those of the regular icosahedron.

Here the minimum eigenvalue is $-\sqrt{5}$, and so from Theorem 3.1, $\theta(G) \leq 3(\sqrt{5} - 1) = 3.7082$. On the other hand $\alpha(G) = 3$, so we have $3 \leq \theta(G) \leq 3.7082$. We can actually say more in this case, however[20]. Let H be the graph whose vertex set V is the same as G's, and in which v and v' are adjacent iff they have distance 2 in G. Note that H is isomorphic to G. Let π be a permutation of V mapping G to H, and let S = $\{(v, \pi(v))\}; v \in V\}$. Then S is an independent set in G^2, and so $\alpha(G^2) \geq 12$. Thus we get finally

$$\sqrt{12} \leq \theta(G) \leq 3 (\sqrt{5} - 1)$$

$$3.4641 \leq \theta(G) \leq 3.7082.$$

• The Dodecahedron Graph. This is the graph of the regular dodecahedron, with $N = 20$, $r = 3$ (see Fig. 3.3). Here $\lambda_{min} = -\sqrt{5}$ also; hence Theorem 3.1 gives $\theta(G) \leq 15 \sqrt{5} - 25 = 8.5410$. On the other hand $\alpha(G) = 8$, as shown[*]. Thus $8 \leq \theta(G) \leq 8.5410$.

---

[*]For a proof that $\alpha(\text{a}) = 8$ for this graph, see Sec. 4.4.

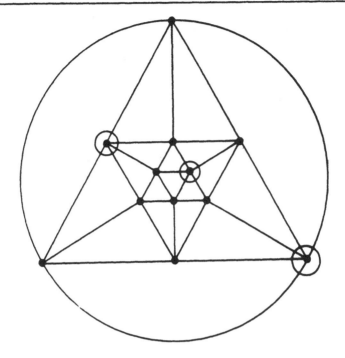

Figure 3-2.   The Icosahedron Graph

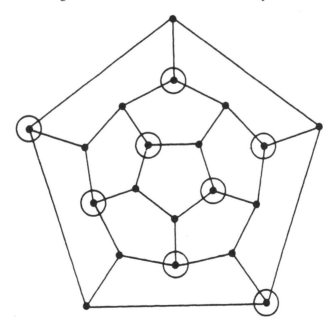

Figure 3.3.   The Dodecahedron Graph

3.6 A Special Graph on Seven Vertices

Consider the graph depicted in Figure 3-4.

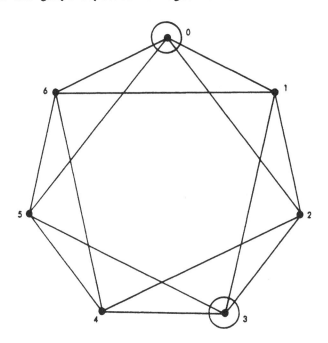

Figure 3-4. A Regular Graph on 7 Vertices

This graph is regular with $N = 7$, $r = 4$, and minimum eigenvalue = $4 \cos \frac{6\pi}{7} \cos \frac{2\pi}{7} = -2.2470$, and hence by Theorem 3.1, $\theta(G) \leq 2.5178$. However, under the action of the symmetries of G, there are two equivalance classes of edges: those of type $\{i, i+1\}$, and those of type $\{i, i+2\}$, modulo 7. In this case the bound of Theorem 3.1 is strictly larger than the Lovasz bound $\theta_L(G)$; in order to compute $\theta_L(G)$, we must apply Theorem 2.5 directly.

Thus let A_0 denote the 7×7 identity matrix; A_1, the incidence matrix for edges of type $\{i, i+1\}$, A_2, for edges of type $\{i, i+2\}$, and A_3, for edges of type $\{i, i+3\}$ (which are not edges of G.)

One easily verifies that the matrices $\{A_0, A_1, A_2, A_3\}$ satisfy conditions (2.29) - (2.31). If $C = \{1,2\}$, the graph G_C is the graph of Figure 3-4. Also, the 7 vectors of the form $x(\zeta) = (1, \zeta, \ldots, \zeta^6)$, where ζ is a complex 7-th root of unity, form a set of common eigenvectors for the A's:

$$A_0 \times (\zeta) = x(\zeta),$$

$$A_1 \times (\zeta) = (\zeta + \zeta^{-1}) \times (\zeta),$$

$$A_2 \times (\zeta) = (\zeta^2 + \zeta^{-2}) \times (\zeta),$$

$$A_3 \times (\zeta) = (\zeta^3 + \zeta^{-3}) \times (\zeta).$$

Thus according to Theorem 3.5, if μ_1 and μ_2 satisfy $1 + \mu_1(\zeta + \zeta^{-1}) + \mu_2(\zeta^2 + \zeta^{-2}) \geq 0$ for all 7-th roots of unity ζ, then $\theta(G) \leq 7/(1 + 2\mu_1 + 2\mu_2)$. To get the best possible such bound we must maximize the function $\mu_1 + \mu_2$ subject to the above set of inequalities. This is easily done by hand, and we get the largest possible value with $\mu_1 = 0.8020$, $\mu_2 = 0.3569$. The resulting bound is $\theta(G) \leq 2.1098$.

3.7 Concluding Remarks

We have seen in this section that the Lovász bound $\theta_L(G)$ is a very powerful tool for studying the function $\theta(G)$. For most graphs G, $\theta_L(G)$ is the best known upper bound on $\theta(G)$, and in many cases $\theta_L(G)$ coincides with a previously computed lower bound, and hence gives the value of $\theta(G)$ exactly. The most spectacular example of this phenomena is the case of Shannon's "Pentagon", the graph C_5 (or Q_5).

It may be that $\theta_L(G) = \theta(G)$ in many other cases as well. Perhaps, for example, $\theta(C_7) = \theta_L(C_7) = 7/(1 + \cos(\frac{\pi}{7})^{-1})$. But if this should turn out to be true, an entirely new behavior of the function $\alpha(G^n)$ will occur. For in all cases for which $\theta(G)$ is presently known, $\theta(G)$ is achieved for a finite value of n, i.e.,

$$\theta(G) = \alpha(G^n)^{1/n}$$

for some particular n. (In fact, $n = 1$ or 2 always, so far as is known.) But the Lovasz bound $\theta_L(G)$ can only be the n-th root of an integer if $n = 1$ or 2. This is because θ_L is always a rational function of the eigenvalues of symmetric matrix. These eigenvalues are necessarily real, and so the algebraic conjugates of θ_L will all be real. On the other hand, the algebraic conjugates of a number of the form $M^{1/n}$ will include complex numbers unless $n = 1$ or 2.

Thus in particular $\theta_L(C_7)$ is not of the form $M^{1/n}$ for any n, M, and so if $\theta_L(C_7) = \theta(G)$, it must be the case that

$$\theta(G) > \alpha(G^n)^{1/n}, \quad n = 1, 2, \ldots \ .$$

In other words, there would be essentially new constructions for $\alpha(G^n)$ for infinitely many values of n. This behavior has never been observed.

In any event, it is definitely not true that $\theta(G) = \theta_L(G)$ for all G. Unfortunately, the smallest graph G for which $\theta(G)$ is definitely known to be strictly less than $\theta_L(G)$ is rather complicated, but let us briefly sketch a description of it. The result is due to Haemers[21].

Let $P^3(C)$ be complex projective 3-space. The points of $P^3(C)$

are 4-tuples $\underline{z} = (z_1, z_2, z_3, z_4)$ of complex numbers, not all zero, and

two points $\underline{z}$ and $\underline{z}'$ are called equivalent if $z = \gamma \underline{z}'$ for some nonzero

complex number γ. The set of points of $P^3(C)$ satisfying the equation

$$z_1^3 + z_2^3 + z_3^3 + z_4^3 = 0 \qquad (3.2)$$

forms a nonsingular cubic surface in $P^3(C)$.

A <u>line</u> in $P^3(C)$ is a set of points of the form

$$L = \{\lambda_1 \underline{z}_1 + \lambda_2 \underline{z}_2 : \lambda_1, \lambda_2 \in C\} \qquad (3.3)$$

where $\underline{z}_1$ and $\underline{z}_2$ are distinct points of $P^3(C)$. This line is said to

lie on the surface (3.2) provided each point on the line satisfies (3.2).

It turns out there are just 27 such lines. A typical one is given by

$$\underline{z}_1 = (1, -\rho, 0, 0)$$

$$\underline{z}_2 = (0, 0, 1, -\sigma),$$

where ρ and σ are complex cube roots of unity. All others are obtained by permuting coordinates and using different roots of unity.

Any such line L intersects exactly ten others. Thus we can define

a graph whose vertex set is the set of these 27 lines, two vertices being

connected by an edge iff the corresponding two lines intersect. This graph

is usually called the <u>Schläfli graph</u>, since the underlying geometric config-

uration was discovered by Ludwig Schläfli in 1858.

From the above description one can compute the 27 x 27 incidence

matrix B for G. Its eigenvalues then turn out to be $(-5, 1, 10)$ with

multiplicities $(6, 20, 1)$. Hence by Theorem 3.1,

$$\theta_L(G) \leq \frac{27}{1 + \frac{10}{5}} = 9.$$

On the other hand the group of symmetries of G (which has order 51840) is known to permute the edges transitively[22] and so by the corollary to Theorem 3.1, $\theta_L(G)$ = 9. However, we shall now show that in fact $\theta(G) \leq$ 7. To do this we will first state a theorem due to Haemers[21] which gives a bound on $\theta(G)$ quite different from Lovasz'.

Theorem 3.2:

Let A = A(v,v') be a symmetric matrix indexed by the vertices of the graph G, such that

A(v,v) = 1, all v ϵ V

A(v,v') = 0, if {v,v'} $\notin$ E.

Then $\theta(G) \leq$ rank (A).

Proof:

Suppose $\alpha(G)$ = M, and that Y = {$v_1, v_2, \ldots, v_M$} is a maximal independent set in G. Then the submatrix of A formed by the rows and columns corresponding to the elements of Y will be a M x M idenity matrix. Thus rank (A) $\geq$ M.

Similarly, if $\alpha(G^n)$ = M_n, the matrix $A^{[n]}$ = A × A × ... × A (n factors) will have an $M_n \times M_n$ identity submatrix, and so

rank ($A^{[n]}$) $\geq \alpha(G^n)$, all n.

But it is well-known[23] that rank (A × B) = rank (A) · rank (B), and so

$\alpha(G^n) \leq$ (rank (A))^n, n = 1,2,... .

Taking n-th roots of this last equation and recalling the definition

(Eq. (1.13)) of $\theta(G)$, we get

$\theta(G) \leq \text{rank} (A),$

as desired.   ∎

Let us now apply Theorem 3.2 to the Schläfli graph, with $A = I - B$,
B being the incidence matrix of the graph. Clearly A satisfies the
hypotheses of Theorem 3.2. Since as we stated above, B has eigenvalues
-5, 1, 10 with multiplicities 6, 20, 1 if follows that A has eigenvalues 6, 0, -9 with multiplicities 6, 20, 1. In particular A has
exactly twenty eigenvalues equal to 0. Since A, being symmetric, is
diagonalizable, it follows that rank (A) = 27 - 20 = 7. Thus according
to Theorem 3.2, $\theta(G) \leq 7$. Since we have previously showed that $\theta_L(G) =$
9, this shows that $\theta(G) < \theta_L(G)$ for the Schläfli graph. (It turns out
that $\alpha(G) = 6$ for the Schläfli graph, and so the bounds $6 \leq \theta(G) \leq 7$
are presently the best known.)

It seems very strange that a simple argument like Theorem 3.2 can
sometimes be better than the Lovasz bound, but there it is. Several interesting questions immediately suggest themselves:

1. Calling the best bound obtainable for a given graph G from
    Theorem 3.2 the <u>Haemers Bound</u> $\theta_H(G)$, what are the general pro-
    perties of θ_H? Clearly θ_H must always be an integer, and for
    example $\theta_H(C_5) = 3$, so θ_H is not always better than θ_L.

2. There is a close similarity between the conditions which must be
    satisfied by the matrix A in the Lovász bound, Theorem 2.3, and
    those that must be satisfies in the Haemers bound, Theorem 3.2.
    Does this mean that there is a more general result that includes

them both?

Finally, let us mention a beautiful result about $\theta_L(G)$ which is proved by Lovasz[9], but whose proof we cannot include here. It concerns the complementary graph $\overline{G}$ of G. $\overline{G}$ is defined as the graph with the same vertex set as G, but with the complementary set of edges.

Theorem 3.3 (Lovász)

For any graph G with N vertices, it must be true that

$$\theta_L(G) \; \theta_L(\overline{G}) \geq N.$$

Furthermore, if the symmetry group of G is transitive on the vertices, then

$$\theta_L(G) \; \theta_L(\overline{G}) = N.$$

There are many applications of Theorem 3.3. For example if $G = C_N$ with odd N, it follows from the results of Section 3.3 and Theorem 3.3 that

$$\theta_L(\overline{C}_N) = 1 + (\cos \frac{\pi}{N})^{-1}.$$

For $N = 7$, this is the result we obtained via linear programming in Section 3.6. If $G = Q_p$, as defined in Section 3.4, then one easily verifies that G and $\overline{G}$ are isomorphic. Furthermore, the symmetry group is vertex-transitive, and so $\theta_L(Q_p)^2 = p$, i.e., $\theta_L(Q_p) = \sqrt{p}$, as we already observed.

4. Applications to the A(n,d) Problem

4.1 Introductory Remarks

In this section, we will use Theorem 2.4 to prove the key result, Theorem 1.1, needed to derive the asymptotic bound on $R(\delta)$ which we have given in Eq.(1.8). This derivation occupies Section 4.2. In Section 4.3, we will derive the bound (1.8) from Theorem 1.1. In Section 4.4 we will give a brief description of how (1.8) can be improved using more advanced techinques (which can still be derived from Theorem 4.2, incidentally). Finally, Appendix A contains a list of properties of the numbers $K_j^{(n)}(i)$ which are needed for tne derivation in Section 4-3.

4.2 A Graph G with $\alpha(G) = A(n,d)$

Our object in this section is for a fixed pair of integers (n,d) to have a closer look at the graph $G = H_{n,d}$ described at the end of Sec. 1.3. This graph will turn out to be of the form treated in Theorem 2.4. We will then apply Theorem 2.4, and after some computation arrive at the linear programming bound, Theorem 1.1.

From now on, then, think of n and d as fixed positive integers with $d \leq n$. Let V denote the set of all binary n-tuples, and for each $i \in \{0,1,\ldots,n\}$ let

$$E_i = \{\{v,v'\} : \| v - v' \| = i\}, \tag{4.1}$$

where we recall that $\| x \|$ denotes the Hamming weight of x. The graph G is defined to be the graph with vertex set V and edge set

$$E = \bigcup_{i=0}^{d-1} E_i. \tag{4.2}$$

By definition, $\{v, v'\} \in G$ iff $\| v - v' \| \le d - 1$. Thus $\{v, v'\} \notin G$ iff $\| v - v' \| \ge d$. Since $A(n, d)$ is by definition the largest possible set $\{v_1, v_2, \ldots\}$ of elements of V such that $\| v_i - v_j \| \ge d$ for all $i \ne j$, it follows that

$$\alpha(G) = A(n, d). \tag{4.3}$$

G therefore has the desired property. Now let us show how to apply Theorem 2.4 to G.

For each $i \in \{0, 1, \ldots, n\}$, let A_i denote the edge-incidence matrix for E_i:

$$A_i(v, v') = 1 \quad \text{if} \quad \| v - v' \| = i$$

$$= 0 \quad \text{if not.}$$

The A_i's clearly satisfy conditions (2.31) and (2.32), and so in order to apply Theorem 2.4 all that remains is to verify that the A_i's have a common set of 2^n orthogonal eigenvectors. This fact will certainly imply that the A_i's commute (for they will then be simultaneously diagonalizable), and will as a bonus give us the eigenvalues $\{\lambda_{j,m}\}$ required by Theorem 2.4.

We shall denote these eigenvectors by ξ_u, where $u \in V$. They are defined by

$$\xi_u(v) = (-1)^{u \cdot v}, \tag{4.4}$$

where in (4.4) $u \cdot v = \Sigma u_k v_k$ is the ordinary dot product. We omit the easy verification that the vectors $\{\xi_u\}$ are orthogonal and independent (they are in fact the characters of the additive group of V), and move directly to the verification that they are simultaneous eigenvectors for the A_i's.

Theorem 4.1:

For each $i \in \{0,1,\ldots,n\}$, $u \in V$,

$$A_i \xi_u = K_i(j) \xi_u,$$

where the numbers $K_i(j) = K_i^{(n)}(j)$ are as defined in Eq. (1.2), and $j = \|u\|$.

Proof:

For $v \in V$, the v-th component of the vector $A_i \xi_u$ is given by

$$A_i \xi_u(v) = \sum_{w \in V} A_i(v,w) \xi_u(w) \qquad (4.5)$$

$$= \sum_{w:\ \|w-v\| = i} (-1)^{u \cdot w}$$

In terms of the variable $x = w-v$, this last sum is

$$\sum_{x:\ \|x\| = i} (-1)^{u \cdot (x+v)} = (-1)^{u \cdot v} \sum_{\|x\| = i} (-1)^{u \cdot x}$$

This shows that $A_i \xi_u = g_i(u) \xi_u$, where

$$g_i(u) = \sum_{\|x\| = i} (-1)^{u \cdot x} \qquad (4.5)$$

It remains only to show that the eigenvalue $g_i(u)$ of Eq. (4.5) is equal to $K_i(j)$.

To do this, let us examine the relationship between u and an arbitrary vector x with $\| x \| = i$. With the aid of an appropriate coordinate permutation, we can depict u and x as follows:

$$u = \overbrace{11111111111}^{j}\ \overbrace{000000000}^{n-j}$$

$$x = \underbrace{11111110000}_{k}\ \underbrace{111100000}_{i-k}$$

In this sketch the parameter k denotes the number of coordinates in which u and x are both equal to 1. The contribution of this particular x to the sum in (4.5) is obviously $(-1)^k$ and equally clearly from the picture, the number of vectors of weight i which have exactly k ones in common with u is $\binom{j}{k}$ $\binom{n-j}{i-k}$. Summing over the possible values of k, we get

$$g_i(u) = \sum_{k=0}^{i} (-1)^k \binom{j}{k} \binom{n-j}{i-k}$$

$$= K_i(j),$$

and this completes the proof of Theorem 4.1.   ∎

Armed with facts in Theorem 4.1, we can now apply Theorem 2.4 to get an upper bound on $\alpha(G) = A(n,d)$.

Theorem 4.2.

Let μ_1, μ_2,...,μ_n be n real numbers satisfying

$$\mu_i \leq 0 \quad \text{if } i \in \{d,d+1,\ldots,n\} \tag{4.6}$$

$$1 + \sum_{i=1}^{n} \mu_i K_i(j) \geq 0 \quad \text{if } j \in \{0,1,\ldots,n\}. \tag{4.7}$$

Then

$$A(n,d) \leq \frac{2^n}{1 + \sum_{i=1}^{n} \mu_i \binom{n}{i}} \qquad (4.8)$$

Proof:

This is essentially a restatement of Theorem 2.4 for the graph G under current consideration, but perhaps one or two comments are in order.

First, although there are 2^n eigenvectors for the matrices, there are only $n + 1$ inequalities in (4.7). This is of course because, as shown in Theorem 4.1, the eigenvalue of A_i corresponding to the eigenvector ξ_u depends only on i and the weight of u.

Second, note that the all-ones vector is the eigenvector ξ_0, with corresponding eigenvalues $K_i(0) = \binom{n}{i}$ by definition. Thus the eigenvalues $\lambda_{i,1}$ required in Theorem 2.4 are merely the binomial coefficients.

Theorem 4.2 is essentially equivalent to our desired result, Theorem 1.1. To make the transformation, however, we will need to invoke certain elementary properties of the eigenvalues $K_i(j)$*. Thus we restate Theorem 1.1 and present a formal proof.

Theorem 4.3 (= Theorem 1.1)

Let $(\lambda_0, \lambda_1, \ldots, \lambda_n)$ be $n + 1$ real numbers satisfying

$$\lambda_0 > 0, \quad \lambda_j \geq 0, \quad j \in \{1, 2, \ldots, n\} \qquad (4.9)$$

---

*In order not to interrupt our development more than necessary, we have relegated the list of needed properties of $\{K_i(j)\}$ to Appendix A. This list contains 20 entries, labeled (A.1) – (A.20).

$$\sum_{j=0}^{n} \lambda_j K_j(i) \leq 0, \quad i \in \{d, d+1, \ldots, n\}. \tag{4.10}$$

Then

$$\Delta(n,d) \leq \frac{1}{\lambda_0} \sum_{j=0}^{n} \lambda_j \binom{n}{j} \tag{4.11}$$

Proof:

For $i \in \{0, 1, \ldots, n\}$ define

$$\mu_i' = \sum_{j=0}^{n} \lambda_j K_j(i). \tag{4.12}$$

Then $\mu_i' \leq 0$ for $i \geq d$, from (4.10). We assert further that

$$\sum_{i=0}^{n} \mu_i' K_i(j) \geq 0, \text{ all } j. \tag{4.13}$$

This fact is a result of the following lemma.

Lemma:

$$\sum_{i=0}^{n} \mu_i' K_i(j) = 2^n \lambda_j.$$

Proof of Lemma:

Using the definition (4.12),

$$\sum_{i=0}^{n} \mu_i' K_i(j) = \sum_{k=0}^{n} \lambda_k \sum_{i=0}^{n} K_i(j) K_k(i).$$

From property (A.10), $K_i(j) = \binom{n}{j}^{-1} \binom{n}{i} K_j(i)$. Hence,

$$\sum_{i=0}^{n} \mu_i' K_i(j) = \binom{n}{j}^{-1} \sum_{k=0}^{n} \lambda_k \sum_{i=0}^{n} \binom{n}{i} K_k(i) K_j(i).$$

From property (A.11), the inner sum above is $2^n \binom{n}{j} \delta_{k,j}$. This completes

the proof of the lemma.   ∎

Returning to the proof of Theorem 4.3: the Lemma, combined with

(4.9), implies the desired result (4.13). Hence if we define parameters

μ_i, $i \in \{0,1,\dots,n\}$ by

$$\mu_i = \frac{\mu_0'}{\mu_0'}$$

$$= \frac{\sum_{j=0}^{n} \lambda_j K_j(i)}{\sum_{j=0}^{n} \lambda_j \binom{n}{j}} \ .$$

It follows that these numbers satisfy the hypotheses of Theorem 4.2. But

by the Lemma, the denominator in the bound (4.8) is

$$1 + \sum_{i=1}^{n} \mu_i \binom{n}{i} = \sum_{i=0}^{n} \mu_i \binom{n}{i}$$

$$= \frac{1}{\mu_0'} \sum_{i=0}^{n} \mu_i' K_i(0) = \frac{2^n \lambda_o}{\mu_o'} \ ,$$

Hence by (4.8)

$$A(n,d) \le \frac{\mu_0}{\lambda_0} = \frac{1}{\lambda_0} \sum_{j=0}^{n} \lambda_j \binom{n}{j},$$

using (4.12) with $i = 0$. This completes the proof of Theorem 4.3.

In the next section we will use Theorem 4.3 to derive the McEliece-

Rodemich-Rumsey-Welch bound (1.8).

4.3 Proof of the MRRW Bound (1.8)

Armed with Theorem 4.3, and the results listed in Appendix A, we now proceed to prove that $R(\delta) \leq g\left((1 - 2\delta)^2\right)$.

Our first remark is that for a fixed j and n, $K_j(i)$ turns out to be a polynomial of degree j in the argument i. These polynomials, which we denote by $K_j(x)$, are called <u>Krawtchouk</u> polynomials, in honor of their discoverer (1929!). (The fact that $K_j(x)$ is a polynomial of degree j appears implicitly in Eq. (A.2)).

At first, n and d will be fixed integers; later, after we have derived the bound (4.22) on $A(n,d)$, we will proceed to an asymptotic analysis.

Let t be an integer, $1 \leq t \leq n/2$, and let a be a real number in the interval $[0,n]$. (They will be specified more precisely later.) Define

$$P^*(x) = K_{t+1}(x)K_t(a) - K_t(x)K_{t+1}(a).$$

According to property (A.16),

$$P^*(x) = \frac{2(a - x)}{t + 1} \binom{n}{t} \sum_{k=0}^{t} \frac{K_k(x)K_k(a)}{\binom{n}{k}} . \tag{4.14}$$

Now define

$$P(x) = \frac{P^*(x)^2}{a-x} \tag{4.15}$$

$$= \frac{2}{t + 1} \binom{n}{t} [K_{t+1}(x)K_t(a) - K_t(x)K_{t+1}(a)] \sum_{k=0}^{t} \frac{K_k(x)K_k(a)}{\binom{n}{k}} \tag{4.16}$$

Now (see Appendix A) for each j, $K_j(x)$ has j distinct real zeros in the interval $(0,n)$. Denote by $x_1^{(j)}$ the smallest such zero. Then by (A.17), $x_1^{(t+1)} < x_1^{(t)}$. Let us now choose a so that

$$x_1^{(t+1)} < a < x_1^{(t)}. \tag{4.17}$$

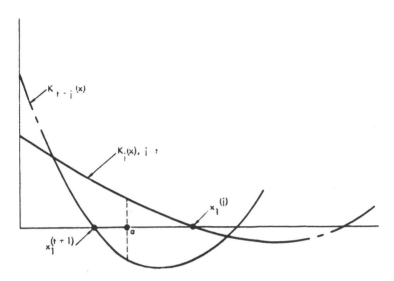

Figure 4-1. Relationship between $K_{t+1}(x)$ and $K_j(x)$, $j \le t$.

Then since $K_j(0) = \binom{n}{j} > 0$ (A.8), it follows that $K_j(a) > 0$, for $j \le t$, and $K_{t+1}(a) < 0$. (See Figure 4-1) Hence in (4.16) $P(x)$ is expressed as a sum, with nonnegative coefficients, of products of Krawtchouk polynomials. By (A.19), any product $K_i(x)K_j(x)$ can be expressed as a sum $\Sigma \alpha_k K_k(x)$ with each $\alpha_k \ge 0$. We conclude that $P(x)$ itself has an expansion in Krawtchouk polynomials with nonnegative coefficients.

Next, observe from (4.15) that $P(x) \le 0$, if $x \ge a$. Hence if we assume $a \le d$, it follows that $P(x) \le 0$ if $x \ge d$. Hence if $P(x) = \Sigma_0^n \lambda_j K_j(x)$, the λ_j satisfy the hypotheses of Theorem 4.3 and so $A(n,d) \le P(0)/\lambda_0$. From (4.15) we have

$$P(0) = \frac{1}{a}\left[\binom{n}{t+1} K_t(a) - \binom{n}{t} K_{t+1}(a) \right]^2$$

$$= \frac{1}{a} \binom{n}{t}^2 K_t(a)^2 \left[\frac{n-t}{t+1} - Q \right]^2 , \tag{4.18}$$

$$\left(Q = \frac{K_{t+1}(a)}{K_t(a)} \right) .$$

To compute λ_0 we use the formula (A.12) $\lambda_0 = \int P(x) \, d\beta$ and the orthogonality properties (A.11) and conclude

$$\lambda_0 = - \frac{2}{t+1} \cdot K_{t+1}(a) K_t(a) \int K_t^2(x) \, d\beta \tag{4.19}$$

$$= - \frac{2}{t+1} \binom{n}{t} K_t(a)^2 Q.$$

Combining (4.18) and (4.19), we get the following bound:

$$A(n,d) \leq \binom{n}{t} \frac{(n - t - (t+1) \, Q)^2}{-2a(t+1) \, Q} ,$$

where

$$\left\{ \begin{array}{l} Q = K_{t+1}(a)/K_t(a) \\[2mm] x_1^{(t+1)} < a < x_1^{(t)} \\[2mm] a < d. \end{array} \right. \tag{4.20}$$

To simplify this, choose t so that $x_1^{(t)} \leq d$ and a so that $Q = K_{t+1}(a)/K_t(a) = -1$ (see Fig. 4-1). Then (4.20) becomes

$$A(n,d) \leq \binom{n}{t} \frac{(n+1)^2}{2a(t+1)} \tag{4.21}$$

(provided $x_1^{(t)} \leq d$, $t \leq n/2$). Now, since $a \geq x_1^{(t+1)}$ and by (A.18) $x_1^{(t+1)} \geq 1$, we get

$$A(n,d) \leq \binom{n}{t} \frac{(n+1)^2}{2(t+1)} \leq \binom{n}{t} (n+1)^2 \tag{4.22}$$

(provided $x_1^{(t)} \leq d$, $t \leq n/2$).

We now proceed to an asymptotic analysis of (4.22). Choose τ so that $1/2 - \sqrt{\delta(1 - \delta)} < \tau < 1/2$, and let (d_n) and (t_n) be sequences of integers such that $d_n/n \to \delta$ and $t_n/n \to \tau$. Now, according to (A.20), $\lim x_1^{(t_n)}/n \leq 1/2 - \sqrt{\tau(1 - \tau)} < \delta$, and so, for sufficiently large n, the hypotheses of (4.22) will be satisfied. Thus

$$\overline{\lim_{n \to \infty}} \frac{1}{n} \log_2 A(n,d_n)$$

$$\leq \overline{\lim_{n \to \infty}} \left[\frac{1}{n} \log_2 \binom{n}{t_n} + \frac{1}{n} \log_2 (n + 1)^2 \right]$$

$$= \overline{\lim_{n \to \infty}} \frac{1}{n} \log_2 \binom{n}{t_n}$$

$$= H_2(\tau), \tag{4.23}$$

since $n^{-1} \log_2 \binom{n}{t_n} \to H_2(\tau_n)$. Combining (4.23) and (1.6), we see that $R(\delta) \leq H_2(\tau)$ whenever $1/2 - \sqrt{\delta(1 - \delta)} < \tau < 1/2$. Since $H_2(\tau)$ is a continuous function of τ, this implies $R(\delta) \leq H_2(1/2 - \sqrt{\delta(1 - \delta)}) = g((1 - 2\delta)^2)$, which is the promised bound (1.8).

4.4   Sketch of a Proof of the MRRW Bound (1.9)

In this section we will indicate how the bound (1.9) is derived. For full details, however, the reader must look elsewhere[7].

The idea is to study the A(n,d) problem using constant-weight codes. The combinatorial result that makes this possible is usually called the Elias argument. Here we present the Elias argument in more generality that is strictly necessary for our purposes.

Let   X   be a finite set, and let   P   be a transitive group of permutations on   X.   Now let   C   be a collection of subsets of   X, such that:

$$Y \in C, \quad Z \subseteq Y \Longrightarrow Z \in C \qquad\qquad (4.24)$$
$$C$$
$$Y \in P, \quad \pi \in P \Longrightarrow Y^{\pi} \in C, \qquad\qquad (4.25)$$

where in (4.25) Y^{π} denotes the image of   Y   under the action of the

permutation π.   If $Y \subseteq X$, we denote by   A(Y)   the cardinality of the

largest subset of   Y   belonging to   C.

Theorem (the Elias Argument):

Let $Y \subseteq X$ be arbitrary.   Then

$$A(X) \le \frac{|X|}{|Y|} A(Y).$$

Proof: Let   K   be an element of   C   with largest possible cardinality.

Then $|K| = A(X)$ by definition.   For the given subset   Y,

$$\sum_{\pi \in P} |K^{\pi} \cap Y| = \sum_{\pi \in P} \sum_{k \in K} |\{k\}^{\pi} \cap Y|$$

$$= \sum_{k \in K} \sum_{\pi \in P} |\{k\}^{\pi} \cap Y|$$

$$= |K| \cdot \frac{|G|}{|H|} \cdot |Y|,$$

since as π runs through   P, k^{π} covers each element of   X $|P| \; |X|$

times.   Hence

$$\frac{1}{|P|} \sum_{\pi \in P} |K^{\pi} \cap Y| = \frac{|Y|}{|X|} |K|.$$

Hence for at least one $\pi \in P$,

$$|K^{\pi} \cap Y| \geq \frac{|Y|}{|X|} |K|.$$

Let Y' denote the set $K^{\pi} \cap Y$ for this particular π. Then $Y' \subseteq Y$

and $Y' \in C$ by (4.24) and (4.25). Thus

$$A(Y) \geq \frac{|Y|}{|X|} |K| = \frac{|Y|}{|X|} A(X). \qquad \blacksquare$$

Example 1. Let X = the vertex set of the dodecahedron graph of Fig.

3.3, let P = the group of symmetries of the dodecahedron, and let C =

the subsets of X which are independent sets in the dodecahedron graph.

Let Y = one of the sets of 5 vertices forming a pentagon. Then clearly

$A(Y) = 2$, and so $\alpha(G) = A(X) \leq \frac{20}{5} \cdot 2 = 8$. On the other hand $\alpha(G) \geq 8$,

since the 8 circled vertices in Fig. 3.3 are independent. Hence $\alpha(G) = $

8, as previously asserted.

Example 2. Let X = the set of binary n-tuples, let P be the group of

translations of the form $\pi y : x \to x + y$. For a fixed integer d let C

be defined as follows:

$$C = \{Y \subseteq X : y_1, y_2 \in Y, \ y_1 \neq y_2, \implies \| y_1 - y_2 \| \geq d\}.$$

Clearly $A(X) = A(n,d)$. For a fixed integer w, let Y denote the sub-

set of X consisting of all vectors of weight w. Then $|Y| = \binom{n}{w}$, and

so the Elias argument gives

$$A(X) \leq \frac{2^n}{\binom{n}{w}} A(Y).$$

But $A(Y)$ = the largest possible number of vectors of weight w with

mutual Hamming distances $\geq d$, and we denote this quantity by $A(n,d,w)$.

We thus have

$$A(n,d) \leq \frac{2^n}{\binom{n}{w}} A(n,d,w).$$
(4.26)

What this means is that any bound on $A(n,d,w)$ (such bounds are usually called bounds on <u>constant weight</u> codes) immediately yields a bound on $A(n,d)$.

McEliece, Rodemich, Rumsey, and Welch[7] derived an asymptotic bound on $A(n,d,w)$ which, combined with (4.26) leads to (1.9). Although the techniques of Section 2 of this paper were not available to those authors (they used Delsarte's results), we can describe their approach using the newer machinery.

For fixed n,d,w, one easily constructs a graph G for which $\alpha(G) = A(n,d,w)$. Its vertices are the binary n-tuples of weight w, two vertices being connected iff the distance between them is $< d$. One defines a family of incidence matrices $\{A_i\}$; A_i corresponds to pairs of vertices of G at distance i. These matrices are simultaneously diagonalizable, and so one gets a "linear programming" bound on $\alpha(G)$ from Theorem 2.4. From here on the work is quite similar to that of Section 4.3, but technically a little more difficult. Fortunately for M.R.R. and W., the most essential properties of the simultaneous eigenvectors and eigenvalues for the A_i were previously derived by Delsarte[15]. Using Delsarte's results and the general technique they developed for the $A(n,d)$ problem, M.R.R. and W. were then able to derive the bound (1.9).

Appendix A.   Some Properties of Krawtchouk Polynomials

In this appendix we collect for reference purposes several important properties of the Krawtchouk polynomials $K_j(x)$ defined in Sections 1.2, 4.3. First we recall the definition[*]

$$K_j(x) = \operatorname*{coef}_{y^j} (1 - y)^x (1 + y)^{n-x} \tag{A.1}$$

From (A.1), it follows that

$$K_j(x) = \sum_{k=0}^{j} (-1)^k \binom{x}{k} \binom{n - x}{j - x} . \tag{A.2}$$

If in (A.1) we write $(1 - y)^x = (1 + y - 2y)^x$ and expand, we get the alternative formula

$$K_j(x) = \sum_{k=0}^{j} (-2)^k \binom{x}{k} \binom{n - k}{j - k} \tag{A.3}$$

From (A.2) or (A.3), it follows that $K_j(x)$ is a polynomial of degree j in x, and it is easily verified that

$$K_0(x) = 1, \tag{A.4}$$

$$K_1(x) = -2x + n, \tag{A.5}$$

$$K_2(x) = 2x^2 - 2xn + (n^2 - n)/2, \tag{A.6}$$

$$K_j(x) = \frac{(-2)^j}{j!} x^j + \text{lower degree terms}, \tag{A.7}$$

$$K_j(0) = \binom{n}{n}. \tag{A.8}$$

$$K_j(1) = \frac{n - 2j}{j} \binom{n - 1}{j - 1}, \text{ if } j \neq 0. \tag{A.9}$$

From (A.1), it is easy to verify that $\binom{n}{i} K_j(i) = \operatorname{coef}$ of $y^j z^i$ in

---

[*]The dependence of $K_j(x)$ on n will usually be suppressed, but, if necessary (e.g., in the proof (A.20)), we will use the notation $K_n^{(n)}(x)$.

$(1 + y + z - yz)^n$; since this is symmetric in y and z, it follows that

$$\binom{n}{i} K_j(i) = \binom{n}{j} K_i(j). \tag{A.10}$$

We come now to the crucial orthogonality properties. Let $\beta(x)$ be a step function with jumps of $2^{-n} \binom{n}{k}$ at $x = 0,1,\ldots,n$. Regard $\beta(x)$ as a Stieltjes integrator, i.e., for any polynomial $P(x)$, define $\int P(x)\, d\beta = 2^{-n} \sum_k P(k) \binom{n}{k}$. The polynomials $K_j(x)$ are orthogonal with respect to β, i.e.,

$$\int K_i(x) K_j(x)\, d\beta = \binom{n}{i} \delta_{ij}, \tag{A.11}$$

(see Szegö[24], §2.82). Hence for any $P(x)$ of degree at most n,

$$P(i) = \sum_{k=0}^{n} a_k K_k(i), \quad i = 0,1,\ldots,n,$$

$$a_k = \binom{n}{k}^{-1} \int P(x)\, d\beta. \tag{A.12}$$

Many important facts follow from this orthogonality. (Formulas (A.13) – (A.18) are all derived from facts in Szegö[24], §§3.2 – 3.4.

For example, there is a __recurrence formula__:

$$(j + 1) K_{j+1}(x) - (n - 2x) K_j(x) + (n - j + 1) K_{j-1}(x) = 0. \tag{A.13}$$

By using the reciprocity formula (A.10), it is easy to transform (A.13) into a __difference equation__:

$$(n - i) K_j(i + 1) - (n - 2j) K_j(i) + i K_j(i - 1) = 0. \tag{A.14}$$

Also, we have the __Christoffel–Darboux__ formula, which says that if $P_0, P_1, \ldots$, are polynomials orthogonal with respect to the Stieltjes integrator $\alpha(x)$, i.e., $\int P_i(x) P_j(x)\, d\alpha(x) = \delta_{ij} \lambda_j$, then

$$\sum_{k=0}^{j} \frac{P_k(x)P_k(y)}{\mu_k} = \frac{1}{\mu_j} \frac{L_j}{L_{j+1}} \left[\frac{P_{j+1}(x)P_j(y) - P_j(x)P_{j+1}(y)}{x - y} \right], \qquad (A.15)$$

where L_j is the leading coefficient of $P_j(x)$. For the Krawtchouk polynomials, $\mu_k = \binom{n}{k}$ by (A.11), and $L_j/L_{j+1} = -(j+1)/2$ by (A.7), and (A.15) becomes

$$K_{j+1}(x)K_j(y) - K_j(x)K_{j+1}(y) = \frac{2(y-x)}{j+1} \binom{n}{j} \sum_{k=0}^{j} \frac{K_k(k)K_k(y)}{\binom{n}{k}} \qquad (A.16)$$

Furthermore, $K_j(x)$ has j distinct real zeros $x_1^{(j)} < x_2^{(j)} < \ldots < x_j^{(j)}$ in the open interval $(0,n)$, and the zeros of K_j and K_{j+1} are interlaced:

$$x_{i-1}^{(j)} < x_i^{(j+1)} < x_i^{(j)}, \qquad i = 1, 2, \ldots, j+1, \qquad (A.17)$$

where in (A.17) we have defined $x_0^{(j)} = 0, x_{j+1}^{(j)} = n$. In addition, each interval $(x_i^{(j)}, x_{i+1}^{(j)})$ must contain a point of increase of $\beta(x)$, i.e., an integer. Since by (A.8), $K_j(0) > 0$ and by (A.9), $K_j(1) > 0$ if $j < n/2$, it follows that

$$x_1^{(j)} \geq 1, \quad \text{if } j < n/2. \qquad (A.18)$$

The next two results about Krawtchouk polynomials we shall derive in detail. Our first result is that any product $K_i(x)K_j(x)$ can be expressed as a linear combination of the K_k with nonnegative coefficients,[*] i.e.,

---

[*]Formula (A.19) must be taken to mean that the polynomials on the left and right are equal for $x = 0, 1, \ldots, n$, since, viewed as a polynomial, $K_i(x)K_j(x)$ has degree $i + j$, which may exceed n.

$$K_i(x)K_j(x) = \sum_{k=0}^{n} \alpha_k K_k(x), \quad \alpha_k \geq 0. \tag{A.19}$$

To prove (A.19), observe that $K_i(x)K_j(x)$ is the coefficient of $y^i z^j$

in $(1 - y)^x(1 + y)^{n-x}(1 - z)^x(1 + z)^{n-x} = (1 + yz)^n(1 - (y + z)/$

$(1 + yz))^x(1 + (y + z)/(1 + yz))^{n-x} = (1 + yz)^n \sum_{k=0}^{n} K_k(x)((y + z)/$

$(1 + yz))^k = \sum_{k=0}^{n} K_k(x)(y + z)^k \cdot (1 + yz)^{n-k}$. The coefficients of this

last polynomial in y and z are obviously nonnegative and in fact this

shows that in (A.19).

$$\alpha_k = \binom{n - k}{(i + j - k)/2} \binom{k}{(i - j + k)/2},$$

where a binomial coefficient with fractional or negative lower index is

to be interpreted as zero.*

Finally, we come to an important result about the asymptotic behavior

of the smallest zero $x_1^{(j)}$ of $K_j^{(n)}(x)$. Let (j_n) be a sequence of

integers for which $j_n/n \to \tau$, $0 \leq \tau \leq 1$, and let $x_1^{(j)_n}$ denote the

smallest zero of $K_{j_n}^{(n)}(x)$. Then

$$\limsup_{n \to \infty} \frac{x_1^{(j)_n}}{n} \leq 1/2 - \sqrt{\tau(1 - \tau)}. \tag{A.20}$$

(Actually it is possible to prove that for $\tau \leq 1/2$, the limit in (A.20)

exists and equals $1/2 - \sqrt{\tau(1 - \tau)}$ (for $\tau \geq 1/2$, the limit is 0), but

the present estimate is sufficient for our purposes and is much easier to

prove.)

---

*Note that α_k is the number of vectors of weight i in V_n at distance j from a fixed vector of weight k.

To prove (A.20), observe that if it is false, then for all sufficiently small ϵ, there exists an infinite sequence of n such that
$x_1^{(j_n)} \geq n(r + 2\epsilon)$, where $r = r(\tau) = 1/2 - \sqrt{\tau(1 - \tau)}$. Define for each n
in this sequence integers i and j by

$$i = i_n = \left\lfloor n(r + \epsilon) \right\rfloor \tag{i}$$

$$j = j_n. \tag{ii}$$

Let $K_j(x) = (-2)^j/j! \ (x - x_1)(x - x_2) \ \cdots \ (x - x_j)$. Then

$$\log \frac{K_j(i + 1)}{K_j(i)} = \sum_{k=1}^{j} \log\left(1 + \frac{1}{i - x_k}\right).$$

But from (i) $|i - x_k| \geq \epsilon n$, and so $\log(1 + (i - x_k)^{-1}) = (i - x_k)^{-1} + 0(n^{-2})$. Therefore,

$$\log \frac{K_j(i + 1)}{K_j(i)} = \sum_{k=1}^{j} \frac{1}{i - x_k} + 0(n^{-1}).$$

Similarly,

$$\log \frac{K_j(i - 1)}{K_j(i)} = - \sum_{k=1}^{j} \frac{1}{i - x_k} + 0(n^{-1}).$$

Hence

$$\log \frac{K_j(i + 1)}{K_j(i)} - \log \frac{K_j(i)}{K_j(i - 1)} = 0(n^{-1}),$$

and so

$$\frac{K_j(i + 1)}{K_j(i)} = \frac{K_j(i)}{K_j(i - 1)} \ (1 + 0 \ (n^{-1})). \tag{iii}$$

Now the difference equation (A.14) can be written as

$$(n - i) \frac{K_i(i + 1)}{K_j(i)} \cdot \frac{K_i(i)}{K_j(i - 1)} - (n - 2j) \frac{K_i(i)}{K_j(i - 1)} + i = 0.$$

If we denote the ratio $K_j(i)/K_j(i - 1)$ by ρ, this becomes

$$(n - i)\rho^2(1 + 0 (n^{-1})) - (n - 2j)\rho + i = 0. \tag{iv}$$

Since ρ is real, the discriminant of (iv) must be nonnegative, i.e.,

$$(n - 2j)^2 - 4i(n - i) + 0 (n) \geq 0.$$

However, by (i) and (ii), this is equivalent to

$$(1 - 2\tau)^2 - 4(r + \varepsilon)(1 - r - \varepsilon) + 0 (n^{-1}) \geq 0,$$

but $(1 - 2\tau)^2 = 4r(1 - r)$ and so

$$-\varepsilon(1 - 2r) + \varepsilon^2 + 0 (n^{-1}) \geq 0. \tag{v}$$

But, if ε is selected so that $-\varepsilon(1 - 2r) + \varepsilon^2 < 0$, i.e., $\varepsilon < 1 - 2r$, (v) is clearly violated for sufficiently large n. This completes the proof of (A.20).

References:

1. MacWilliams, F. J., and Sloane, N. J. A., *The Theory of Error-Correcting Codes* (2 vols.), North-Holland, Amsterdam, 1977.

2. Gass, S. I., *Linear Programming*, McGraw-Hill, New York, 1958.

3. Best, M. R.; Brown, A. E.; MacWilliams, F. J.; Odlyzko, A.M.; and Sloane, N. J. A., Bounds for binary codes of length less than 25, *IEEE Trans. Inform. Theory* IT-24, 81, 1978.

4. Berlekamp, E. R., ed., *Key Papers in the Development of Coding Theory*, IEEE Press, New York, 1974.

5. Sidelnikov, V. M., Upper bounds on the cardinality of a code with a given minimum distance, (in Russian) *Problemy Peredachi Informatsii*, 10, 43, 1974. (English translation appears in *Information and Control*, 28, 292, 1975.)

6. Levenshtein, V. I., On the minimal redundancy of binary error-correcting codes (in Russian), *Problemy Peredachi Informatsii*, 10, 26, 1974. (English translation appears in *Information and Control*, 28, 268, 1975.

7. McEliece, R. J., Rodemich, E. R., Rumsey, H. C., Welch, L. R., New upper bounds on the rate of a code via the Delsarte-MacWilliams inequalities, *IEEE Trans. Inform. Theory* IT-23, 157, 1977.

8. Shannon C., The zero error capacity of a noisy channel, *IRE Trans. Inform. Theory* IT-2, 8, 1956.

9. Lovász, L., On the Shannon capacity of a graph, *IEEE Trans. Inform. Theory*, IT-24, 1978, *in press*.

10. McEliece, R. J. Rodemich, E. R., Rumsey, H. C., The Lovász bound and some generalizations, *J. Combinatorics, Information, and System Science*, 3, 1978, 134.

11. Birkhoff, G., and MacLane, S., *A Survey of Modern Algebra* (2nd ed.), MacMillian, New York, 1960, chapters 8 and 9.

12. MacDuffee, C., *The Theory of Matrices*, Chelsea, New York, 1956, Section VII.

13. Wielandt, H., *Finite Permutation Groups*, Academic Press, New York, 1964, chapter 5.

14. Hoffman, K., and Kunze, R., *Linear Algebra*, Prentice-Hall, Englewood Cliffs, 1961, chapter 6.

15. Delsarte, P., An algebraic approach to the association schemes of coding theory, *Philips Res. Reports.*, Supplement 1973, No. 10.

16. Goethals, J.-M., Association schemes, this volume, pp. 243-283

17. Schriver, A., A comparison of the bounds of Delsarte and Lovász, IEEE Trans. Inform. Theory, IT-24, 1978, *in press*.

18. Baumert, L. D., et. al., A combinatorial packing problem, in *Computers in Algebra and Number Theory*, American Mathematical Society, Providence, 1971, p. 97.

19. Weyl, H., *Algebraic Theory of Numbers* (Annals of Math. Studies No. 1), Princeton University Press, Princeton, 1940, section 11.

20. Hickerson, D., private communication.

21. Haemers, W., On the problems of Lovász concerning the Shannon capacity of a graph, *IEEE Trans. Inform. Theory*, IT-24, 1978, *in press*.

22. Dickson, L. E., *Linear Groups*, Dover Publications, New York, 1958, sec. 283.

23. Marcus, M., and Minc, H., *A Survey of Matrix Theory and Matrix Inequalities*, Allyn and Bacon, Boston, 1967, p. 28.

24. Szegö, G., *Orthogonal Polynomials*, American Math. Society, Providence, 1939.

AN INTRODUCTION TO ANTICODES

P.G. Farrell
Electronics Laboratories
The University of Kent at Canterbury
Canterbury, Kent, CT2 7NT,
England

1:   Code-Words, Code-Books & Code-Columns

The N code-words of a binary block error-correcting code[1,2] of
block length n can be tabulated as the rows of an Nxn matrix: this
is the *code-book* of the code. The N rows of the code-book are the codewords; the n columns of the code-book are also of interest, and may be
called the *code-columns*. For example, the code-book of the N=6, n=6 code
mentioned by Hamming[3] is:

	0	0	0	0	0	0
	0	1	0	1	0	1
	1	0	0	1	1	0
N=6 code-words (rows)	1	1	1	0	0	0
	0	0	1	0	1	1
	1	1	1	1	1	1

n=6 code-columns

This code has *Hamming* or *minimum distance*[3] d=3; that is, any pair of code-words will differ in at least d positions, though many pairs will differ in more than d positions (e.g., the first and last words differ in all six positions). Thus the minimum distance is the minimum value among the possible pair-wise distances between code words.

If the code is *linear*[1,2,4], then each n-digit code word consists of k information digits, and n-k=c check or redundant digits which are linear (modulo-2 addition) combinations of some or all of the information digits. Thus k of the code-columns are information columns, and c are check or redundant columns. It is convenient to consdier the *systematic* form of the code-book, in which the information columns are grouped together on the left, and the redundant columns on the right. The number of code-words in a linear code-book is $N=2^k$. Thus the code-book for the Hamming[3] single-error-correcting code with k=2, c=3, n=5, $N=2^2=4$ and d=3 is:

	k_1	k_2		c_1	c_2	c_3	
	O	O		O	O	O	
$N=2^k=2^2=4$	1	O		1	1	O	n=5, d=3
code words	O	1		1	O	1	
	1	1		O	1	1	
	k=2			c=3			
	information columns			redundant columns			

The rate[1,2,4], or efficiency, of a linear code is given by R=k/n; in general, $R=\log_2 N/n$. A code is *optimum* if it has the maximum possible rate for a given minimum distance and block length.

A relatively novel way of constructing a code with a given N is to adjoin suitable code-columns until a code-book with the desired minimum distance or block length has been achieved. In the case of a linear code it is only necessary to ensure that each code word used (except the null word) has the desired *weight*. In the general case (i.e., a non-linear code), there are 2^N-2 possible distinct code-columns to choose from, since the all-ZERO and all-ONE columns are useless because they do not add to the minimum distance of a code-book. The first example previously given, with N=6 and n=6, is made up from 6 distinct columns. Notice that the number of ONES in each column is 3; that is, the weight of each column is 3. It will be shown below that it is efficient to use columns with weight near or equal to N/2 to construct a code, in the sense that the use of such columns minimises the total number of columns required to achieve a given minimum distance. If the code is linear, then there are 2^k-1 distinct columns to choose from, since there are 2^k linear combinations of k information columns but the null combination (i.e., the combination which results in the all-ZERO column) is useless. Thus in the second example above, with k=2, n=5 and $N=2^2=4$, there are only 3 possible distinct columns, so that two columns (c_2 and c_3) are duplicates of other columns. Linear code-books with $n > 2^k-1$ must have repeated columns; code books with $n \leq 2^k-1$ need not. Notice that all the possible columns in a linear code-book have weight $N/2 = 2^{k-1}$. This is because:-

(i) all information columns have weight 2^{k-1};

(ii)   exactly half the weights of the rows of a code-book made up-exclusively of information columns are an even value, and half are an odd value;

(iii) Thus any linear combination of one or more information columns always results in a column with weight 2^{k-1}.

This property (a more elegant proof is given in reference 5) of linear code-books seems to be a good one, in that it must lead to efficient codes in the sense mentioned above. Unfortunately, however, the property goes with two further constraints:-

(a)   no column may have a ONE at the top;

(b)   all columns have one of the following two symmetries:

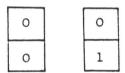

that is, either the top and bottom halves of the column are identical (e.g., k_1 and c_2 in the second example), or the bottom half is the inverse (logical complement) of the top half (e.g. k_2, c_1 and c_3 in the second example). Thus the following column is not permissible in a k=3 code-book:

$$
\begin{array}{ll}
0 & \\
1 & \\
1 & k=3 \\
0 & N = 2^k = 8 \\
0 & \\
1 & \\
0 & \\
1 &
\end{array}
$$

For a given k (i.e., for a given $N=2^k$), of the 2^k-1 possible distinct

columns, $2^{k-1}-1$ have $\boxed{\begin{matrix}0\\0\end{matrix}}$ symmetry, and 2^{k-1} have $\boxed{\begin{matrix}0\\1\end{matrix}}$ symmetry. Thus,

if all 2^k-1 possible columns are known for a given value of k, those for

k+1 can easily be found by doubling the height of each of the columns

of height 2^k using either the $\boxed{\begin{matrix}0\\0\end{matrix}}$ symmetry or the $\boxed{\begin{matrix}1\\1\end{matrix}}$ symmetry, and

finally adjoining the $\begin{matrix}2k\ \text{ZEROS} \qquad 2k\ \text{ONES}\\ \{00\ \ldots\ldots \quad : \quad 11\ \ldots\ldots\}\end{matrix}$ column.

This will give:

$$2(2^k-1) + 1 = 2^{k+1}-1$$

distinct columns. The process can be represented by

O	O	O
1	1	o

where $O \equiv$ columns of height 2^k

$I \equiv$ inverses of the columns of height 2^k

$o \equiv$ all-ZERO column of height 2^k

$1 \equiv$ all-ONE column of height 2^k;

and it can begin with the simplest possible case, the only permissible

column for k=1:

$$\begin{matrix}0\\1\end{matrix}$$

Thus, the permissible columns for k=2 are:

O	O	O
O	1	1
1	1	O
1	O	1

for k=3

O	O	O	O	O	O	O
O	O	1	1	O	1	1
O	1	1	O	1	1	O
O	1	O	1	1	O	1
1	1	1	1	O	O	O
1	1	O	O	O	1	1
1	O	O	1	1	1	O
1	O	1	O	1	O	1

and so on.

The linear code that results from a linear code-book consisting of all permissible columns for a given k has parameters:-

$$n = 2^k - 1 \qquad\qquad d = 2^{k-1}$$

$$N = 2^k \qquad \text{and} \qquad R = k/n = k/(2^k - 1)$$

The parameters of these codes, for k=1-10, are given in Table 1 below:

		TABLE 1 : m-sequence code parameters		
k	n	N	d	R
1	1	2	1	1
2	3	4	2	0.667
3	7	8	4	0.429
4	15	16	8	0.267
5	31	32	16	0.161
6	63	64	32	0.095
7	127	128	64	0.055
8	255	256	128	0.031
9	511	512	256	0.018
10	1023	1024	512	0.010

That the minimum distance of these codes is 2^{k-1} may be proved by induction, starting with the code for k=1 and noting the properties of the $\begin{array}{c}0\\0\end{array}$ and $\begin{array}{c}0\\1\end{array}$ symmetries. These well-known codes[1,2,5] are simplex[6], because the normalised cross-correlation between any two code words is given by

$$c(x_i, x_j) = \frac{-1}{2^k - 1} \quad , \quad \text{all } i \neq j \quad .$$

This is equivalent to saying that the Hamming distances between all pairs of code-words are equal, and given by

$$d_{ij} = \frac{n}{2} \{ 1 - \rho(x_i, x_j) \}$$

$$= \frac{2^{k-1}}{2} \{ 1 + \frac{1}{2^k - 1} \}$$

$$= 2^{k-1} = \dot{d} .$$

Thus the average and minimum distances of the codes are equal, so the codes are *equidistant*, or *uniform*. The codes are *optimum*, because they exactly meet the Plotkin bound[7]. An alternative derivation of the codes is by means of the theory of Hadamard matrices[5,6]. The codes may also be called maximum-length-sequence or *m-sequence* codes[1,5] because the code words for each value of k may be generated, after suitable re-arrangement of the code columns, by taking the linear m-sequence[6] of length $n=2^k-1$ and all its cyclic translates (cyclic shifts) together with the null (all-ZERO) word. Thus these codes are *cyclic*[1,4,5]. The m-sequence codes (as they shall be called in the remainder of this text) also exactly meet the Griesmer bound[8], so clearly they are optimum codes of fundamental importance to the theory of error-control coding.

A convenient way of reducing the block length of a code is to puncture[9,10] (i.e. delete or remove) columns from the code book, without altering the number of code words. Any column may be removed, provided at least k columns remain; in the case of linear code, if an information column is removed, then the order of the code words can be re-arranged to restore the code-book to systematic form. Puncturing one column reduces the minimum distance of the code by one; and puncturing two columns reduces it by two. If m columns are punctured, however, where

m > 2, then it is possible to so choose the columns removed in such a way
that the distance is reduced by less than m. For example, puncturing any
two columns together with the column which is the mod-2 sum of the two
columns chosen, reduces the distance by only two (see example below).

Solomon & Stiffler[9] have shown that optimum binary linear codes can
be constructed by puncturing certain columns from an m-sequence code-book.
The parameters of these punctured codes (which are also cyclic) are

$$n = 2^k - 1 - \sum_i (2^{\ell_i} - 1),$$

$$d = 2^{k-1} - \sum_i 2^{\ell_i - 1} ,$$

and $N = 2^k$;

where the ℓ_i are integers such that

$$1 \leq \ell_i \leq k - 1 ,$$

$$\ell_i \neq \ell_j ,$$

and $\sum_i \ell_i \leq k$.

Values of ℓ_i, 2^{ℓ_i}, $2^{\ell_i} - 1$ and 2^{i-1} are given in Table 2.

TABLE 2 : Values of ℓ_i, etc.			
ℓ_i	2^{ℓ_i}	2^{ℓ_i-1}	$2^{\ell_i}-1$
1	2	1	1
2	4	3	2
3	8	7	4
4	16	15	8
5	32	31	16
6	64	63	32
7	128	127	64
8	256	255	128
9	512	511	256
10	1024	1023	512

From Table 2, values of $\sum_i 2^{\ell_i-1}$ and $\sum_i 2^{\ell_i-1}$ may be calculated, for each value of k, as given in Table 3.

TABLE 3 : Values of $\sum 2^{\ell_i-1}$ and $\sum 2^{\ell_i-1}$ for $2 \le k \le 7$	
k — $\sum_i 2^{\ell_i-1}$	$\sum_i 2^{\ell_i-1}$
2 — 1	1
3 — 1 3 4	1 2 3
4 — 1 3 4 7 8	1 2 3 4 5
5 — 1 3 4 7 8 10 15 16	1 2 3 4 5 6 8 9
6 — 1 3 4 7 8 10 11 15 16 18	1 2 3 4 5 6 7 8 9 10
7 — 1 3 4 7 8 10 11 15 16 18 19 22	1 2 3 4 5 6 7 8 9 10 11 12

Hence, for example, if k=3, the punctured codes which result are:

$$(n,d) = (6,3), \ (4,2) \ \text{and} \ (3,1)$$

Expressed in terms of the code-book:-

n		3			4		6		7
	0	0	0		0		0	0	0
	1	0	0		1		1	1	0
k=3	0	1	0		1		1	0	1
	1	1	0		0		0	1	1
N=2^k=8	0	0	1		1		0	1	1
	1	0	1		0		1	0	1
	0	1	1		0		1	1	0
	1	1	1		1		0	0	0
d		1			2		3		4

It is interesting to speculate if the m-sequence code-books for all values of k can be similarly partitioned. If k=4, the punctured codes are:

$$(n,d) = (14,7), \ (12,6), \ (11,5), \ (8,4) \ \text{and} \ (7,3);$$

and so on for higher values of k. Notice, however, that not necessarily all values of d, $1 \leq d \leq 2^{k-1}$, can be achieved by means of the Solomon and Stiffler (S/S) construction, for a given value of k. When k=5, for instance, there is no construction for d=7. Once a value of d is achieved, though, it is then available for all larger values of k. An extended table of S/S construction parameters will be found in Appendix 1. How to choose the appropriate columns for each construction will be made clear in the next Section.

This idea of puncturing certain columns from a code-book to form shorter code-books can be generalised and extended in interesting ways, as will be shown in the succeeding sections.

2: Anticodes

In the previous section, m-sequence codes were defined. These are optimum linear codes with code-books made up of every possible linear code-column, without any repeated columns. The idea of puncturing columns from an m-sequence code-book was also introduced; by partitioning off the punctured columns from an m-sequence code-book, another code is found, with reduced block length and minimum distance, but having the same number of code-words as the "parent" m-sequence code:-

In this section, attention will be focussed on the properties of the array consisting of the punctured columns.

The m-sequence codes are optimum, and also equidistant; that is, all the code-words have weight 2^{k-1}, except the null word. The ultimate intention of puncturing is to construct an optimum, but shorter, code. Thus, if m columns are to be punctured, it is desirable that the maximum weight, δ, of the rows of the array of punctured colums should be as small as possible, as this maximum value of row

weight will determine the minimum weight, and hence the minimum

distance, of the resulting code.   If an array of m colums, with

maximum row weight ε, is punctured from an m-sequence code with k

information digits then a code with block length 2^k-1-m of minimum

distance $2^{k-1}-\varepsilon$ results:-

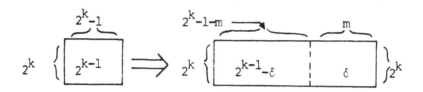

Returning to the example of the previous section, with k=3, the

relationships between n and m, and d and ε, can clearly be seen:-

				m = 4	3	1	
n			3	4	6	7	
	0	0	0	0	0 0	0	
	1	0	0	1	1 1	0	
k=3	0	1	0	1	1 0	1	
	1	1	0	0	0 1	1	
N=2^3=8	0	0	1	1	0 1	1	
	1	0	1	0	1 0	1	
	0	1	1	0	1 1	0	
	1	1	1	1	0 0	0	
d			1	2	3	4	
				3	2	1	ε

The array of punctured columns should have minimum value of δ for a given m; alternatively, for a given value of δ, a maximum value of m is sought. These properties are exactly the opposite of those of a code, which are that a maximum value of d for a given n, or a minimum value of n for a given d are desirable. Thus the array of punctured columns will be called a *linear anti-code*:-

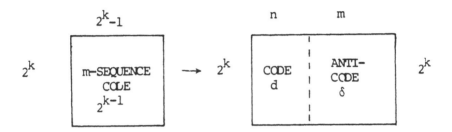

The 2^k rows of the anti-code are the anticode *words*; its m columns are the anticode *columns*; the maximum value of anticode-word weight (i.e., the maximum value of Hamming distance between all pairs of anticode-words) is the *maximum distance*, δ, of the anticode. An anticode is optimum if it has the *minimum* value of δ for a given m and k. Clearly, and as pointed out in the previous chapter, the optimum values of δ for m=1,2,3 and 4 are δ=1,2,2 and 3. More generally, an anticode may be defined as an array of N rows and m columns, constructed such that the maximum Hamming distance between any pair of rows is less than or equal to a certain value, δ. Clearly, in the case of a linear anticode

$\delta = \max_i (w_i)$, where

w_i = weight of anticode word i.

This is because the words of an anticode form a group, like those of a

linear code. In the anticode case, however, the group may consist of

only 2^j distinct words, where $1 \le j \le k$, and then each distinct word

will appear 2^{k-j} times in the anticode. For example, this k=3, m=3,

δ=2 anticode has j=2; i.e. each word appears twice:-


```
        0   0   0
        1   1   0
        1   0   1     k=3
        0   1   1     m=3
        0   1   1     δ=2
        1   0   1     j=2
        1   1   0
        0   0   0
```


This rather startling property of anticodes is in direct opposition to

that of codes, which of course cannot have separated words. The

properties of codes and anticodes are compared and contrasted in

Appendix 2.

An anticode can be constructed from 2^k-1 different columns. If all

the columns are used, without duplication, then all the rows except

the null row have weight 2^{k-1}. Hence optimum anticodes with parameters

$N = 2^k$, $m = 2^k-1$, and $\delta = 2^{k-1}$ exist, with maximum distance equal to the

average distance between pairs of rows (i.e. they are uniform or equi-

distant anticodes). It will be noticed that these parameters and

properties are also those of m-sequence codes, so that identical optimum

m-sequence codes and anticodes exist for these parameters. If $m > 2^k-1$, then some columns must be repeated.

An anticode may contain information as well as parity check columns; this does not invalidate the anticode, since any deletion code constructed from it will have the correct Hamming distance, and the missing information columns can be restored by suitable re-arranging of the rows. (This corresponds to the process of transforming the generator matrix of a group code into standard echelon form[1]).

The Plotkin upper bound on d for optimum codes can also be applied to anticodes. In the anticode case the bound is a lower bound on δ, given by:

$$\delta \geq \frac{m.2^{k-1}}{2^k-1} \quad .$$

It can be derived by noting that the maximum distance of an anticode must exceed the average distance between pairs of words in the anticode. This bound also implies that an anticode can only meet the bound exactly if it is uniform (equidistant) and therefore has δ even. Also, clearly $\delta \to m/2$ as $k \to \infty$. Thus the following lower bound on the length of a code, for a given k and d, can be derived:-

$$n \geq 2^k-1-2\delta, \text{ where } \delta=2^{k-1}-d$$

$$\geq 2d-1$$

which is, of course, the Plotkin bound re-stated as a lower bound on n. MacWilliams[25] has shown that all codes which meet the Plotkin bound

cannot have repeated columns. Hence neither will anticodes which meet
the bound. It is a strong conjecture,[13,16] furthermore, that all
optimum codes and anticodes can be constructed without requiring repeated
columns, provided $n \leq 2^k-1$. It is also possible to derive a Griesmer[8]
anticode bound, and MacWilliams & Sloane[2] show that all anticodes which
meet the bound cannot have repeated columns if $n < 2^k-1$, thus strengthening
the above conjecture.

A linear anticode is a subspace of the vector space V_m. Hence a set
of basis vectors (anticode-words) can be found to describe the subspace;
that is, a linear anticode can be described by means of a *generator matrix*
in exactly the same way as a linear code can. Each column in the "parent"
m-sequence code-book corresponds to a column in the m-sequence code
generator matrix. The generator matrix of the anticode is formed from
the columns of the m-sequence code generator matrix corresponding to
those columns punctured from the m-sequence code book. The anticode
generator matrix will not necessarily be in standard echelon form (SEF),
but it can be reduced to SEF by suitable row operations. If the anticode
has repeated code-words (that is, if $j < k$) then the SEF generator
matrix has k-j all-zero (null) rows, and a j x j unit matrix instead of
a k x k unit matrix. For example, the k=3 m-sequence code generator
matrix (see previous example) is:

$$
\left[G_{m-SEQ} \right] =
\begin{bmatrix}
1 & 0 & 0 & | & 1 & 1 & 1 & 0 \\
0 & 1 & 0 & | & 1 & 1 & 0 & 1 \\
0 & 0 & 1 & | & 1 & 0 & 1 & 1
\end{bmatrix}
$$

The three right-hand columns of this matrix form the generator matrix of

a k=3, m=3, δ=2 anticode:

$$\begin{bmatrix} G_{A1} \end{bmatrix} \quad = \quad \begin{bmatrix} 1 & 1 & 0 \\ 1 & 0 & 1 \\ 0 & 1 & 1 \end{bmatrix}$$

Converting to SEF:

$$\begin{bmatrix} G_{A1/SEF} \end{bmatrix} \quad = \quad \left[\begin{array}{cc|c} 1 & 0 & 1 \\ 0 & 1 & 1 \\ \hline 0 & 0 & 0 \end{array} \right]$$

the single all-zero row and 2x2 unit matrix arise from the fact that j=2

in this case. The four right-hand columns of G_{m-SEQ} form the generator

matrix of a k=3, m=4, δ=3 anticode:

$$\begin{bmatrix} G_{A2} \end{bmatrix} \quad = \quad \begin{bmatrix} 1 & 1 & 1 & 0 \\ 1 & 1 & 0 & 1 \\ 1 & 0 & 1 & 1 \end{bmatrix} \quad , \quad \begin{bmatrix} G_{A2/SEF} \end{bmatrix} \quad = \quad \left[\begin{array}{ccc|c} 1 & 0 & 0 & 0 \\ 0 & 1 & 0 & 1 \\ 0 & 0 & 1 & 1 \end{array} \right]$$

In this case j=3, so there are no null rows. If the generator matrix of

an anticode can be converted, by row operations and column transposition,

into that of another anticode, then the anticodes are *equivalent*, that

is, they will have the same δ. This result parallels that for equivalent

codes. If there are any null rows, these can effectively be deleted,

since the properties of the anticode, apart from the number of words,

are unaltered. This permits formulation of a parity check matrix for an anticode; the two examples given above have the parity check matrices:

$$\left[H_{A1/SEF}\right] = \begin{bmatrix} 1 & 1 & \vdots & 1 \end{bmatrix} \quad \text{and} \quad \left[H_{A2/SEF}\right] = \begin{bmatrix} 0 & 1 & 1 & \vdots & 1 \end{bmatrix}$$

Hashim[11] has shown that a constructional upper bound on δ, for a given m and sufficiently large value of k, can be divided for anticodes. The derivation parallels that of the Varshamov- Gilbert[12] constructional lower bound on d for codes.

If the minimum distance of an optimum code (linear or non-linear) is an odd value, then it can be increased by unity by adjoining an overall parity check, and vice-versa; i.e. :-

N(n,d) <==> N(n+1, d+1), d odd.

The corresponding rule for anticodes is:-

N(m,δ) <==> N(m-1, δ-1), δ odd;

that is, deleting an appropriate column from an optimum anticode with δ odd gives an optimum δ-1 anticode. In practice, this rule is best implemented in reverse, by noting that addition of any column to an optimum δ even anticode gives an optimum δ+1 anticode. Thus, even values of δ are of importance in the search for new anticodes, just as odd values of d are of importance in the search for new codes.

Anticodes have been studied by Farrell,[5,13] Farrell and Farrag[14,15], and by Farrag[16]. Examples of maximum-distance linear codes have been studied by Maki and Tracey[17], and extended to the general (non-linear) case by Reddy[18]. Some of the construction techniques for anticodes described in the next chapter have been systematised by Hashim & Pozdniakov[19]. The book by MacWilliams & Sloane[2] has a section on anticodes.

3:   Linear Anticode Constructions

In the previous section, the concept of an anticode was introduced and defined, and the properties of anticodes were discussed. Methods of constructing optimum and near-optimum linear binary anticodes will be described in this section. It is convenient to describe the parameters of an anticode in a similar way to those of a code, by means of a triple (m, k, δ), where m is the word length, 2^k is the number of words, and δ is the maximum distance, of the linear binary anticode. Where necessary, an anticode triple will be preceded by the abbreviation AC, and a code triple by the abbreviation C. Initially, anticodes without repeated columns will be considered.

3.1 Short Anticodes

As has already been mentioned, optimum anticodes for m = 1,2,3 and 4, with δ = 1,2,2 and 3, are easily constructed as follows:

m = 1 , any column, $k \geq 1$;

m = 2 , any two columns, $k \geq 2$;

m = 3 , any two columns and their mod-2 sum, $k \geq 2$;

m = 4 , the anticode for m = 3, adjoined to any other column, $k \geq 3$.

Thus optimum (1, $\geq$1, 1), (2, $\geq$2, 2), (3, $\geq$2, 2) and (4, >3, 3) anticodes

exist. AC(2, $\geq$2, 2) is just a "shortened" version of AC(3, $\geq$2, 2); in

paractice it is sufficient to concentrate on finding the longest anticode

with a given value of δ. Notice that for these simple anticodes, the

value of k (provided it is large enough) does not affect the other

parameters of the anticode.

3.2   m-Sequence Anticodes

As pointed out in the previous section, the class of m-sequence codes

is identical with the class of m-sequence anticodes, with parameters

$$m = 2^k - 1 \ (= n)$$
$$\delta = 2^{k-1} \ (= d)$$

Thus optimum anticodes (7, >3, 4), (15, $\geq$4, 8), (31, $\geq$5, 16), ... etc,

exist. These are equidistant anticodes, and in each case they are made up

of all possible columns for the particular value of k. The $\geq$ signs

indicate that these anticodes may have repeated words (rows), for values

of k greater than the minimum indicated. Because of the equidistance

property, these codes/anticodes have $\delta = d$. In general, for an array

of words/columns, $\delta \geq d$ (δ can never be less than d). The array is

optimum as a code if d is maximised, as an anticode if δ is minimised;

it is interesting to note that d and δ are simultaneously optimised

in the case of the m-sequence arrays.

The generator matrix of an m-sequence anticode consists of every possible k-tuple column, k the minimum value for which the anticode exists, and as many null rows as required to complete the required number of words. For example, AC(7, 4, 4) has:

$$[G] \quad = \quad \begin{bmatrix} 1 & 0 & 0 & 1 & 1 & 1 & 0 \\ 0 & 1 & 0 & 1 & 1 & 0 & 1 \\ 0 & 0 & 1 & 1 & 0 & 1 & 1 \\ \hline 0 & 0 & 0 & 0 & 0 & 0 & 0 \end{bmatrix}$$

3.3 Solomon and Stiffler Construction

S/S anticode constructions[9] exist, as indicated in section 1, with parameters:

$$m = \sum_i 2^{l_i} - 1$$

$$\delta = \sum_i 2^{l_i - 1} ,$$

where the l_i are integers such that

$$1 \leq l_i \leq k-1$$

$$l_i \neq l_j$$

and

$$\sum_i l_i \leq k$$

Thus anticodes with the parameters given in Table 3, Chapter 1, exist, and are optimum. These S/S construction anticodes consist of i adjoined m-sequence anticodes. For example, AC(10, >5, 6) consists of AC(7, >3,4) adjoined to AC(3, >2, 2):-

(7, >3, 4) m-sequence anticode	(3, >2, 2) m-sequence anticode

$$\underbrace{\qquad\qquad}\quad AC(10, \geq 5, 6)$$

Since there are at least five information columns, the two m-sequence anticodes can be constructed independently, thus ensuring that the overall anticode has no repeated columns: three of the information columns and associated parity check columns form AC(7, >3, 4), the remaining two and their associated check columns form AC(3, >2, 2).

The generator matrix of a S/S construction anticode consists of adjoined m-sequence generator matrices, with suitable numbers of null sub-words. For AC(10, 5, 6):-

$$[G] = \begin{bmatrix} 1 & 0 & 0 & 1 & 1 & 1 & 0 & 0 & 0 & 0 \\ 0 & 1 & 0 & 1 & 1 & 0 & 1 & 0 & 0 & 0 \\ 0 & 0 & 1 & 1 & 0 & 1 & 1 & 0 & 0 & 0 \\ 0 & 0 & 0 & 0 & 0 & 0 & 0 & 1 & 0 & 1 \\ 0 & 0 & 0 & 0 & 0 & 0 & 0 & 0 & 1 & 1 \end{bmatrix}$$

Note that the null sub-words occur in different rows of the generator matrix. This is to ensure that there are no repeated columns.

The (m, δ) parameters of S/S constructions are identical with the Griesmer anticode bound. This is, of course, why the S/S constructions are optimum.

3.4 Simple Stacking

Notice that the component anticodes of AC(10, ≥ 5, 6) example, given in the previous section, both have repeated rows. Also, the fact that an anticode may have repeated rows was mentioned and discussed in the previous two chapters. Thus a legitimate way of constructing an anticode with m columns and 2^{k+1} words is to take an anticode with m columns and 2^k words, and double the height of each of its columns by repeating each word once.

For example:-

$$
\text{AC}(3, 2, 2) \quad
\begin{array}{ccc}
0 & 0 & 0 \\
1 & 0 & 1 \\
0 & 1 & 1 \\
1 & 1 & 0
\end{array}
\quad
\begin{array}{ccc}
0 & 0 & 0 \\
1 & 0 & 1 \\
0 & 1 & 1 \\
1 & 1 & 0 \\
\hline
0 & 0 & 0 \\
1 & 0 & 1 \\
0 & 1 & 1 \\
1 & 1 & 0
\end{array}
\quad \text{AC}(3, 3, 2)
$$

This process will be called "simple stacking"; it can be repeated as many times as required. Simple stacking (S/STK) does not alter the maximum distance of the anticode, as no new rows are generated in the process. The generator matrix of a simple stack is the generator matrix of the original anticode, over as many null rows are required. For the above example, AC(3, 3, 2)

$$[G] = \begin{bmatrix} 1 & 0 & 1 \\ 0 & 1 & 1 \\ \hline 0 & 0 & 0 \end{bmatrix}$$

Thus null rows generate repeated words, as mentioned previously in section 2.

It is convenient to use the notation introduced in section 1 to indicate simple stacking; i.e.:-

$$\boxed{0} \Rightarrow \begin{array}{|c|} \hline 0 \\ \hline 0 \\ \hline \end{array}$$

where, e.g. $0 \equiv$ AC(3, 2, 2).

3.5 Map Stacking

An alternative way of introducing repeated words, and thus of increasing the value of k of an anticode, is to map[16] each word of the original anticode as many times as required. For example, an alternative AC(3, 3, 2), equivalent to that given in section 3.4 above is:-

```
                                       0 0 0
                                       0 0 0
                                       ─────
                                       1 0 1
                    0 0 0              1 0 1
                    1 0 1              ─────    AC(3, 3, 2)
    AC(3, 2, 2)     0 1 1     =>       0 1 1
                    1 1 0              0 1 1
                                       ─────
                                       1 1 0
                                       1 1 0
```

Note that the columns of this anticode are different from those in the
previous example, though the (m, k, δ) parameters of the result are
identical. This fact will be useful later. The generator matrix now
has a null row above the original matrix:-

$$
\begin{bmatrix} G \end{bmatrix} \Rightarrow
\begin{bmatrix}
0 & 0 & 0 \\
\hline
1 & 0 & 1 \\
0 & 1 & 1
\end{bmatrix}
$$

Thus S/S constructions are combinations of simple and map stacking
(M/STK).

Simple or map stacking of an optimum anticode does not necessarily
result in an optimum anticode, because the larger value of k makes
available additional distinct columns which may permit a larger value
of m for the same δ. For example, an optimum (17, 5, 10) anticode is
known (for derivation, see below), but the (17, 6, 10) anticode formed
by stacking it is not optimum, because the S/S construction with

parameters (18, $\geq$6, 10) is the appropriate optimum anticode. It is a matter of observation, however, that stacking of an optimum anticode (which does not have repeated columns) always results in an anticode with at worst only one less column than the appropriate optimum anticode for the stacked value of k (see the short table of anticodes below). If the original optimum anticode has repeated columns, then the stacked anticode may be several columns short of the optimum value of m.

The following notation may be used to denote mapped stacking[16]:-

$$\boxed{O} \quad \Rightarrow \quad \boxed{O_M}$$

3.6 Inversion Stacking

Another method of using a given anticode to construct an anticode with a higher value of k, is to stack the original anticode upon an inverted version of itself. Using the notation developed in Chapter 1:-

$$\boxed{O} \quad \Rightarrow \quad \boxed{\begin{matrix} O \\ I \end{matrix}} \quad \Rightarrow \quad \boxed{\begin{matrix} O \\ I \\ O \\ 1 \end{matrix}}$$

where   O   represents AC(m, k, δ),

and   I   is the anticode with words (or columns) which are the logical complements of those of AC(m, k, δ).

For example, :-

$$
AC(3, 2, 2) \quad
\begin{matrix}
0\ 0\ 0 \\
1\ 0\ 1 \\
0\ 1\ 1 \\
1\ 1\ 0
\end{matrix}
\quad \Rightarrow \quad
\begin{matrix}
0\ 0\ 0 \\
1\ 0\ 1 \\
0\ 1\ 1 \\
1\ 1\ 0 \\
\overline{} \\
1\ 1\ 1 \\
0\ 1\ 0 \\
1\ 0\ 0 \\
0\ 0\ 1
\end{matrix}
\quad AC(3, 3, 3)
$$

Inversion stacking (I/STK) alters the value of δ, making it equal to m, because of the null word (or words) in a linear anticode. Thus inversion stacking on its own is not an effective way of generating anticodes. Used in combination with simple stacking, however, it becomes a powerful method for generating good new anticodes. The generator matrix of an inversion stacked anticode consists of the matrix for the original anticode, over a row of ONES. For the above example:-

$$
\begin{bmatrix} G \end{bmatrix} \;=\;
\begin{bmatrix}
1 & 0 & 1 \\
0 & 1 & 1 \\
\hline
1 & 1 & 1
\end{bmatrix}
$$

Inversion stacks are sometimes useful codes, see section 4; the minimum distance of the I/STK is given by $d = m - \delta$, where δ_o is the maximum distance of the original AC.

3.7 Combined Stacking

Simple (or map) stacking and inversion stacking may be combined in a number of ways to construct optimum and near-optimum anticodes. One way is:-

$$(m, k, \delta) \quad \boxed{O} \quad => \quad \begin{array}{|c|c|} \hline O & O \\ \hline 1 & O \\ \hline \end{array} \quad (2m, k+1, 2\delta)$$

The maximum distance of the lower half of this anticode book is m (all the words in the lower half have weight m), so the overall δ is 2δ, since $\delta > m/2$ (Plotkin anticode bound, Chap. 1). Precisely because $\delta > m/2$, it is always possible to adjoin the $\{0\ 0 --- 0 \mid 1\ 1 -- 1\}$ column without increasing the maximum distance of theanticode so constructed:-

$$(m, k, \delta) \quad \boxed{O} \quad => \quad \begin{array}{|c|c|c|} \hline O & O & O \\ \hline 1 & 1 & O \\ \hline \end{array} \quad (2m, k+1, 2\delta)$$

This is an important and useful method of combined stacking, as it permits construction of many new anticodes from previously known ones; as such, it will be called canonical combined stacking (CC/STK). If O is an m-sequence anticode, then another m-sequence anticode results from a CC/STK, as pointed out, in a different context in section 1. The similarity of this construction to the Kroeneker product of Hadamand matrices is not coincidental: m-sequences can be used to generate $2^k \times 2^k$ Hadamand matrices[6]. In general, it does not follow that an optimum anticode will result from a CC/STK of an optimum "parent" anticode, though many can be found. For example, a CC/STK of optimum AC(8, 4, 5) gives AC(17, 5, 10), which is also optimum (see why in the next section). The generator matrix of a CC/STK is:

$$
[G] = \begin{bmatrix}
O & & & \\
O & & & \\
O & & g & g \\
\hline
1 & 1\ 1\text{---}1 & 0\ 0\text{---}0
\end{bmatrix}
$$

where $[g]$ is the generator matrix of the "parent" anticode.

Combined stacking can be extended to an infinite variety of combinations of simple, mapped, and inversion stacking, and column adjacency. Thus many optimum and good anticodes can be constructed from simple anticodes with small k (in principle, from the (1,1,1) anticode!). As an example, optimum AC(3, 2, 2) can be used to construct optimum AC(10, 4, 6) as follows:

	O	O	O
O	I	I	O
	I	O	O
1	O	I	O

Another example is that the adjacency of AC(63, 6, 32) map stacked to AC(63, 11, 32), and AC(25, 5, 14) simple stacked to AC(25, 11, 14), gives optimum (because it meets the Griesmer[8] bound) AC(88, 11, 46).

3.8 Anticodes Derived from Codes

Anticodes can, of course, be derived from known codes. If an
(n, k, d) code exists, then a $(2^k-1-n, k, 2^{k-1}-d)$ anticode also exists.
If the code is optimum, then so is the anticode. It may seem trivial
to find an anticode in this way. Once the anticode has been found,
however, then it can be stacked in various ways to form anticodes with
larger k, from which other, possibly new codes can be derived. Thus
optimum $C(11, 5, 4)$ leads to optimum $AC(21, 5, 12)$, which when simple
stacked becomes possibly optimum $AC(21, 6, 12)$, which in turn leads to
$C(42, 6, 20)$, which is confirmed by Baumert and McEliece[20] to be
optimum. So this method of anticode derivation can be used to confirm
the optimality of a previously found anticode. As another example,
optimum single-parity-check codes with parameters $(5, 4, 2)$ and
$(6, 5, 2)$ are known; hence $AC(10, 4, 6)$ (see section 3.7) and
$AC(25, 5, 14)$ are optimum. For a final example, $C(14, 5, 6)$ is
optimum[2,21]; therefore $AC(17, 5, 10)$ is also optimum (see section 3.7).

3.9 A Short Table of Optimum Anticodes

Using the methods and examples quoted in the previous section,
a short table of optimum linear binary anticodes may be derived.
Notes on Table 4:-

    (i) Abbreviations

        S/S : Solomon & Stiffler construction (section 3.3)

       S/STK : Simple stacking (section 3.4)

      CC/STK : Canonical combined stacking (section 3.7)

k \ m	1	2	3	4	5	6	Derivation
1	1	1	1	1	1	1	m-seq. AC & S/S and S/STK
2							
3		2	2	2	2	2	m-seq. AC and S/STK
4			3	3	3	3	Rule 1
5							
6							
7			4	4	4	4	m-seq. AC & S/S and S/STK
8				5	5	5	Rule 1
9							
10				6	6	6	C(5,4,2) & S/S and S/STK
11				7	7	7	Rule 1
12							
13							
14							
15				8	8	8	m-seq. AC & S/S and S/STK
16					9	9	Rule 1
17					10		CC/STK of (8, 4, 5), and S/STK
18					11	10	11 : Rule 1 ; 10 : S/S & S/STK
19						11	Rule 1
20							
21					12	12	C(11, 5, 4) and S/STK
22					13	13	Rule 1
23							
24							
25					14	14	C(6, 5, 2) and S/STK
26					15	15	Rule 1
27							
28							
29							
30							
31					16	16	m-seq. AC & S/S and S/STK

Table 4 : Short Table of Linear Binary Anticodes : values of δ

(ii) Rule 1 is the relationship

$$N(m, \delta) \iff N(m+1, \delta+1), \quad \delta \quad \text{even},$$

introduced in section 2.

(iii) Anticodes to the right of the dotted line do not have repeated
columns; anticodes to the left would necessarily have
repeated columns.

(iv) Where values of δ have been omitted (for clarity), the value
is the even number next below; e.g., for $m = 5$, $k = 3$, 4 and 5
$\delta = 4$; for $m = 19$, $k = 5$, $\delta = 12$; etc.

(v) A table of the codes corresponding to (punctured with) this
table of anticodes is given in Appendix 3; it is interesting
to note all the values of n, k and d that must be listed,
in contrast to the above table which has at most two values
of δ for each m. Note that the codes derived from simple
stacks of m-sequence anticodes are all bi-orthogonal[5,6] and
Reed-Muller[2,22] codes.

4:   Codes Derived From Anticodes

4.1 Additional Methods of Constructing Anticodes

In order to extend the list of optimum anticodes given in Table 4,
it is necessary to consider additional ways of constructing anticodes.

The ultimate aim is always to find anticodes (hopefully optimum) from which

new optimum and good codes can be derived.

4.1.1 Pseudo Solomon and Stiffler Costructions

Solomon and Stiffler[9] constructions consist of adjoined stacked

m-sequence anticodes (section 3.3). There is no need for the m-sequence

restriction. Any two or more anticodes $(m_1, \geq k_1, \delta_1)$, $(m_2, \geq k_2, \delta_2)$,....,

may be adjoined to form an anticode with parameters which are the sum

of the individual anticode parameters, e.g. $AC(m_1 + m_2 + ... , k_1 + k_2 +$

$..., \delta_1 + \delta_2 + ...)$ results.   These pseudo Solomon & Stiffler

constructions (PS/S) sometimes extend the range of useful anticodes.

For example, AC(31, 5, 16) + AC(21, 5, 12) = AC(52, 10, 28), which is

optimum, since it may be also derived from C(11, 6, 4). Also AC(63, 6, 32)

+ AC(10, 4, 6) = AC(73, 10, 38) which has the same parameters as the

optimum S/S construction AC(73, 11, 38), but with smaller k. As a final

example, AC(63, 6, 32) + AC(25, 5, 14) = AC(88, 11, 46), which is an

laternative derivation to the map stacking given in section 3.7. A table

of PS/S constructions with values of k less than the S/S construction

with the same value of δ, and the same, or one less, value of m, is in

Appendix 4. PS/S constructions, unlike S/S constructions, are not all

necessarily optimum, though it is a strong conjecture that they are.

Certainly they are all near optimum, in that they are at most one column

short of optimum, when constructed from optimum constituent anticodes.

4.1.2 Combined Stacking of Distinct Anticodes

Combined stacks need not be constructed from just one "parent" anticode, but can be formed from two or more anticodes with different parameters. An example is the following construction:

$$O_1 \equiv (m_1, k, \delta_1)$$

$$O_2 \equiv (m_2, k, \delta_2)$$

O_2	O_1
I_2	O_1

$(m_1+m_2, k+1, \delta_1+\delta_2)$

Inverting O_2 ensures that the complete anticode has no repeated columns. This construction is only successful if the minimum weight of O_2 is such that $m_2 - d_2 \leq \delta_2$, otherwise the maximum weight of the lower half of the construction, and therefore of the whole anticode, exceeds $\delta_1 + \delta_2$. If, e.g. $O_1 \equiv AC(15, 4, 8)$, and $O_2 \equiv (10, 4, 6)$ for which $d_2 = 4$, then optimum $AC(25, 5, 14)$ results. Thus it is often necessary to know d as well as δ for an array, and it is important for d to be as large as possible.

4.1.3 Shortening of S/S or PS/S Constructions

The generator matrix of an S/S or PS/S construction is in general made up of two or more adjoined sub-matrices (see Chap. 3, section 3.3 and section 4.1.1 above), the rows of which do not overlap. If one of the sub-matrices is allowed to overlap by one row with another, then the k (and thus the number of words) of the overall construction is reduced by one. The construction now has one repeated column (there are two identical information columns), but removal of one of these then gives an (m-1, k-1, δ) anticode. For example, the matrix for S/S AC(10, 5, 6) is

$$
G \;=\; \begin{bmatrix}
1 & 0 & 0 & 1 & 1 & 0 & 1 & 0 & 0 & 0 \\
0 & 1 & 0 & 1 & 0 & 1 & 1 & 0 & 0 & 0 \\
0 & 0 & 1 & 0 & 1 & 1 & 1 & 0 & 0 & 0 \\
0 & 0 & 0 & 0 & 0 & 0 & 0 & 1 & 0 & 1 \\
0 & 0 & 0 & 0 & 0 & 0 & 0 & 0 & 1 & 1
\end{bmatrix}
$$

Shifting the left-hand sub-matrix down one row gives

$$
\begin{bmatrix}
1 & 0 & 0 & 1 & 1 & 0 & 1 & 0 & 1 & 1 \\
0 & 1 & 0 & 1 & 0 & 1 & 1 & 0 & 0 & 0 \\
0 & 0 & 1 & 0 & 1 & 1 & 1 & 0 & 0 & 0 \\
0 & 0 & 0 & 0 & 0 & 0 & 0 & 1 & 0 & 1
\end{bmatrix}
$$
$$\quad\uparrow\hspace{9em}\uparrow$$

The arrowed columns are identical: deleting one of them gives AC(9, 4, 6).
If there are i sub-matrices, then the process may be repeated i-1 times;
i.e., AC(m-i+1, k-i+1, δ) results. These anticodes are normally sub-
optimum, but sometimes this is the only way of constructing a useful
anticode with the given parameters. Thus, AC(73, 10, 38), for which
i = 3, gives AC(71, 8, 38), which corresponds to C(184, 8, 92).

4.1.4 Computer Search

     Computer search techniques may be used to find optimum and
near-optimum anticodes, in ways similar to computer searches for good
codes. Farrag[16] carried out a search for optimum anticodes by writing

and running a programme which successively synthesised all possible
anticodes with given parameters. All anticodes with $k \leq 6$, and many with
$k = 7$, were found. The computation time for this technique becomes excessive
for the larger values of m with $k = 7$, and for $k \geq 8$. It may therefore
be more effective to process anticode generator or parity-check matrices[11].

4.2 Extended Table of Anticodes

Table 4 in section 3 is extended in Appendix 5. In order to save
space, only the highest value of m for which an anticode with a given δ
is known is given, and anticodes with δ odd are omitted.

4.3 Anticodes and Codes with Repeated Columns

Discussion so far has concentrated on anticodes and codes which do
not have repeated code-columns; that is, all the columns of their code-
books are distinct. If, however, in the case of a code $n > 2^k-1$, then the
code-book must have repeated columns.

Codes with duplicate (repeated) columns can be generated from
anticodes with non-repeated columns. If a code with $2^k-1 < n < 2(2^k-1)$
and $2^{k-1} < d < 2.2^{k-1}$ is required, then it may be constructed by
puncturing an (m, k, δ) anticode, with $m < 2^k-1$ and $\delta < 2^{k-1}$, from two
adjoined m-sequence codes:-

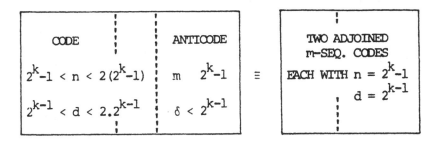

In general, if a code with $r(2^k-1) < n < (r+1)(2^k-1)$ and

$r.2^{k-1} < d < (r+1)2^{k-1}$ is required, then the anticode is punctured

from r+1 adjoined m-sequence codes. If the anticode meets the Griesmer[8]

bound, then the repeated column code will also be optimum. For example,

puncturing AC(10, 4, 6), which meets the Griesmer bound, from two

adjoined C(15, 4, 8) gives C(20, 4, 10), which is an optimum repeated

column code. AC(17, 5, 10) does not meet the Griesmer bound, however,

even though it is optimum, so puncturing it from two adjoined m-sequence

codes with k = 5 produces non-optimum C(45, 5, 22) (the optimum code

is (44, 5, 22). Notice that because the anticode has no repeated columns,

the repeated column code consists of r adjoined m-sequence codes,

adjoined to another code with $n < 2^k-1$. Thus C(20, 4, 10) ≡ (15, 4, 8)

+ (5, 4, 2). Once the code is permitted repeated columns, however, then

the anticode used to puncture from the r+1 adjoined m-sequence codes

need not be restricted to having distinct columns. It may with

advantage be allowed to have repeated columns, since this means that

anticodes which meet the Griesmer bound can be used to puncture with,

thus generating optimum repeated column codes. Specifically, anticodes with the parameters of S/S constructions, or PS/S constructions which meet

the Griesmer bound, may be used, with repeated columns permitted, but with

the restriction that $k(r+1) \geq \sum_i z_i$. This result was also discovered by

Belov, et al,[23] independently. Thus, for example, S/S construction

(18, 6, 10) may be formed with k = 5 if repeated columns are allowed, i.e.

repeated column (each column appearing not more than twice) anticode

RAC(18, 5, 10), when punctured from two adjoined m-sequence codes, gives

the optimum repeated column code RC(44, 5, 22). Codes formed by

puncturing with repeated column anticodes do not contain as many as r

adjoined m-sequence codes, since the anticode is punctured from more

than one of the r+1 adjoined m-sequence codes:-

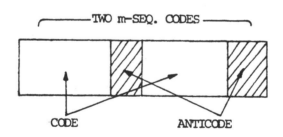

Repeated column codes containing and not containing m-sequence codes

have been studied by Patel[24]. It is interesting to conjecture

whether it would be possible to construct codes that meet the

Griesmer bound for all $n > 2^k-1$, $d > 2^{k-1}$. Certainly the above results

confirm the observation by Baumert and McEliece[20] that their theorem

is rather conservative in predicting the value of d large enough for the

Griesmer bound to be tight.

4.4 Codes Constructed from Inversion Stacks of Anticodes or Codes

If the minimum distance of an anticode is d, then the minimum

distance of the code formed by inversion stacking (Chap. 3, section 3.6)

an anticode with parameters (m, k, δ) is $\min\{\delta, m-d\}$; that is, a

code with parameters $(m, k+1, \min\{\delta, m-d\})$ is formed. This result

highlights the remark made at the end of section 4.1.2 above about the

importance of knowing both the maximum and minimum distance of any code/

anticode book. Thus, though inversion stacking is not in general a

good method of anticode generation, it can be a useful code construction.

For example, AC(56, 6, 30) has d = 26; hence C(56, 7, 26) results, which

has distance only one less than the lowest upper bound[21]. Codes may also

be inversion stacked, provided the maximum distance is known.

Codes may also be constructed by canonical combined stacking of

code/anticode books (which may have repeated columns). If the book has

parameters (n, k, d), then C(2n+1, k+1,{min n+1, 2d} results. It may be

possible to adjoin more than one {00 ... 0 ⋮ 11 ... 1} column.

4.5 New Codes Derived from Anticodes

A number of new codes, with and without repeated columns, have been

found as a result of puncturing anticodes from m-sequence codes. The

parameters of these new codes are listed in Appendix 6, together with

their derivation. The codes tend to be of low rate, because calculations

have not, at present, gone beyond $k \leq 8$, for codes with block lengths

less than approximately 300. High rate codes can in principle be found,

however. An advantage of anticodes methods is that the weight structure

of a code derived from an anticode is easily computed. The codes listed
in Appendix 6 include those presented in references 13, 14 and 15,
together with some additional ones. A very extensive list will be found
in reference 16. Note that the codes with block lengths which exceed
the Griesman bound by unity are conjectured to be optimum (see section 2).

4.6 Multi-level Anticodes

The theory of anticodes developed so far generalises quite easily
to the q-nary or multi-level case. Stacking procedures can also be
generalised, so that tables of multi-level anticodes, and codes derived
from them, can be produced. Farrag[16] has compiled such tables for q = 3
and $1 \leq k \leq 4$. Anticode theory is of particular interest in the multi-
level case, because of the relative lack of systematic multi-level
code synthesis procedures, compared to the binary case.

References

1.   Peterson, W.W. and Weldon, E.J., Error-correcting codes, M.I.T.,
     1972.

2.   MacWilliams, F.J. and Sloane, N.J.A, *The Theory of Error-Correcting
     Codes*, Vols. I & II, North-Holland, 1977.

3.   Hamming, R.W., Error-correcting and error-detecting codes, *Bell
     Syst. Tech. Jour.*, 1950, Vol. 26, pp. 147-160.

4.   Longo, G., An introduction to algebraic coding theory, CISM Report
     No. 23, April 1977.

5. Farrell, P.G., Coding for noisy data links, Ph.D. Thesis, University of Cambridge, 1969.

6. Golomb, S.W. (Ed), *Digital Communications with Space Applications*, Prentice-Hall, 1964.

7. Plotkin, M., Binary codes with specified minimum distance, *IRE Trans.*, 1960, Vol. IT-6, pp. 445-450.

8. Griesmer, J.H., A bound for error-correcting codes, *I.B.M. Jour.*, 1960, Vol. 4, No. 5, p. 532.

9. Solomon, G. and Stiffler, V.J., Algebraically punctured cyclic code, *Information and Control*, 1965, Vol. 8, pp. 170-179.

10. Berlekamp, E.R., *Algebraic coding theory*, McGraw-Hill, 1968.

11. Hashim, A.A., Maximum distance bounds for linear anticodes, *Proc. IEE*, Vol. 123, No. 3, pp. 189-190, March, 1976.

12. Gilbert, E.N., A comparison of signalling alphabets, *BSTJ*, Vol. 31, No. 3, May, 1952, pp. 504-522.

13. Farrell, P.G., Linear binary anticodes, *Elec. Letters*, 1970, Vol. 6, No. 13, pp. 419-421.

14. Farrell, P.G. and Farrag, A., Further properties of linear binary anticodes, *Elec. Letters*, Vol. 10, No. 16, 8 Aug. 1974, p. 340.

15. Farrell, P.G. and Farrag, A., New error-control codes derived from anticodes, presented at IEEE Symp. on Info. Theory, Ronneby, June 1976.

16. Farrag, A., Anticodes and optimum error-correcting codes, Ph.D. Thesis, University of Kent at Canterbury, 1976.

17. Maki, G.K. and Tracey, J.H., Maximum distance linear codes, *IEEE Trans.*, 1971, Vol. IT-17, No. 5, p.637.

18. Reddy, S.M., On block codes with specified maximum distance, *IEEE Trans.*, 1972, Vol. IT-18, No. 6, pp. 823-824.

19. Hashim, A.A. and Podzniakov, V.S., On the stacking techniques of linear codes, paper submitted for publication to IEE.

20. Baumert, L.D. and McEliece, R.J., A note on the Griesmer bound, *IEEE Trans.*, Vol. IT-19, pp. 134-135, No. 1, January 1973.

21. Helgert, H.J. and Stinaff, R.D., Minimum-distance bounds for binary linear codes, *IEEE Trans.*, 1973, Col. IT-19, No. 3, pp. 344-356.

22. Reed, I.S., A class of multiple-error-correcting codes and the decoding scheme, *IRE Trans.*, Vol. IT-4, No. 5, Sept. 1954, p. 38.

23. Belov, B.I., Logachev, V.N. and Sandimirov, V.P., The construction of a class of binary linear codes which achieve the Varshamov-Griesmer bound, *Prob. Pered. Infor.*, Vol. 10, No. 3, pp. 36-44.

24. Patel, A.M., Maximal group codes with specified minimum distance, *I.B.M. Jour. Res. Dev.*, Vol. 14, No. 4, pp. 434-443.

25. MacWilliams, J., Error-correcting codes for multiple-level transmission, *Bell. Syst. Tech. Jour.*, 1961, Vol. 40, pp. 281-308.

Appendix 1: Parameters of the Solomon and Stiffler Constructions

$2^{\ell_i}-1,\ 2^{\ell_i}-1$	least value of k (for no repeated columns)	number of ℓ_i			
			81, 42	12	3
			82, 43	13	4
			85, 44	13	3
1, 1	2	1	86, 45	14	4
3, 2	3	1	88, 46	15	4
4, 3	3	2	89, 47	16	5
7, 4	4	1	94, 48	11	2
8, 5	4	2	95, 49	12	3
10, 6	5	2	97, 50	13	3
11, 7	6	3	98, 51	14	4
15, 8	5	1	101, 52	14	3
16, 9	5	2	102, 53	15	4
18, 10	6	2	104, 54	16	4
19, 11	7	3	105, 55	17	4
22, 12	7	2	109, 56	15	3
23, 13	8	3	110, 57	16	4
25, 14	9	3	112, 58	17	4
26, 15	10	4	113, 59	18	5
31, 16	6	1	116, 60	18	4
32, 17	6	2	117, 61	19	5
34, 18	7	2	119, 62	20	5
35, 19	8	3	120, 63	21	6
38, 20	8	2	127, 64	8	1
39, 21	9	3			
41, 22	10	3			
42, 23	11	4			
46, 24	9	2			
47, 25	10	3			
49, 26	11	3			
50, 27	12	4			
53, 28	12	3			
54, 29	13	4			
56, 30	14	4			
57, 31	15	5			
63, 32	7	1			
64, 33	7	2			
66, 34	8	2			
67, 35	9	3			
70, 36	9	2			
71, 37	10	3			
73, 38	11	3			
74, 39	12	4			
78, 40	10	2			
79, 41	11	3			

Appendix 2: A Comparison of the Properties of Codes and Anticodes

CODES	ANTICODES
- block length n	- block length m
- minimum distance d : $d = \min(d_{ij})$, $i \neq j$, $\quad = \min_i(w_i)$ if a linear code	- maximum distance δ $\delta = \max(d_{ij})$, $i \neq j$, $\quad = \max_i(w_i)$ if a linear anticode
- optimum if has the greatest d for a given n and N (or k)	- optimum if has the least δ for a given m and N (or k)
- deleting a redundant (parity check) column in general reduces d by unity	- deleting a column in general does not reduce δ
- adding a redundant column does not in general increase d	- adding a column in general does increase δ
- adding an overall parity check to a code with d odd increases d by unity: $N(n,d) \iff N(n+1,d+1)$, d odd	- adding any column to an anticode with δ even increases δ by unity: $N(m,\delta) \iff N(m+1,\delta+1)$, δ even
- the words of a code are all distinct; hence the $[G]$ matrix of a code has no null rows	- an anticode may have repeated rows; hence the $[G]$ matrix of an anticode may have null rows

Appendix 3: Table of linear Binary Codes Derived from Table 4
            (A Short Table of Linear Binary Anticodes):
            Values of (n, d)

m \ k	1	2	3	4	5	6
1	(0,0)	(2,1)	(6,3)	(14,7)	(30,15)	(62,31)
2						
3		(0,0)	(4,2)	(12,6)	(28,14)	(60,30)
4			(3,1)	(11,5)	(27,13)	(59,29)
5						
6						
7			(0,0)	(8,4)	(24,12)	(56,28)
8				(7,3)	(23,11)	(55,27)
9						
10				(5,2)	(21,10)	(53,26)
11				(4,1)	(20,9)	(52,25)
12						
13						
14						
15				(0,0)	(16,8)	(48,24)
16					(15,7)	(47,23)
17					(14,6)	
18					(13,5)	(45,22)
19						(44,21)
20	BI-ORTHOGONAL & REED MULLER					
21					(10,4)	(42,20)
22					(9,3)	(41,19)
23						
24						
25					(6,2)	(38,18)
26					(5,1)	(37,17)
27						
28						
29						
30						
31					(0,0)	(32,16)

Appendix 4:   Parameters of Pseudo Solomon and Stiffler Constructions

m, k, δ	m, k for S/S constructions	Derivation
25, 8, 14	25, 9	15, 4, 8 + 10, 4, 6
41, 9, 22	41, 10	31, 5, 16 + 10, 4, 6
48, 10, 26	49, 11	" + 17, 5, 10
52, 10, 28	53, 12	" + 21, 5, 12
56, 10, 30	56, 14	" + 25, 5, 14
73, 10, 38	73, 11	63, 6, 32 + 10, 4, 6
80, 11, 42	81, 12	" + 17, 5, 10
84, 11, 44	85, 13	" + 21, 5, 12
88, 11, 46	88, 15	" + 25, 5, 14
96, 12, 50	97, 13	" + 33, 6, 18
100, 12, 52	101, 14	" + 37, 6, 20
103, 12, 54	104, 16	" + 40, 6, 22
108, 12, 56	109, 15	" + 45, 6, 24
111, 12, 58	112, 17	" + 48, 6, 26
115, 12, 60	116, 18	" + 52, 6, 28
119, 12, 62	119, 20	" + 56, 6, 30

Appendix 5:   Extended Table of Anticode Parameters

m	δ	k	Derivation
3	2	≥ 2	m-seq. AC
7	4	≥ 3	"
10	6	≥ 4	C(5,4,2) or C/STK
15	8	≥ 4	m-seq. AC
17	10	≥ 5	CC/STK of (8,4,5)
18	10	≥ 6	S/S
21	12	5-6	C(11,5,4)
22	12	≥ 7	S/S
25	14	≥ 5	C(6,5,2)
31	16	≥ 5	m-seq. AC
33	18	6	CC/STK
34	18	≥ 7	S/S
37	20	7	C(26,6,12) or computer search
38	20	≥ 8	S/S
40	22	6-8	C(23,6,10) or computer search
41	22	≥ 9	PS/S
45	24	6-8	C(18,6,8) or computer search
46	24	≥ 9	S/S
48	26	6-10	C(15,6,6) or computer search
49	26	≥ 11	S/S
52	28	6-11	C(11,6,4)
53	28	≥ 12	S/S
56	30	≥ 6	C(7,6,2)
63	32	6	m-seq. AC
65	34	7	C/STK
66	34	≥ 8	S/S
68	36	7	Shortened AC(69,8,36)
69	36	8	CC/STK

Appendix 5: (continued)

70	38	≥ 9	S/S
71	38	7-8	I/STK[16]
72	38	9	Shortened PS/S
73	38	≥ 10	PS/S
77	40	7-9	C(52,7,24)[21]
78	40	≥ 10	S/S
79	42	7-9	I/STK[16]
80	42	10-11	C/STK
81	42	≥ 12	S/S
82	44	7-9	C/STK
83	44	1 10	CC/STK
84	44	11-12	PS/S
85	44	≥ 13	S/S
86	46	7-9	C(41,7,18)[19]
87	46	10	Shortened PS/S
88	46	≥ 11	BS/S
91	48	7-9	I/STK[16]
93	48	10	CC/STK
94	48	≥ 11	S/S
95	50	7-10	C(32,7,14)[19]
96	50	11	C/STK
97	50	≥ 12	PS/S
100	52	7-13	C(27,7,12)[21]
101	52	≥ 14	S/S
103	54	7-15	C(24,7,10)[19]
104	54	≥ 16	S/S
108	56	7-14	C(19,7,8) or computer search)
109	56	≥ 15	S/S
111	58	7-16	C/STK
112	58	≥ 17	S/S
115	60	7-17	C(12,7,4)
116	60	≥ 18	S/S
119	62	≥ 7	C(8,7,2)
127	64	≥ 7	m-seq. AC

Appendix 6:   New Linear Binary Codes Derived from Anticodes

All the codes are optimum;   except those marked °, which
have a block length which exceeds the Griesmer bound by
unity;   and those marked *, which exceed the Griesmer
bound by more than unity.

n, k, d	AC derived from	n, k, d	AC derived from
44,6,21	19,6,11	228,7,113	26,7,13
72,6,35	54,6,29 repeated col.	231,7,115	23,7,13
76,6,37	50,6,27 "	235,7,117	19,7,11
		238,7,119	16,7,9
*55,7,25	56,7,30 I/STK	243,7,121	11,7,7
*58,7,27	68,7,36	246,7,123	8,7,5
*61,7,29	66,7,35	250,7,125	4,7,3
°74,7,35	53,7,29	253,7,127	1,7,1
°78,7,37	49,7,27		
°81,7,39	46,7,25	135,8,65	120,8,63
°86,7,41	41,7,23	°139,8,67	116,8,61
°89,7,43	38,7,21	°143,8,69	112,8,59
92,7,45	35,7,19	°146,8,71	109,8,57
104,7,51	23,7,13	°151,8,73	104,8,55
108,7,53	19,7,11	°154,8,75	101,8,53
138,7,67	116,7,61 repeated col.	188,9,93	67,8,35
140,7,69	114,7,59 "	191,8,95	64,8,33
143,7,71	111,7,57 "	198,8,97	57,8,31
148,7,73	106,7,55 "		
152,7,75	102,7,53 "		
156,7,77	98,7,51 "		
159,7,79	95,7,49 "		
165,7,81	89,7,47 "		
168,7,83	86,7,45 "		
172,7,85	82,7,43 "		
175,7,87	79,7,41 "		
180,7,89	74,7,39 "		
183,7,91	71,7,37 "		
187,7,93	67,7,35 "		
190,7,95	64,7,33		
197,7,97	57,7,31		
200,7,99	54,7,29 repeated col.		
204,7,101	50,7,27 "		
207,7,103	47,7,25 "		
212,7,105	42,7,23 "		
215,7,107	39,7,21 "		
219,7,109	35,7,19		
222,7,111	32,7,17		

ARRAY CODES

P. G. Farrell
The Electronics Laboratories,
The University of Kent at Canterbury,
Canterbury, Kent CT2 7NT,
England

1.   Introduction

This contribution is concerned with codes formed by generalising

(or iterating) one or more component codes into arrays in (conceptually)

two or more dimensions (which need not be orthogonal). Array codes can be

used for multiple random-error detection and correction, for burst-error

detection and correction, and for detecting and correcting clusters or

patches of errors. They are particularly useful when the data to be

protected is presented in a rectangular format, such as punched card,

magnetic or paper tape, graphs, maps, or pictures. Many of the array codes

which will be mentioned are well known[1-10], but some new codes and decoding

techniques[11-14] will also be described. The motivation for studying array

codes is that they are relatively simple to decode, and also, at least in

some cases, have relatively high efficiencies (data rates).

Array codes stem, in one way or another, from the single-parity-
check (SPC) code:-

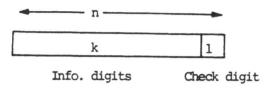

Info. digits   Check digit

This code has block length $n = k+1$; rate $R = k/n = (n-1)/n$; and
Hamming distance $d = 2$. The single check digit (even parity) is the
modulo-2 sum of the k information digits; and the code is capable of
detecting all patterns with an odd number of errors. Thus the simplest
array code proper is the generalisation of the SPC code into two dimensions:-

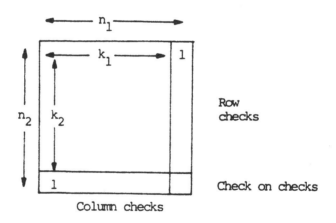

Column checks

This is called a row-and-column-parity code, or two-coordinate code, or
geometric, or matrix code. It has $n = n_1 \cdot n_2$; $R = k_1 \cdot k_2 / n_1 \cdot n_2 = R_1 \cdot R_2$; and $d = 2.2 = 4$. Hence it is capable of detecting all single,
double and triple errors, and any other odd number of errors, or of
correcting all single errors. It can also detect bursts of length
$b \leq k_1$ (if rows are transmitted); if used for burst-error-detection,

then the row checks may be omitted, and the code is equivalent to a set of interleaved SPC codes. It is unnecessary for the array to be square; error detection is most efficient when the array is rectangular[15]. This simple two-dimensional array code can be generalised, or extended, in at least three different ways, which will now be described.

2.   Product Codes

In this type of array code, the row and column SPC codes are replaced by more powerful codes:-

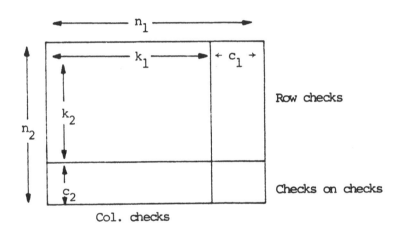

The row and column codes need not be the same, and product codes are not restricted to only two dimensions, so in general $n = n_1 . n_2 . n_3 \cdots$;

$R = k_1 . k_2 . k_3 \cdots / n_1 n_2 n_3 \cdots = R_1 R_2 R_3 \cdots$;   and $d = d_1 . d_2 . d_3 \cdots$.

If the component codes are cyclic, then the product code is also cyclic if n_1, n_2, n_3, etc. are relatively prime.[8] The generator matrix of the product code is the Kroeneker product of the generator matrices of the component codes. Multi-dimensional (> 2) product codes, or iterated codes[9,10], may be decoded with a probability of error that tends to zero

at a finite rate. The decoding of product codes is in general quite
complex, if the full error-control power of the code is to be taken
advantage of. Simpler decoding methods can be used if error-control is
reduced; the simplest decoder has a complexity not much greater than that
of the decoder for the most powerful component code, but the sacrifice
in performance is considerable. The full performance of a product code
may be almost entirely restored, however, if soft-decision techniques
(see contribution on Soft Decision Detection Techniques) can be used;
with a complexity approximately that of the decoder for the component
codes. Thus, for example[16], an $(n,k,d) = (225,121,9)$ code can be decoded
by means of adaptive full soft-minimum-distance decoding of the $(15,11,3)$
component code words.

3.   Burst-Error-Correction Codes

      In order to correct a one-dimensional burst of errors, two sets of
parity checks are required, each taken on "directions" in the array which
are orthogonal to the "direction" of the burst. Thus, in order to
correct a row burst, column and diagonal checks may be used:-

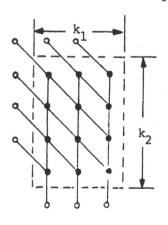

- information digit

o check digit

The burst may be in adjacent rows, provided its length does not exceed k_1.
The number of parity checks required is $2k_1 + k_2 - 1$, so $k_1 < k_2$ is
desirable. Some of the diagonal checks near the corners of the array are
rather inefficient, in that they check relatively few information digits.
The rate of the code can be improved, but with a reduction in the
correctable burst lengths, if these information and check digits are
removed, to give a hexagonal array. Alternatively, if possible bursts
are all confined to one row only, then the diagonal checks may be linked:-

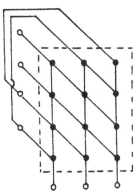

In this case only $k_1 + k_2$ checks are required. If double-row-correction
is desired, then the linked diagonal checks and the column checks may be
interleaved on alternate digits, so that $2(k_1 + k_2)$ checks are required.
Decoding of all these codes is quite simple, because an error in an
information digits causes two parity checks to fail, and proper pairing
of failed checks is ensured by the burst nature of the correctable error
patterns. An alternative strategy would be to use three dimensional
array codes, but in this case the ratio of burst length to block length
can become unacceptably large.

A two-dimensional patch or cluster of e errors, with dimensions
$i \times i$, $1 \le e \le i^2$, can be corrected by interleaving row and column

parity checks to degree i, thus requiring $i(k_1+k_2)$ checks. Much more

efficient schemes can be found[14], however, which require fewer parity

checks, and take into account, as is particularly necessary for patch-

error-correction, the position of the check digits in the array. For

example, a 2 x 2 patch-error-correcting code with k = 6 x 6 = 36,

n = 7 x 7 = 49 and thus R = 0.73, has the following check arrangement:-

1 3	4 9	1 11	2 6	5 3	11 13	C_1
13 6	7 12	13 10	4 8	10 1	4 12	C_2
5 10	11 3	6 1	9 12	13 7	11 5	C_3
2 9	8 13	2 5	4 11	6 3	12 8	C_4
10 7	12 6	7 9	10 8	7 5	1 9	C_5
9 3	2 8	5 1	2 4	6 11	13 4	C_6
C_{13}	C_{12}	C_{11}	C_{10}	C_9	C_8	C_7

The two numbers in each square indicate the two parity check equations

which that information digit is in; e.g. $c_1 = k_1+k_3+k_{11}+k_{15}+k_{30}+k_{33}$.

These codes are quite simple to decode, though not as simple as the inter-

leaved row and column check codes. At the cost of an increase in the number

of checks, patch-error correcting codes which are even simpler to decode

may be devised;[14] failure of any pair of checks uniquely determines an

information digit containing an error. So the decoder consists of a

syndrome calculator, and a set of k^2 AND gates.

4.   Self-Orthogonal Array Codes

A code is self-orthogonal with Hamming distance d if no two information digits appear together in more than one check equation, and each information digit appears in at least d-1 equations[17]. Now consider a two-dimensional array code, with points in the array representing information digits, and straight lines through the points representing check equations[12]. If d-1 lines pass through each point, then the code has distance d. Thus a two-coordinate code, with row and column checks, has 2 lines passing through each point, and so has distance 3. Adding the check-on-checks to the array increases the distance to 4. An array code with row, column, and the two sets of diagonal checks has d = 5. If the 4 "knight's move" lines through each point are added, then d = 9 results. An example of "knight's move" lines is given below:-

Each set of "knight's move" lines requires $k_1 + 2(k_2 - 1)$ checks. These codes are relatively poor in rate, but are easy to decode, and many patterns of more than $\lfloor (d-1)/2 \rfloor$ errors are corrected. They may also be augmented, using the method proposed by Kasahara, et al[18]; this improves the rate considerably. For example, the array code with row, column and diagonal checks, and $k_1 = k_2 = 10$, has k = 100, n = 158, R = 0.633, and d = 5. When augmented, k = 126, n = 158, R = 0.797, d = 5. These codes can also be further improved by adding certain overall parity checks (e.g. as in the trivial check-on-check example given above), and by omitting checks and information digits at the corners of the array[12].

The parity-check "lines" need not be straight in all cases, but can be linked (as for burst-error-correcting codes). This improves the code rate without loss of distance. For example, by linking the diagonal checks, a (38,16,5) rate 0.42 code is improved to a (32,16,5) rate 0.5 code.

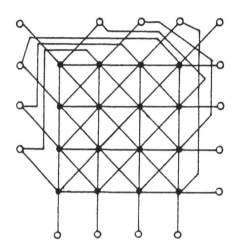

(no two points lie together on more than one line)

For certain values of code parameters, this linking process may be generalised as follows[12,13]:-

(i)   Let the array have p x p information digits, p a prime.

(ii) Label each information digit with the row number r and the column number c, $0 \le r, c, \le p-1$.

(iii) Let $d \le p+1$.

(iv) Attach the d-1 numbers $D_i(r,c) = (r+ic) \bmod p$ to each information digit, $0 \le i \le d-2$ (i.e. $i < p$).

(v) Then, for each vlue of i, each information digit to which a

particular value of $D_i(r,c)$ is attached appears in one parity

check equation (i.e., there are $p(d-1)$ check equations).

(vi) Thus, a $(p^2+p(d-1),\ p^2,\ \le p+1)$ code results.

For example, if $p = 3$ and $d = 4$, the following array results:

r \ c	0	1	2
0	0,0,0	0,1,2	0,2,1
1	1,1,1	1,2,0	1,0,2
2	2,2,2	2,0,1	2,1,0

The numbers in each square are the values of $D_i(r,c)$ for i = 0, 1 and 2,

respectively. There are therefore 9 check equations, so k = 9, n = 18

and R = 0.5. The proof of this result is as follows[12,13]. For any

square (r_1,c_1) and any number $D_j(r_1,c_1)$ in that square, it is required to

prove that any other square (r_2,c_2) with $D_j(r_2,c_2) = D_j(r_1,c_1)$ has

$D_k(r_2,c_2) \neq D_k(r_1,c_1)$, for all $k \neq j$, and j, k < p. Now, if

$$D_j(r_2,c_2) = (D_j(r_1,c_1)$$

then
$$(r_2 + jc_2) \bmod p = (r_1 + jc_1) \bmod p$$

$$\therefore \quad (r_2 - r_1) \bmod p = \{j(c_1 - c_2)\} \bmod p.$$

But if $D_k(r_2,c_2) = D_k(r_1,c_1)$

this implies $(r_2 - r_1) \bmod p = \{k(c_1 - c_2)\} \bmod p$

$$\therefore \quad j \bmod p = k \bmod p$$

$$\text{ie} \quad j = k, \quad j,k < p$$

Thus it has been shown that $D_k(r_2,c_2) \neq D_k(r_1,c_1)$ if $j \neq k$, provided $j,k < p$ and p is a prime. The rates of these codes are often better than those of the best known self-orthogonal codes[19]. The codes are relatively easy to decode[13], and they may be augmented as before[13]. It is also possible to let p be a power of a prime, with the $D_i(r,c)$ now defined over $GF(p)$, at the cost of an increase in decoder complexity[13].

References

1.   Goldberg, M., Easily decoded error-correcting codes and techniques
      for their generation, Ph.D. Thesis, University of London, 1971.

2.   Goldberg, M., Augmentation techniques for a class of product codes,
      IEEE Trans, IT-19, 666, 1973.

3.   N.E. Head, A high-speed data transmission system, *GEC Jour.*, 30
      No. 3, 129, 1963.

4.   N.J.A. Sloane, A simple description of an error-correcting code
      for high-density magnetic tape; *BSTJ*, 55 No. 2, 157, Feb. 1976.

5.   D.T. Brown & F.F. Sellers, Error correction for IBM 800-bit-per-inch
      magnetic tape, *IBM Jour Res Dev*, 384, July 1970.

6.   C.D. Mathers, Digital video recording - some experiments in error
      protection, BBC Res. Dept Rep. 1976/1, Jan. 1976.

7.   P. Calingaert, Two-dimensional parity checking, *Jour Assoc Comp
      Mach*, 8 No. 2, 186, 1961.

8.   H.O. Burton & E.J. Weldon, Cyclic product codes; *IEEE Trans*, IT-11, 433, July 1965.

9.   P, Elias, Error-free coding, *IRE Trans*, IT-4, 29, Sept. 1954.

10. A.B. Cooper, Algebraic codes constructed from other algebraic codes: A short survey and some recent results; Proc. NATO ASI on Comm. Systs and Random Proc. Theory, Ed. J. Skwirzymski, pub. Sijthoff & Noordhoff, 1978.

11. G. Riley, Error control for data multiplex systems; Ph.D. Thesis, Univ. of Kent at Canterbury, 1975.

12. R.J.G. Smith, Easily decoded error-correcting codes, Ph.D. Thesis, 1978.

13. R.J.G. Smith, Easily decoded efficient self-orthogonal block codes, *Elec Letters*, 13 No. 7, 173, 31st March 1977.

14. T. Meshkati, Two-dimensional-burst-error-correcting codes, Postgrad. Dip. Dissertation, Univ. of Kent at Canterbury (in preparation).

15. R. Rowland, Error-detecting capabilities of two-coordinate parity codes; *Electronic Eng.*, 16, Jan. 1968.

16. P.G. Farrell, E. Munday & N. Kalligeros, Digital communications using soft-decision detection techniques; AGARD Symp. on Digital Comms. in Avionics, Munich, June 1978 (Conf. Preprint No. 239).

17. J.L. Massey, Threshold decoding; MIT Press, 1963.

18. M. Kasahara, et al, New class of binary codes constructed on the basis of concatenated codes and product codes; *IEEE Trans*, IT-22, 462, 1976.

19.   R.L. Townsend & E.J. Weldon, Self-orthogonal quasi-cyclic codes;
       IEEE Trans, IT-13, 183, 1967.

ASSOCIATION SCHEMES

J.-M. Goethals

MBLE Research Laboratory
Avenue Van Becelaere 2
B-1170   Brussels (Belgium)

INTRODUCTION

We present in these lecture notes a survey of Delsarte's work on
the algebraic theory of association schemes,which has influenced considerably the recent developments in coding theory. We have somewhat upda-
ted Delsarte's original results which are often presented with new proofs.
The material has been divided into three main parts.

The· first Section serves as an introduction to association schemes
in general. The eigenmatrices P and Q which play a fundamental role in
the theory are introduced with a brief discussion of their main properties. The emphasis is then on subsets Y of the point set X of an association scheme. For these subsets the concepts of inner and dual distributions are introduced as well as their characteristic matrices.

The second Section deals with the important case when the point set
X of an association scheme can be given the structure of an Abelian
group. In this case a dual association scheme can be defined for which
the eigenmatrices are obtained by interchanging the role of the matrices
P and Q of the original scheme. For subsets Y which are subgroups of X,
the above duality has a nice interpretation in terms of dual subgroups
and their inner distributions. As a first example, the Hamming schemes
$H(n,q)$ are discussed. A subset here is a code and the above duality leads
to the celebrated MacWilliams identities in this case. As a second
example, we study the association scheme of all symplectic forms on a
vector space and discuss with some details an application of the duality to Reed-Muller codes.

The third Section introduces the concept of a <u>polynomial scheme</u> .
A scheme is P-polynomial if the (i,k)-entry of its P matrix is representable by means of a polynomial $\Phi_k(z_i)$ of degree k in a suitable variable
z_i. A similar definition exists for Q-polynomial schemes. A scheme is
P-polynomial if and only if it is metric. In this case a subset Y is a
<u>code</u> for which the concepts of <u>minimum distance</u> d and <u>external distance</u>
r are well defined. A generalization of Lloyd's theorem for perfect codes
is given. Dually, in a Q-polynomial scheme, the concept of <u>t-design</u> is
introduced and a generalization of Wilson's theorem for tight designs
is given.

No references are given in the text since most results are due to
Delsarte and can be found in the references listed in the Bibliography,
especially in references [2] , [3] ,[4] . In writing these notes, we have

been influenced by the previous accounts of Delsarte's work given by

Cameron and van Lint [1] and Sloane [7] .

1. ASSOCIATION SCHEMES

1.1. Definitions.

An association scheme with n classes on a set X consists of a par-

tition of the set of 2-element subsets of X into n classes $\Gamma_1, \Gamma_2, \ldots, \Gamma_n$,

satisfying the conditions :

(i) given $x \in X$, the number v_i of $y \in X$ with $\{x,y\} \in \Gamma_i$ depends only

on i ;

(ii) given $x, y \in X$ with $\{x,y\} \in \Gamma_k$, the number of $z \in X$ with

$\{x,z\} \in \Gamma_i$ and $\{y,z\} \in \Gamma_j$ is a constant $p_{i,j}^k$ depending only on

i, j, and k.

It is convenient to think of an association scheme on X as a coloring

of the edges of the complete graph on X with colors $c_1, c_2, \ldots, c_n$; an

edge has color c_i if it belongs to Γ_i. The first condition asserts that

each graph (X, Γ_i) is regular ; the second, that the number of triangles

with given coloring on a given base depends only on the coloring and not

on the base. We shall denote by D_i the adjacency matrix of the graph

(X, Γ_i) ; its entries $D_i(x,y)$ are equal to 1 if $\{x,y\} \in \Gamma_i$ and are zero

otherwise. We observe that the (x,y)-entry in the matrix product $D_i D_j$

is equal to the number $z \in X$ such that $\{x,z\} \in \Gamma_i$ and $\{y,z\} \in \Gamma_j$, that

is, equal to $p_{i,j}^k$ if $\{x,y\} \in \Gamma_k$. Moreover the diagonal entries are equal

to zero unless i=j, in which case they all are equal to v_i. Thus by de-

fining $p_{i,j}^0 = \delta_{i,j} v_i$, $p_{i,0}^k = p_{0,i}^k := \delta_{i,k}$, and denoting the unit matrix I by D_0, we may write

$$D_i D_j = D_j D_i = \sum_{k=0}^{n} p_{i,j}^{k} D_k \ .$$ (1.1)

This shows that the commuting symmetric matrices $D_0, D_1, \ldots, D_n$ span an (n+1)-dimensional real algebra (called the <u>Bose-Mesner algebra</u> of the scheme).

1.2. The eigenmatrices P and Q.

The Bose-Mesner algebra of an association scheme is semi-simple, hence admits a basis of mutually orthogonal idempotent matrices $J_0, J_1, \ldots, J_n$. These are, for $k=0,1,\ldots,n$, the matrices of the orthogonal projections $\pi_k : V \rightarrow V_k$ of the space $V=RX$ of all functions from X to the field R of real numbers onto the eigenspaces V_k common to all the matrices in the algebra. These matrices satisfy

$$J_k J_\ell = \delta_{k,\ell} J_k \ ,$$ (1.2)

$$\text{trace } (J_k) = \text{rank } (J_k) = \dim (V_k) \ .$$

The notation is chosen so that V_0 is the space spanned by the all-one vector and thus $J_0 = |X|^{-1} J$ where J is the all-one matrix. We observe that, with respect to the basis $(J_0, \ldots, J_n)$, every D_k has an expression of the form

$$D_k = \sum_{i=k}^{n} p_k(i) J_i \ ,$$ (1.3)

where $p_k(i)$ is the eigenvalue of D_k associated to the eigenspace V_i. Thus these are real numbers and we have

$$D_k J_i = p_k(i) \, J_i \, . \tag{1.4}$$

The square matrix P of order n+1 whose (i,k)-entry is $p_k(i)$, $0 \le i,k \le n$, is called the __eigenmatrix__ of the scheme. The matrix Q defined by

$Q := |X| P^{-1}$, whose (i,k)-entry will be denoted by $q_k(i)$, is called the

__dual eigenmatrix__ of the scheme. Note that from (1.3) we obtain

$$J_k = |X|^{-1} \sum_{i=0}^{n} q_k(i) \, D_i \, . \tag{1.5}$$

As we shall see later on these matrices play a central role in the theory of association schemes. We now briefly discuss a few of their properties.

The following theorem describes some __orthogonality relations__ satisfied by the $p_k(i)$ and $q_k(i)$. We denote by μ_k the dimension of the eigenspace V_k and we assume $v_0 = 1$.

__Theorem 1.1.__   (i) $\displaystyle\sum_{k=0}^{n} \mu_k \, p_i(k) \, p_j(k) = \delta_{i,j} \, v_i |X| \; ;$

(ii) $\displaystyle\sum_{i=0}^{n} v_i \, q_k(i) \, q_\ell(i) = \delta_{k,\ell} \mu_k |X| \, .$

__Proof.__ We prove part (i) by taking the trace of both members in (1.1). The matrix $D_i D_j$ has the eigenvalue $p_i(k) \, p_j(k)$ with multiplicity μ_k. For $k \ne 0$, D_k has a zero diagonal, and D_0 has trace equal to $|X|$. The result follows since $p_{i,j}^0 = \delta_{i,j} \, v_i$. Part (ii) is proved similarly by taking the coefficient of D_0 in both members of (1.2) where J_k and J_ℓ are to be expressed as in (1.5).

__Corollary 1.2.__ $\mu_k \, p_i(k) = v_i \, q_k(i)$.

Proof. This follows at once from theorem 1.1 and the fact that P and Q are related by $PQ=QP=|X|I$.

Remark 1.3. By comparing the eigenvalues on both members of (1.1) we easily obtain

$$p_i(\ell)p_j(\ell) = \sum_k p^k_{i,j} \, p_k(\ell) \,, \qquad \ell=0,1,\dots,n. \qquad (1.6)$$

1.3. The Krein parameters.

The adjacency matrices D_i of an association scheme are mutually orthogonal and idempotent with respect to the Hadamard product $((A \circ B)_{x,y}= A_{x,y} \, B_{x,y})$, that is, we have

$$D_k \circ D_\ell = \delta_{k,\ell} D_k \,. \qquad (1.7)$$

It follows that the Bose-Mesner algebra is closed under Hadamard multiplication. Hence there exist real number $c^k_{i,j}$ such that for the idempotents J_i we have

$$J_i \circ J_i = \sum_k c^k_{i,j} \, J_k \,. \qquad (1.8)$$

These numbers, called the Krein parameters of the scheme, are the eigenvalues of the matrix $J_i \circ J_j$, which is a principal submatrix of the Kronecker product $J_i \otimes J_j$. Therefore the following inequalities hold

$$0 \leqslant c^k_{i,j} \leqslant 1 \,, \qquad (1.9)$$

since the only eigenvalues of $J_i \otimes J_j$ are 0 and 1.

It is sometimes convenient to define :

$$E_i := |X|J_i \,, \qquad q^k_{i,j} := |X| \, c^k_{i,j} \,. \qquad (1.10)$$

Then (1.8) takes the form

$$E_i \circ E_j = \sum_k q_{i,j}^k E_k \ , \tag{1.11}$$

and, from (1.5) we readily obtain

$$q_i(\ell) \ q_j(\ell) = \sum_k q_{i,j}^k \ q_k(\ell) \ . \tag{1.12}$$

It becomes apparent that the $q_{i,j}^k$ play a role which is in a sense dual
to that of the $p_{i,j}^k$ (compare (1.1) to (1.11) and (1.6) to (1.12)). However they need not be integers. When they all are integers it is sometimes possible to define a "dual" association scheme whose parameters
are obtained by interchanging the role of the p's and the q's. This
duality has a simple interpretation when the association scheme admits
a regular Abelian group of automorphisms. An example is provided by the
Hamming schemes (to be discussed in the next section) which are self-
dual.

1.4. Subsets in association schemes.

Let Y be a subset of the point set X of an association scheme. We
shall be concerned with the partition of the set of 2-element subsets
of Y induced by the n classes $\Gamma_1, \ldots, \Gamma_n$ of the association scheme on X.
The inner distribution of Y is defined to be the (n+1)-tuple $\underline{a} = (a_0, a_1, \ldots, a_n)$ of rational numbers given by

$$a_i = |Y|^{-1} \sum_{x \in Y} \sum_{y \in Y} D_i(x,y) \tag{1.13}$$

Thus a_i is the average valency of $\Gamma_i \mid Y$.
Clearly, we have $a_0 = 1$, $\sum a_i = |Y|$, and $a_i \geq 0$. Similarly, the dual dis-

tribution of Y is defined to be the $(n+1)$-tuple $\underline{b}=(b_0,\ldots,b_n)$ of real numbers given by

$$b_i = |Y|^{-2} \sum_{x \in Y} \sum_{y \in Y} E_i(x,y) \ , \qquad (1.14)$$

where E_i is related to the idempotent J_i as in (1.10).

Lemma 1.4. The elements of the dual distribution satisfy : $b_0=1$, $\sum b_i = |X|/|Y|$, and $b_i \geqslant 0$, $1 \leqslant i \leqslant n$.

Proof. We have $E_0(x,y)=1$, $\forall x,y \in X$, $\sum E_i =|X|I$, whence $b_0=1$ and $\sum b_i=|X|/|Y|$. For $i=1,2,\ldots,n$, we may write

$$b_i = |X|/|Y|^2 \ u^T J_i u_Y \ ,$$

where u_Y is the incidence vector of $Y \subset X$. Since J_i is idempotent, b_i is nonnegative.

Theorem 1.5. The inner and dual distributions are related by :

$$b_k =|Y|^{-1} \sum_{i=0}^{n} q_k(i) \ a_i \ ,$$

$$a_k =|Y|/|X| \sum_{i=0}^{n} p_k(i) \ b_i,$$

that is, in matrix form,

$$\underline{b} =|Y|^{-1} \ \underline{a} \ Q, \qquad \underline{a} =|X|^{-1} \ |Y| \ \underline{b} \ P \ .$$

Proof. The result follows at once from the definition, by use of (1.3) and (1.5).

Remark 1.6. From lemma 1.4 and theorem 1.5, it follows that the elements a_i of the inner distribution of any subset $Y \subset X$ satisfy the linear constraints

$$a_0 = 1, \quad a_i \geqslant 0, \quad \sum a_i = |Y|$$

$$\sum_i a_i \, q_k(i) \geqslant 0 \, , \quad k=1,2,\ldots n.$$

This observation is the basis for the linear programming method of obtaining upper bounds on the cardinality $|Y| = \sum a_i$ of subsets $Y \subset X$ satisfying certain conditions which can be expressed as linear constraints on the a_i.

1.5. Characteristic matrices.

The space $V = RX$ of all functions from X to R is the orthogonal direct sum of the eigenspace : $V = V_0 + V_1 + \ldots + V_n$. Let us choose orthogonal bases $(f_{i,1}, \ldots, f_{i,\mu_i})$ for the spaces V_i so that we have :

$$\sum_{x \in X} f_{i,\mu}(x) \, f_{j,\nu}(x) = \delta_{i,j} \, \delta_{\mu,\nu} |X| \, . \tag{1.15}$$

Then, we may write

$$E_i(x,y) = \sum_{\mu=1}^{\mu_i} f_{i,\mu}(x) \, f_{i,\mu}(y), \tag{1.16}$$

with the matrix E_i defined as in (1.10).

Given a subset Y of the point set X, the matrix H_i with rows indexed by the elements of Y and columns by the elements of the basis of V_i, with (x,μ)-entry equal to $f_{i,\mu}(x)$, $x \in Y$, is called the i-th characteristic matrix of Y. From (1.16) and by use of (1.5) and (1.10) , we deduce

$$H_k \, H_k^T = \sum_{i=0}^{n} q_k(i) \, (D_i | Y) \, , \tag{1.17}$$

where $(D_i | Y)$ denotes the restriction to Y of the adjacency matrix D_i.

Theorem 1.7. Assume that, for given integers $i,j \in \{0,1,\ldots,n\}$, the components b_k of the dual distribution of Y satisfy $q_{i,j}^k \, b_k = 0$ for k=1, 2,...,n. Then the following holds for the characteristic matrices of Y :

$$H_i^T H_j = \begin{cases} 0 & \text{if } i \neq j , \\ |Y|I & \text{if } i=j . \end{cases}$$

Proof. The above theorem is a direct consequence of the following lemma.

Lemma 1.8. $\| H_i^T H_j - |Y| \Delta_{i,j} \|^2 = |Y|^2 \sum_{k=1}^{n} q_{i,j}^k \, b_k$, where $\Delta_{i,j}$ denotes the appropriate zero matrix for $i \neq j$ and unit matrix for $i=j$.

Proof. We have, for the norm of $H_i^T H_j$, $\| H_i^T H_j \|^2 = \sum_\mu \sum_\nu (\sum_{x \in Y} f_{i,\mu}(x) f_{j,\nu}(x))^2$, which, by use of (1.16), may be written as

$$\sum_{x \in Y} \sum_{y \in Y} E_i(x,y) E_j(x,y) .$$

By use of (1.11) and (1.14) this becomes :

$$|Y|^2 \sum_{k=0}^{n} q_{i,j}^k \, b_k .$$

For $i \neq j$, we have $q_{i,j}^0 = 0$. For $i=j$, we use

$$\| H_i^T H_i - |Y| I \|^2 = \| H_i^T H_i \|^2 - 2|Y| \| H_i \|^2 + |Y|^2 \| I \|^2$$

$$= \| H_i^T H_i \|^2 - |Y|^2 \, \mu_i .$$

The result now follows since $q_{i,i}^0 = q_i(0) = \mu_i$.

2. ASSOCIATION SCHEMES ON AN ABELIAN GROUP.

Throughout this section we consider the following situation : X is a finite Abelian group (written additively) and the n classes $\Gamma_1,...,\Gamma_n$ of an association scheme on X are invariant under translation, that is, for i=1,2,...,n,

$$(\{x,y\} \in \Gamma_i) \Rightarrow (\{x+z,y+z\} \in \Gamma_i, \forall z \in X).$$

Thus we have a partition of X into n+1 classes $X_0, X_1, \ldots, X_n$, with $X_0 = \{0\}$ and, for i=1,2,...,n,

$$(\{x,y\} \in \Gamma_i) \Longleftrightarrow (\pm(y-x) \in X_i). \qquad (2.1)$$

2.1. Main properties.

We first briefly recall some properties of the characters of a finite Abelian group which we shall need. A character ϕ of the finite Abelian group X is a homomorphism of X into the multiplicative group of complex roots of unity, i.e. $\phi(x+y)=\phi(x)\phi(y)$ holds for every $x,y \in X$. The set X' of all characters forms a group isomorphic to X with respect to multiplication defined as follows : for $\phi, \psi \in X'$,

$$\phi.\psi(x) := \phi(x)\psi(x) , \quad \forall x \in X.$$

The image of $x \in X$ under the isomorphism $X \to X'$ will be denoted by ϕ_x so that we have $\phi_x \phi_y = \phi_{x+y}$ for every $x,y \in X$. It is convenient to use the notation $<x,y>$ to denote the value $\phi_y(x)$. Thus we have

$$<x+y,z> = <x,z><y,z>, \quad <x,y+z> = <x,y><x,z> , \qquad (2.2)$$

for all $x,y,z \in X$. Let S denote the square matrix of order $|X|$ with entries $<x,y>$ indexed by the elements $x,y \in X$. The orthogonality relations satisfied by the characters of X can be expressed by the matrix equation $S\tilde{S}=\tilde{S}S = |X|I$, where $\tilde{S}$ is the conjugate transpose of S. They follow from $<x,y>^* = <-x,y>$ and the relations

$$\sum_{x \in X} <x,y> = \sum_{x \in X} <y,x> = \begin{cases} |X| & \text{if } y=0 , \\ \\ 0 & \text{otherwise} . \end{cases} \qquad (2.3)$$

Lemma 2.1. The columns of S are the eigenvectors of all the matrices in the Bose-Mesner algebra of the association scheme on X.

Proof. It suffices to prove the result for the adjacency matrices D_k of the graphs (X,Γ_k). We have by (2.1) and (2.2)

$$\sum_{y \in X} D_k(x,y) <y,z> = \sum_{u \in X_k} <x+u,z> =$$

$$= <x,z> \sum_{u \in X_k} <u,z> . \qquad (2.4)$$

Hence the column vector with index z in S is an eigenvector of D_k with the eigenvalue given by the summation $\sum<u,z>$ over all $u \in X_k$. This proves the lemma.

For $i=0,1,\ldots,n$, let X_i' be the set of indices $z \in X$ for which the corresponding column of S is in the i-th eigenspace V_i. This defines a partition of X into n+1 classes X_0', $X_1',\ldots,X_n'$ with $X_0' = \{0\}$ and $|X_i'| = \mu_i$, $i=0,1,\ldots,n$.

Theorem 2.2. The elements of the eigenmatrices P and Q of the association scheme on X are given by :

$$p_k(i) = \sum_{u \in X_k} <u,z> , \qquad z \in X_i' , \qquad (2.5)$$

$$q_k(i) = \sum_{u \in X_k'} <x,u> , \qquad x \in X_i . \qquad (2.6)$$

Proof. The first relation follows from (2.4) by definition of X_i' (since

$p_k(i)$ is the i-th eigenvalue of D_k). For the second we refer to (1.16)

which, applied to the present situation, gives

$$E_k(x,y) = \sum_{u \in X'_k} <-x,u><y,u> = \sum_{u \in X'_k} <y-x,u> .$$

The result now follows from (2.1) and the fact that $E_k(x,y)=q_k(i)$ for

all $\{x,y\} \in \Gamma_i$.

Remark 2.3. Strictly speaking the elements of S are complex-valued and

so are the eigenvectors indexed by the elements of X. However since all

matrices in the Bose–Mesner algebra are real symmetric, the complex

eigenvectors occur in complex conjugate pairs indexed by pairs $\{z,-z\}$.

Thus we have

$$(z \in X'_k) \Longleftrightarrow (-z \in X'_k) ,$$

and we may define a partition of the set of 2-element subsets of X into

n classes $\Gamma'_1, \Gamma'_2, \ldots, \Gamma'_n$ by defining, for $i=1,2,\ldots,n$,

$$(\{x,y\} \in \Gamma'_i) \Longleftrightarrow (\pm(y-x) \in X'_i) . \tag{2.7}$$

Theorem 2.4. The n classes Γ'_i form an association scheme on X.

Proof. By using an argument similar to the one used in the proof of

lemma 2.1, one easily shows that the rows of S are eigenvectors of the

adjacency matrices D'_k of the graphs (X,Γ'_k). The corresponding eigenvalues

of D'_k are given by (2.6) for every row of S with index $x \in X_i$. Having

common eigenspaces the matrices D'_k commute with each other, and from the

relations (1.2) one easily deduces that they satisfy

$$D'_i D'_j = \sum_k q^k_{i,j} D'_k , \tag{2.8}$$

which proves the theorem.

The association schemes on X defined by the Γ_i and the Γ_i', respectively, are called <u>dual</u>. The parameters of one scheme are obtained from those of the other by interchanging $p_{i,j}^k$ with $q_{i,j}^k$ and $p_k(i)$ with $q_k(i)$ for all i,j,k.

2.2. Subgroups and duality.

Let Y be a non-trivial subgroup of X. The set

$$Y' := \{y \in X \mid \langle x,y \rangle = 1, \forall\, x \in Y\}$$

is itself a subgroup of X, called the <u>dual</u> of Y ; it is isomorphic to the factor group X/Y. We shall need the following result which is a generalization of (2.3) :

$$\sum_{x \in Y} \langle x,y \rangle = \begin{cases} |Y| & \text{if } y \in Y' , \\ 0 & \text{otherwise.} \end{cases} \qquad (2.9)$$

Let $\underline{a}=(a_0,a_1,\ldots,a_n)$ and $\underline{a}'=(a_0',\ldots,a_n')$ denote the inner distributions of Y and Y' respectively, with respect to the association schemes defined on X by the Γ_i and the Γ_i' respectively. Similarly, let us denote by $\underline{b}$ and $\underline{b}'$ their respective dual distributions. The following theorem shows how these distributions are related.

<u>Theorem 2.5.</u> $\underline{a}'=\underline{b}$, $\underline{b}'=\underline{a}$.

<u>Proof.</u> We first observe that, since Y is a subgroup, we have by (2.1) : $a_i= |X_i \cap Y|$; similarly, we have $a_i' = |X_i' \cap Y'|$. We now consider the double summation $\sum \langle x,y \rangle$ with respect to all $x \in Y$ and all $y \in X_k'$. By first summing with respect to x and then with respect to y, we obtain by

(2.9) the value $|Y|$ a_k'. By summing in reverse order, we obtain by (2.6)

the value $\sum_i q_k(i)a_i$. Hence we have

$$|Y| \ a_k' = \sum_i q_k(i) \ a_i \ ,$$

and by theorem 1.5 we have $a_k'=b_k$. The other relations are proved similar-

ly.

Remark 2.6. The relations of theorem 2.5 constitute a generalization of

the MacWilliams identities for linear codes, which will be investigated

in the next paragraph.

2.3. First example : the Hamming schemes.

Let $X=F^n$ be the set of all n-tuples $x=(x_1,x_2,\ldots,x_n)$ from a finite

set F of cardinality $q \geqslant 2$. We make X a metric space by defining the

Hamming distance $d(x,y)$ between two n-tuples to be the number of compo-

nents in which they differ, i.e.

$$d(x,y) = |\{i \mid 1 \leqslant i \leqslant n, \ x_i \neq y_i\}| \ .$$

For $i=1,\ldots,n$, we define Γ_i to be the set of pairs of n-tuples at distan-

ce i, i.e.

$$\Gamma_i =\{\{x,y\} \mid d(x,y)=i; \ x,y \in X\} \ . \qquad (2.10)$$

Simple counting arguments show that the n classes $\Gamma_1,\ldots,\Gamma_n$ form an asso-

ciation scheme on X, with $v_i=\binom{n}{i} (q-1)^i$ and

$$p_{i,j}^k = \sum_{\lambda,\mu} \binom{n-k}{\lambda}\binom{k}{\mu}\binom{k-\mu}{i-\lambda-\mu}(q-1)^\lambda(q-2)^\mu,$$

where the summation is extended to all λ,μ satisfying $2\lambda+\mu = i+j-k$ (and

$\mu=0$ if $q=2$). This association scheme will be denoted by $H(n,q)$.

It is convenient to provide F with the structure of an Abelian group (in an arbitrary way) and then extend it to $X=F^n$ by taking n copies of F. We shall use an additive notation for the group operation and denote by 0 (zero) the identity element. Then, by definition, the <u>Hamming weight</u> w(x) of an element x in the group X is the number of its nonzero components x_i. For the distance d(x,y) between two elements we now have

$$d(x,y) = w(x-y) , \qquad \forall \, x,y \in X ,$$

which shows that the n classes (2.10) are invariant under translation in X. Thus we are in the situation described at the beginning of this section, cf. (2.1), where here X_i is the set of all elements of weight i in X.

We shall now use the results of theorem 2.2 to obtain an explicit expression for the elements of the eigenmatrices P and Q. We first give a description of the characters of X. For $\alpha,\beta \in F$, we let the map $\alpha \to <\alpha,\beta>$ denote the character of F associated to β. With $F^*=F\backslash\{0\}$, we have

$$\sum_{\alpha \in F^*} <\alpha,\beta> = \begin{cases} q-1 & \text{if } \beta=0 , \\ \\ -1 & \text{otherwise} , \end{cases} \qquad (2.11)$$

which follows from (2.3) applied to F. The characters of X are obtained by defining, for $x,y \in X$,

$$<x,y> = \prod_{i=1}^{n} <x_i,y_i> . \qquad (2.12)$$

It is convenient to define, for elements of F,

$$w(\alpha) = \begin{cases} 0 & \text{if } \alpha = 0 , \\ \\ 1 & \text{if } \alpha \in F^* . \end{cases}$$

Then, we have, for an element $x \in X$,

$$w(x) = \sum_{i=1}^{n} w(x_i) . \qquad (2.13)$$

Lemma 2.7. For an indeterminate λ and an arbitrary $y \in X$, we have

$$\sum_{x \in X} <x,y>\lambda^{w(x)} = (1-\lambda)^{w(y)}(1+(q-1)\lambda)^{n-w(y)}$$

Proof. By use of (2.12) and (2.13) we may write

$$\sum_{x \in X} <x,y>\lambda^{w(x)} = \prod_{i=1}^{n} (\sum_{x_i \in F} <x_i,y_i>\lambda^{w(x_i)}),$$

where, by (2.11), each term of the product is equal to $(1+(q-1)\lambda)$ or $(1-\lambda)$ according as y_i is equal to zero or not. This proves the lemma.

Let us denote by $K_k(i)$ the coefficient of λ^k in the expansion of

$$(1-\lambda)^i(1+(q-1)\lambda)^{n-i} = \sum_{j} \binom{n-i}{j} q^j \lambda^j (1-\lambda)^{n-j} .$$

Thus we have

$$K_k(i) = \sum_{j=0}^{k} (-1)^{k-j} \binom{n-j}{k-j} \binom{n-i}{j} q^j , \qquad (2.4)$$

which shows that $K_k(i)$ is a polynomial of degree k in i, called a Krawtchouk polynomial.

Theorem 2.8. The Hamming scheme $H(n,q)$ is self-dual and the elements of its eigenmatrices P and Q are given by

$$p_k(i) = q_k(i) = K_k(i) .$$

Proof. Let us examine the equality of lemma 2.7. Clearly the coefficient of λ^k only depends on $w(y)$. For $w(y)=i$, it is equal to $K_k(i)$ (by definition) in the right-hand side. In the left-hand side, it is given by

$$\sum_{x \in X_k} <x,y> \, ,$$

which is equal to $p_k(i)$ for any $y \in X_i'$, cf. theorem 2.2. Thus we have $X_i'=X_i$ for every i, and the theorem is proved.

By applying theorem 1.1 and corollary 1.2 to the Hamming scheme, we obtain the following theorem on Krawtchouk polynomials.

Theorem 2.9. The Krawtchouk polynomials satisfy the orthogonality conditions :

$$\sum_{k=0}^{n} K_i(k)K_j(k)\binom{n}{k}(q-1)^k = \delta_{i,j}\binom{n}{i}(q-1)^i q^n \, .$$

In addition, $\binom{n}{k}(q-1)^k K_i(k)=\binom{n}{i}(q-1)^i K_k(i)$ holds.

Also, by applying the relations (1.6) with i=1 to Krawtchouk polynomials, we obtain the following recurrence relation :

$$(k+1)K_{k+1}(u)=(K_1(u)-(q-2)k)K_k(u)-(q-1)(n-k+1)K_{k-1}(u), \quad (2.15)$$

where $K_1(u)=n(q-1)-qu$. This shows that $K_k(u)$ can also be expressed as a polynomial of degree k in $K_1(u)$.

We now turn to the problem of subsets in the Hamming schemes. A subset Y of the point set X of the Hamming scheme H(n,q) is called a code of length n over F. The inner distribution a of a code Y is called the distance-distribution of Y. We observe that a_i is the average number of codewords at distance i from a given codeword. When Y is a subgroup of X it is called a group-code. When F is a field, X is a vector space over F and a code Y is said to be linear whenever it is a linear subspace of X. Clearly a linear code is a group-code but the converse needs not to be true. When Y is a group-code, we are in the situation studied in § 2.2.

The relations of theorem 2.5 then become the __MacWilliams identities__ which

we shall now describe. We first remark that, for a group-code Y, the

element a_i of its distance-distribution is equal to the number of code-

words of weight i. Thus the coefficient of λ^i in its __weight-enumerator__

$W_Y(\lambda)$,

$$W_Y(\lambda) = \sum_{x \in Y} \lambda^{w(x)} ,$$

is simply given by a_i.

The __dual code__ of the group-code Y is the dual subgroup Y' of Y,

that is,

$$Y' = \{y \in X \mid <x,y> = 1, \forall x \in Y\} .$$

__Theorem 2.10.__ The weight-enumerators of a pair of dual codes Y,Y' are

related by (MacWilliams identities) :

$$|Y| \ W_{Y'}(\lambda) = \sum_{i=0}^{n} a_i(1-\lambda)^i(1+(q-1)\lambda)^{n-i} ,$$

with $W_Y(\lambda) = \sum a_i \lambda^i$.

__Proof.__ Let a_k' be the number of codewords of weight k in Y'. By theorem

2.2 we have $|Y| \ a_k' = \sum_i a_i q_k(i)$, where $q_k(i)$ is the Krawtchouk polynomial

$K_k(i)$, cf. theorem 2.8. Thus we have

$$|Y| \ W_{Y'}(\lambda) = \sum_i \sum_k a_i \ K_k(i) \ \lambda^k$$

$$= \sum_i a_i(1-\lambda)^i(1+(q-1)\lambda)^{n-i} ,$$

by definition of the Krawtchouk polynomials, and the theorem is proved.

2.4. __Second example : symplectic forms.__

Let $V=V(m,q)$ be an m-dimensional vector space over the field

F=GF(q). A function f from V×V to F satisfying

$$(\sum a_i \xi_i, \sum b_j \eta_j) = \sum \sum a_i b_j f(\xi_i, \eta_j) \ , \quad \forall \, a_i, b_j \in F, \ \forall \, \xi_i, \eta_j \in V \ ,$$

is called a <u>bilinear</u> <u>form</u> on V. The bilinear form f is <u>symplectic</u> (or alternate) if

$$f(\xi, \xi) = 0 \ , \quad \forall \, \xi \in V \ ,$$

which implies

$$f(\xi, \eta) + f(\eta, \xi) = 0, \quad \forall \, \xi, \eta \in V.$$

The bilinear form f is uniquely determined by the square matrix of order m with entries $f_{i,j} = f(\delta_i, \delta_j)$ for a fixed basis $(\delta_1, \ldots, \delta_m)$ of V. The matrix of a symplectic form satisfies

$$f_{i,i} = 0 \ , \quad f_{i,j} + f_{j,i} = 0 \ ,$$

hence is skew-symmetric. There is a one-to-one correspondence between the set of all symplectic forms on V and the set X of all skew-symmetric matrices of order m over F. From now on we shall identify symplectic forms with elements of X. Clearly X is an $\binom{m}{2}$-dimensional vector space over F.

The <u>rank</u> of a form is the rank of its matrix. Thus symplectic forms have even rank. We shall consider the partition of X into the n+1 subsets

$$X_i = \{x \in X \mid rk(x) = 2i\} \ , \quad i=0,1,\ldots,n,$$

where n= [m/2] . Accordingly, we define a partition of the set of 2-element subsets of X into the n classes $\Gamma_1, \ldots, \Gamma_n$,

$$\Gamma_i = \{\{x,y\} \mid rk(x-y)=2i \ ; \ x,y \in X\} \ . \qquad (2.16)$$

We shall show that these n classes form an association scheme on X which will be denoted by $S(m,q)$ and called a **symplectic scheme**. Clearly the n

classes (2.16) are invariant under translation in X and so we are in the

situation described at the beginning of this section. In particular, by

an argument similar to the one used in lemma 2.1, it is easily shown that

the character matrix S of X provides eigenvectors for the adjacency ma-

trices D_k of the graphs (X,Γ_k). It remains to be shown that there are

exactly n+1 common eigenspaces for these matrices.

Let the characters of F be defined as for the Hamming schemes,

cf. (2.11). Then the character matrix of X is obtained by defining,

$$\text{for } x,y \in X, \ x = (x_{i,j}), y = (y_{i,j}) \ ,$$

$$<x,y> = \prod_{i=1}^{m-1} \prod_{j=i+1}^{m} <x_{i,j}, \ y_{i,j}> \ .$$

We shall use the following facts about the group $GL(m,q)$ of all nonsin-

gular matrices of order m over F.

Proposition 2.11.

(i) For any $u \in GL(m,q)$, the map

$$x \to u^T x u \tag{2.17}$$

is a rank preserving permutation on X ;

(ii) The group $GL(m,q)$, acting by permutations on X as in (2.17),

is transitive on each set X_k ;

(iii) For any $u \in GL(m,q)$ and $x,y \in X$, the following holds :

$$<u^T x u, y> = <x, u y u^T>. \tag{2.18}$$

Corollary 2.12. The sum $\sum <x,y>$ over all $x \in X_k$ only depends on the rank

of $y \in X$.

Proof. The map (2.17) is a permutation on X_k, and so we have, by (2.18)

$$\sum_{x \in X_k} <x,y> = \sum_{x \in X_k} <u^T x\, u, y> = \sum_{x \in X_k} <x, u\, y\, u^T> .$$

We may choose u arbitrarily in GL(m,q). In particular, since this group is transitive on any X_i, we may choose u so that $u\, y\, u^T$ is any given matrix with the same rank as y. This proves the lemma.

Theorem 2.13. S(m,q) is a self-dual association scheme, and so its eigenmatrices satisfy P=Q.

Proof. It follows from the above corollary that the matrices D_k have exactly n+1 common eigenspaces. These are, for i=0,1,...,n, the spaces spanned by the columns of the character matrix S with indices in X_i, cf. the proof of lemma 2.1. Thus we have $X'_i = X_i$ for all i, and the theorem is proved.

The derivation of the actual values of the elements $p_k(i) = q_k(i)$ is rather technical and we shall omit the details (which can be found in the literature). We shall merely give the results. These are expressed in terms of the Gaussian coefficients which are defined as follows. For an integer s > 1 and nonnegative integers n,k, the s-ary Gaussian coefficients $[\begin{smallmatrix} n \\ k \end{smallmatrix}]$ are defined by :

$$[\begin{smallmatrix} n \\ 0 \end{smallmatrix}] = 1 \ , \ [\begin{smallmatrix} n \\ k \end{smallmatrix}] = \prod_{i=0}^{k-1} (s^n - s^i)/(s^k - s^i), \quad k \geqslant 1.$$

They satisfy

$$[\begin{smallmatrix} n \\ k \end{smallmatrix}] = [\begin{smallmatrix} n \\ n-k \end{smallmatrix}] \ , \ \lim_{s \to 1} [\begin{smallmatrix} n \\ k \end{smallmatrix}] = \binom{n}{k} \ ,$$

and, for an indeterminate λ,

$$(1-\lambda)(1-\lambda s)\dots(1-\lambda s^{n-1}) = \sum_{k=0}^{n} (-1)^k\, s^{\binom{k}{2}} [\begin{smallmatrix} n \\ k \end{smallmatrix}] \lambda^k .$$

Let $G_k(i)$ denote the coefficient of λ^k in the expansion of

$$\sum_{j=0}^{n-i} \begin{bmatrix} n-i \\ j \end{bmatrix} c^j \lambda^j (1-\lambda)(1-\lambda s) \ldots (1-\lambda s^{n-j-1}) ,$$

that is,

$$G_k(i) = \sum_{j=0}^{k} (-1)^{k-j} s^{\binom{k-j}{2}} \begin{bmatrix} n-j \\ k-j \end{bmatrix} \begin{bmatrix} n-i \\ j \end{bmatrix} c^j , \qquad (2.19)$$

where c is an arbitrary nonzero constant. We observe that, for $s \to 1$ and

$c=q$, $G_k(i)$ becomes the Krawtchouk polynomial $K_k(i)$, cf. (2.14). For that

reason $G_k(i)$ is called a <u>generalized Krawtchouk polynomial</u>. In fact $G_k(i)$

is a polynomial of degree k in the variable s^{-i}. This follows from the

definition of the Gaussian coefficients. We now give the parameters of

the symplectic scheme $S(m,q)$.

<u>Theorem 2.14.</u> For the symplectic scheme $S(m,q)$, the elements of the

eigenmatrices are given by

$$p_k(i) = q_k(i) = G_k(i) ,$$

where $G_k(i)$ is the generalized Krawtchouk polynomial (2.19) with

$$s=q^2 \quad \text{and} \quad c=q^{m(m-1)/2n} .$$

We observe that, for the cardinality of the set X_k, we have

$|X_k| = G_k(0)$, that is,

$$|X_k| = \begin{bmatrix} n \\ k \end{bmatrix} (c-1)(c-s)\ldots(c-s^{k-1}) .$$

For future use, we quote without giving a proof the following **property**

of generalized Krawtchouk polynomials

$$\sum_{k=0}^{t} \begin{bmatrix} n-k \\ n-t \end{bmatrix} G_k(i) = \begin{bmatrix} n-i \\ t \end{bmatrix} c^t , \qquad (2.20)$$

which holds for $t=0,1,\ldots,n$.

2.5. <u>Duality is symplectic schemes. An application to Reed-Muller codes.</u>

Let Y, Y' be a pair of dual subgroups in the point set X of the symplectic scheme S(m,q). By theorem 2.5, we know that their inner distributions are related by

$$|Y| \, a_k' = \sum_{i=0}^{n} G_k(i) \, a_i \, ,$$

where a_i, a_i' denote the number of elements of rank 2i in Y, Y', respectively. We shall now describe an application to Reed-Muller codes in the case when q=2.

From now on we let F be the binary field GF(2) and, as before, V denotes an m-dimensional vector space over F. A <u>linear form</u> on V is a function L from V to F satisfying

$$L(\sum a_i \xi_i) = \sum a_i \, L(\xi_i), \, \forall a_i \in F, \, \forall \xi_i \in V.$$

The set $\mathcal{L}$ of all linear forms on V is an m-dimensional vector space over F, usually called the dual space of V. A <u>quadratic form</u> on V is a function Q from V to F with the properties :

(i) $Q(\xi) = 0$ for $\xi = 0$;

(ii)   the function $f : V \times V \to F$ defined by $f(\xi,\eta) = Q(\xi+\eta)+Q(\xi)+Q(\eta)$,

       $\forall \xi, \eta \in V$, is a bilinear form on V, which will be denoted by $\phi(Q)$.

We observe that, for any quadratic form Q, the bilinear form $f=\phi(Q)$ is symplectic since $f(\xi,\xi)=0$ holds for all $\xi \in V$. Moreover f is identically zero iff Q is linear.

<u>Proposition 2.16.</u>

(i) The set $\mathcal{Q}$ of all quadratic forms on V is a vector space of dimen-
     sion $m+\binom{m}{2}$ over F ;

(ii) The map $Q \rightarrow \phi(Q)$ is a vector space homomorphism from $\mathcal{Q}$ to the
     set X of all symplectic forms on V ;

(iii) The kernel Ker(ϕ) of the homomorphism $\phi: \mathcal{Q} \rightarrow X$ is the set $\mathcal{L}$ of
      all linear forms on V.

Thus we have $X \simeq \mathcal{Q}/\mathcal{L}$ and the map ϕ identifies every coset of $\mathcal{L}$ in $\mathcal{Q}$
with a given symplectic form.

     Let $V^* := V\backslash\{0\}$ and let us denote by FV^* the set of all functions
from V^* to F. Elements of FV^* will be represented by the (2^m-1)-tuples
of their values in V^*. In this way the elements of $\mathcal{L}$ and $\mathcal{Q}$ may be viewed
as vectors of length 2^m-1 over F, and the sets $\mathcal{L}$ and $\mathcal{Q}$ become linear codes of length 2^m-1 and dimensions m and $m+\binom{m}{2}$, respectively, over F.
They are called the first- and second order Reed-Muller codes, respectively. Every nonzero element $L \in \mathcal{L}$ has weight (= number of its nonzero
values in V^*) equal to 2^{m-1}. The weight-distribution of a given coset
of $\mathcal{L}$ in $\mathcal{Q}$ only depends on the rank of the symplectic form associated to
it. Specifically, we have the following proposition.

Proposition 2.17.

     Let f be any given symplectic form in X_k. Then, among the 2^m
quadratic froms $Q \in \phi^{-1}(f)$ (= satisfying $\phi(Q)=f$), there are

$$2^{k-1}(2^k+1) \text{ forms with weight } 2^{m-1} - 2^{m-1-k} ,$$

$$2^m-2^{2k} \quad \text{ forms with weight } 2^{m-1} ,$$

$$2^{k-1}(2^k-1) \text{ forms with weight } 2^{m-1} + 2^{m-1-k} .$$

We shall be concerned with subsets Y of the set X of all symplectic forms and the codes $C(Y)$ they define as follows. We let $C(Y)$ be the
set of all quadratic forms Q satisfying $\phi(Q) \in Y$. Thus $C(Y)$ is a union
of $|Y|$ cosets of $\mathcal{L}$ in $\mathcal{Q}$, in other words, a code of length 2^m-1 consis-
ting of $|Y|$ cosets of the first-order RM code, all contained in the se-
cond-order RM code. The distance-enumerator $W_{C(Y)}(\lambda)$ of the code $C(Y)$,

$$W_{C(Y)}(\lambda) = \frac{1}{|C(Y)|} \sum_{u,v \in C(Y)} \lambda^{d(u,v)} \quad ,$$

is related to the inner distribution of Y as indicated in the following
theorem.

Theorem 2.18. Let $\underline{a}=(a_0,\ldots,a_n)$ be the inner distribution of $Y \subset X$ in
the symplectic scheme. Then the distance-enumerator of the code $C(Y)$ is
given by $\sum_{k=0}^{n} a_k W_k(\lambda)$, where $W_k(\lambda)$ is the weight-enumerator of the set
of 2^m quadratic forms obtained from any given symplectic form in X_k (as
indicated in proposition 2.17).

Proof. Since, for any two vectors u,v, we have $d(u,v)=w(u-v)$, the distribution of distances in the code $C(Y)$ is given by the distributions of
weights $w(Q-Q')$, $Q,Q' \in C(Y)$. Given any two symplectic forms $f,f' \in Y$
with $f-f' \in X_k$, the distribution of distances in the set $\phi^{-1}(f) \times \phi^{-1}(f')$
is obtained by taking 2^m times the distribution of weights in the set
$\phi^{-1}(f-f')$, which is given by proposition 2.17. Since there are $|Y| \, a_k$
pairs $f,f' \in Y$ with $f-f' \in X_k$, the theorem is proved.

Corollary 2.19. For a pair of dual subgroups Y, Y' of X, the weight-enumerators of the codes $C(Y)$, $C(Y')$ are given by

$$\sum_k a_k \, W_k(\lambda) \; , \quad \sum_k a_k' \, W_k(\lambda) \; ,$$

respectively, where the inner distributions $\underline{a}$ and $\underline{a}'$ of Y, Y' are related by

$$|Y| a_k' = \sum_i G_k(i) \, a_i \quad .$$

Proof. This follows from theorems 2.5 and 2.14.

Example 2.20. The dual code of the BCH code of length 63 and minimum weight 5 is a linear (63,12) code. It is a subcode of the second-order and a supercode of the first-order RM code. Its weight-enumerator can be given the form

$$(1+63\lambda^{32}) + 21(10\lambda^{24}+48\lambda^{32}+6\lambda^{40})+42(36\lambda^{28}+28\lambda^{36}) \; ,$$

which shows that it corresponds to a linear space Y of symplectic forms consisting of 42 forms of rank 6, 21 of rank 4, and the zero form. The dual Y' of Y in X has inner distribution given by

$$|Y| a_k' = G_k(0)+21 \, G_k(2)+42 \, G_k(3) \; ,$$

that is,

$$a_0' = 1, \; a_1' = 0, \; a_2' = 315, \; a_3' = 196 \; .$$

The code C(Y') is a (63,15) code with weight-enumerator

$$(1+63\lambda^{32})+315(10\lambda^{24}+48\lambda^{32}+6\lambda^{40})+196(36\lambda^{28}+28\lambda^{36}) \; .$$

3. POLYNOMIAL SCHEMES

3.1. Definitions.

Let P and Q denote the eigenmatrices of an association scheme with n classes. Clearly, given any set of n+1 distinct nonnegative real

numbers $z_0=0$, $z_1,\ldots,z_n$, there exists for every k a unique polynomial

$\Phi_k(z)$ of degree n or less with coefficients in R, such that

$$\Phi_k(z_i) = p_k(i), \quad i=0,1,\ldots,n,$$

where $p_k(i)$ denotes the (i,k)-entry of P. The association scheme is said

to be __P-polynomial__ with respect to $z_0,\ldots,z_n$ if, for every k, the polyno-

mial Φ_k has degree k exactly. A __Q-polynomial scheme__ is defined analogous-

ly from the matrix Q.

       From the relations (1.6) one easily deduces that a P-polynomial

scheme can be characterized by the following properties of its intersec-

tion numbers :

   (i) $p_{i,1}^{i+1} \neq 0$ for $i=1,\ldots,n-1$;

                                                                                    (3.1)

   (ii) $p_{i,j}^k \neq 0$ only if $|i-j| \leq k \leq i+j$.

A similar characterization exists for Q-polynomial schemes in terms of the

parameters $q_{i,j}^k$. An association scheme with the n classes $\Gamma_1,\ldots,\Gamma_n$ on X

is called __metric__ if, for $i=1,2,\ldots,n$, Γ_i is the set of pairs of vertices

at distance i in the graph (X,Γ_1). (This latter graph is then called a

metrically regular, or perfectly regular, graph).

__Theorem 3.1.__ An association scheme is P-polynomial if and only if it is

metric.

__Proof.__ This follows from the fact that an association scheme is metric

if and only if the adjacency matrix D_i of the graph (X,Γ_i) is a polyno-

mial in D_1 of degree i (equivalently iff (3.1) holds for the intersec-

tion numbers).

No such combinatorial characterization is known for Q-polynomial schemes. However one might expect that any "algebraic" property of a P-polynomial scheme should have its counterpart in a Q-polynomial scheme. This is the case, for example, with the concepts of perfect codes (in a P-polynomial scheme) and tight designs (in a Q-polynomial scheme) which will be discussed in the next paragraphs. Before going into further details, let us mention at this point that the Hamming and symplectic schemes discussed previously are examples of schemes which are both P- and Q-polynomial.

3.2. P-polynomial (= metric) schemes.

A nonempty subset Y of the point set X in a metric scheme is called a code. The mapping d from X^2 into $\{0,1,\ldots,n\}$ defined by $d(x,y)=i$ iff $\{x,y\} \in \Gamma_i$, is a distance function on X. The minimum distance $d(Y)$ of a code Y is the smallest nonzero distance between elements of Y. It can be defined to be the index of the first nonzero component of the inner distribution (hereafter called distance-distribution) $\underline{a}$ of Y, not counting $a_0=1$. The external distance $r(Y)$ of the code Y is defined to be the number of nonzero components of the dual distribution $\underline{b}$ of Y, not counting $b_0=1$. The outer distribution of Y is defined as follows. For any $x \in X$, let $b_i(x)$ denote the number of elements of Y at distance i from x, and let B_i denote the vector with components indexed by the elements of X and with x-entry equal to $b_i(x)$. The outer distribution (or distribution matrix) of Y is the matrix $B=(B_0,B_1,\ldots,B_n)$.

Lemma 3.2. Let Δ be the diagonal matrix $\Delta= \text{diag} \{b_0,b_1,\ldots,b_n\}$ constructed from the dual distribution $\underline{b}$ of a code Y. Then, for the distribution matrix of Y, the following holds :

$$|X| B^T B = |Y|^2 P^T \Delta P.$$

Proof. Let u_Y be the incidence vector of $Y \subset X$. Then we have $B_i = D_i u_Y$, whence

$$B_i^T B_j = u_Y^T D_i D_j u_Y = \sum_k p_{i,j}^k u_Y^T D_k u_Y .$$

Now, by use of $D_k = \sum_\ell p_k(\ell) J_\ell$, cf. (1.3), and $u_Y^T J_\ell u_Y = b_\ell |Y|^2 / |X|$, cf. (1.14), we obtain

$$|X| B_i^T B_j = |Y|^2 \sum_\ell b_\ell \sum_k p_{i,j}^k p_k(\ell) ,$$

which, from (1.6), becomes

$$|X| B_i^T B_j = |Y|^2 \sum_\ell b_\ell p_i(\ell) p_j(\ell) .$$

This proves the lemma.

The following theorem justifies the terminology adopted for the parameter $r(Y)$ of a code.

Theorem 3.3. For a code Y with external distance $r(Y) = r$, every element of X is at distance less than or equal to r from at least one point of Y.

Proof. We shall prove the result by showing that the submatrix $\bar{B} = (B_0, B_1, \ldots, B_r)$ of the distribution matrix B of the code Y has the same rank as B, which by the preceding lemma is equal to $r+1$. So the columns of $\bar{B}$ span the column space of B and clearly for no element $x \in X$ we may have $b_0(x) = b_1(x) = \ldots = b_r(x) = 0$.

Let K,L denote the following subsets of $\{0, 1, \ldots, n\}$, $K = \{0, 1, \ldots, r\}$, $L = \{k | b_k \neq 0\}$, where $\underline{b} = (b_0, \ldots, b_n)$ is the dual distribution of Y. Thus we have $|K| = |L| = r+1$. Let $\bar{P}$, $\bar{\Delta}$ denote the restriction of P,Δ

to the sets L×K and L×L, respectively. Then, by lemma 3.2, we may write

$$|X| \; \bar{B}^T \bar{B} = |Y|^2 \; \bar{P}^T \bar{\Delta} \bar{P} \; .$$

Clearly $\bar{\Delta}$ is nonsingular and so is $\bar{P}$ by the polynomial property of P.
Hence $\bar{B}$ has rank r+1 and the theorem is proved.

<u>Corollary 3.4.</u> For any code Y with minimum distance d(Y)=d and external
distance r(Y)=r, the following holds :

$$r \geqslant (d-1)/2.$$

<u>Proof.</u> Let e= $\left[(d-1)/2\right]$ and let us choose an element x ∈ X at distance e
from some element y ∈ Y. Then x is at distance e+1 or more from the other
elements y' of Y by the triangle inequality d(y,y') ⩽ d(x,y)+d(x,y').
Hence e ⩽ r by theorem 3.3, and the corollary is proved.

For a code Y with dual distribution <u>b</u>, let L= {k | 1 ⩽ k ⩽ n ;
$b_k \neq 0$} . The <u>characteristic polynomial</u> of Y is the polynomial

$$F_Y(z) = \frac{|X|}{|Y|} \; \prod_{k \in L} \; (1-z/z_k)$$

of degree r=r(Y). With respect to the basis $(\Phi_0, \Phi_1, \ldots, \Phi_n)$ we may write
F_Y in the form

$$F_Y(z) = \sum_{k=0}^{r} \alpha_k \Phi_k(z) \; , \tag{3.2}$$

where the coefficients α_k are uniquely determined. Since $\Phi_k(z_i)=p_k(i)$,
we have, by definition of F_Y,

$$\sum_{k=0}^{r} \alpha_k p_k(i)=F_Y(z_i)= \begin{cases} \dfrac{|X|}{|Y|} & \text{if } i=0 \; , \\ \\ 0 & \text{if } i \in L. \end{cases} \tag{3.3}$$

Lemma 3.5. $\sum_{k=0}^{r} \alpha_k b_k(x) = 1$, $\forall\, x \in X$.

Proof. We have $B_k = D_k\, u_Y = \sum_i p_k(i)\, J_i\, u_Y$, whence

$$\sum_{k=0}^{r} \alpha_k B_k = \sum_{i=0}^{r} F_Y(z_i)\, J_i\, u_Y .$$

From the definition of b_i, cf. (1.14), it follows that $(b_i=0) \Rightarrow (J_i u_Y=0)$. Hence the above summation reduces to the single term

$$F_Y(z_0)\, J_0 u_Y = \frac{|X|}{|Y|} \cdot \frac{1}{|X|}\, J\, u_Y = u_x ,$$

and the lemma is proved.

Corollary 3.6. For a code Y with minimum distance $d(Y)=d$ and external distance $r(Y)=r$ satisfying $d > r$, the coefficients α_k of its characteristic polynomial (3.2) satisfy :

$$\alpha_0 = \alpha_1 = \ldots = \alpha_{d-r-1} = 1 .$$

Proof. For any $i < d-r$, let us choose an element $x \in X$ at distance i from some element $y \in Y$. Then by the triangle inequality every other $y' \in Y$ is at distance greater than r from x. Thus we have $b_i(x)=1$ and $b_j(x)=0$ for all $j \leqslant r$, $j \neq i$. From lemma 3.5 it follows that $\alpha_i=1$. Since this holds for $i=0,1,\ldots,d-r-1$, the corollary is proved.

We can now state our main theorem.

Theorem 3.7. Let Y be a code with minimum distance $d(Y)=d$ and external distance $r(Y)=r$. Let $e = [\frac{1}{2}(d-1)]$. Then

$$\sum_{i=0}^{e} v_i \leqslant |X|/|Y| \leqslant \sum_{i=0}^{r} v_i .$$

If one of these bounds is attained, then so is the other, the code is called <u>perfect</u>, and its characteristic polynomial is the <u>sum polynomial</u>

$$\Psi_e(z) = \sum_{k=0}^{e} \Phi_k(z) \ .$$

<u>Proof</u>. For any nonnegative integer s, the "sphere of radius s" centred on a point $x \in X$ contains $\sum_{i=0}^{s} v_i$ points. The spheres of radius e centred on points of Y are pairwise disjoint, while those of radius r cover X. The inequalities follow. If equality holds on one side, the above reasoning shows that is also holds on the other side. We then have r=e and d=2e+1, whence, by corollary 3.6, $\alpha_0 = \alpha_1 = \ldots = \alpha_e = 1$, and the theorem is proved.

<u>Corollary 3.8</u>. If a perfect code Y with minimum distance $d(\cdot) = 2e+1$ exists, then the zeros of the sum polynomial $\Psi_e(z)$ are contained in the set $\{z_1, \ldots, z_n\}$.

<u>Proof</u>. This follows from theorem 3.7 by definition of the characteristic polynomial.

<u>Remark 3.9</u>. The Hamming schemes H(n,q) are P-polynomial with respect to $\{0,1,\ldots,n\}$ with $\Phi_k(z) = K_k(z)$ (the Krawtchouk polynomials) and with the Hamming distance as distance function. The sum polynomial $\Psi_e(z)$ is the Lloyd polynomial $L_e(z) = \sum_{k=0}^{e} K_k(z)$. By using the necessary conditions of corollary 3.8, several authors (mainly van Lint and Tietäväinen) were able to show the non-existence of perfect codes. It is now known that, when q is a power of a prime, perfect codes only exist for the following sets of parameters :

(i)   e=1 , $n=(q^m-1)/(q-1)$, $m \geqslant 2$, q any power of a prime ;

(ii)   e=m ,   n=2m+1, q=2 ;

(iii)   e=2 , n=11, q=3 ;

(iv)   e=3 , n=23, q=2.

In the last three cases a unique code is known to exist. In the last
two cases there are the celebrated Golay codes.

We conclude this paragraph with an example of a perfect code in
a metrically regular graph.

Example 3.10. Let X be the set of 3-subsets of a 7-set. We define a
graph (X,Γ) on X by defining $\{x,y\} \in \Gamma$ if and only if x and y are disjoint 3-subsets. This graph is metrically regular, hence defines an association scheme on X which is P-polynomial. The three classes of this
scheme can be defined as follows :

$$\Gamma_1 = \Gamma, \; \Gamma_2 = \{\{x,y\} \subset X; \; |x \cap y| = 2\} ,$$

$$\Gamma_3 = \{\{x,y\} \subset X; \; |x \cap y| = 1\} .$$

The eigenmatrix P is given by

$$P = \begin{bmatrix} 1 & 4 & 12 & 18 \\ 1 & 2 & 0 & -3 \\ 1 & -1 & -3 & 3 \\ 1 & -3 & 5 & -3 \end{bmatrix} ,$$

and it is easily verified that the scheme is P-polynomial with respect
to $z_0=0$, $z_1=2$, $z_2=5$, $z_3=7$, with $\phi_1(z)=4-z$, $\phi_2=\phi_1^2-4$, $\phi_3 = \frac{1}{2} \phi_1(\phi_1^2-7)$.
The sum polynomial $\Psi_1(z)=1+\phi_1(z)$ has the single zero $z_2=5$, hence satis-
fies the condition of corollary 3.8. A perfect code Y with minimum distance 3 should satisfy :

(i) $|X|/|Y| = 5$,   i.e. $|Y| = 7$;

(ii) $\forall \, x,y \in Y, \; x \neq y$, $|x \cap y| = 1$.

Hence Y is the set of blocks of a Steiner system $S(2,3,7)$.

3.3. Q-polynomial schemes.

We consider an association scheme with n classes on X which is Q-polynomial with respect to $z_0=0,z_1,\ldots,z_n$. Thus we assume there exist, for $k=0,1,\ldots,n$, polynomials Φ_k of degree k satisfying

$$\Phi_k(z_i)=q_k(i) , \quad i=0,1,\ldots,n. \tag{3.4}$$

A nonempty subset Y of the point set X will be called a _design_ ; it will be characterized by two parameters (which are the dual concepts of minimum and external distances for a code in a metric scheme). Let $\underline{a}$ and $\underline{b}$ denote the inner and dual distributions of Y. The design Y is said to have _strength_ t if, for its dual distribution, $b_1=b_2=\ldots=b_t=0$ hold. The _maximum_ _strength_ $t(Y)$ is the largest t for which Y has strength t. The degree $s(Y)$ of Y is defined to be the number of nonzero components of its inner distribution, not counting $a_0=1$.

Lemma 3.11. The characteristic matrices of a design Y with maximum strength $t(Y)=t$ satisfy $H_i^T H_j=|Y| \Delta_{i,j}$ for $i+j \leqslant t$, where $\Delta_{i,j}$ denotes the appropriate zero matrix for $i \neq j$ and unit matrix for $i=j$.

Proof. This follows from theorem 1.7, since for a Q-polynomial scheme with strength t we have $b_1=b_2=\ldots=b_t=0$ and $q_{i,j}^k \neq 0$ only if $i+j \leqslant k$.

For a design Y with degree $s(Y)=s$, let $L= \{k \mid 1 \leqslant k \leqslant n ; a_k \neq 0\}$. The _annihilator_ _polynomial_ of Y is the polynomial

$$G_Y(z) = |Y| \prod_{k \in L} (1-z/z_k)$$

of degree s. Let us write

$$G_Y(z) = \sum_{k=0}^{s} \beta_k \, \Phi_k(z) \, , \tag{3.5}$$

where the coefficients β_k with respect to the basis $(\Phi_0,\ldots,\Phi_n)$ are uniquely determined. By definition of the annihilator polynomial and by use of (3.4), we have

$$G_Y(z_i) = \sum_{k=0}^{s} \beta_k \, q_k(i) = \begin{cases} |Y| & \text{if } i=0 \, , \\ \\ 0 & \text{if } i \in L \, . \end{cases} \tag{3.6}$$

Lemma 3.12. $\sum\limits_{k=0}^{s} \beta_k \, H_k \, H_k^T = |Y| I$.

Proof. By (1.17) we have

$$\sum_{k=0}^{s} \beta_k \, H_k \, H_k^T = \sum_{i=0}^{n} \left(\sum_{k=0}^{s} \beta_k \, q_k(i) \right) \, (D_i|Y) \, ,$$

where by (3.6) the only nonzero term in the summation with respect to i occurs for i=0. This proves the lemma.

Theorem 3.13. Let Y be a design with degree s(Y)=s and maximum strength t(Y)=t. Let $e = [\frac{1}{2} t]$. Then the following hold :

$$\sum_{i=0}^{e} \mu_i \leq |Y| \leq \sum_{i=0}^{s} \mu_i \, .$$

Proof. For an integer c let G_c denote the matrix $G_c = [H_0, H_1, \ldots, H_c]$ of order $|Y| \times (\mu_0 + \ldots + \mu_c)$; also let Δ_s denote the diagonal matrix

$$\Delta_s = \beta_0 I_0 \oplus \beta_1 I_1 \oplus \ldots \oplus \beta_s I_s$$

obtained from the coefficients of the annihilator polynomial (3.5), where I_k denotes a unit matrix of order μ_k. By lemmas 3.11 and 3.12 we have

$$G_e^T \, G_e = |Y| \, I \ , \qquad G_s \, \Delta_s \, G_s^T = |Y| \, I \ , \qquad \qquad (3.7)$$

which imply the inequalities and prove the theorem.

Lemma 3.14. Let the degree s(Y)=s and maximum strength t(Y)=t of a design Y satisfy $t \geqslant s$. Then, for the coefficients of the annihilator polynomial of Y, the following holds :

$$\beta_0 = \dots = \beta_{t-s} = 1 \ .$$

Proof. By theorem 3.13, we have $t \leqslant 2s$. Let i be any integer in the range (0,t-s). Thus $2i \leqslant t$ holds and by lemma 3.11 we have $H_i^T \, H_i = |Y| \, I$. Multiplying the two members of the equality in lemma 3.12 by H_i^T on the left and H_i on the right, we obtain

$$\sum_{k=0}^{s} \beta_k \, H_i^T \, H_k \, H_k^T \, H_i = |Y|^2 \, I \ .$$

By lemma 3.11 we have $H_i^T \, H_k = |Y| \, \Delta_{i,k}$ for k=0,...,s. It follows that $\beta_i = 1$ and the lemma is proved.

Theorem 3.14. If one of the bounds of theorem 3.13. is attained, then so is the other, the design is called tight, and its annihilator polynomial is the sum polynomial $\psi_e - \sum_{k=0}^{e} \hat{P}_k$.

Proof. Let us assume first that $|Y| = \sum_{i=0}^{e} \mu_i$. Then G_e is a square matrix and, by (3.7), we have

$$G_e \, G_e^T = \sum_{k=0}^{e} H_k \, H_k^T = |Y| \, I \ ,$$

that is, cf. (1.17),

$$\sum_{i=0}^{n} \left(\sum_{k=0}^{e} \Phi_k(z_i) \right) (D_i | Y) = |Y| \, I \ ,$$

which shows that $\Psi_e = \sum\limits_{k=0}^{e} \Phi_k$ is the annihilator polynomial of Y and

proves the first part of the theorem. Assume now that we have $|Y| = \sum\limits_{k=0}^{s} \mu_k$.

We may observe that G_s is a square matrix and form (3.7) we deduce

$G_s^T G_s = |Y| \Delta_s^{-1}$, that is,

$$H_i^T H_j = |Y| \beta_i^{-1} \Delta_{i,j} , \qquad i,j \in \{0,1,\ldots,s\} .$$

By comparing the traces of $H_k^T H_k$ and $H_k H_k^T$ we deduce $\beta_k = 1$ for $k=0,1,\ldots,$

s. Then, from lemma 1.8 it follows that we have $b_1 = b_2 = \ldots = b_{2s} = 0$, which

implies $t(Y) \geqslant 2s$, whence $t(Y)=2s$ and the theorem is proved.

Corollary 3.16. If a tight design Y with maximum strength $t(Y)=2e$ exists,

then the zeros of the sum polynomial $\Psi_e(z)$ are contained in the set

$\{z_1,\ldots,z_n\}$.

Proof. This follows from theorem 3.14 by definition of the annihilator

polynomial.

   Let Y be a design with degree $s(Y) = s$ and let L be defined as

before. Then the restriction to Y of the classes Γ_i, $i \in L$, is a parti-

tion of the set of 2-element subsets of Y. The following theorem gives

a sufficient condition for these s classes to form an association scheme

on Y.

Theorem 3.17. If the degree $s(Y)=s$ and maximum strength $t(Y)=t$ of a

design Y satisfy $t \geqslant 2s-2$, then the restriction to Y of the given scheme

is an association scheme on Y, which is Q-polynomial with respect to

$z_0=0$ and the s zeros of its annihilator polynomial.

Proof. With the hypothesis of the theorem, the matrix G_{s-1} (defined

as in theorem 3.13) is non-square and satisfies $G_{s-1}^T G_{s-1} = |Y| \ 1$ (by

lemma 3.11). Hence G_{s-1} can be completed to a square orthogonal matrix
$G = [G_{s-1}, K]$. Thus we have

$$G\ G^T = K\ K^T + \sum_{k=0}^{s-1} H_k\ H_k^T = |Y|\ I\ . \qquad (3.8)$$

From lemma 3.11 it also follows that the s+1 matrices $J_k' = |Y|^{-1}\ H_k\ H_k^T$,
k=0,...,s-1, and $J_s' = |Y|^{-1}\ K\ K^T$ are mutually orthogonal and idempotent.
Moreover we have, by (1.17),

$$J_k' = |Y|^{-1} \sum q_k(i)\ (D_i|Y)\ ,\quad k=0,\ldots,s-1, \qquad (3.9)$$

where the summation can be restricted to the s+1 indices i for which
$(D_i|Y) \neq 0$. This and (3.8) show that the (s+1)-dimensional algebra generated by these idempotent matrices is also generated by the s+1 nonzero
$(D_i|Y)$. This suffices to show that we have an association scheme with
s classes on Y. Moreover, for the elements $q_k'(i)$ of the eigenmatrix Q
of this scheme, we have by (3.9) and (3.8),

$$q_k'(i) = q_k(i) = \Phi_k(z_i),\quad k=0,\ldots,s-1;\quad i \in \{0\} \cup L\ ,$$

$$\text{and } q_s'(i) = |Y| - \sum_{k=0}^{s-1} \mu_k \quad \text{for } i = 0\ ,$$

$$-\sum_{k=0}^{s-1} q_k(i) \quad \text{for } i \in L\ .$$

Clearly there exists a polynomial Φ_s' of degree s satisfying $\Phi_s'(z_i) = q_s'(i)$,
$i \in \{0\} \cup L$. This proves the theorem.

Example 3.18. Let the graph (X, Γ_1) be defined on the set X of all n-sub-
sets of a v-set (with $v \geqslant 2n$) by $(\{x,y\} \in \Gamma_1) \Longleftrightarrow (|x \cap y| = n-1)$. This
graph is metrically regular and defines an n-classes association scheme

which is both P- and Q-polynomial (and was called by Delsarte a <u>Johnson</u> <u>scheme</u> J(n,v)). The n classes are defined, for i=1,...,n, by

$$(\{x,y\} \in \Gamma_i) \Longleftrightarrow (|x \cap y| = n-i) \;.$$

A design with maximum strength t is nothing but a <u>t-design</u> in the usual sense, i.e. a collection of n-subsets, called blocks, having the property that every t-subset is contained in a constant number of blocks. The multiplicities μ_i are given by $\mu_i = \binom{v}{i} - \binom{v}{i-1}$, i=1,...,n, so that the bounds of theorem 3.13 become

$$\binom{v}{e} \leqslant |Y| \leqslant \binom{v}{s} \quad \text{(the Wilson bounds)}$$

<u>Example 3.19</u>. Let Y be a group-code in the Hamming scheme H(n,q). Then Y (as a design) has maximum strength t(Y)=t if and only if its dual code Y' has minimum distance d(Y')=t+1. Moreover s(Y)=r(Y') (and conversely). By comparing theorems 3.7 and 3.13 one easily sees that Y is tight if and only if Y' is perfect. It is perhaps worth mentioning that a design with maximum strength t is nothing but an <u>orthogonal array</u> of strength t (in the sense of Rao). If t(Y) ⩾ 2s(Y)-2 holds for the group-code Y, the restriction to Y of the Hamming scheme is an association scheme with s classes (on the group Y) which is invariant under translations. Hence it admits a dual association scheme which can be defined on the set of cosets of Y' in X by using the isomorphism Y ≃ X|Y' .

BIBLIOGRAPHY.

[1]   Cameron, P. J. and van Lint, J. H., <u>Graph Theory</u>, <u>Coding Theory</u> and <u>Block Designs</u>, London Math. Soc. Lecture Note Series, N°19, Cam-

bridge University Press, London, 1975, Chap. 15.

[2]   Delsarte, P., "An algebraic approach to the association schemes
      of coding theory", Philips Res. Repts. Supplements, N°10, 1973.

[3]   Delsarte, P., "The association schemes of coding theory", in Com-
      binatorics, Mathematical Centre Tracts, n°55, M. Hall, Jr. and
      J. H. van Lint, Eds., Math. Centrum, Amsterdam, 1974, p. 139.

[4]   Delsarte, P. and Goethals, J.-M., "Alternating bilinear forms over
      GF(q)", J. Combinatorial Theory, Ser. A, vol. 19, pp. 26-50, 1975.

[5]   Goethals, J.-M., "Nonlinear codes defined by quadratic forms over
      GF(2)", Information and Control, Vol. 31, pp. 43-74, 1976.

[6]   MacWilliams, F.J. and Sloane, N. J. A., The Theory of Error-Correc-
      ting Codes, North-Holland Mathematical Library, Vol. 16, North-Hol-
      land, Amsterdam, 1977, Chap. 21.

[7]   Sloane, N. J. A., "An introduction to association schemes and coding
      theory", in Theory and Applications of Special Functions, R. A.
      Askey, Ed., Academic Press, New York, 1975, p.225.

Generalized quadratic-residue codes

J.H. van Lint

Department of Mathematics

Eindhoven University of Technology

I. INTRODUCTION

At the 1975 CISM Summer School on Information Theory P. Camion (cf. [1])

introduced "global quadratic abelian codes" which are a generalization of

(classical) quadratic residue codes (QR-codes). A year earlier H.N. Ward

(cf. [8]) had used symplectic geometry to introduce a generalization of

QR-codes. Both presentations rely heavily on abstract algebra. Essential-

ly such codes (at least in the binary case) were introduced by Ph. Del-

sarte in 1971 (cf. [2]) as codes generated by the adjacency matrices of

finite miquelian inversive planes. Recently J.H. van Lint and F.J. Mac-

Williams (cf. [4]) showed that the methods that are used to treat QR-codes can

easily be generalized to give a completely analogous treatment of the so-

called *generalized quadratic residue codes* (GQR-codes).

In many cases the miquelian inversive planes then appear as the supports of the words of minimum weight in GQR codes, thus providing the link with Delsarte's construction.

In these lectures we aim to present this elementary exposition of GQR-codes after a quick survey of the theory of classical QR-codes. Furthermore we shall consider some t-designs connected with QR-codes. We do not consider the question of decoding of QR-codes at all. For this we refer to the literature (e.g. [5]).

II. QUADRATIC RESIDUE CODES

Although we assume that the reader is familiar with the theory of cyclic codes (in fact even with QR-codes) we briefly mention a few facts to be used in the sequel (cf. MacWilliams and Sloane [5] or Van Lint [3]).

The isomorphism which maps a vector $\underline{a} = (a_0, a_1, \ldots, a_{n-1})$ in GF(ℓ) (where $(n, \ell) = 1$) onto $a_0 + a_1 x + \ldots + a_{n-1} x^{n-1}$ in the polynomial ring GF(ℓ)[x] mod ($x^n - 1$) associates with a cyclic (n,k)-code an ideal in this ring. This ideal is a principal ideal generated by a polynomial $g(x)$, where $g(x) \mid (x^n - 1)$. In many important examples of cyclic codes the generator $g(x)$ is specified by giving sufficiently many (or all) of the zeros of this polynomial in some extension field of the alphabet GF(ℓ). Usually the code C and the corresponding ideal are identified. If $x^n - 1 = g(x)h(x)$ then $h(x)$ is the generator for a cyclic code which is equivalent to the dual of the code with generator $g(x)$, the equivalence being established by the permutation $x \rightarrow x^{-1}$.

Every cyclic code has a unique element $e(x)$, called the idempotent, which has the properties:

i) $e(x) = e^2(x)$,

ii) $e(x)$ generates C,

iii) for all code words $f(x)$ we have $e(x)f(x) = f(x)$, i.e. $e(x)$ is a unit.

Remark: The name "idempotent" is slightly confusing because a code can contain many elements with property i). However, the properties ii) and iii) make $e(x)$ unique among the idempotent elements of the code.

To introduce QR-codes we now assume that the word length n is a prime p ($n = p$) and we make the (unnecessary) restriction that ℓ is also a prime (in fact little is known if $\ell > 3$). We also assume that ℓ is a quadratic residue mod p. Let U denote the set of nonzero squares in GF(p) and let V denote the set of nonsquares. If α is a primitive n-th root of unity in some extension field of GF(ℓ), then

$$g_0(x) := \prod_{u \in U} (x - \alpha^u) \quad \text{and} \quad g_1(x) := \prod_{v \in V} (x - \alpha^v)$$

are polynomials with coefficients in GF(ℓ) and we have

$$x^n - 1 = (x - 1)g_0(x)g_1(x) .$$

Definition 2.1. The quadratic residue codes A^+, A, B^+, B are the cyclic codes with generators $g_0(x)$, $(x - 1)g_0(x)$, and $(x - 1)g_1(x)$ respectively.

Since the permutation π_j : $GF(p) \to GF(p)$ defined by $\pi_j(k) = jk$ maps

U into V (and vice versa) when $j \in V$, we see that the codes A and B

(respectively A^+ and B^+) are equivalent. This equivalence can be realized

by taking $j = -1$ in the case $p \equiv -1 \pmod 4$. From this it follows that if

$p \equiv -1 \pmod 4$ then $A^+ = A^\perp$, $B^+ = B^\perp$. If $p \equiv 1 \pmod 4$ then $A^\perp = B^+$,

$B^\perp = A^+$. From the QR-codes we obtain the extended QR-codes of word length

$p + 1$ by adding an overall parity check bit in the following way:

Definition 2.2. The extended QR-codes A_∞ and B_∞ are defined by adding an

overall parity check bit a_∞ (resp. b_∞) to A^+ (resp. B^+) such that

i) A_∞ and B_∞ are self-dual if $p \equiv -1 \pmod 4$.

ii) $A_\infty^\perp = B_\infty$ if $p \equiv -1 \pmod 4$.

That this is possible (and how to do this) will be shown for GQR-codes in

the next section (also see [5]).

The following lemma will enable us to establish a bound for the mini-

mum distance of QR-codes.

Lemma 2.3. If $c(x) = \sum_{i=0}^{p-1} c_i x^i$ is a code word of weight d in $A^+ \backslash A$ then:

i) $d^2 \geq p$,

ii) $d^2 - d + 1 \geq p$ if $p \equiv -1 \pmod 4$.

<u>Proof.</u> Let $\hat{c}(x) = c(x^j)$ where $j \in V$. Then $\hat{c}(1) \neq 0$, $c(x)$ is a multiple of

$g_0(x)$ and $\hat{c}(x)$ is a multiple of $g_1(x)$. Therefore $c(x)\hat{c}(x)$ is a nonzero multiple of $g_0(x)g_1(x)$ which implies $c(x)\hat{c}(x) = c. (1 + x + x^2 +...+ x^{p-1})$.

On the other hand the product $c(x)\hat{c}(x)$ contains at most d^2 nonzero terms

$$cx^k = (c_a x^d).(c_d x^{bj}) .$$

This proves i). If $p \equiv -1$ (mod 4) we may take $j = -1$ and then the d

products $(c_a x^a).(c_a x^{-a})$ where $c_a \neq 0$ all contribute to the term of degree

0 in the product of $c(x)$ and $\hat{c}(x)$. This proves ii). Observe that it is'

essential in the proof to require that $c(x) \notin A$.   □

A more detailed analysis of the number of distinct values which $a + bj$

can take than we used in the proof of (2.3) ii) leads to several general-

izations of the lemma. We refer the reader to Van Lint [3] and Van Tilborg

[7].

The most important tool needed to study a QR-code is its idempotent.

Here we briefly introduce the simplest case, namely $\ell = 2$ (binary alphabet).

We define a polynomial $e(x)$ by

$$e(x) := \sum_{u \in U} x^u . \qquad\qquad (2.4)$$

Since $2 \in U$ we see that $e(x^2) = e^2(x) = e(x)$. Therefore $e(\alpha) \in GF(2)$.

It is not possible that every choice of α yields $e(\alpha) = 1$ so we may assume

that α has been chosen in such a way that $e(\alpha) = 0$. Clearly $e(\alpha^j) = 0$ for

every $j \in U$. If, on the other hand, $j \in V$ then

$$e(\alpha^j) + e(\alpha) = \sum_{u \in U} \alpha^u + \sum_{v \in V} \alpha^v = \sum_{i=1}^{p-1} \alpha^i = 1 \, , \quad \text{i.e.}$$

$e(\alpha^j) = 1$ if $j \in V$. Finally observe that

$$e(1) = \tfrac{1}{2}(p - 1) = \begin{cases} 0 & \text{if } p \equiv 1 \pmod 8 \, , \\[2mm] 1 & \text{if } p \equiv -1 \pmod 8 \end{cases}$$

(when $\ell = 2$ we must have $p \equiv \pm 1 \pmod 8$). These facts establish the follow-ing lemma.

Lemma 2.5. If α is suitably chosen in the definition of QR-codes then the polynomial $e(x)$ defined in (2.4) is the idempotent of A^+ if $p \equiv -1 \pmod 8$ and of A if $p \equiv 1 \pmod 8$.

Lemma 2.5 makes it possible to find a simple set of vectors which span A_∞. We shall consider this in detail in the next section. As an example we consider $p \equiv -1 \pmod 8$. Let C be the circulant matrix with the vector $\underline{e}$ corresponding to $e(x)$ as its first row. We border C with a row and column of 1's to obtain the matrix M. Then the rows of M clearly span A_∞. The positions $0, 1, \ldots, p-1, \infty$ which we have used to number the coordinates for A correspond to points of the projective line of order p. We now con-sider the permutations $x \to (ax + b)/(cx + d)$ with a, b, c, d in $GF(p)$ and $ad - bc = 1$, acting on the coordinate places. It is not difficult to show that each such permutation sends a row of M into a linear combination of at most three rows of M (cf. [3]).

In fact it is sufficient to show this for the permutations x → x + 1 (trivial since the code is cyclic) and x → -1/x. This establishes the following theorem.

Theorem 2.6. A_∞ is invariant under the group PSL(2,p) acting on the positions.

We then have the following consequence.

Theorem 2.7. For the binary QR-code A^+ the minimum weight is an odd number d satisfying

i) $d^2 > p$ if $p \equiv 1 \pmod{8}$,

ii) $d^2 - d + 1 \geq p$ if $p \equiv -1 \pmod{8}$.

<u>Proof</u>. Since PSL(2,p) is doubly transitive on the positions there are words of minimum weight in A_∞ with a 1 in position ∞. Therefore the minimum weight in A^+ is odd and the result now follows from lemma 2.3.   □

This theorem and slight extensions mentioned earlier have made it possible to determine the minimum distance of binary QR-codes of length p for all primes $p \equiv \pm 1 \pmod 8$ with $p \leq 103$ (cf. [5]). For small p the binary QR-codes are all extremely good codes. This requires some explanation. Again we consider only $p \equiv -1 \pmod 8$. Then every row of the matrix M introduced above has weight divisible by 4. Therefore this also holds for the code A which is self-dual by (2.2) i). It was shown by

C.L. Mallows and N.J.A. Sloane (cf. [5]) that a binary self-dual code of

length n, for which all weights are divisible by 4, has minimum distance

d satisfying

$$d \leq 4[n/24] + 4$$

and furthermore that equality can hold for small n only. The extended QR-

codes corresponding to p = 7,23,31,47 all meet this bound. For p = 71 no

code is known which meets the bound; the QR-code has d = 12, i.e. it is

the best known code for these parameters. It is clear that if the bound of

theorem 2.7 is near to the true minimum distance, then for large p the

QR-codes are bad codes. The behaviour of d for QR-codes with large p is

still a completely open problem.

III. GENERALIZED QUADRATIC RESIDUE CODES

In this section we consider linear codes of length q where q now is

a prime power: $q = p^m$. The restrictions on the alphabet $\mathbb{F} = GF(\ell)$ will

be described later. In order to describe these codes we consider the

additive group G of the field $GF(q)$. We remind the reader that the group

algebra $\mathbb{F}G$ is the ring $(\mathbb{F}G, \oplus, \star)$ consisting of formal sums, written as

$$\sum_{g \in G} a_g g \qquad (a_g \in \mathbb{F})$$

with the following rules for addition and multiplication

$$\left(\sum_{g\in G} a_g g\right) + \left(\sum_{g\in G} b_g g\right) := \sum_{g\in G} (a_g + b_g)g \; , \tag{3.1}$$

$$\left(\sum_{g\in G} a_g g\right) \star \left(\sum_{g\in G} b_g g\right) := \sum_{g\in G} \left(\sum_{g_1+g_2=g} a_{g_1} b_{g_2}\right)g \; . \tag{3.2}$$

The elements of G are used to number the positions of a code and a code word $\underline{a} = (a_0, a_1, \ldots)$ is identified with the element $\sum_{g\in G} a_g g$ of $\mathbb{F}G$. A subset S of G is identified with the element $\sum_{g\in G} a_g g$ with $a_g = 1$ if $g \in S$, $a_g = 0$ if $g \notin S$. We define the elements U,V,O of $\mathbb{F}G$ as the elements corresponding to the subset U of nonzero squares in G, the subset V of nonsquares in G, and the set O := {0}. The inner product of two vectors $\underline{c}$ and $\underline{c}'$ is denoted by $<\underline{c}.\underline{c}'>$.

In order to define the GQR-codes we need a special representation of the character group G^* of G. Let ξ be a primitive p-th root of unity in some extension field $\hat{\mathbb{F}}$ of $\mathbb{F}$ and let α be a primitive element of GF(q). If $g = i_0 + i_1\alpha + \ldots + i_{m-1}\alpha^{m-1} \in GF(q)$, $(i_s \in GF(q))$, we define $\psi_1 : G \to \hat{\mathbb{F}}$ by

$$\psi_1(g) := \xi^{i_0} \; .$$

Furthermore we define for each $h \in G$

$$\psi_h(g) := \psi_1(gh) \; .$$

Remark: Usually the characters of a group G are defined to be mappings from G into $\mathbb{C}$. Here we have replaced $\mathbb{C}$ by $\hat{\mathbb{F}}$. This does not alter the theory which we review below.

The mapping $h \leftrightarrow \psi_h$ is an isomorphism between G and G^*. It is well known that

$$\sum_{g \in G} \psi_f(g) = \begin{cases} q & \text{if } f = 0 , \\ 0 & \text{if } f \neq 0 . \end{cases} \tag{3.3}$$

A character ψ_f on G is extended to a linear functional on $\mathbb{F}G$ by

$$\psi_f(\sum_{g \in G} \alpha_g g) := \sum_{g \in G} \alpha_g \psi_f(g) . \tag{3.4}$$

In fact ψ_f is a homomorphism of the ring $\mathbb{F}G$ into $\hat{\mathbb{F}}$. We shall often use this and also the fact that two elements c and c' of $\mathbb{F}G$ for which $\psi_f(c) = \psi_f(c')$ for every f are the same, i.e. c = c'.

We are now in a position to define the GQR-codes A^+ and B^+.

Definition 3.5.

i) A^+ consists of all $\underline{c} = \sum_{g \in G} c_g g$ for which $\psi_u(\underline{c}) = 0$ for all $u \in U$.

ii) B^+ is defined in the same way, replacing U by V.

iii) A and B have the additional requirement that $\psi_0(\underline{c}) = 0$.

It is clear that A^+ and B^+ are linear codes of dimension $\frac{1}{2}(q + 1)$. If $m = 1$, i.e. $q = p$, this definition coincides with (2.1). If $v \in V$ then the permutation of coordinate positions given by $g \to vg$ maps A^+ into B^+, i.e. these codes are equivalent.

Since $\mathbb{F}G$ is a semisimple algebra the ideals A^+ and B^+ are principal ideals, generated by idempotents E_A, E_B, $(E_A * E_A = E_A)$.

Lemma 3.6. Let the constants c_0, c_1 be defined by

i) $c_0 := \frac{1}{2}(-1 - \sqrt{q})$, $c_1 := \frac{1}{2}(-1 + \sqrt{q})$ if $-1 \in U$,

ii) $c_0 := \frac{1}{2}(-1 - \sqrt{-q})$, $c_1 := \frac{1}{2}(-1 + \sqrt{-q})$ if $-1 \in V$.

Then (if ξ is suitably chosen)

$$\psi_u(U) = c_0, \ \psi_u(V) = c_1 \qquad \text{for all} \ \ u \in U ,$$

$$\psi_v(U) = c_1, \ \psi_v(V) = c_0 \qquad \text{for all} \ \ v \in V .$$

Proof. If $u \in U$ then

$$\psi_u(U) = \sum_{g \in U} \psi_1(ug) = \sum_{h \in U} \psi_1(h) = \psi_1(U) .$$

This shows that $\psi_u(U)$ is a constant which we denote by c_0.

The other cases are proved in the same way. The value of c_0 and c_1 depends on the choice of ξ in the definition of ψ_1. Let $n \in V$. Then

$$\sum_{\psi \in G^*} \psi(U) \psi(-n) = \sum_{\psi \in G^*} \sum_{u \in U} \psi(u - n) = 0$$

by (3.3). On the other hand

$$\sum_{\psi \in G^*} \psi(U)\psi(-n) = \psi_0(U)\psi_0(-n) + \sum_{u \in U} \psi_u(U)\psi_u(-n) + \sum_{v \in V} \psi_v(U)\psi_v(-n) =$$

$$= (q - 1)/2 + c_0 \sum_{u \in U} \psi_1(-un) + c_1 \sum_{v \in V} \psi_1(-vn) =$$

$$= \begin{cases} (q - 1)/2 + 2c_0c_1 & \text{if } -1 \in U , \\ \\ (q - 1)/2 + c_0^2 + c_1^2 & \text{if } -1 \in V . \end{cases}$$

Furthermore, we have from

$$\psi_1(0 \oplus U \oplus V) = \sum_{g \in G} \psi_1(g) = 0$$

that $1 + c_0 + c_1 = 0$. So c_0 and c_1 are roots of a quadratic equation. The values stated in the lemma are the solutions of this equation.   □

Lemma 3.7. The idempotents of the GQR-codes are given by

$$qE_A = \begin{cases} \tfrac{1}{2}(q + 1)0 \oplus -c_0U \oplus -c_1V & \text{if } -1 \in U , \\ \\ \tfrac{1}{2}(q + 1)0 \oplus -c_1U \oplus -c_0V & \text{if } -1 \in V . \end{cases}$$

The idempotent qE_B is obtained by interchanging c_0 and c_1.

Proof. We prove only the first case (the others are similar). By lemma 3.6
we have, for the element E_A defined above, $\psi_0(E_A) = 1$, $\psi_u(E_A) = 0$ for
$u \in U$, $\psi_v(E_A) = 1$ for $v \in V$. Thus $\psi_g(E_A) = 0$ or 1 for all $g \in G$, which
shows that E_A is idempotent. Since E_A has the same zeros as the idempotent
of A^+ it must be equal to this idempotent.   □

The last two lemmas show us which conditions we have to put on our
alphabet $\mathbb{F} = GF(\ell)$. Clearly we must have $(q, \ell) = 1$. For the idempotents
to be code words the constants c_0 and c_1 have to be elements of $\mathbb{F}$. If q
is a square this is always so. If $q = p^m$ with m odd we must require that
$\sqrt{p} \in GF(\ell)$ if $p \equiv 1 \pmod 4$ and that $\sqrt{-p} \in GF(\ell)$ if $p \equiv -1 \pmod 4$.

Example 3.8. Let $q = 3^3$ and $\ell = 7$. Then we find $\sqrt{-q} = \pm 1$. The choice in
(3.6) ii) depends on ξ. We may take $\sqrt{-q} = -1$. Then $c_0 = 0$, $c_1 = -1$ and
$E_A = -U$.

With the aid of the idempotent E_A (which generates A^+) we can now
construct a matrix M (generalizing the construction following (2.5)) such
that the rows of M span A^+. The rows and columns of M are labeled by the
elements $0, 1, \alpha, \ldots, \alpha^{q-2}$ of $GF(q)$. The first row of A is the code word qE_A.
The other rows are obtained by the action of G, i.e. the entry in place
(α^i, α^j) is the coordinate of qE_A in place $\alpha^j - \alpha^i$. The rank of M is $\frac{1}{2}(q + 1)$.

Example 3.9. We construct the GQR-code of length 9 over an arbitrary field
$\mathbb{F}$ (with characteristic $\neq 3$). By (3.6) i) we have $c_0 = -2$, $c_1 = 1$. Let

$GF'(9)$ be generated by a primitive element α with $\alpha^2 = 1 - \alpha$. Then we find for M:

		0	1	α	α^2	α^3	α^4	α^5	α^6	α^7
(00) = 0		5	2	-1	2	-1	2	-1	2	-1
(10) = 1		2	5	2	-1	2	2	-1	-1	-1
(01) = α		-1	2	5	-1	2	-1	-1	2	2
(12) = α^2		2	-1	-1	5	2	-1	2	2	-1
(22) = α^3		-1	2	2	2	5	-1	2	-1	-1
(20) = α^4		2	2	-1	-1	-1	5	2	-1	2
(02) = α^5		-1	-1	-1	2	2	2	5	-1	2
(21) = α^6		2	-1	2	2	-1	-1	-1	5	2
(11) = α^7		-1	-1	2	-1	-1	2	2	2	5

We now show that extended GQR-codes A_∞, B_∞ can be defined in the manner announced in (2.2).

Definition 3.10. We define the extended codes A_∞, B_∞ by adding a "parity check" bit c_∞ to each code word $\underline{c} = \sum_{g \in G} c_g g$ of A^+ (resp. B^+) where:

i) $c_\infty := \dfrac{\sqrt{-q}}{q} \sum_{g \in G} c_g$ if $-1 \in V$,

ii) $c_\infty := \begin{cases} \dfrac{\sqrt{q}}{q} \sum\limits_{g \in G} c_g & \text{if } c \in A^+ \text{ and } -1 \in U , \\[2mm] -\dfrac{\sqrt{q}}{q} \sum\limits_{g \in G} c_g & \text{if } c \in B^+ \text{ and } -1 \in U . \end{cases}$

Lemma 3.11. If $-1 \in V$ then A_∞ and B_∞ are self-dual; if $-1 \in U$ then $A_\infty = B_\infty^\perp$.

<u>Proof</u>. First we observe that the element $I := q^{-1}(0 \oplus U \oplus V)$ is characterized by the property that $\psi_0(I) = 1$ and $\psi_h(I) = 0$ for all $h \neq 0$. Now assume $-1 \in V$. Let $\underline{c} = (\sum_{g \in G} c_g g, c_\infty)$ and $\underline{c}' = (\sum_{g \in G} c'_g g, c'_\infty)$ be two code words of A_∞. For all $v \in V$ we have

$$\psi_v \left(\sum_{g \in G} c'_g(-g) \right) = \psi_{-v} \left(\sum_{g \in G} c'_g g \right) = 0 \; .$$

Hence

$$\psi_h \left(\sum_{g \in G} c_g g \; * \; \sum_{g \in G} c'_g(-g) \right) = 0 \qquad \text{for all } h \neq 0 \; .$$

Furthermore

$$\psi_0 \left(\sum_{g \in G} c_g g \; * \; \sum_{g \in G} c'_g(-g) \right) = (\Sigma c_g)(\Sigma c'_g) = -q c_\infty c'_\infty \; .$$

Hence

$$\sum_{g \in G} c_g g \; * \; \sum_{g \in G} c'_g(-g) = -q c_\infty c'_\infty I \; .$$

Therefore

$$\sum_{g \in G} c_g c'_g = -c_\infty c'_\infty \; , \text{ i.e. } <\underline{c}.\underline{c}'> = 0 \; .$$

This proves that A_∞ is self-dual. The second statement is proved in a similar way.   □

We now prove a generalization of theorem 2.6. We shall show that A_∞
and B_∞ are invariant under a group of monomial transformations for which
the underlying group of permutations (of coordinate positions) is $PSL(2,q)$.
This group is generated by the following transformations:

T_1: the additive group of $GF(q)$, i.e. G,

T_2: $i \to ui$ where $u \in U$,

T_3: $i \to -1/i$.

By construction of A_∞ and B_∞ the transformations of T_1 and T_2 leave
the code invariant. So it suffices to find a monomial transformation τ
for which the underlying permutation is T_3 which preserves A_∞. We consider the case $-1 \in V$ and only look at A_∞. The other cases are similar.
We define τ as follows: multiply the coordinates in the positions of
$V \cup \{\infty\}$ by -1 and then apply T_3. We consider the matrix M defined after
(3.8) and add a column ∞ corresponding to the parity check. The elements
in this column are all $\sqrt{-q}$. Call the new matrix M_∞.

a) The first row of M_∞ is mapped by τ into

$$(-\sqrt{-q} \ 0 \oplus c_0 U \oplus -c_1 V, \ \tfrac{1}{2}(q + 1)) \ .$$

For any $u \in U$

$$\psi_u(-\sqrt{-q} \ 0 \oplus c_0 U \oplus -c_1 V) = -\sqrt{-q} + c_0^2 - c_1^2 = 0$$

by lemma 3.6. The coordinate $2(q + 1)$ is in accordance with the rule (3.10)
i). Therefore the image of the first row of M_∞ is in A_∞.

b) Let s be a square in GF(q) and let r_{-s} be a row of M corresponding to s. Then r_{-s} has coordinate $-c_0$ in position 0 (because $-s \in V$), $\frac{1}{2}(q + 1)$ in position s, $-c_1$ in position $u + s$ for all $u \in U$, $-c_0$ in position $v + s$ for all $v \in V$, and finally $\sqrt{-q}$ in position ∞. From this we find the coordinates of the permuted row $(r_{-s})^{\tau}$:

position	coordinate of row $(r_{-s})^{\tau}$
0	$-\sqrt{-q}$
-1/s	$\frac{1}{2}(q + 1)$
-1/(u + s)	$-c_1$ if $u + s \in U$
	c_1 if $u + s \in V$
-1/(v + s)	$-c_0$ if $v + s \in U$
	c_0 if $v + s \in V$
∞	$-c_0$

We compare this with the entries in row r' which has label -1/s.

position	coordinate of row r'
0	$-c_1$
-1/s	$\frac{1}{2}(q + 1)$
u - 1/s ($u \in U$)	$-c_1$
v - 1/s ($v \in V$)	$-c_0$
∞	$\sqrt{-q}$

We now determine $X = (r_{-s})^{\tau} - r'$. Clearly position -1/s has a 0 (remark that $-1/s \in V$). Let $u + s \in U$. Then $\dfrac{u}{s(u + s)} = \dfrac{1}{s} - \dfrac{1}{u + s} \in U$, i.e.

$-\dfrac{1}{u+s} = u' - 1/s$ for some $u' \in U$. Therefore in this case $\underline{X}$ has a 0 in

position $-1/(u+s)$, which is in V. In exactly the same way we see that $\underline{X}$

has coordinate $c_0 + c_1 = -1$ in position $-1/(u+s)$ if $u + s \in V$. The

positions $-1/(v+s)$ are treated analogously. The result is that

$\underline{X} = (c_0 0 \oplus -U, -c_1)$. Since $\psi_u(c_0 0 \oplus -U) = 0$ for all $u \in U$ and since the

entry $-c_1$ in position ∞ is in accordance with (3.10) i) we see that $\underline{X} \in A_\infty$

and hence $(\underline{r}_s)^\tau \in A$. A row $\underline{r}_t$ where $t \in V$ is treated in the same way. We

omit the details.

We have therefore proved the following theorem.

Theorem 3.12. The codes A_∞ and B_∞ are invariant under a group of monomial

transformations for which the underlying group of permutations is PSL$(2,q)$.

Corollary 3.13. The minimum weight of A_∞ is one more than the minimum

weight of A^+.

<u>Proof.</u> PSL$(2,q)$ is transitive on the positions. Hence A_∞ has words of mini-

mal weight with $c_\infty \neq 0$.   □

We are now in a position to generalize theorem 2.7.

Theorem 3.14. Let A^+ be the GQR-code of length $q = p^m$ over some field $\mathbf{F}$.

Let d be the minimum distance of A^+. Then

i) $d^2 \geq q$,

ii) $d^2 - d + 1 \geq q$ if $-1 \in V$,

iii) $d^2 = q$ if m is even.

<u>Proof.</u> Let $\underline{c} = \sum\limits_{g \in G} c_g g$ be a code word of minimum weight d in A^+. Let $n \in V$.

Define $\underline{c}' = \sum\limits_{g \in G} c_g ng$. Then $\underline{c}'$ is a word of weight d in B^+. By (3.13) we

have $\psi_0(\underline{c}) = \sum\limits_{g \in G} c_g \neq 0$ and in the same way $\psi_0(\underline{c}') \neq 0$ and therefore

$\psi_0(\underline{c} \star \underline{c}') \neq 0$. However $\psi_h(\underline{c} \star \underline{c}') = 0$ for all $h \neq 0$. This implies that

$\underline{c} \star \underline{c}'$ is a non-zero multiple of $0 \oplus U \oplus V$. The rest of the proof of i)

and ii) is exactly the same as in (2.7). Now let $m = 2t$. Define $K := GF(p^t)$

and $U_i := \{\alpha^{2i} k \mid k \in K^*\}$ for $i = 0, 1, \ldots, \frac{1}{2}(p^t - 1)$; (then $K^* = U_0$). Since all

the elements of K^* are squares in $GF(q)$ we see that $U = \sum\limits_i U_i$. For any

$u \in U$ we have

$$\psi_u(U_i) = \sum\limits_{g \in K^*} \psi_u(\alpha^{2i} g) = \sum\limits_{g \in K^*} \psi_{\alpha^{2i} u}(g) .$$

This is the sum of the values of a character over all nonzero elements of

a field. Hence it is -1 or $|K| - 1 = p^t - 1$. But

$$\sum\limits_i \psi_u(U_i) = \psi_u(U) = c_0 = \frac{1}{2}(-1 - p^t) .$$

This is possible only if $\psi_u(U_i) = -1$ for all values of i. It follows that

$$\psi_u(\sum\limits_{g \in K} g) = 1 + \psi_u(K) = 0, \quad \text{i.e.} \quad \sum\limits_{g \in K} g \in A^+ .$$

This proves iii).   □

In this section we have completely generalized the theory presented in

section 2. We mentioned there that it is not known whether QR-codes of

large length are good. This is also true for GQR-codes of length $q = p^m$

where m is odd. Theorem 3.14 iii) shows that GQR-codes are bad if $q = p^m$,

m even. Nevertheless they have interesting combinatorial properties as we

shall see in the next section.

IV. GQR-CODES AND t-DESIGNS

The most famous of all QR-codes is the Golay-code, i.e. the binary QR-

code of length 23. By (2.7) ii) this code has minimum distance 7. Since

$2^{12} \cdot \sum_{i=0}^{3} \binom{23}{i} = 2^{23}$ this code is perfect. Let us consider a list A of the

code words of weight 8 in the extended code G_{24}. The fact that the Golay

code is perfect determines its weight enumerator. Hence we know that the

list is a 759 by 24 (0,1)-matrix in which every row has sum 8 and no two

rows overlap in more than four positions. Therefore the rows cover $759\binom{8}{5}$

distinct fivetuples. This number is exactly $\binom{24}{5}$. Hence A is the incidence

matrix of a 5-design. This design is the famous Steiner system S(5,8,24).

We remark that this property is used in some of the decoding procedures

of the Golay code. Since 5-designs are hard to construct (and not too

long ago only a few were known) it is not surprising that one tried to

find others using QR-codes and certain generalizations such as the

symmetry codes (cf. [5]). For QR-codes with large minimum distance this

has led to several new 5-designs. We mention the cases q = 47, ℓ = 2 and

q = 11,23,47, and 59 with ℓ = 3. In each of these cases the supports of the code words of some suitable fixed weight produced the 5-design.

We now consider some other connections between GQR-codes and design theory. We aim to show a connection between extended GQR-codes of length $p^2 + 1$ (p prime) and certain 3-designs known as inversive planes. An inversive plane is a 3-design with parameters $(n^2 + 1, n + 1, 1)$, i.e. an extension of an affine plane. The so-called miquelian inversive planes are constructed as follows.

Consider the projective line of order q^2, i.e. $GF(q^2) \cup \{\infty\}$. Take the subset $GF(q) \cup \{\infty\}$ and let the group $PGL(2,q^2)$ act on this set. This produces the 3-design. From theorem 3.12 and the proof of theorem 3.14 iii) the reader should already expect a connection with GQR-codes. We shall show that the miquelian plane consists of the supoorts of code words of minimal weight in $A_\infty \cup B_\infty$. To do this it is clearly sufficient to consider A_∞ only and to find all code words of minimal weight with a 1 in some fixed position, say ∞.

Let A_∞, B_∞ be the extended GQR-codes of length $p^2 + 1$, let $K := GF(p)$ and let $\underline{c} := \sum_{g \in K} g$ be the code word of minimal weight defined in the proof of theorem 3.14. We are in the case that $A_\infty^\perp = B_\infty$. From theorem 3.12 we know that for $\underline{u} \in U$ and $b \in GF(p^2)$ the vector $(\sum_{g \in uK+b} g, 1)$, is in A_∞ and similarly $(\sum_{g \in vK+b} g, -1)$ is in B_∞ if $v \in V$. From the definition of a miquelian plane we then see that we must show that these words are the only words of minimal weight in A_∞ with a 1 in position ∞. For this purpose we need some lemmas.

Lemma 4.1. Let $\underline{a} := \sum\limits_{g \in G} a_g g$ be a code word of weight p in A^+ such that $(\underline{a}, 1) \in A_\infty$. Then $a_g = 0$ or 1 for all $g \in G$.

Proof. The vector $(\underline{a}, 1)$ is orthogonal to each vector $(\sum\limits_{g \in vK+b} g, -1)$ since these are in B. It is easy to see that for a fixed v there are p choices for b such that no two of the vectors $(\sum\limits_{g \in vK+b} g, -1)$ have a non-zero coordinate in the same position, except in position ∞. Therefore for each of these there is exactly one a_g which is 1, accounting for the inner product 0.

Lemma 4.2. Let $\underline{a}$ be as in lemma 4.1. Let $a_0 = 1$. Then $a_g = 1$ implies that g is a square in $GF(p^2)$.

Proof. Consider the vector in B_∞ corresponding to the idempotent E_B. This is $p^{-2}(\frac{1}{2}(p^2 + 1)0 \oplus -c_1 U \oplus -c_0 V, -p)$. This vector is orthogonal to $(\underline{a}, 1)$. Let $\underline{a}$ have $a_g = 1$ for s values of g in U and $t = p - 1 - s$ values of g in V. Apparently

$$\tfrac{1}{2}(p^2 + 1) - sc_1 - tc_0 - p = 0 ,$$

i.e. $s = p - 1$. This proves the lemma.   □

Lemma 4.3. If $\underline{a}$ is a code word of weight p in A^+ with $a_0 = 1$ then $\underline{a} = \sum\limits_{g \in uK} g$ for some $u \in U$.

Proof. By lemmas 4.1 and 4.2 we have $\underline{a} = 0 \oplus \sum\limits_{i=1}^{p-1} u_i$ where each $u_i \in U$. By translating we obtain the vectors

$$\underline{a}^{(j)} := -u_j \oplus \sum_{i=1}^{p-1} (u_i - u_j)$$

which are also in A^+. Now lemma 4.2 implies that the set

$U_0 := \{0, u_1, u_2, \ldots, u_{p-1}\}$ has the property that the difference of any two

distinct elements of U_0 is in U. Let $v \in V$. Define $V_0 := \{vx \mid x \in U_0\}$.

Suppose that $u_i + vu_j = u_s + vu_t$. Then $u_i - u_s = v(u_t - u_j)$. Since $u_i - u_s$

and $u_t - u_j$ are squares if $i \neq s$, $t \neq j$ we see that $i = s$, $t = j$. This

implies that the set

$$U_0 + V_0 = \{x + y \mid x \in U_0, y \in V_0\}$$

has exactly p^2 elements, i.e. $U_0 + V_0 = GF(p^2)$. It is known (cf. A.D.

Sands [6]) that an abelian group of type (p,p) can be written as $U_0 + V_0$

only if one of U_0, V_0 has the property $X + \lambda = X$ for some λ. This implies

that U_0 is periodic, i.e. $U_0 = \{0, u, 2u, \ldots, (p-1)u\}$. This proves the

lemma. $\square$

Theorem 4.4. Let A_∞, B_∞ be the extended GQR-codes of length $p^2 + 1$ over

GF(ℓ). Each of these codes contains $\frac{1}{2}p(p^2 + 1)(\ell - 1)$ code words of mini-

mum weight $p + 1$. The $p(p^2 + 1)$ supports of these code words form the

miquelian plane $3 - (p^2 + 1, p + 1, 1)$.

<u>Proof</u>. The theorem follows immediately from lemma 4.3 by counting arguments.

We use the fact that PSL($2, p^2$) is 2-transitive. $\square$

Remark. We do not know whether theorem 4.4 is also true if we replace p
by a power of p.

Example 4.5. We consider the GQR-code defined in example 3.9. We reorder
the rows and columns as follows: $0,1,\alpha^2,\alpha^4,\alpha^6,\alpha,\alpha^3,\alpha^5,\alpha^7$. Then we add the
parity check column to obtain the matrix M_∞. The first five rows of this
matrix are

$$
\begin{pmatrix}
5 & 2 & 2 & 2 & 2 & -1 & -1 & -1 & -1 & 3 \\
2 & 5 & -1 & 2 & -1 & 2 & 2 & -1 & -1 & 3 \\
2 & -1 & 5 & -1 & 2 & -1 & 2 & 2 & -1 & 3 \\
2 & 2 & -1 & 5 & -1 & -1 & -1 & 2 & 2 & 3 \\
2 & -1 & 2 & -1 & 5 & 2 & -1 & -1 & 2 & 3
\end{pmatrix}
$$

Since the first five columns of this matrix are independent we can obtain
a generator matrix of the code of the form $(I_5 C)$. We find

$$
C = \begin{pmatrix}
-1 & -1 & -1 & -1 & -1 \\
1 & 1 & 0 & 0 & 1 \\
0 & 1 & 1 & 0 & 1 \\
0 & 0 & 1 & 1 & 1 \\
1 & 0 & 0 & 1 & 1
\end{pmatrix} .
$$

It is then easily established by hand that the GQR-code has fifteen codewords of weight 4 with all non-zero coordinates equal to 1 (independent of
F) . These words and the corresponding fifteen words of the dual code form
the thirty blocks of the miquelian plane 3-(10,4,1), the extension of the

affine plane of order 3.

The connection with the codes defined by Delsarte (cf. [2]) is as
follows. The construction of the inversive plane defined above yields two
subdesigns (taking $PSL(2,p^2)$ instead of $PGL(2,p^2)$). We have already seen
that these correspond to the words of minimal weight in A_∞ resp. B_∞. The
codes are defined by the mod 2 span of the rows of these subdesigns. Our
treatment shows that the alphabet is irrelevant.

As a final result we consider the case $-1 \in V$.

Theorem 4.6. Let A_∞ be the extended GQR-code of length $q + 1$ and suppose
-1 is not a square in $GF(q)$. Then the supports of the words of minimum
weight in A_∞ form a 3-design.

Proof. If $-1 \in V$ then $PSL(2,q)$ is 3-homogeneous. Hence the result follows
immediately from theorem 3.12.   ☐

Example 4.7. We consider once again the GQR-code of example 3.8. By computer search it was shown that the extended code has minimum distance 9.
There turn out to be 1092 supports of code words of weight 9. Now, by
divisibility conditions one easily sees that a $3 - (28,9,\lambda)$ has $\lambda \equiv 0$
(mod 28) and therefore at least 1092 blocks. Hence, the smallest possible
design for $v = 28$, $k = 9$ is provided by the words of minimum weight in
this extended GQR-code.

REFERENCES

1. Camion, P., *Global Quadratic Abelian Codes,* in Information Theory,
    CISM Courses and Lectures <u>219</u>, G. Longo, ed., Springer-Verlag, Wien
    1975.

2. Delsarte, P., *Majority Logic Decodable Codes Derived from Finite Inver-*
    sive Planes, Inf. and Control <u>18</u>, 1971, 319-325.

3. van Lint, J.H., *Coding Theory,* Lecture Notes in Math. <u>201</u>, Springer-
    Verlag, Berlin, 1971.

4. van Lint, J.H. and F.J. MacWilliams, *Generalized Quadratic Residue*
    Codes, IEEE Trans. on Information Theory <u>24</u> (1978).

5. MacWilliams, F.J. and N.J.A. Sloane, *The Theory of Error-Correcting*
    Codes, North-Holland, Amsterdam, 1977.

6. Sands, A.D., *On the Factorization of Finite Abelian Groups,* Acta Math.
    Acad. Sci. Hung. <u>13</u>, 1962, 153-159.

7. van Tilborg, H.C.A., *On Weights in Codes,* Report 71-WSK-03, Dept. of
    Mathematics, Technological University Eindhoven, 1971.

8. Ward, H.N., *Quadratic Residue Codes and Symplectic Groups,* J. of
    Algebra <u>29</u>, 1974, 150-171.

SOFT DECISION DETECTION TECHNIQUES

P. G. Farrell
Electronics Laboratories,
The University, Canterbury, Kent, CT2 7NT,
England.

1.   Probabilistic Decoding

It is well known that an optimum method of detection (demodulation
and decoding), for a data transmission system with channel (error-
correction) coding, is coherent correlation detection (or matched
filtering) of the sequence of signal elements corresponding to the block
length, in the case of a block code, or to the decoder search length,
in the case of a convolutional code (see fig. 1(a)). In practice,
unless the block or search length (and therefore the constraint length)
is very short, this ideal detector is too complex to realise, because
of the difficulty of generating, storing and correlating the large
number of analogue signal elements required. Thus most practical
detectors consist of an analogue demodulator, possibly coherent, operating
on individual signal elements, followed by a purely digital decoder

operating on blocks of the digits produced by the "hard" decisions of the
demodulator (see fig. 1(b)). However, some of the information which would
be lost by only correlating over a signal element can be used to assist
and improve the decoding process, and vice-versa. Additional information
can be fed forward from the demodulator to improve operation of the decoder,
or fed back from the decoder to improve operation of the demodulator
(see fig. 1(c)). The advantage of these forms of partially combined
demodulation and decoding (or inter-active demodulation and decoding) is
that they are much less complex to implement than fully combined forms
of demodulation and decoding such as coherent correlation detection or
matched filter detection. In addition, under certain circumstances the
performance of some inter-active demodulation and decoding methods (or
probabilistic decoding methods, as they were collectively called)[54]
is asymptotically close to that of ideal detection[15,29].

Null-zone, or forced erasure detection, or failure correction
decoding[3,6,21,22,23,28,30,34,39,40,51] are all ways of implementing
feedforward between the demodulator and the decoder: processed signal
elements with values lying near the threshold level of the demodulator,
and thus of doubtful worth, are passed forward to the demodulator labelled
as erasures. The decoder now has some knowledge of where errors are
likely to be in the block, and can decode accordingly. In this way the
error-correcting power of a code can be approximately doubled (a code
with Hamming distance d can correct d-1 errors in a block transmitted
over a binary erasure channel, but only $\lfloor (d-1)/2 \rfloor$ on a BSC, where
$\lfloor x \rfloor$ is the largest integer $\leq x$). Feedback from the decoder could be
used to adaptively adjust demodulator thresholds levels, for example.[47]

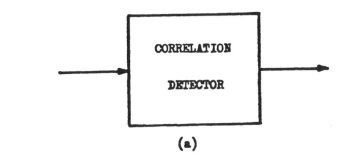

(a)

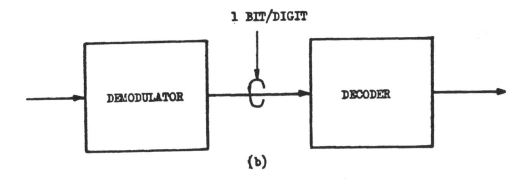

1 BIT/DIGIT

(b)

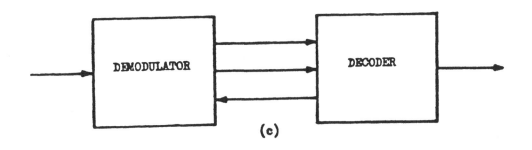

(c)

Fig. 1 : Detectors, Demodulators and Decoders

In a binary symmetric system, if errors seem to occur more often in ones than in zeros, then the threshold could be altered to restore symmetry (i.e., approximately equal numbers of one and zero errors).

Null-zone detection can be extended to double-null-zone detection with an improvement in performance[4], and can be generalised to more than two "null-zones", though with gradually diminishing rise in performance as the number of zones is increased. This general form of null-zone detection is called soft-decision decoding.[5,9,16,19,42,43,45] Thus, strictly speaking, soft-decision decoding is a type of probabilistic decoding. Because of its importance, however, the term "soft-decision" has come to replace the word "probabilistic", which has fallen into disuse. Thus soft-decision decoding not only refers to the particular method, but also has come to mean the whole field of decoding with confidence (reliability) information. This is fortunate in a way, because the term probabilistic deocding has also been applied to sequential decoding of convolutional codes.[10] Work in the field of soft-decision (probabilistic) decoding was initiated by Balser and Silverman[1], and some of the early work in this field is summarised by Schwartz.[38]

2.   Soft-Decision Decoding

Instead of making a hard decision, on each binary signal received, a soft-decision demodulator first of all decides whether it is above or below the decision threshold, and then computes a "confidence" number which specifies how far from the decision threshold the demodulator output is. This number could in theory be an analogue quantity, but in practice, if it is to be useful it must be quantised. Thus the output of the demodulator is still quantised, but into many more than the two regions of a hard-decision device.

An example of an 8-region device is given in figure 2. In this case the input to the demodulator is a binary signal, and the signal space is quantised into eight regions, deliniated by one decision threshold and three pairs of confidence thresholds. Each input signal is thus demodulated into an output character consisting of one binary hard decision digit and two binary confidence digits. In general, each binary signal is demodulated into a character consisting of $\log_2 Q$ binary digits (see figure 3) at the output of the demodulator, if there are Q regions in the quantised output signal space (normally Q is a power of 2). A binary code word of n digits is thus represented by $\log_2 Q = r$, say, binary code words, each of n digits. One of these consists of the (hard) decision digits, the others consist of the confidence digits of appropriate weighting. If the signal falls in a region of complete confidence, then the confidence digits of the corresponding output character are all ONES. The soft-decision-distance, d_s, between an output character and each of the two highest confidence output characters is then the Euclidean distance between the output character and each of the highest confidence characters; the distance between characters corresponding to adjacent regions being unity. Thus, for example, if a signal is demodulated as 0 0 0, then the soft-decision distances to 1 1 1 and 0 1 1 are respectively 4 and 3 (see figure 2). A convenient

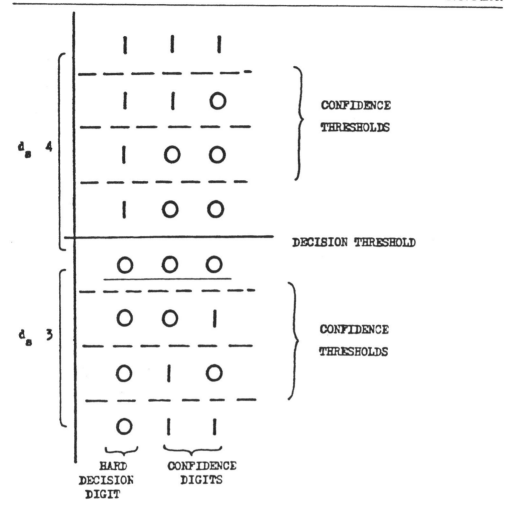

Fig. 2 : 8-region Soft-Decision Quantisation

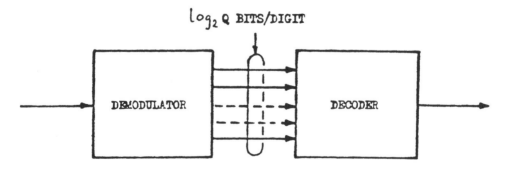

Fig. 3 : Soft-Decision Detector

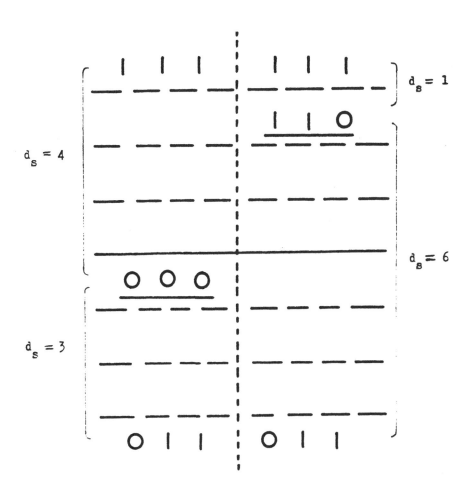

Fig. 4 : Soft-Decision Decoding Example

way of computing the soft-decision distance between two characters,
when the regions and characters are mapped as in figure 2, is to invert
the confidence digits of one of the characters if their decision digits
are different, then modulo-2 add the resulting characters, and finally
interpret the result as a binary number. Thus

$$d_s(0\ 0\ 0,\ 1\ 1\ 1) = 0\ 0\ 0\ \oplus\ 1\ 0\ 0 = 1\ 0\ 0 \equiv 4,\ \text{and}$$

$$d_s(0\ 0\ 0,\ 0\ 1\ 1) = 0\ 0\ 0\ \oplus\ 0\ 1\ 1 = 0\ 1\ 1 \equiv 3.$$

The soft-decision distance (SDD) between a received code word and a
possible transmitted code word may be computed by summing the appropriate
soft-decision distances for each digit (character) of the code word.
Thus, by computing the soft-decision distances to all possible code
words, the one most likely to have been transmitted may be determined by
selecting the one with lowest SDD, in a manner exactly analogous to
minimum Hamming distance decoding. For example, using the demodulator
arrangement of figure 2, together with a single repetition code, assume
that the code word 1 1 is transmitted. Imagine that the first ONE is
demodulated as 0 0 0, and the second ONE as 1 1 0. Then the SDD to
1 1 1 1 1 1 is $4 + 1 = 5$, and the SDD to 0 1 1 0 1 1 is $3 + 6 = 9$ (see
figure 4). The minimum SDD value is 5, so the soft-decision decoder
outputs the correct code word, 1 1, in spite of the error in the first
digit. A hard-decision decoder, given 0 1, could only detect the error,
without being able to correct it. The soft-decision method of decoding
described above is called minimum soft-decision distance (MSDD) decoding.
It is then equally applicable to block and convolutional codes (see
below).

It should be noted that the confidence thresholds need not be
linearly (equally) spaced; Massey[32], Lee[24], Harrison[19] and Rappaport
& Kurz[35] amongst others, have shown that a non-linear spacing array may
be optimum. Alternatively, or in addition, soft-decision distances may
be calculated as weighted sums of the demodulator output characters, as
in generalised minimum distance decoding[14] and threshold decoding[31].
Finally, a different mapping of characters on to regions than that given
in figure 2 may be used, either to pre-weight the characters or to make
SDD computation easier. Alternative distance functions may also be used.[36]

The above example shows that a simple single-error-detecting
repetition code (d = 2) is capable of single-error-correction when used
with soft-decision demodulation (d_s = 14). This confirms the statement
in section 1 that the error control power of a code is almost doubled
by the use of soft-decision detection: an e-error-detecting code
approximates to an e-error-correcting code, or a t-error-correcting
code approximates to a 2t-error-correcting code. In general

$$d_s = d(Q-1)$$

$$\approx d.Q \text{ for large } Q.$$

In practice values of $\log_2 Q$ greater than 4 or 5 (16 or 32 regions)
are unnecessary, as the increase in performance is only marginal[2]. In
terms of decoder output error rate, the improvement due to soft-decision
demodulation depends on the particular code and channel error statistics,
but one to two orders of magnitude or more decrease in output error rate,
for white Gaussian noise channels with error rates in the range 10^{-2} to
10^{-4}, is typical. This corresponds to 1.5 to 2 dB improvement in

signal-to-noise ratio (see figure 5). In non-Gaussian noise the
improvement is considerably greater[7], see for example figure 6 (Farrell
& Munday[13]).

Soft-decision decoding became of practical importance with the
discovery of the Viterbi algorithm (VA) for maximum likelihood (minimum
distance) decoding of convolutional codes[48]. Use of soft-decision
demodulation does not significantly increase the complexity of a VA
decoder, which is a function of the rate and constraint length of the
code. The present development of integrated circuit micro-electronics
permits implementation of half-rate convolutional codes with encoding
constraint lengths of up to about 12, with soft-decision decoding. More
powerful convolutional codes, particularly if for use on bursty channels,
require sequential decoding.[53] Use of soft-decision sequential decoding
was initially found to be impractical, but pioneering work by Jordan[25];
the advent of stack decoding algorithms[18,24]; and more recent research
into algorithms which make efficient use of the structural and distance
properties of convolutional codes[33], indicate that soft-decision
sequential decoding is feasible. Soft-decision threshold decoding of
convolutional codes is also possible.[17]

Soft-decision techniques were less generally applicable to block
codes until comparatively recently. The early work previously mentioned
was concerned with quite simple block codes (e.g. the Wagner code - a
single-parity-check code with soft-decision demodulation - of Balser &
Silverman[1]. Single-error-correcting codes with soft-decision decoding
have been studied by Sundberg[45], Harrison[19], and Kalligeros[27]. Work by

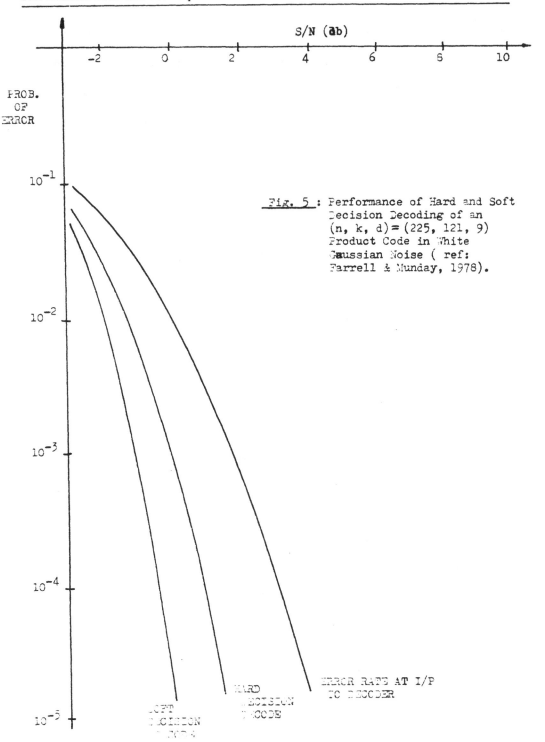

PROB.
OF
ERROR

S/N (ab)

Fig. 5 : Performance of Hard and Soft
Decision Decoding of an
(n, k, d) = (225, 121, 9)
Product Code in White
Gaussian Noise (ref:
Farrell & Munday, 1978).

ERROR RATE AT I/P
TO DECODER

HARD
DECISION
DECODE

SOFT
DECISION
DECODE

Forney[14] on generalised minimum distance decoding led to the application
of soft-decision techniques to iterated and concatenated codes[37], algebraic
decoders[9] and error-trapping decoders[16] based on successive erasure
decoding. Weldon[50] developed a method of weighted erasure (multiple
syndrome) decoding, a soft-decision decoding technique applicable in
principle to any block code for which a decoding procedure is known.
This work was extended by Wainberg & Wolf[49] for burst errors, and by
Reddy[36]. Massey's work on thresholf decoding[31] has led to the
combination of soft-decision techniques with majority logic decoding[43].
A quite different approach was discovered by Hartmann & Rudolph[20], which
may be called soft-decision dual-code-domain decoding. It is an optimum
decoding method in a symbol-by-symbol sense in that it minimises the
symbol error probability, rather than the code-word error probability.
It is important because it applies to codes of high rate, unlike most of
the methods mentioned previously. More general application of soft-
decision decoding to block codes is possible if full (comparison of
received word with all possible code words) minimum distance decoding
or MSDD, is used. This has recently become feasible in practice because
of the availability of cheap integrated circuits and microprocessors.
It is particularly feasible if the code used has some internal structure
which can simplify MSDD decoding: for example, if the code is a product
or concatenated code[8,11,12,13] (see figures 5 & 6). Also Wolf[32] has
shown that any linear block code can be soft-decision decoded using the
Viterbi algorithm. Thus a very wide range of block error-correcting
codes can be decoded efficiently by means of soft-decision techniques.

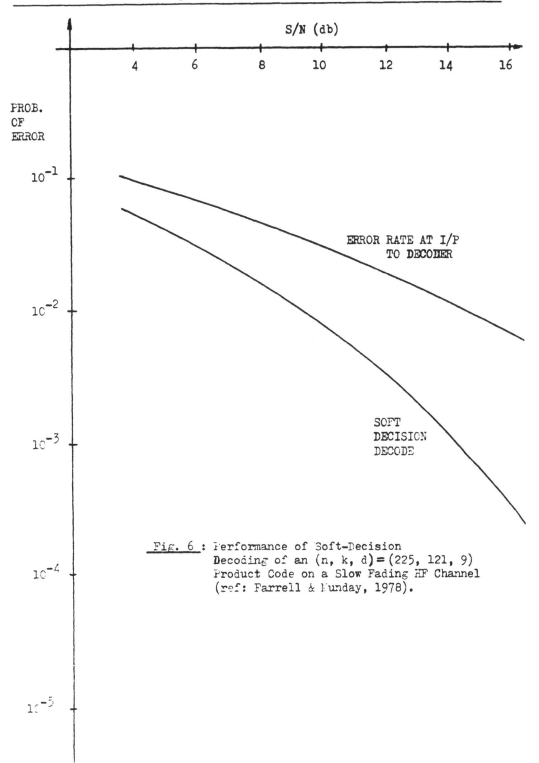

Fig. 6 : Performance of Soft-Decision
         Decoding of an (n, k, d) = (225, 121, 9)
         Product Code on a Slow Fading HF Channel
         (ref: Farrell & Munday, 1978).

The discussion so far has concentrated on error-correcting codes; it is of interest to note that soft-decision techniques can also be used to improve the efficiency of error detection codes, and therefore of automatic request for repeat (ARQ) systems[41,44].

3.   Conclusions

The performance results for experimental soft-decision decoding systems confirm the results predicted by theory. The advantages of using soft-decision techniques are clear, and may be listed as:-

  (i)   soft-decision decoding is applicable to a wide range of
        error-correcting codes, both block and convolutional;

  (ii) soft-decision techniques are also appropriate for use with
        error-detection/ARQ systems;

 (iii) there is a substantial increase in performance ($\sim$ 2db in SNR)
        where soft-decision techniques are applied to the Gaussian
        channel, but the increase is even more marked in a non-Gaussian
        environment;

  (iv) the performance of the best soft-decision algorithms
        asymptotically approaches that of the equivalent optimum
        detector;

   (v) in the case of a non-Gaussian (e.g., impulse noise) channel,
        the optimum detector may be unknown or unrealisable: a soft-
        decision detector may then be the best practical device to
        use;

  (vi) the implementation of a soft-decision decoder is not

substantially more complex than that of the corresponding
minimum distance decoder;

(vii)   use of a soft-decision demodulator may be traded for additional
decoding complexity.

It is of particular value to have demonstrated that soft-decision
techniques can be effectively applied to block codes. Though in many
circumstances convolutional codes outperform block codes, there are
certain situations in which block codes are more appropriate, such as
when relatively short messages are to be transmitted, or when system
synchronisation has to be achieved very rapidly, or when a relatively
simple coding method is sufficient. Use of soft-decision decoding in
these cases enables achievement of the highest possible performance.

A reason often quoted for rejecting the use of soft-decision
decoding is that it requires modification or replacement of the hard-
decision demodulator in a receiver. This modification, however, is
normally quite simple; merely the provision at an additional output
terminal of the demodulated signal (suitably buffered if necessary)
before hard-decision, limiting or pulse regeneration. The reward for
this modification could be a doubling of coding gain, since many
practical hard-decision decoding schemes can only offer up to about
2db of coding gain. As Massey[32] has pointed out, to use a hard-decision
demodualtor can, in overall system performance terms, cancel out most
or all of the gain provided by the coding scheme. Thus soft-decision
demodulation should be adopted or provided for wherever possible.

References

1. Balser, M. & Silverman, R.A.: Coding for constant-data-rate systems, Part I: A new error-correcting code; *Proc IRE*, Vol 42, No 9 (September, 1954), p 1428; Part II: Multiple-error-correcting codes; *Proc IRE*, Vol 43, No 6 (June, 1955), p 728.

2. Batson, B.H., Moorehead, R.W. & Taqvi, S.Z.H.: Simulation results for the Viterbi decoding algorithm, *NASA Report* to TR R-396, 1972.

3. Bloom, F.J. et al: Improvement of binary transmission by null-zone reception; *Proc IRE*, vol 45, p 963, 1957.

4. Cahn, C.R.: Binary decoding extended to Nonbinary demodulation of phase shift keying; *IEE Trans*, Vol COM-17, No 5 (Oct.), p 583, 1969.

5. Chase, D.: A class of algorithms for decoding block codes with channel measurement information; *IEEE Trans*, Vol IT-18, No 1 (Jan.), p 170, 1972.

6. Chase, D.: A combined coding and modulation approach for communication over dispersive channels; *IEEE Trans*, Vol COM-21, No 3 (March), pp 159-174, 1973.

7. Chase, D.: Digital signal design concepts for a time-varying Rician Channel; *IEEE Trans*, Vol COM-24, No 2 (Feb), pp 164-172, 1976.

8. Dorsch, B.: A decoding algorithm for binary block codes and J-ary output channels; *IEEE Trans*, Vol IT-20, No 3 (May), pp 391-394, 1974.

9. Einarsson, G. & Sundberg, C.E.: A note on soft-decision decoding with successive erasures; *IEEE Trans*, Vol IT-22, No 1 (Jan.), p 88, 1976.

10.   Fano, R.M.:   A Heuristic discussion of probabilistic decoding;
      IEEE Trans, Vol IT-9, pp 64-74, 1963.

11.   Farrell, P.G.:   Soft-decision minimum-distance decoding; *Proc NATO
      ASI on Communications Systems and Random Process Theory*,
      Darlington, England, Aug. 1977.

12.   Farrell, P.G. & Munday, E.:   Economical practical realisation of
      minimum-distance soft-decision decoding for data transmission;
      Proc. Zurich Int. Seminar on Digital Communications, March 1976,
      pp 135.1-6.

13.   Farrell, P.G. & Munday, E.:   Variable redundancy HF digital
      communications with adaptive soft-decision minimum-distance
      decoding;   final report on MOD (ASWE) RES. Study Contract
      AT/2099/05/ASWE, 1978.

14.   Forney, G.:   Generalised minimum distance decoding; *IEEE Trans*,
      Vol IT-12, No 2 (April, 1966), pp 125-131, and in *"Concatenated
      Codes"*, MIT Res. Memo. No 37, 1966.

15.   Fritchman, B.D., et al: Approximations to a joint detection/
      decoding algorithm; *IEEE Trans*, Vol COM-25, No 2 (Feb), pp 271-
      278, 1977.

16.   Goodman, R.M.F. & Green, A.D.:   Microprocessor controlled soft-
      decision decoding of error-correcting block codes; Proc. *IERE
      Conf. on Digital Processing of Signals in Communications*, No 37,
      pp 37-349, Loughborough, England, 1977.

17. Goodman, R.M.F. & Ng, W.H.: Soft-decision threshold decoding of convolutional codes; *Proc IERE Conf on Digital Processing of Signals in Communications*, No 37, pp 535-546, Loughborough, England, 1977.

18. Haccoun, D. & Ferguson, M.J.: Generalised stack algorithms for decoding convolutional codes; *IEEE Trans*, Vol IT-21, No 6 (November), pp 638-651, 1977.

19. Harrison, C.N.: Application of soft decision techniques to block codes; *Proc IERE Conf on Digital Processing of Signals in Communications*, Loughborough, England, No 37, pp 331-336, 1977.

20. Hartmann, C.R.P. & Rudolph, L.D.: An optimum symbol-by-symbol decoding rule for linear codes; *IEEE Trans*, Vol IT-22, No 5 (Sept.), pp 514-517, 1976.

21. Heller, R.M.: Forced-erasure decoding and the erasure reconstruction spectra of group codes; *IEEE Trans*. Vol COM-15, No 3 (June), p 390, 1967.

22. Hobbs, C.F.: Universality of blank-correction and error detection; *IEEE Trans*, Vol IT-13, No 2 (April), p 342, 1967.

23. Jayant, N.S.: An erasure scheme for atmospheric noise burst interference; *Proc IEEE*, Vol 54, No 12 (Dec.), p 1943, 1966.

24. Jelinek, F.: A fast sequential decoding algorithm using a stack; *IBM Jour. Res. Dev.*, Vol 13, Nov., pp 675-685, 1969.

25. Jordan, K.L.: The performance of sequential decoding in conjunction with efficient modulation; *IEEE Trans*, Vol COM-14, No 3 (June) pp 283-297, 1966.

26. Justesen, J.: A class of constructive asymptotically good algebraic codes, *IEEE Trans*, Vol IT-18, No 5 (Sept.), pp 652-56, 1972.

27. Kalligeros, N.: *Soft-Decision Error-Correction*; M.Sc. Dissertation, University of Kent at Canterbury, England, 1977.

28. Kazakov, A.A.: A method of improving the noise immunity of redundant binary code reception; *Telecoms (trans of Elec. & Radioteknika)* Vol 22, No 3 (March), p 51, 1968

29. Lee, L.N.: On optimal soft-decision demodulation; *IEEE Trans*, Vol IT-22, No 4 (July), pp 437-444, 1976.

30. Marquart, R.G.: The performance of forced erasure decoding; *IEEE Trans*, COM-15, No 2 (June), p 397, 1967.

31. Massey, J.L.: *Threshold Decoding*; MIT Press, 1963.

32. Massey, J.L.: Coding and modulation in digital communications; *Proc. Zurich Int. Seminar on Digital Communications*, pp E2(1)-(4), 1974.

33. Ng, W.H. & Goodman, R.M.F.: An efficient minimum distance decoding algorithm for convolutional error-correcting codes, *Proc. IEE*, Vol 125, No 2, Feb. 1978, pp 97-103.

34. Pettit, R.H.: Use of the null-zone in voice communications; *IEEE Trans*, Vol COM-13, No 2 (June), p 175, 1965.

35. Rappaport, S.S. & Kurz, L.: Optimal decision thresholds for digital signalling in non-Gaussian noise; *IEEE Int. Conv. Rec.*, Part 2, p 198, 1965.

36. Reddy, S.M.: Further results on decoders for Q-ary output, *IEEE Trans*, Vol IT-20, No 4 (July), pp 552-4, 1974.

37. Reddy, S.M. & Robinson, J.P.: Random error and burst correction by
     iterated codes; *IEEE Trans*, Vol IT-18, No 1 (Jan), pp 182-191,
     1972.

38. Schwartz, L.S.: Some recent developments in digital feedback
     systems; *IRE Trans*, Vol CS-9, No 1 (March), pp 51-7, 1961.

39. Smith, J.S.: Error control in duobinary data systems by means of
     null-zone detection; *IEEE Trans*, Vol COM-16, No 6 (Dec.),
     p 825, 1968.

40. Sullivan, N.J. & Heaton, A.G.: Transient frequency response of
     transmittance peaked I.F. filters with application to null-zone
     detection; *Elec. Letters*, Vol 5, No 18, p 423, 4th Sept, 1969.

41. Sundberg, C.E.: Soft-decision error-detection for binary antipodal
     signals on the Gaussian channel; Dept. Telecom. Th., Lund. Univ.,
     Sweden, Tech. Rep. TR-65, 1974.

42. Sundberg, C.E.: Reliability numbers matching binary symbols for
     Gray-coded MPSK and MDPSK signals; as above, TR-66, 1975.

43. Sundberg, C.E.: One-step majority logic decoding with symbol
     reliability information; *IEEE Trans*, IT-21, pp 235-242, No 2
     (March), 1975.

44. Sundberg, C.E.: A class of soft-decision error detectors for the
     Gaussian channel; *IEEE Trans*, Vol COM-24, No 1 (Jan), pp 106-112,
     1976.

45. Sundberg, C.E.: Asymptotically optimum soft-decision decoding
     algorithms for Hamming codes; *Elec. Letters*, Vol 13, No 2, p 38,
     20th Jan, 1977.

46. C.C.I.T.T.: Control of errors for data transmission on switched telephone connections. *"Blue Book"* (Supplement No. 66), 1964.

47. Thiede, E.C.: Decision hysteresis reduces digital Pe; *IEEE Trans*, Vol COM-20, No 5 (Oct) p 1038, 1972.

48. Viterbi, A.J.: Error Bounds for convolutional codes and an asymptotically optimum decoding algorithm; *IEEE Trans*, Vol IT-13, No 2 (April), pp 260-269, 1967.

49. Wainberg, S. & Wolf, J.K.: Burst decoding of binary block codes on Q-ary output channels; *IEEE Trans*, Vol IT-18, No 5 (Sept), p 684, 1972.

50. Weldon, E.J.: Decoding binary block codes on Q-ary output channels; *IEEE Trans*, Vol IT-17, No 6 (Nov.), pp 713-718, 1971

51. White, H.E.: Failure-correction decoding; *IEEE Trans*, Vol COM-15, No 1 (Feb.), p 23, 1967.

52. Wolf, J.K.: Efficient maximum-likelihood decoding of linear block codes using a trellis; *IEEE Trans*, Vol IT-24, No 1 (Jan), pp 76-80, 1977.

53. Wozencraft, J.M.: Sequential decoding for reliable communication; *IRE Nat. Conv. Rec.*, Part II, pp 11-25, 1957.

54. Wozencraft, J.M. & Kennedy, R.S.: Modulation and demodulation for probabilistic coding; *IEEE Trans*, Vol IT-12, No 4 (July), pp 291-297, 1966.

SOFT DECISION DECODING

Carlos R. P. Hartmann
School of Computer and Information Science
Syracuse University
Syracuse, New York

1. INTRODUCTION

In a digital communication system with one level of coding
(modulation-demodulation), Figure 1, it is natural to design the demodulator to make hard decisions in such a way that the probability of
symbol error is minimized.

Figure 1: Digital Communication System with One Level of Coding

However, when a second level of coding (error-control encoding-
decoding) is added, Figure 2, this demodulation strategy is no longer

appropriate.

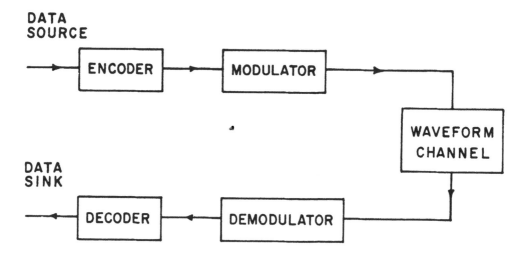

Figure 2:   Digital Communication System with Two Levels of Coding

In a communication system using two-level coding, the transmitted bit
stream usually must satisfy known algebraic constraints.   To make hard
decision without regard to these constraints is to throw information
away and degrade the performance of the system.   This situation was
tolerated for a time because it was thought that the loss in
performance at the output of the demodulator was justified by the
simplicity of the digital decoder that followed.   This has come into
question recently, however, and there have been many proposals for reducing this performance loss through a modified decoder which takes
advantage of the additional information provided by the demodulator.
We refer the reader to Massey [1] for an excellent discussion of the
philosophic point involved.

     In this series of lectures we will present an algebraic soft decision decoding technique whose complexity varies inversely with the code rate. It will be shown that by using all of the p^{n-k} parity-check of an (n,k) linear block code it is possible to obtain a soft decision decoding rule which minimizes the probability of symbol error. Asymptotic performance of this decoding rule for the additive white Gaussian noise channel will be presented. A simplified soft decision decoder for L-step orthogonalizable codes will also be described. The complexity of such a decoder is comparable to that of a conventional hard decision majority decoder. For codes in which the number of orthogonal parity checks is exactly d_H-1, where d_H is the minimum distance of the code, the performance of the soft decision decoder is asymptotically optimum for the Gaussian channel. An iterative decoding technique will also be discussed.

2. BACKGROUND

   We may consider the modulator, waveform channel and demodulator of Figure 1, as one entity which will be called the channel (Figure 3).

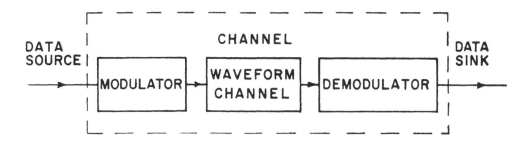

Figure 3: The Channel. (Communication System with One Level of Coding)

Most of the definitions given in this section are due to
Massey [2] or Forney [3].

The *discrete memoryless channel* (or DMC) is a channel, with a
finite input alphabet and a finite output alphabet, that acts
independently on each input symbol and whose statistics do not vary with
time. Letting $A = \{a_1, a_2, \ldots, a_{q_1}\}$ and $B = \{b_1, b_2, \ldots, b_{q_2}\}$ be the input
and output alphabets respectively, we can specify a DMC by stating the
conditional probability $\Pr(b_j|a_i)$ of receiving b_j when a_i is trans-
mitted for $j = 1, 2, \ldots, q_2$ and $i = 1, 2, \ldots, q_1$. A DMC is often shown by
a directed graph in which the edge from node a_i to node b_j is labelled
with $\Pr(b_j|a_i)$. Figure 4 shows the binary symetric channel (BSC) for
which $A = B = \{0,1\}$. The quantity ϵ is called the "crossover
probability" of the BSC.

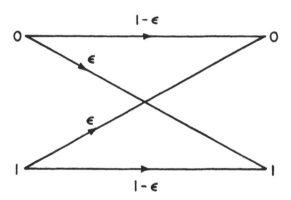

Figure 4: The Binary Symetric Channel

A *block code* of length n and $M = 2^{n\bar{R}}$ codewords is an ordered set
of M n-tuples $\{\underline{c}_1, \underline{c}_2, \ldots, \underline{c}_M\}$ over the input alphabet A of the DMC.
We will write $\underline{c}_j = (c_{j0}, c_{j1}, \ldots, c_{j,n-1})$ where $c_{ji} \in A$. The parameter $\bar{R}$

is the code *rate*. We say that $\bar{R}$ is the rate in "bits per channel use" because, when the M codewords are equiprobable, we send $\log_2 M = n\bar{R}$ bits of information in n uses of the DMC. For a block code of length n the maximum value of $\bar{R}$ is $\bar{R}_{max} = \log_2 q_1$. It is frequently convenient to use the *dimensionless rate* R defined by $R = \bar{R}/\bar{R}_{max}$, where $0 \le R \le 1$.

If $A = GF(q)$, where q is a power of a prime number, and the block code is a subspace of V_n, the vector space of all n-tuples over $GF(q)$, we say that the block code is a *linear block code*. In this case $M = q^k$ and the linear block code of length n is denoted by (n,k). The dimensionless rate of the code is $R = k/n$.

The *Hamming distance* between two vectors $\underline{x}$ and $\underline{y}$ is the number of places in which they differ. It will be denoted by $d_H(\underline{x},\underline{y})$.

The *minimum distance* of a block code is the least number of places in which two distinct codewords differ. It will be denoted by d_H. That is,

$$d_H = \min\{d_H(\underline{c}_i,\underline{c}_j) \mid i \ne j, \ \underline{c}_i \text{ and } \underline{c}_j \text{ are codewords}\} .$$

An *encoder*, Figure 5, is a device which accepts one of the $2^{n\bar{R}}$ commands from a data source and generates the corresponding codeword $\underline{c} = (c_0, c_1, \ldots, c_{n-1})$, $c_j \in A$, for transmission over the channel. Commonly the data source will be a continuous stream of binary data; for every $n\bar{R}$ binary digits the encoder generates a codeword.

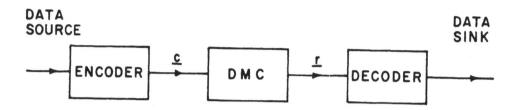

DATA
SOURCE

DATA
SINK

Figure 5:   Communication System with Two Levels of Coding

A *decoder*, Figure 5, is a device which observes an output sequence

$\underline{r} = (r_0, r_1, \ldots, r_{n-1})$, $r_j \in B$, processes this sequence, and presents the

result to the data sink or user in the desired form.   The result pre-

sented by the decoder is called an *estimate*.   Commonly the user wants to

know which codeword was transmitted or what the mth symbol of the trans-

mitted codeword was.   The event in which the estimate of a codeword is

not identical with the input codeword is called a *word error*, and

analogously we define a *symbol error*.

For a broader treatment of block codes the reader is referred to

[4].

We will restrict the derivation of the optimal decoding rules, in

the next section, to the DMC in order to simplify the presentation.

3.   OPTIMUM DECODING RULES FOR BLOCK CODES

A codeword $\underline{c} = (c_0, c_1, \ldots, c_{n-1})$, $c_j \in A$ is transmitted over a DMC.

The received word is $\underline{r} = (r_0, r_1, \ldots, r_{n-1})$, $r_j \in B$.   The decoding

problem is:

(a)   given $\underline{r}$, compute an estimate $\hat{\underline{c}}$ of the transmitted codeword $\underline{c}$

in such a way that the probability of word (codeword) error

(or P_{WORD}) is minimized. Or

   (b) given $\underline{r}$, compute an estimate $\hat{c}_m$ of transmitted code symbol c_m in such a way that the probability of symbol error (or P_{SYMBOL}) is minimized.

   We now derive a decoding rule which minimizes P_{WORD}. Let $Pr(\underline{r}|\underline{c}_j)$ be the probability of receiving $\underline{r} = (r_0, r_1, \ldots, r_{n-1})$ given that the j codeword is transmitted. For a DMC

$$Pr(\underline{r}|\underline{c}_j) = \prod_{i=0}^{n-1} Pr(r_i|c_{ji}) \, .$$

   Let $Pr(\underline{c}_j)$ be the probability of $\underline{c}_j$ being transmitted. Thus

$$Pr(\underline{c}_j|\underline{r}) = \frac{Pr(\underline{r}|\underline{c}_j)Pr(\underline{c}_j)}{Pr(\underline{r})}$$

where $Pr(\underline{r}) = \sum_{j=1}^{M} Pr(\underline{c}_j)Pr(\underline{r}|\underline{c}_j)$.

   If the decoder decodes $\underline{r}$ into $\underline{c}_j$, then the probability (given $\underline{r}$) that the decoding of the transmitted word is incorrect is $1 - Pr(\underline{c}_j|\underline{r})$. Thus, to minimize P_{WORD} we must maximize $Pr(\underline{c}_j|\underline{r})$ [12].

   So, the decoding rule to minimize P_{WORD} may be stated as follows:

Decoding Rule 1: Set $\hat{\underline{c}} = \underline{c}_j$ where the codeword $\underline{c}_j$ maximizes the expression $Pr(\underline{c}_j|\underline{r})$.

Decoding Rule 2: (maximum-likelihood word decoding - MLWD): Set $\hat{\underline{c}} = \underline{c}_j$, where the codeword $\underline{c}_j$ maximizes the expression $Pr(\underline{r}|\underline{c}_j)$.

   MLWD minimizes P_{WORD} when all the codewords have equal probability of being transmitted, that is, are equiprobable.

   We now define a decoding rule to minimize P_{SYMBOL}. Let $S_m(a_i)$ be the set of codewords for which $c_m = a_i$. Then

$$\Pr(c_m = a_i | \underline{r}) = \sum_{\underline{c} \in S_m(a_i)} \Pr(\underline{c} | \underline{r}) \ .$$

If the decoder decodes r_m into a_i, then the probability (given $\underline{r}$) that the decoding of the mth symbol of the transmitted word is incorrect is $1 - \Pr(c_m = a_i | \underline{r})$. Thus, to minimize P_{SYMBOL} we must maximize $\Pr(c_m = a_i | \underline{r})$.

So, the decoding rule to minimize P_{SYMBOL} may be stated as follows:

Decoding Rule 3: Set $\hat{c}_m = a_i$, where $a_i \in A$ maximizes the expression $\Pr(c_m = a_i | \underline{r})$.

Decoding Rule 4 (maximum-likelihood symbol decoding - MLSD): Set $\hat{c}_m = a_i$, where $a_i \in A$ maximizes the expression

$$\sum_{\underline{c} \in S_m(a_i)} \Pr(\underline{r} | \underline{c}) \ .$$

MLSD minimizes P_{SYMBOL} when all the codewords are equiprobable.

Although in practice MLWD and MLSD are used in conjunction with linear codes, neither decoder makes any essential use of the linear property. Both decodes are exhaustive in the sense that the $\Pr(\underline{r} | \underline{c})$ has to be computed for every codeword $\underline{c}$. For this reason, these techniques can be used in practice only with codes having a small number of codewords.

We now present a decoding rule for <u>linear codes</u> which minimizes P_{SYMBOL} for any DMC when the codewords are equiprobable. It is also exhaustive, but in the sense that every word in the dual code is used in the decoding process. This means that in practice this decoding rule can be used only with codes whose dual codes have a small number of codewords.

Let $\underline{c} = (c_0, c_1, \ldots, c_{n-1})$ be any codeword of an (n,k) linear block code C over GF(p) and $\underline{c}_j' = (c_{j0}', c_{j1}', \ldots, c_{j,n-1}')$ the jth codeword of the $(n,n-k)$ dual code C'. Let $\omega = \exp[2\pi\sqrt{-1}/p]$ (primitive complex p^{th} root of unity) and $\delta_{ij} = 1$ if $i = j$ and zero otherwise. Unless otherwise stated, the elements of GF(p) are taken to be the integers $0,1,\ldots,p-1$, and all arithmetic operations are performed in the field of complex numbers.

Decoding Rule 5: Set $\hat{c}_m = s$, where $s \in$ GF(p) maximizes the expression

$$A_m(s) = \sum_{t=0}^{p-1} \omega^{-st} \sum_{j=1}^{p^{n-k}} \left[\prod_{\ell=0}^{n-1} \sum_{i=0}^{p-1} \omega^{-i(c_{j\ell}'-t\delta_{m\ell})} Pr(r_\ell|i) \right] .$$

Theorem 1 [5]. Decoding Rule 5 minimizes P_{SYMBOL} when the codewords are equiprobable.

The Decoding Rule 5 takes a comparatively simple form in the binary case: set $\hat{c}_m = 0$ if $A_m(0) > A_m(1)$ and $\hat{c}_m = 1$ otherwise. It is more convenient however to state the rule in terms of the *likelihood ratio* $\phi_m = Pr(r_m|1)/Pr(r_m|0)$.

Binary Decoding Rule 5: Set $\hat{c}_m = 0$ if

$$2^{n-k} \sum_{j=1}^{n-1} \prod_{\ell=0}^{n-1} \left(\frac{1-\phi_\ell}{1+\phi_\ell} \right)^{c_{j\ell}' \oplus \delta_{m\ell}} > 0 \tag{1}$$

and $\hat{c}_m = 1$ otherwise. Where $\oplus$ denotes modulo 2 addition.

The optimum decoder which implements Binary Decoding Rule 5 for a binary cyclic code is shown in Figure 6. The received word

$\underline{r} = (r_0, r_1, \ldots, r_{n-1})$ is processed by the "demodulation function"

$f(r_\ell) = (1-\phi_\ell)/(1+\phi_\ell)$. The resulting vector

$f(\underline{r}) = (f(r_0), f(r_1), \ldots, f(r_{n-1}))$ is stored in the ring-connected analog

shift register. All 2^{n-k} possible estimates of the transmitted code bit

c_0 are formed by taking real products in accordance with (1). The

final step is to apply the decision function

$$\hat{c}_0 = \begin{cases} 0 \text{ if } \bar{\textstyle\sum} > 0 \\[2em] 1 \text{ otherwise} \end{cases}$$

where $\bar{\textstyle\sum}$ is the real sum of the 2^{n-k} estimates. The remaining $k-1$

information digits are decoded simply by cyclically permuting the

received word $\underline{r}$ in the buffer store.

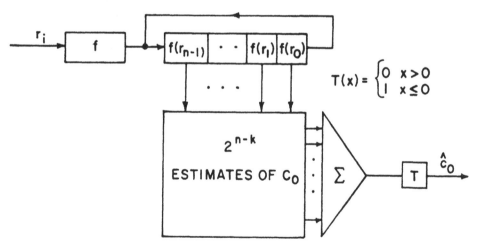

Figure 6 [6]: Optimum Symbol-by-Symbol Decoder for a

Binary Cyclic (n,k) Code

Example 1: (3,2) binary code

We will illustrate the decoding rule for the received symbol r_0.

The Binary Decoding Rule 5 (1) in this case becomes

$$\hat{c}_0 = 0 \text{ iff } \sum_{j=1}^{2} \prod_{\ell=0}^{2} \left(\frac{1-\phi_\ell}{1+\phi_\ell}\right)^{c'_{j\ell} \oplus \delta_{0\ell}} > 0 .$$

Or

$$\hat{c}_0 = 0 \text{ iff } \left(\frac{1-\phi_0}{1+\phi_0}\right) + \left(\frac{1-\phi_1}{1+\phi_1}\right)\left(\frac{1-\phi_2}{1+\phi_2}\right) > 0 .$$

Now

$$\left(\frac{1-\phi_0}{1+\phi_0}\right) + \left(\frac{1-\phi_1}{1+\phi_1}\right)\left(\frac{1-\phi_2}{1+\phi_2}\right) =$$

$$= \frac{(1-\phi_0)(1+\phi_1)(1+\phi_2) + (1+\phi_0)(1-\phi_1)(1-\phi_2)}{(1+\phi_0)(1+\phi_1)(1+\phi_2)} =$$

$$= \frac{2(1+\phi_1\phi_2 - \phi_0\phi_1 - \phi_0\phi_2)}{(1+\phi_0)(1+\phi_1)(1+\phi_2)}$$

Thus,

$$\hat{c}_0 = 0 \text{ iff } 1 + \phi_1\phi_2 > \phi_0\phi_1 + \phi_0\phi_2 \qquad (2)$$

Substituting in (2) the value of $\phi_\ell = \Pr(r_\ell|1)/\Pr(r_\ell|0)$, manipulating

the inequality and using the fact that the channel is memoryless we

obtain

$$\hat{c}_0 = 0 \text{ iff } \Pr(\underline{r}|(000)) + \Pr(\underline{r}|(011)) > \Pr(\underline{r}|(110)) + \Pr(\underline{r}|(101)) .$$

If the codewords are equiprobable we can conclude that

$$\hat{c}_0 = 0 \text{ iff } \Pr(c_0=0|\underline{r}) > \Pr(c_0=1|\underline{r}) .$$

Example 2 [5]: (7,4) Hamming code

We will illustrate the decoding rule for the received symbol r_0.

Since the (7,4) code is cyclic, $r_1,\ldots,r_6$ may be decoded simply by

cyclically permuting the received word $\underline{r}$ in the buffer store.

The Binary Decoding Rule 5 (1) in this case becomes

$$\hat{c}_0 = 0 \text{ iff } \sum_{j=1}^{8} \prod_{\ell=0}^{6} \left(\frac{1-\phi_\ell}{1+\phi_\ell} \right)^{c'_{j\ell} \oplus \delta_{0\ell}} > 0 . \tag{3}$$

The parity check matrix H of the (7,4) code and its row space C' are

shown below.

$$H = \begin{bmatrix} 1 & 1 & 1 & 0 & 1 & 0 & 0 \\ 0 & 1 & 1 & 1 & 0 & 1 & 0 \\ 0 & 0 & 1 & 1 & 1 & 0 & 1 \end{bmatrix} \begin{matrix} (a) \\ (b) \\ (c) \end{matrix}$$

	c_0	c_1	c_2	c_3	c_4	c_5	c_6		
	0	0	0	0	0	0	0		
	1	1	1	0	1	0	0	(a)	
C':	0	1	1	1	0	1	0	(b)	
	1	0	0	1	1	1	0	(a⊕b)	
	0	0	1	1	1	0	1	(c)	(4)
	1	1	0	1	0	0	1	(a⊕c)	
	0	1	0	0	1	1	1	(b⊕c)	
	1	0	1	0	0	1	1	(a⊕b⊕c)	

Let $\rho_\ell = (1-\phi_\ell)/(1+\phi_\ell)$. Then substituting (4) into (3) gives

$$\hat{c}_0 = 0 \text{ iff } \rho_0 + \rho_1\rho_2\rho_4 + \rho_2\rho_5\rho_6 + \rho_1\rho_3\rho_6 + \rho_3\rho_4\rho_5 + \tag{5}$$
$$+ \rho_0\rho_1\rho_2\rho_3\rho_5 + \rho_0\rho_2\rho_3\rho_4\rho_6 + \rho_0\rho_1\rho_4\rho_5\rho_6 > 0 .$$

The decoder configuration corresponding to (5) is shown in Figure 7.

The reader will probably recognize the similarity between the

decoder of Figure 7 and a one-step majority decoder using nonorthogonal

parity checks [7]. And in fact if the "soft decision" function

$(1-\phi(x))/(1+\phi(x))$ were replaced by the "hard decision" function

$f(x) = -1$ if $x > \frac{1}{2}$ and $+1$ otherwise, and if the last three parity

checks in the decoder were deleted, then the resulting circuit would be

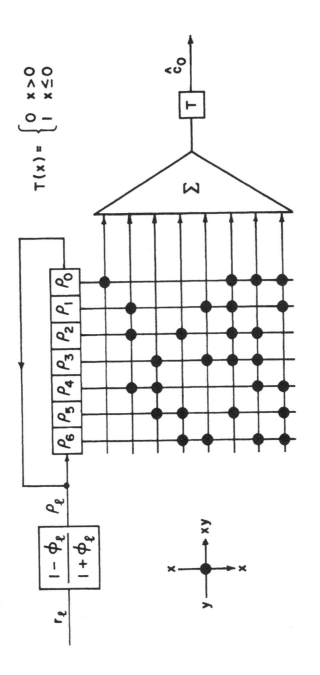

Figure 7 [5]:   Decoder for the (7,4) code

mathematically equivalent to a conventional one-step majority decoder.
Parity checks in the circuit of Figure 7 would be computed by taking
products of +1's and -1's, rather than by taking modulo 2 sums of 0's
and 1's as would be the case in a conventional digital decoding circuit.

Finally, we remark that the Decoding Rule 5 presented here for
linear codes over GF(p) can be generalized in a straightforward fashion
to linear codes over GF(q) [5].

Another decoding method which minimizes P_{SYMBOL} was proposed by
Bahl et al [8]. It uses the dual code to compute $Pr(\underline{r}|\underline{c})$, thus,
its complexity is also proportional to the number of codewords in the
dual code.

Now let us restrict our attention to linear binary block codes with
equiprobable codewords transmitted over the additive white Gaussian
noise (or AWGN) channel by antipodal signaling. We will present
asymptotic expressions for P_{WORD} and P_{SYMBOL}. The AWGN channel is a
memoryless channel with a finite input alphabet and a infinite output
alphabet. In the case under consideration, A = {0,1} and B is the set
of real numbers.

When c_m is transmitted, the mth received component of $\underline{r}$ is

$$r_m = (-1)^{c_m}\sqrt{E} + e_m$$

where E is the signal energy per channel bit and e_m is a noise sample of
a Gaussian process with single-sided noise power per hertz N_0. The
variance of e_m is $N_0/2$ and the signal-to-noise ratio (or SNR) for this
channel is $\gamma = E/N_0$. In order to account for the redundancy in codes

of different rates, we will use the SNR per transmitted bit of infor-

mation $\gamma_b = E_b/N_0 = \gamma n/k = \gamma/R$, in our formulations.

Let C be a binary linear code with dimensionless rate R. If the

dual code of C has minimum distance greater than 2, then the asymptotic

behavior of P_{SYMBOL} as γ_b decreases (or $AB_{\gamma_b \to 0}(P_{SYMBOL})$) is

$$AB_{\gamma_b \to 0}(P_{SYMBOL}) \approx Q(\sqrt{2R\gamma_b}) = \frac{1}{\sqrt{2\pi}} \int_{\sqrt{2R\gamma_b}}^{\infty} \exp(-x^2/2)dx \qquad [9],$$

which is the probability of symbol error before decoding.

If C is a binary linear cyclic code with dimensionless rate R and

minimum distance d_H, then the asymptotic behavior of P_{SYMBOL} as γ_b

increases (or $AB_{\gamma_b \to \infty}(P_{SYMBOL})$) is

$$AB_{\gamma_b \to \infty}(P_{SYMBOL}) \approx Q(\sqrt{2Rd_H\gamma_b}) \qquad [9] \quad .$$

But, $Q(\sqrt{2Rd_H\gamma_b})$ is also the asymptotic behavior of P_{WORD} as γ_b increases

[3]. This result tends to support the conjective in [5] and [8] that

optimum symbol-by-symbol decoding and optimum word decoding give, for

all practical purposes, the same performance on discrete memoryless

channels.

In most practical applications the linear (n,k) code required in

the communication system makes prohibitive the use of a decoder which

implements any of the decoding rules previously stated.

Since the complexity of the decoder illustrated in Figure 6 depends
almost exclusively upon the number of estimates used, an obvious
modification is to use a proper subset of the set of all 2^{n-k}
estimates. Except for certain degenerate cases (e.g. (n,n-1) codes),
it appears that all 2^{n-k} estimates must be used in order to minimize
P_{SYMBOL}. So the use of a proper subset will result in some loss of
performance. The problem is to achieve the best trade-off between the
number of estimates used and P_{SYMBOL}.

In the next section we will present a suboptimum decoding scheme
for binary linear (n,k) codes.

4. SUBOPTIMUM DECODING SCHEME FOR BINARY LINEAR CODES

When all 2^{n-k} estimates are used, the demodulation function
$f(r_i) = (1-\phi_i)/(1+\phi_i) = \tanh(\beta r_i)$, where β is a function of the SNR,
minimizes P_{SYMBOL} on the AWGN channel for any binary linear code.
However, when a proper subset of the estimates is used, this function is
not necessarily optimum, and in fact is not necessarily even
asymptotically optimum [10, Figure 3.17]. Determining the best
demodulation function for a given set of estimates appears to be a very
difficult problem.

In this section we will use fixed demodulation functions. Nevertheless, it is intuitively clear that the best demodulation function
for a given set of estimates would have to be adaptive as it is in
the case when all of the estimates are used.

In the case of an analog decoder, we have to define error-correcting capability over the real numbers (or RE). The natural

distance measure over $(RE)^n$ is the Euclidean metric, and it is easily

seen that a binary (n,k) code with minimum Hamming distance d_H has

minimum Euclidean distance $d_E = \sqrt{d_H}$. We say that a decoding function

is a *radius-s decoding rule* if it maps a received vector onto a nearest

word in the code whenever the vector is within Euclidean distance s of

a code word. The maximum radius possible without having overlapping

spheres is $s < d_E/2$, and a radius-s decoding rule which achieves

this radius is called a *maximum-radius decoding rule*. (Note the

obvious analogy with t-error-correction in digital decoding.) The

importance of a maximum-radius decoding rule stems from the following

theorem.

Theorem 2 [6]. A symbol-by-symbol decoding scheme for binary block

codes is asymptotically optimum (SNR→∞) for the AWGN channel if and

only if it is a maximum-radius decoding rule.

We now present a class of demodulation functions, with their

associated estimate sets, which achieve maximum-radius decoding.

In the development which follows, the received word

$\underline{r} = (r_0, r_1, \ldots, r_{n-1})$ is the real sum of the transmitted binary code

word $\underline{c} = (c_0, c_1, \ldots, c_{n-1})$, $c_i \in \{0,1\}$, and an error vector

$\underline{e} = (e_0, e_1, \ldots, e_{n-1})$, $e_i \in R^n$. As defined before the binary (n,k)

code is denoted by C and its (n,n-k) dual code by C'. The jth code

word of C' is $\underline{c}'_j = (c'_{j0}, c'_{j1}, \ldots, c'_{j,n-1})$.

The class of demodulation functions we now consider consists of all continuous functions $f: R \to R$ which satisfy the following three

conditions:

(A1) $f(x) = - f(1-x)$.

(A2) $\displaystyle\prod_{i=1}^{v} f(x_i) \geq f(\sqrt{\sum_{i=1}^{v} x_i^2})$ for any integer $v \geq 1$.

(A3) For any integer $b \geq 1$

$$(\sum_{i=1}^{b} x_i^2 < b/4) \to \sum_{i=1}^{b} f(x_i) > 0 .$$

The following examples will give the reader an idea of the sorts of

demodulation functions contained in this class.

$$f(x) = \begin{cases} 1 & x \leq 0 \\ \cos(\pi x) & 0 < x < 1 \\ -1 & 1 \leq x \end{cases} ,$$

$$f(x) = \begin{cases} 1 & x \leq a \\ \dfrac{1-2x}{1-2a} & a < x < 1-a, \ \dfrac{3-2\sqrt{2}}{2} < a < 1 - \dfrac{1}{\sqrt{2}} \\ -1 & 1-a \leq x \end{cases} .$$

It is shown in [6] that these functions satisfy conditions

(A1) - (A3).

We consider the case where the set of estimates is derived from

parity checks which satisfy a combinatorial constraint. Suppose there

are J parity checks, each checking the first digit position and at most

λ of the checks checking any other digit position. Let the J parity

checks be

$$\underline{c}'_1 = (c'_{10}, c'_{11}, \ldots, c'_{1,n-1})$$

$$\underline{c}'_2 = (c'_{20}, c'_{21}, \ldots, c'_{2,n-1})$$

$$\vdots$$

$$\underline{c}'_J = (c'_{J0}, c'_{J1}, \ldots, c'_{J,n-1})$$

where $c'_{j0} = 1$ and $c'_{ji} \in \{0,1\}$ for all $1 \le j \le J$ and $1 \le i < n$. Let

$$\lambda_i = \sum_{j=1}^{J} c'_{ji} \text{ for } i = 1,2,\ldots,n-1. \text{ Then } \lambda = \max\{\lambda_1, \lambda_2, \ldots, \lambda_{n-1}\}. \text{ Let}$$

$$F_0(\underline{r}) = \lambda f(r_0) + \sum_{j=1}^{J} \prod_{i=1}^{n-1} (f(r_i))^{c'_{ji}} ,$$

where f satisfies conditions (A1) - (A3), with the convention that $0^0 = 1$.

Decoding Rule 6:

$$\hat{c}_0 = \begin{cases} 0 \text{ if } F_0(\underline{r}) > 0 \\ \\ 1 \text{ otherwise} . \end{cases}$$

The main result of this section is given by the following theorem:

Theorem 3 [6]. If $d_E(\underline{r}, \underline{c}) < \frac{1}{2} \sqrt{\frac{J+\lambda}{\lambda}}$, then Decoding Rule 6 gives $\hat{c}_0 = c_0$.

The next example gives the idea of the proof of Theorem 3.

Example 3: Consider the (7,3) binary code. Let

$$\underline{c}'_1 = (1\ 0\ 1\ 1\ 0\ 0\ 0)$$

$$\underline{c}'_2 = (1\ 1\ 0\ 0\ 0\ 1\ 0)$$

$$\underline{c}'_3 = (1\ 0\ 0\ 0\ 1\ 0\ 1)$$

In this case, $J = 3$ and $\lambda = 1$.

Thus

$$\frac{1}{2} \sqrt{\frac{J+\lambda}{\lambda}} = 1 .$$

Assume the transmitted codeword is $\underline{c}_0 = (00...0)$. Hence

$$F_0(\underline{r}) = f(e_0) + f(e_2)f(e_3) + f(e_1)f(e_5) + f(e_4)f(e_6) . \qquad (6)$$

Furthermore assume $\qquad \sum_{i=0}^{6} e_i^2 < 1 .$

By Condition (A2)(v=2) we may write (6) as

$$F_0(\underline{r}) \geq f(e_0) + f(\sqrt{e_2^2 + e_3^2}) + f(\sqrt{e_1^2 + e_5^2}) + f(\sqrt{e_4^2 + e_6^2}) .$$

By Condition (A3)(b=4) we may conclude that if

$\sum_{i=0}^{6} e_i^2 < 1$, then $F_0(\underline{r}) > 0$. Hence, if $d_E(\underline{r},\underline{c}_0) < 1$, then

$\underline{\hat{c}} = (00...0)$. In general we can say that if $d_E(\underline{r},\underline{c}) < 1$ then Decoding

Rule 6 give $\underline{\hat{c}} = \underline{c}$. But the minimum Euclidean distance of the (7,3)

code is 2, hence this is a maximum-radius decoding rule.

Example 4 [6]: Consider the (7,4) binary Hamming code. Let

$$\underline{c}_1' = (1110100)$$

$$\underline{c}_2' = (1101001)$$

$$\underline{c}_3' = (1010011)$$

$$\underline{c}_4' = (1001110)$$

In this case, J = 4 and λ = 2. By Theorem 1, if $d_E(\underline{r},\underline{c}) < \frac{\sqrt{3}}{2}$, then

Decoding Rule 6 gives $\underline{\hat{c}} = \underline{c}$. But the minimum Euclidean distance of the

(7,4) code is $\sqrt{3}$, hence this is a maximum-radius decoding rule. The

corresponding algebraic analog decoder is shown in Figure 8.

As a consequence of Theorem 3 we have the following corollary:

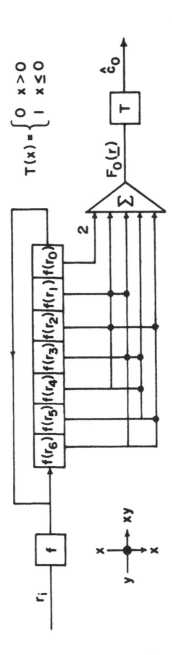

Figure 8 [6]: One-Step Algebraic Analog Decoder for the (7,4) Code

with Nonorthogonal Parity Products

Corollary 1 [6]: A 1-step orthogonalizable code can be maximum-radius decoded using only the disjoint estimates.

The extension of this result to L-step orthogonalizable codes is given by the following theorem:

Theorem 4 [6]. An L-step orthogonalizable code can be maximum-radius decoded using only the disjoint estimates provided that the subcode to be decoded at the second step is (L-1)-step orthogonalizable with minimum distance at least $2d_H - 1$.

In digital majority logic decoding, it is often advantageous to convert a conventional L-step majority decoder into an L-stage sequential code reduction decoder [11]. This conversion goes through in the case of algebraic analog decoding. A two-stage analog sequential code reduction decoder for the (7,4) code is shown in Figure 9.

One of the features of algebraic analog decoding is that it lends itself naturally to iterative extensions.

If we replace the threshold element at the output of an algebraic analog decoder by the function $g(x) = \frac{1-x}{2}$ (which converts a code word in (+1,-1)-form to (0,1)-form), we have, in effect a nonlinear filter operating in $(RE)^n$ which accepts as input a point $\underline{r}^{(0)}$ (the received word) and produces as output another point $\underline{r}^{(1)}$. Hopefully, $\underline{r}^{(1)}$ is closer to the nearest code word than was the received word $\underline{r}^{(0)}$. It is a natural next step to feed $\underline{r}^{(1)}$ back into the decoder input and then to continue this procedure. At some appropriate point, the output of the decoder is fed through the threshold element thereby producing $\underline{\hat{c}}$. A

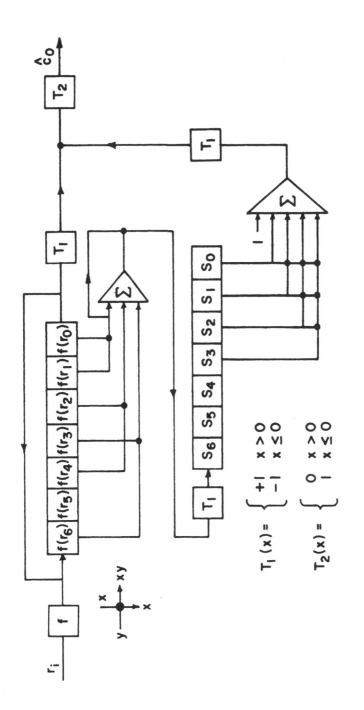

Figure 9 [6]:   Two-Stage Sequential Code Reduction Algebraic

Analog Decoder for the (7,4) Code

block diagram of this iterative extension is shown in Figure 10.

The following theorem assures us that P_{WORD} can never be increased by iteration.

Theorem 5 [6]. If $\underline{r}^{(\ell)}$ can be correctly decoded by the basic algebraic analog decoder, then $\underline{r}^{(\ell+m)}$ will also be correctly decoded, for $\ell=0,1,\ldots,$ and $m = 1,2,\ldots$.

The fact that maximum-radius decoding is asymptotically optimum on the AWGN channel does not mean that the scheme is necessarily attractive from a practical point of view, since in many applications the input SNR is relatively low. To see whether maximum-radius decoding, and algebraic analog decoding in general, performs well at low as well as high SNR, we simulated the performance of the (21,11),(73,45) and (17,9) binary codes over the AWGN channel. We assumed antipodal signalling in the transmission. The demodulation function used in all cases was

$$f(x) = \begin{cases} 1 & x \leq 0 \\ \cos(\pi x) & 0 < x < 1 \\ -1 & 1 \leq x \end{cases}$$

Figures 11 and 12 show the performance of a maximum-radius decoder and its iterative extension for the (21,11) projective geometry code. The decoder in this case uses six disjoint estimates. Figures 13 and 14 show the performance of maximum-radius decoding of the (73,45) projective geometry code. The decoder in this case uses ten disjoint estimates. The performance of radius-s decoding of the (17,9) quadratic-residue code is shown in Figure 15 and 16.   The decoder in

this case uses 25 nondisjoint estimates and, we suspect, does not

achieve maximum-radius decoding.   The dotted curves in Figures 12

through 14 show the asymptotic behavior of optimum decoding [3].

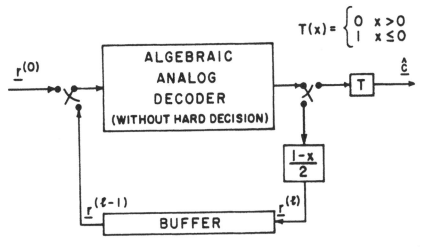

Figure 10 [6]:   Iterative Extension of an Algebraic Analog Decoder

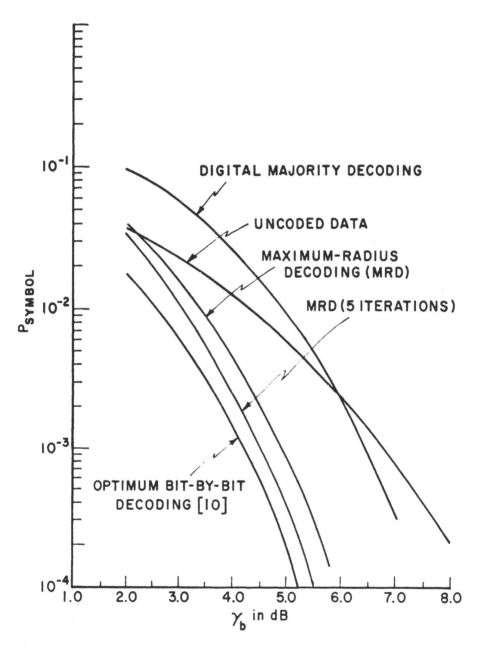

Figure 11 [6]:   Symbol Error Rate of the (21,11) P.G.

Code over the AWGN Channel

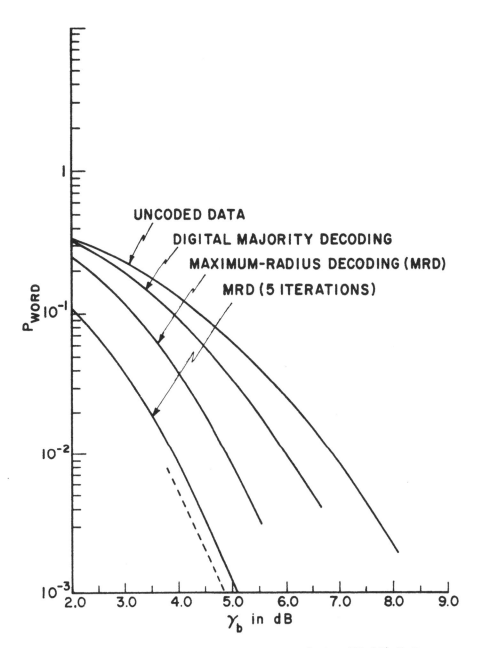

Figure 12 [6]: Word Error Rate of the (21,11) P.G.

Code over the AWGN Channel

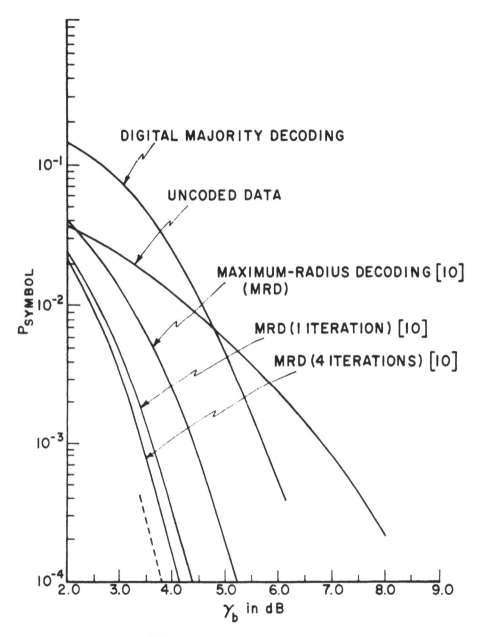

Figure 13 [6]:   Symbol Error Rate of the (73,45) P.G.

Code over the AWGN Channel

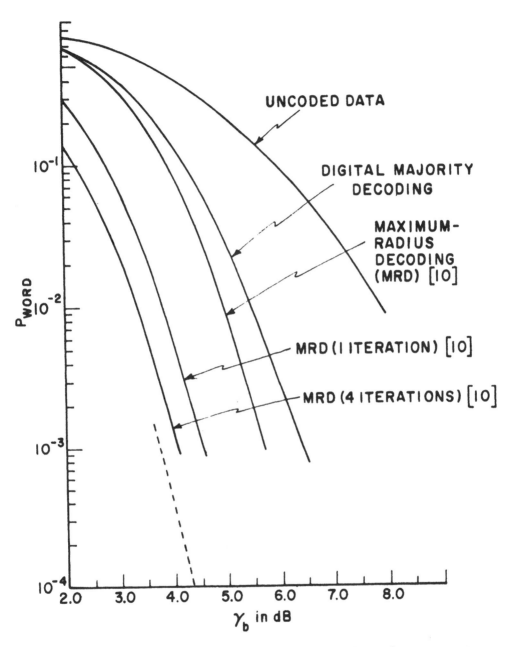

UNCODED DATA

DIGITAL MAJORITY
DECODING

MAXIMUM-
RADIUS
DECODING
(MRD) [IO]

MRD (I ITERATION) [IO]

MRD (4 ITERATIONS) [IO]

Figure 14 [6]:   Word Error Rate of the (73,45) P.G.

Code over the AWGN Channel

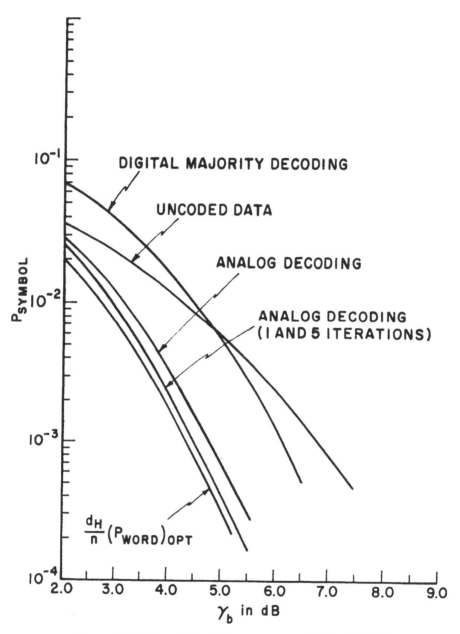

Figure 15 [6]:   Symbol Error Rate of the (17,9) Code

over the AWGN Channel

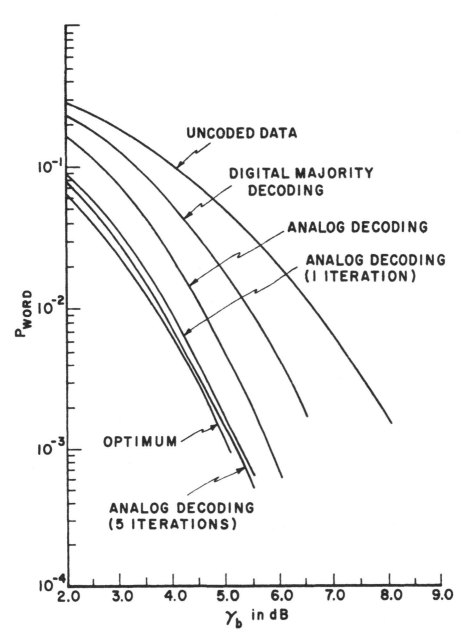

Figure 16 [6]: Word Error Rate of the (17,9) Code

over the AWGN Channel

REFERENCES

1. Massey, J.L., Coding and demodulation in digital communication,
    *Proceedings of the International Zurich Seminar on Digital
    Communication*, Switzerland, 1974.

2. Massey, J.L., Error bounds for tree codes, trellis codes, and
    convolutional codes with encoding and decoding procedures, in
    Coding and Complexity, CISM courses and lectures No. 216, Longo, G.,
    Springer-Verlag, Vienna, 1975, 2.

3. Forney, G.D., Jr., *Concatenated Codes*, M.I.T. Research Monograph
    No. 37, The M.I.T. Press, Cambridge, 1966.

4. Peterson, W.W. and Weldon, E.J., Jr., *Error-Correcting Codes*,
    2nd edition, The M.I.T. Press, Cambridge, 1972.

5. Hartmann, C.R.P. and Rudolph, L.D., An optimum symbol-by-symbol
    decoding rule for linear codes, *IEEE Transactions on Information
    Theory*, IT-20, 514, 1976. Copyright ⓒ by IEEE.

6. Rudolph, L.D., Hartmann, C.R.P., Hwang, T.Y. and Duc, N.Q.,
    Algebraic analog decoding of linear binary codes, accepted for
    publication in the *IEEE Transactions on Information Theory*.
    Copyright ⓒ by IEEE.

7. Rudolph, L.D., A class of majority logic decodable codes, *IEEE
    Transactions on Information Theory*, IT-13, 305, 1967.

8. Bahl, L.R., Coke, J., Jelinek, F. and Raviv, J., Optimal decoding
    of linear codes for minimizing symbol error rate, *IEEE Transactions
    on Information Theory*, vol. IT-20, 284, 1974.

9. Hartmann, C.R.P., Rudolph, L.D. and Mehrotra, K.G., Asymptotic
    performance of optimum bit-by-bit decoding for the white Gaussian
    channel, *IEEE Transactions on Information Theory*, IT-23, 520, 1977.
    Copyright ⓒ by IEEE.

10. CNR, Incorporated, demod/decoder integration, RADC final technical report on Contract F30602-76-C-0361, 1978.

11. Rudolph, L.D. and Hartmann, C.R.P., Decoding by sequential code reduction, *IEEE Transactions on Information Theory*, IT-19, 549, 1973.

12. Gallager, R.G., *Information Theory and Reliable Communication*, 5th edition, John Wiley and Sons, New York, 1968, 120.

- ADDENDUM -

This work was supported by National Science Foundation Grant

ENG 75-07709 and Rome Air Development Contract F30607-75-C-0121.

Towards the maximum-likelihood decoding of long
convolutional codes.

R.M.F. Goodman, B.Sc., Ph.D.,
University of Hull,
Hull HU6 7RX
England.

Abstract

Minimum distance decoding of convolutional codes has generally been
considered impractical for other then relatively short constraint length
codes, because of the exponential growth in complexity with increasing
constraint length. The minimum distance decoding algorithm proposed in
the paper, however, uses a sequential decoding approach to avoid an
exponential growth in complexity with increasing constraint length, and
also utilises the distance and structural properties of convolutional
codes to considerably reduce the amount of tree searching needed to find
the minimum distance path. In this way the algorithm achieves a complexity that does not grow exponentially with increasing constraint length,
and is efficient for both long and short constraint length codes. The

algorithm consists of two main processes. Firstly, a direct mapping
scheme which automatically finds the minimum distance path in a single
mapping operation, is used to eliminate the need for all short back-up
tree searches. Secondly, when a longer back-up search is required, an
efficient tree searching scheme is used to minimise the required search
effort. By extending the approach used in the paper to the effective
utilisation of soft-decision decoding, the algorithm offers the
possibility of maximum-likelihood decoding long convolutional codes.

1.   Introduction

It is well known that convolutional codes are capable of performing
better than block codes in most error control applications. For a
particular application, the realisation of this superiority depends on
the efficiency and practicability of the decoding algorithms used. In
general, maximum-likelihood decoding of short constraint length codes can
be achieved by using the Viterbi algorithm. However, in order to achieve
low probabilities of sink bit error rate with minimum signal-to-noise
ratio requirements, it is necessary to use codes with long constraint
length, and this renders the usual Viterbi decoder impractical on the
grounds of complexity. In this case non-maximum-likelihood sequential
decoding[1] is usually used, as its complexity is insensitive to constraint
length. Unfortunately, the number of computations required to complete
the decoding is highly variable, and although several efficient
sequential decoding algorithms have been proposed[2,3], the performance of
a sequential decoder is directly related to the time available for

searching the code tree, that is, the probability of buffer overflow.

The algorithm presented in this paper requires much less computation than sequential decoding, and features a non-exponential increase in complexity with constraint length. In addition, operation is maximum-likelihood in that at every node the path chosen is guaranteed to be the path at the minimum distance from the received sequence. On the face of it such a decoding scheme would appear to be impractical because every path in the entire code tree would have to be tested at every forward node extension to guarantee minimum distance from the received sequence. However, the advantage to be gained from minimum distance decoding is the capability of spotting incorrect decoding paths as early as possible. This has the effect of halving the number of branch search operations for every one segment reduction in back-up distance. The algorithm presented differs from other convolutional decoding schemes in that it finds the minimum distance path, and utilises the distance and structural properties of the particular convolutional code used, to eliminate the need for testing the whole tree, and also to substantially reduce the required decoding effort in two ways. Firstly, all short searches with a back-up distance of up to b_m nodes are eliminated by a direct mapping scheme which guarantees that the path chosen is at minimum distance from the received sequence. Thus a maximum of $2 \cdot {}^{(b_m+1)} - 2$ branch searches is replaced by a single mapping operation. Secondly, when a back-up is required (because the path we are searching for diverges at more than b_m nodes back and cannot therefore be mapped to) we not only can derive

a maximum back-up distance, but also determine the exact nodes at which
the divergence might have occurred. As the number of these nodes is
considerably less than the total number of nodes between b_m and the maximum back-up distance, the number of searches required (which increases
exponentially with every node back) is very significantly reduced.

For reasons of brevity the discussion in this paper is limited to hard-
decision decoding of binary half-rate single generator convolutional
codes. The approach used, however, can be extended to other codes and to
soft-decision decoding, thus opening the way to optimum maximum-likelihood decoding of long constraint length convolutional codes. This paper
develops in the following way. Firstly we introduce the distance and
structural properties of convolutional codes that are utilised in the
algorithm, and describe the basic decoding strategy. Next, the concept
of decoding with permissible paths is described, and then this is
developed into the direct mapping scheme for eliminating all short back-
up searches. The technique for minimising the number of actual back-up
searches is then outlined, and finally the algorithm is summarised and
discussed.

2.   Convolutional Codes and their Structural Properties

In this section we introduce some of the distance and structure
properties of single-generator convolutional codes, that are utilised in
the decoding algorithm.

A single-generator convolutional code is one in which each message digit is

encoded individually into V code digits, where V is a positive integer,
giving a maximum information rate of 1/V. The V code digits for each
message digit depend on both the present message digit and the K-1 previous message digits, where K is the constraint length of the code in
segments. Such a code is generated by a K-segment generator sequence
$g = g(2^0)g(2^1)g(g^2) \ldots g(2^{K-1})$ and is a systematic code if the first
digit of each code segment is the same as the corresponding message
digit. The code can be represented by its tree structure, the branches
of which can be extended indefinitely from any node (Fig. 1). Each
branch has one segment of code digits associated with it, and the code
digits of the two branches stemming from an arbitrary node are always
one-complements of each other. Figure 2 shows the first five segments
of the code tree for the rate one-half code used as an example in this
paper, which has a fifty segment generator sequence.

The encoding operation is one of selecting a path through the tree in
accordance with the message digits. At each node the upper branch is
taken if the message digit is a zero, or the lower branch is taken if it
is a one.

Consider, for any node in the infinite tree, all the paths that extend k
segments forward from that node. The resulting subtree is referred to as
a truncated tree, or k-unit, and is divided into two half-trees depending
on which branch was chosen at the first node. The initial code tree (S)
is the k-unit stemming from the very first node, and is divided into the
upper and lower half initial code trees (S_0 and S_1 respectively).

We may now summarise several useful properties of these codes.

(i)   The code is a group code. That is, if w and w' are two equal-length code paths, belonging to the initial truncated tree S, it implies there is a x such that $x = w \oplus w'$ is within S.

(ii)   If w and w' are paths in <u>opposite</u> halves of <u>any</u> k-unit, then $x = w \oplus w'$ is a code path in the lower half <u>initial</u> code tree S_1.

(iii) Fundamental distance property. The minimum distance between half-trees of <u>any</u> k-unit is equal to the weight of the minimum weight path in S_1. We can then define a distance function d(.) such that d(k) is the minimum distance between half-trees of any k-unit, and depends only on k, and not on which k-unit is chosen. The guaranteed error-correcting capability of any k-unit is then T(k), where T(k) is the largest integer such that $T(k) \leq [d(k)-1]/2$. Table 1 shows the distance function d(.) for the half-rate code used in this paper.

3.   The Basic Decoding Strategy

Consider the notation:

v the received sequence, which differs from the transmitted sequence due to errors.

w the tentatively decoded sequence, a path in the code tree which is the decoder's tentative version of the transmitted sequence.

$t = w \oplus v$ the test-error sequence, which has ones in the positions where w and v differ.

t_b the sequence consisting of the last b branches of the sequence t.

Our basic decoding strategy is then as follows. We always seek a code path w which is at minimum distance $|t|$ from the received sequence v. In other words, a w is accepted to be the decoded sequence if and only if for all other paths w' in the corresponding truncated tree, w has minimum test-error weight. That is $|t| = |w \oplus v| \leq |w \oplus v| = |t'|$.

We define the basic branch operation (BBO) to be the decoding action of a single branch forward extension in order to select the latest segment w_1 of w. Whenever a decoded path w is accepted as being the minimum distance path, the decoder shifts out the earliest segment of w which is assumed to be a correct representation of the corresponding segment of the transmitted sequence, and shifts in the newly received segment v_1 of v. The BBO then selects w_1 to be the segment closest in distance to v_1.

For the half-rate code, the BBO results in a w_1 that always has a test-error weight $|t_1| = |w_1 \oplus v_1| \leq 1$. The $|t_1|$ is either 0 or 1. If $|t_1| = 1$, then in addition we impose a constraint on the BBO such that $t_1 = 01$, or in terms of quaternary digits which we use from now on, $t_1 = 1$ and not 2 (nothing is affected in terms of distance by doing this). If we assume that the new segment w_1 results from the extension of a path that has minimum test-error weight, the following are implied. Firstly, if $|t_1| = 0$, the new path is guaranteed to have minimum test-error weight, and the decoder returns to the BBO. Alternatively, if $|t_1| = 1$, it is possible that there exists some other path w' with smaller test-error weight $|t'| = |w' \oplus v| < |t|$, and if so $|t_1'| = 0$ and $|t'| = |t| - 1$. (ref. 4).

Thus whenever the BBO results in a $|t_1| = 1$ the decoder either auto-
matically utilises the direct mapping scheme to eliminate the need to
search for w', or else determines whether or not a back-up search for w'
is needed, and if so, how far to back-up and how to conduct the search.

4. Permissible Path Decoding

Let us assume that the decoder needs to search the b-unit which spans the
last b segments of the code tree, for a w' with smaller test-error weight.
Following sequential decoding practice, this would require a step-by-
step back-up, with the basic branch-by-branch encoding and examining
method being used to calculate test-error weights. This is obviously a
very lengthy process. We now introduce a systematic procedure for
searching the b-unit, which requires considerably less effort than the
method outlined above.

The procedure is based on code property (ii). This states that w' can be
directly derived by the modulo-2 operation $w' = w \oplus x$, where x is a
truncated path in the lower-half initial code tree. In addition,
$t' = w' \oplus v = w \oplus x \oplus v = t \oplus x$, and so if w and w' are in opposite
halves of a k-unit we can derive the test-error weight of w' by direct
modulo-2 addition of t and the k-segment path x. This is still a cumbersome process, however, if all $2^b - 1$ truncated paths with length $k \leq b$ in
the lower-half initial b-unit have to be used to search for w'. We now
introduce several conditions which the x must satisfy because of the code
structure[4]. This serves to reduce the number of x required to search

the b-unit to a very small number in most cases of interest. The reduced
set of paths needed to search the b-unit are called permissible paths,
and denoted P.

Condition a. $|P|$ must be odd.

Condition b. $|P_1| = 1$.

Condition c. $|P| \leq 2|t|-1$.

Condition d. $P_1 = 1$, (quaternary).

Condition e.   If P is longer than two segments, $P_2 = 01$.   (quaternary)

Figure 3 shows the first six segments of the lower-half initial code tree.
Each segment is represented as a quaternary digit, and the number in the
upper right-hand corner gives the weight of the code path up to that segment. A number in the lower right-hand corner indicates a permissible
path, and gives the sequential order i of the permissible path $P_{(i)}$. It
can be seen that there are only three permissible paths which satisfy the
conditions on P. These are: $P_{(1)} = 31$, $P_{(2)} = 32201$ and $P_{(3)} = 310101$.
It is therefore possible to search the entire 6-unit without back-up, by
making only three test-error weight comparisons based on $|t'| = |t \oplus P|$.
In the next section we eliminate the need for even this small number of
comparisons.

5.   Direct Mapping Decoding

In this section we introduce a direct mapping scheme to eliminate all short back-up searches. Consider that the last two segments of t are $t_2 = 11$; we can always find a path with smaller test-error weight, $|t'| = |t| - 1 < |t|$, by directly changing w to $w' = w \oplus P_{(1)}$. The direct mapping scheme is an extension of this in which a set of test-error patterns and corresponding permissible paths are stored, and utilised to directly change w to $w' = w \oplus P_{(i)}$.

In order to specify which test-error patterns do not have minimum weight, and should therefore be replaced by some t' during the decoding process, we need to build up a minimum test-error pattern tree. The tree is shown in Fig. 4 and starts with the BBO from the very beginning. At each node in the tree the length of the test-error pattern increases by one segment. Also, we know that there are only two possibilities for t_1 at each BBO extension, and so two branches stem from each node in the tree.

Starting from the first node, there are only two possible one-segment test-error sequences, 0 and 1. After the next BBO extension there are four possible test-error sequences, 00, 01, 10 and 11. However, $t_2 = 11$ is not a minimum test-error pattern because there is a $t_2' = t_2 \oplus P_{(1)} = 20$ with smaller weight. We therefore replace $t_2 = 11$ by $t_2' = 20$ in the tree and assume that whenever a $t_2 = 11$ is encountered, the decoder directly maps t to $t' = t \oplus P_{(1)}$, and w is mapped to $w' = w \oplus P_{(1)}$. We continue building up the tree in a similar manner, such that each entry is guaranteed to be a minimum test-error pattern. In this way, we can build up a set of test-error patterns t_b and corresponding permissible paths $P_{(i)}$, for which $|t'| = |t \oplus P_{(i)}| = |t| - 1 < |t|$. Note that the test-error patterns in the upper-half of the tree are the same as those in the lower-half, preceeded with one or more zeroes. The search for the t_b can therefore be confined to the lower-half tree only.

Fig. 4 shows the first 5 segments of the minimum test-error pattern tree. The under-lined sequences show were a t_b has been mapped to $t'_b = t_b \oplus P_{(i)}$, and the value of i is given in the lower right corner of that entry. The weight of each minimum test error pattern t is given in the upper corner of each entry. Table 2 shows all the t_b for $b \leq 10$ segments, together with their corresponding $t'_b = t_b \oplus P_{(i)}$. The $P_{(i)}$ used are shown in Table 3.

A direct mapping decoder operating on this principle would therefore store the t_b and corresponding $P_{(i)}$ in memory. Decoding proceeds by using the BBO, and whenever the tentatively decoded sequence w has a t whose last b segments exactly match a pattern t_b stored in memory, we directly map t to $t' = t \oplus P(i)$ and w to $w' = w \oplus P_{(i)}$. No searching for w' is therefore necessary. If t is such that its tail sequence does not match any stored t_b, then either t has minimum test-error weight, in which case the decoder can return to the BBO; or else the required t_b and $P_{(i)}$ are ones which have not been stored. This latter case is dealt with in more detail later.

An example of direct mapping decoding is shown in Fig. 5. The received sequence v has been obtained from an all-zero transmitted sequence, and

contains 4 errors. The decoder starts by using the BBO, and whenever the
tail of the test-error sequence matches one of the patterns in Table 2 a
mapping operation is performed. The lines show the path taken by the
decoder through the code tree. Each segment of w is given above the
path, and the corresponding segment of t appears below the path. It can
be seen that to correctly decode the twelve segment received sequence, it
is only necessary to perform twelve BBOs and four mapping operations.
This is considerably less than the decoding effort required by other
sequential decoding schemes to correct the same pattern of errors.

The range over which direct mapping can be operated in a practical decoder depends on the storage requirements of the t_b and $P_{(i)}$. This
range, in segments, will be denoted b_m. For example, Table 2 shows that
thirty t_b and eleven $P_{(i)}$ are needed to operate direct mapping over
b_m = 10 segments.

It can be seen from Table 2, and from the condition $|P| < 2 |t|$, that the
number of required P increases only slowly with increasing k. The slow
growth in the number of new P that must be stored as b_m is extended, also
limits the growth rate of the number of new t_b that must be stored. Thus
although the number of possible mappings increases exponentially with k,
most of these are performed with permissible paths of length less than k.
It is therefore the number of applications of existing t_b (and
correspondingly $P_{(i)}$) that grows exponentially with k, rather than the
number of new t_b. This is shown in Table 3. For example, in developing
the minimum test-error pattern tree from 1 segment to 2 segments deep,

$P_{(i)}$ is used once. However, when extending the tree from 9 segments to 10, $P_{(1)}$ is used 83 times.

Note that direct mapping can be used by itself as a sub-optimum minimum-distance decoding procedure. In this case, if $t_1 = 1$ and the tail sequence of t does not match any pattern in store, we must consider the possibility that w' (which has $|t'| = |t| - 1$) diverges from w at greater than b_m nodes back. The earliest segment of w (which may or may not be in error) is then shifted out of the decoder, which reverts to the BBO and direct mapping. A sub-optimum direct mapping decoder of this type therefore does no searching at all, but will sometimes accept errors and then recover to the correct path in time.

The algorithm proposed in this paper, however, uses direct mapping to eliminate all short back-up searches, up to a maximum range of b_m nodes. If $t_1 = 1$ and no direct mapping is possible, then either w has minimum test-error weight or else w' diverges from w at greater than b_m nodes back. The next section deals with the method for determining whether or not w has minimum test-error weight, and if not, how to determine the nodes at which it is possible for a w' with $|t'| = |t| - 1 < |t|$ to diverge from w.

6. Determination of the Back-Up Distance

In this section we examine the course of action to be taken if $|t_1| = 1$ and direct mapping is not possible. Some of the results utilised are based on our previous work[5], and are therefore only summarised here.

The first question to be answered is whether or not a back-up search is necessary. That is, is there a possible w' with $|t'| = |t| - 1$ that diverges from w at greater than b_m nodes back. If the answer to this is no, then w is at minimum distance from the received sequence v, and the decoder returns to the BBO.

To answer this question we utilise an upper bound b_t on the back-up distance. The bound states that when w (with $|t_1| = 1$) is the BBO extension of a path having minimum test-error weight, and if there exists a w' with $|t'| < |t|$, then w' diverges from w at most b_t nodes back, where b_t is the minimum value of i such that

$$d(i) = 2|t| - 1. \qquad (1)$$

Thus if $b_t \leq b_m$ no search is necessary. Table 4 shows b_t for various $|t|$. If $b_t > b_m$ then it is still possible that a search for w' will be needed. In this case we examine each node between $b_m + 1$ and b_t by means of a simple threshold value, to see whether or not it is possible that w' diverges from w at that node. The end result is a small set of nodes, whose back-up distances are denoted b_t^*, at which w' may have diverged from w.

The b_t^* are found as follows. By using the code structure properties in conjunction with the upper bound on back-up distance (equation 1), we can establish a threshold condition $T^*(b)$ which $|t_b|$ must satisfy in order for it to be possible that w' diverges from w at b nodes back. This threshold condition is as follows. It is only possible for w' to diverge from w at $b_t^* = b$ nodes back if $|t_b| \geq T^*(b) = [d(j) + 1]/2$, where j is the minimum value such that $d(j) \geq d(b)$ and $d(j)$ is odd. Table 5 shows values of b, and $T^*(b)$.

An example of applying Table 6 is as follows. Suppose we have $b_t = 11$, and $t_{11} = 10010000101$. This gives $t_b < T^*(b)$ for $b \leq 10$, and $t_b = T^*(b)$ for $b = 11$.

The method of specifying the b_t^* given in this section considerably cuts down the amount of tree searching needed to find w'. In the next section we outline an efficient method of searching for w' with the aid of direct mapping.

7. Utilising Direct Mapping in the Tree Search

Having established the values of b_t^* at which w' may have diverged from w, we instigate a search of the $b_t^* - 1$ segment truncated tree stemming from the complement branch of w, for each value of b_t^*, starting with the smallest value greater than b_m.

Each truncated tree is searched in the following manner. First of all the current test-error sequence t is put into storage for later use. At the node b_t^* we force the decoder to take the complement branch to w, and at the same time start a new test-error sequence t^*, which has $|t^*| = 0$ at the node b_t. The search of the truncated tree continues by using the BBO, direct mapping, and the back-up operation, as follows.

Assume that the decoder has reached a point c segments from the node b_t^*, and that the test-error weight $|t*|$ has just become equal to $|t_{b_t^*}|$. If $c \leq b_m + 1$, and the direct mapping decoder cannot perform a mapping, then the search of the truncated tree is abandoned because no path in it can have $|t'| = |t| - 1$. If $c > b_m + 1$ it is possible that the path w' diverges from the present path being followed somewhere between $b_m + 1$ and $c - 1$ nodes back. In this case we can determine the possible nodes at which w' might have diverged by using the $T*(b)$ threshold conditions on $t*$. If the threshold conditions state that the smallest back-up distance is greater than or equal to c, then the search of the truncated tree is abandoned. Otherwise, a back-up is instigated, and we carry out the search using the BBO, direct mapping, and the back-up operation. If each of the possible nodes between $b_m + 1$ and $c - 1$ have been searched, and no path of length $c = b_t^*$ with test-error weight $|t_c^*| = |t_{b_t^*}| - 1$ can be found, there is no w' with $|t'| = |t| - 1$ in the truncated tree corresponding to the present value of b_t^*. In this case the back-up distance is increased to the next value of b_t^* and the search procedure is repeated.

If we run out of search time during the back-up search, then we force the decoder to accept the earliest segment of w, and return to the BBO and direct mapping. Thus an error may be accepted, but the decoder will recover to the correct path in time.

8. Conclusions

In this paper we have presented a minimum distance decoding algorithm

for convolutional codes. Initial simulation tests have confirmed that

the amount of decoding effort is considerably less than other

convolutional decoding schemes. The advantages of the proposed algorithm

are best seen in relation to sequential decoding. Firstly, from the

performance part of view; since our algorithm is minimum distance de-

coding, it is clear that for any received sequence v, the test-error

weight obtained by the decoding algorithm will be always less than or

equal to the test-error weight obtained from sequential decoding.

Therefore, the probability of decoding error will be always less than or

equal to that of sequential decoding. Secondly, from the decoding

operations point of view; it is well known that the probability of buffer

overflow ultimately determines the performance of a sequential decoder.

By utilising direct mapping to eliminate all short back-up searches, by

using minimum distance decoding to catch possible decoding errors in the

earliest possible segment, and by using the threshold conditions on back-

up distance to eliminate unnecessary back-up searches, it can be seen

that the proposed algorithm will require much less decoding effort than

other sequential decoding schemes. Therefore when the size of buffer is

fixed, the proposed algorithm will always give a lower probability of

buffer overflow, and hence a better performance. Future work will be

aimed towards analytically establishing the distribution of the number of

computations for the algorithm and in obtaining fuller simulated performance results.

9. <u>References</u>

1. WOZENCRAFT, J.M., and REIFFEN, B.: 'Sequential decoding' (John
    Wiley and Sons, 1961).

2. . FANO, R.M.: 'A heuristic discussion on probabilistic decoding', IEEE
    Trans., 1963, IT-9, pp. 64-67.

3. JELINEK, F.: 'A fast sequential decoding algorithm using a stack',
    IBM J. Res. Develop., 1969.

4. NG, W.H., and GOODMAN, R.M.F.: 'An efficient minimum distance de-
    coding algorithm for convolutional error correcting codes, Proc.
    IEE, Vol. 125, No. 2, Feb. 1978.

5. NG, W.H.: 'An upper bound on the back-up depth for maximum likeli-
    hood decoding of convolutional codes', IEEE Trans., 1976, IT-22,
    pp. 354-357.

k	g	d(k)	k	g	d(k)
1	11	2	26	01	11
2	01	3	27	01	11
3	00	3	28	01	11
4	01	4	29	01	12
5	00	4	30	01	12
6	01	5	31	00	12
7	00	5	32	00	12
8	01	5	33	01	13
9	01	6	34	00	13
10	00	6	35	01	13
11	00	7	36	01	14
12	01	7	37	00	14
13	00	7	38	00	14
14	01	8	39	01	14
15	01	8	40	01	15
16	01	9	41	00	15
17	00	9	42	01	15
18	00	9	43	00	15
19	00	9	44	01	16
20	01	9	45	00	16
21	01	10	46	01	16
22	00	10	47	00	16
23	00	10	48	01	17
24	00	10	49	01	17
25	01	11	50	00	17

Table 1   Distance Function d(.) for the Rate One-Half Code.

Columns under t_b are labelled 11 10 9 8 7 6 5 4 3 2 1; columns under $t'_b = t_b \oplus P_{(i)}$ are labelled 12 11 10 9 8 7 6 5 4 3 2 1.

b	\[11\]	10	9	8	7	6	5	4	3	2	1	i of $P_{(i)}$	\[12\]	11	10	9	8	7	6	5	4	3	2	1
2										1	1	1											2	0
5							1	0	2	0	1	2								2	2	0	0	0
5							2	0	2	0	1	2								1	2	0	0	0
5							1	0	1	0	1	3								3	0	0	0	0
6						1	0	0	1	0	1	3							2	1	0	0	0	0
6						2	0	0	1	0	1	3							1	1	0	0	0	0
8				1	0	0	2	0	1	0	1	4					2	2	1	0	0	0	0	0
8				2	0	0	2	0	1	0	1	4					1	2	1	0	0	0	0	0
8				1	2	0	0	0	1	0	1	4					2	0	1	2	0	0	0	0
8				2	2	0	0	0	1	0	1	4					1	0	1	2	0	0	0	0
8				1	0	2	0	0	2	0	1	4					2	2	0	0	2	0	0	0
8				2	0	2	0	0	2	0	1	5					1	2	0	0	2	0	0	0
8				1	2	0	0	0	2	0	1	5					2	0	2	0	2	0	0	0
8				2	2	0	0	0	2	0	1	5					1	0	2	0	2	0	0	0
9			1	0	0	1	2	0	0	0	1	6				2	1	0	0	1	0	0	0	0
9			1	0	1	0	0	2	0	0	1	7			3	0	0	0	0	2	0	0	0	0
9			1	0	0	2	0	1	0	0	1	8			3	0	0	2	0	0	0	0	0	0
9			1	0	2	0	0	1	0	0	1	8			3	0	0	0	2	0	0	0	0	0
10		1	0	0	1	0	0	2	0	0	1	7			2	1	0	0	0	2	0	0	0	0
10		2	0	0	1	0	0	2	0	0	1	7			1	1	0	0	0	2	0	0	0	0
10		1	1	0	0	0	0	2	0	0	1	7			2	0	0	1	0	2	0	0	0	0
10		1	0	0	0	2	0	1	0	0	1	8			2	1	0	2	0	0	0	0	0	0
10		2	0	0	0	2	0	1	0	0	1	8			1	1	0	2	0	0	0	0	0	0
10		1	1	0	0	0	0	1	0	0	1	8			2	0	0	2	2	0	0	0	0	0
10		2	0	0	2	0	0	1	0	0	1	8			1	1	0	0	2	0	0	0	0	0
10		3	0	0	0	0	0	2	0	0	1	7				1	0	1	0	2	0	0	0	0
10		3	0	0	0	0	0	1	0	0	1	8				1	0	2	2	0	0	0	0	0
10		2	0	1	0	1	0	0	2	0	1	9			1	2	0	1	0	2	0	0	0	0
10		2	3	0	0	0	0	0	1	0	1	10	3	3	0	0	0	0	0	0	0	0	0	0
10		2	3	0	0	0	0	0	2	0	1	11	3	2	0	0	0	0	0	2	0	0	0	0

Table 2   Total t_b and t'_b for the First Ten Segments of the Minimum Test-Error Pattern Tree.

$P_{(i)}$	$P_{(i)}$ b												$\|P_{(i)}\|$	$A[P_{(i)}]$ b									
	12	11	10	9	8	7	6	5	4	3	2	1		10	9	8	7	6	5	4	3	2	1
$P_{(1)}$											3	1	3	83	31	19	11	3	2	2	-	1	-
$P_{(2)}$								3	2	2	0	1	5	8	4	2	1	-	2	-	-	-	-
$P_{(3)}$							3	1	0	1	0	1	5	9	5	4	1	2	1	-	-	-	-
$P_{(4)}$						3	2	1	2	0	1	0	1	7	3	-	4	-	-	-	-	-	-	-
$P_{(5)}$						3	2	2	0	2	2	0	1	7	2	-	4	-	-	-	-	-	-	-
$P_{(6)}$					3	1	0	1	3	0	0	0	1	7	-	1	-	-	-	-	-	-	-	-
$P_{(7)}$				3	1	0	1	0	2	2	0	0	1	7	3	1	-	-	-	-	-	-	-	-
$P_{(8)}$				3	1	0	2	2	0	1	0	0	1	7	4	3	-	-	-	-	-	-	-	-
$P_{(9)}$				3	2	1	1	1	2	0	2	0	1	9	1	-	-	-	-	-	-	-	-	-
$P_{(10)}$			3	1	3	0	0	0	0	0	2	0	1	7	1	-	-	-	-	-	-	-	-	-
$P_{(11)}$		3	2	2	3	0	0	0	0	2	1	0	1	9	1	-	-	-	-	-	-	-	-	-

Table 3   The Required P_i and the Exponential Growth of their Application.

$A[P_{(i)}]$ is the number of applications of $P_{(i)}$ used in developing the bth segment of the minimum test-error pattern tree.

k	$d(k)_{ave}$	$d(k)_{min}$	$|t(k)_{max}|$
1	2	2	1
2	3	3	1
3	4	3	2
4	5	4	2
5	6	4	3
6	7	5	3
7	8	5	3
8	9	5	4
9	10	6	4
10	11	6	4

Table 4   Comparison of Growth Rates Between $d(k)$ and $|t(k)_{max}|$

$|t|$	$d(b_t)$	b_t
1	–	–
2	3	2
3	5	6
4	7	11
5	9	16
6	11	25
7	13	33
8	15	40
9	17	48

Table 5   Maximum Back-Up Distance b_t for Different Values of $|t|$.

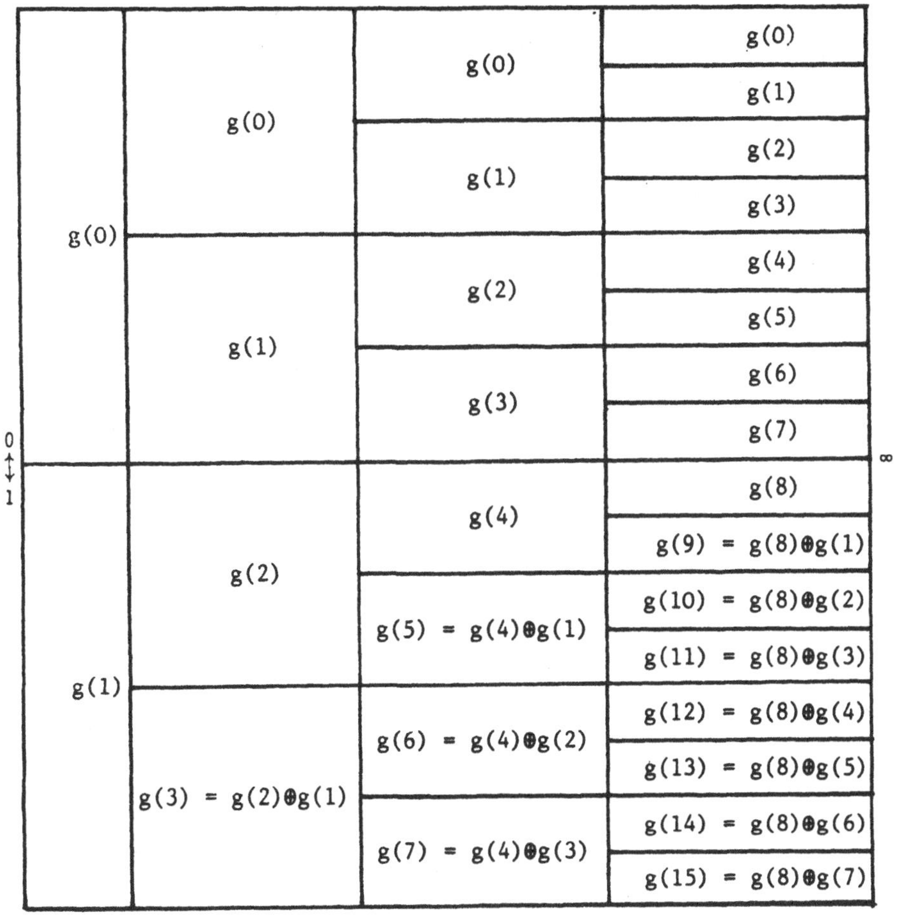

g(0)	g(0)	g(0)	g(0)
			g(1)
		g(1)	g(2)
			g(3)
	g(1)	g(2)	g(4)
			g(5)
		g(3)	g(6)
			g(7)
g(1)	g(2)	g(4)	g(8)
			g(9) = g(8)⊕g(1)
		g(5) = g(4)⊕g(1)	g(10) = g(8)⊕g(2)
			g(11) = g(8)⊕g(3)
	g(3) = g(2)⊕g(1)	g(6) = g(4)⊕g(2)	g(12) = g(8)⊕g(4)
			g(13) = g(8)⊕g(5)
		g(7) = g(4)⊕g(3)	g(14) = g(8)⊕g(6)
			g(15) = g(8)⊕g(7)

0
1

∞

Fig. 1   The development of a single-generator initial code tree,
where $g = g(1)g(2)g(4) \ldots g(2^{K-1})$.

				00
00	00	00	00	11
			11	01
				10
		11	01	00
				11
			10	01
				10
	11	01	00	01
				10
			11	00
				11
		10	01	01
				10
			10	00
				11
g——11	01	00	01	00
				11
			10	01
				10
		11	00	00
				11
			11	01
				10
	10	01	01	01
				10
			10	00
				11
		10	00	01
				10
			11	00
				11

0 ↕ 1   ∞

Fig. 2   The development of the initial code tree for the half-
rate code with g = 11 01 00 01 00 ... $g(2^{K-1})$

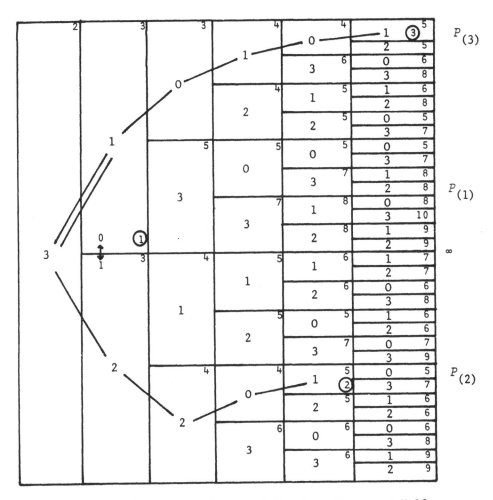

Figure 3   Selection of Permissible Paths from the Lower-Half
Initial Code Tree.

0	00	000	0000	00000
				00001
			0001	00010
				00020
		001	0010	00100
				00101
			0020	00200
				00201
	01	010	0100	01000
				01001
			0101	01010
				01020
		020	0200	02000
				02001
			0201	02010
				02020
1	10	100	1000	10000 ·1
				10001 ·2
		101	1001	10010 ·2
				10020 ① ·2
			1010	10100 ·2
				300000 ③ ·2
			1020 ①	10200 ·2
				22000 ② ·2
	20 ①	200	2000	20000 ·1
				20001 ·2
			2001	20010 ·2
				20020 ① ·2
		201	2010	20100 ·2
				20101 ·3
			2020 ①	20200 ·2
				12000 ② ·2

Fig. 4 The minimum test-error pattern tree up to 5 segments.

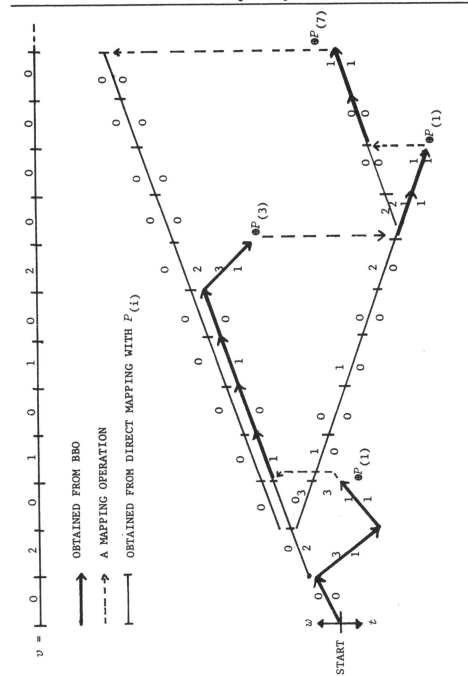

Fig. 5   Direct mapping search of a given received sequence.

On the design of practical minimum distance
convolutional decoders.

R.M.F. Goodman, B.Sc., Ph.D.,
University of Hull,
Hull HU6 7RX
England.

Abstract

In this paper we consider the hardware and computational requirements of

practical decoders designed to implement our efficient minimum distance

algorithm for convolutional codes. Firstly, we derive and evaluate

upper bounds for the number of decoding operations required to advance

one code segment, and show that significantly fewer operations are

required than in the case of sequential decoding. This implies a signifi-

cant reduction in the severity of the buffer overflow problem. Secondly,

we propose modifications to the algorithm in order to further reduce the

computational effort required at long back-up distances, at the expense

of only a small loss in coding gain, and discuss the trade-off between

coding gain and storage requirement as an aid to quantitative decoder

design. Finally, the performance and construction of decoders that
utilise hard and soft-decision sub-optimum forms of the algorithm are
described.

1.   Introduction

In a previous paper[1] we proposed a new minimum distance decoding scheme
for convolutional codes, which uses the distance and structural
properties of convolutional codes in order to achieve a significant
reduction in computational effort, when compared with sequential decoding.
In this paper we quantitatively assess the decoding effort required by
our algorithm and show that this is indeed much less than that required
by sequential decoding. In addition, by dividing the decoding procedure
into several regions in terms of required back-up distance, we propose
modifications to the algorithm which result in even further computational
reductions.

In sequential decoding, the progress of the decoder is highly variable
involving both forward extensions and back-up searches in order to find a
tentatively decoded path satisfying the current metric conditions. Since
data is transmitted at a constant rate, a buffer is required, and this
then raises the possibility of buffer overflow. Indeed, with sequential
decoding it is the possibility of buffer overflow that limits the effective user output bit error rate of the decoder. Any decoding scheme which
reduces the number of computations required per message bit therefore
reduces decoding delay and improves the output error rate achievable with

a fixed buffer, or conversely, reduces the size of buffer needed to achieve a given output error rate. Hence, by utilising our decoding algorithm, a much more advantageous trade-off between buffer size and output bit error rate can be established than in the case of sequential decoding.

For sequential decoding, the average number of computations per message bit tends to infinity with increasing message sequence length for rates above the computation rate R_{comp}, and is bounded above by a constant for rates less than R_{comp}, where R_{comp} is a function of the channel transition probabilities, and hence signal-to-noise ratio, only. Therefore, for rates R less than R_{comp} the probability of error can be made to approach zero by increasing constraint length without incurring excessive computation. The limiting factor on output bit error rate is then the probability of dismissal or buffer overflow, and this problem becomes severe when the ratio of R/R_{comp} tends to one. That is, at low E_b/N_o. Fig. 1 shows the probability of dismissal for the Fano decoder under conditions of $R \simeq R_{comp}$. The probability of the number of computations required per branch N_r, exceeding the number of allowed computations per branch N_a, is plotted; where the unit of computation is taken to be the examination of one branch of the code tree by the decoder. It can be seen for $R \simeq R_{comp}$ that unless the buffer size is sufficient to allow the maximum number of computations to be of the order of up to 2^{20}, the coding gain achievable with a long constraint length half rate code will be severely reduced from the maximum of 5.1dB (at an output bit error rate of 10^{-5}).

The basic strategy adopted in our decoding algorithm is to always seek a path at minimum distance from the received sequence, at every node extension. Compared with the above type of sequential decoding, this enables our algorithm to achieve a significant reduction in the maximum number of decoding operations, in two main ways. Firstly, a direct mapping scheme is utilised to directly find the minimum distance path in a single mapping operation without the need for a back-up search. Secondly, when a back-up search is required, an efficient search procedure that directly identifies the possible nodes at which path divergence might have occurred, is instigated.

In this paper we analyse the maximum number of computations required to advance one branch when using the algorithm, and compare this to the maximum required for sequential decoding; thereby showing a significant reduction in effort. Secondly, by dividing the decoding procedure to be adopted into several ranges of back-up distances, we introduce modifications of the algorithm to achieve even further reductions in the computational effort.

This paper develops in the following way. Firstly, we review the basic decoding procedure as described in reference 1. Secondly, a loose upper bound on the maximum computational effort is developed and compared with sequential decoding. Next, the upper bound is considerably tightened, showing a marked decrease in the computational effort required. We then

propose modifications to the algorithm to reduce the computational effort
at long back-up distance, and finally discuss the trade-off between
buffer size, coding gain, and decoder memory requirement, for full and
sub-optimum decoding.

2.   The Basic Minimum Distance Algorithm

Consider the following notation:

v the received sequence, which may differ from the transmitted

             sequence due to channel errors.

w the tentatively decoded path, a path in the code tree which is

             being compared with v, and is the decoder's current estimate of

             the corresponding transmitted path.

$t = w \oplus v$ the test-error sequence, which has ones in those positions were

             w and v differ

$|t|$ the weight of t

t_b the last b branches of t.

The code studied in this paper and in reference 1 is a systematic half-
rate code with constraint length k = 50 segments. The generator sequence
is g = 31010101100101110001100011111100101100110101010110 in quaternary
form, that is, [00] = 0, [01] = 1, [10] = 2, and [11] = 3.

We now review the basic procedures used in the algorithm.

(i)   The basic branch operation[1] (BBO). Whenever a w is found which is
known to be a minimum distance $|t|$ from v, the decoder carries out the
BBO to select the next segment of w, w_1, which is the tentative version

of the corresponding transmitted segment. For the code in this study we impose a rule that the BBO must choose a w_1 which results in a $t_1 = 0$ or 1, and eliminate the possibility of $t_1 = 2$. Hence we always have $|t_1| \leq$ 1.

(ii) Maximum back-up distance[1,2]. When the BBO results in a $t_1 = 0$ we can be sure that w has minimum test-error weight, and the decoder can return to the BBO after out-putting the oldest segment of w as the final decoded version of the corresponding transmitted segment. However, if $t_1 = 1$ it is possible that another path w' may have smaller test-error weight $|t'| = |t| - 1$. In this case we must determine whether or not a back-up search is needed, and if so, how far to back-up. The maximum back-up distance in branches, b_t, depends on the current value of $|t|$, and is tabulated in Table 1.

(iii) Required back-up distance. If the value of b_t is $\leq b_m$, the range over which direct mapping operates, then no search is needed and w' is found by a single mapping operation. If $b_t > b_m$ then we can identify a set of nodes $b_t^* \leq b_t$ at which w' may have diverged from w, and instigate the search procedure[1] at each of these nodes to try to find w'. The necessary condition for instigating a subsearch at back-up distance $b_t^* = b$ is $|t_b| \geq T^*(b)$, where $T^*(b)$ depends on the distance profile of the code and is tabulated in Table 2.

(iv) Permissible path decoding[1]. Assume that there is a w with test error weight $|t|$, and we are searching for a w' of the same length as w but belonging to the opposite half truncated tree, and having a smaller test error weight $|t'|$. In this case

w' and t' can be derived from $w' = w \oplus P$ and $t' = t \oplus P$, where P is a truncated path in the lower-half initial code tree and is called a permissible path. Searching for w' with the aid of a specially selected set of P will be used to modify the basic algorithm in order to reduce decoding effort, and is described later in the paper.

(v)   Direct mapping[1] (DM). Consider a set of test-error patterns t and their corresponding minimum test-error patterns t', where $|t'| = |t \oplus P|$ $< |t|$, and the maximum length of P is $\leq b_m$, the range over which direct mapping operates. In the decoder we store two sets of t and P into memory. During the decoding process, whenever the tentatively decoded sequence w has a test-error sequence t whose last b segments t_b exactly match a pattern stored in memory, we directly map t to $t' = t \oplus P$, and w' to $w \oplus P$. This guarantees that the new tentatively decoded sequence w' has minimum test-error weight. Once a direct mapping takes place, no more searching is needed and the decoder returns to the BBO. If t is such that its tail sequence does not match any stored t_b, that either t has minimum test-error weight, in which case the decoder returns to the BBO, or else the required t_b and P are not in the memory. Hence, only when $b_t^* \geq b_m + 1$ do we need to use the back-up search procedures. Otherwise, at most one direct mapping is all we need to acquire the path having minimum test-error weight.

3.   Upper bounds on the Maximum Number of Computations

In this section we upper bound the maximum number of computations required to advance one segment with the use of our algorithm, and compare this with the equivalent number of sequential decoding.

The code used is as detailed in the last section, and the search length L is assumed to be equal to the constraint length K, so that a valid comparison with the equivalent sequential decoder (which achieves 5.1dB coding gain at an output bit error rate of 10^{-5}) is ensured.

Considering that our decoding algorithm proceeds with basic branch operations (BBOs) and direct mappings (DMs), the BBO is taken to be the unit of our computation. We therefore assume that one DM takes the same amount of time as one BBO. The underlying assumption is that it takes approximately the same time to compare two paths, regardless of length, in the range from one to L segments.

Whenever the BBO results in $t_1 = 0$, which guarantees the path w being followed is at minimum distance from the received sequence v, the decoder returns to the BBO; thus the minimum computation for advancing one branch is one BBO. If $t_1 = 1$ and the decoder indicates that one DM has taken place to find w', the decoder also returns to the BBO. In this case it takes two computations, one BBO and one DM, to advance one branch. However, if $t_1 = 1$, and the decoder indicates that no direct mapping has taken place and that $b_t > b_m$, then a back-up search for w' is needed. We develop an equation for the maximum number of computations, N, as follows.

Firstly, let us assume that we have to search the complete $(b_t - b_m)$ unit at back-up distance b_t, by examining every path in the unit. (Note that this assumption is for simplicity in calculating the bound, and is not the actual search procedure adopted in the algorithm). As there are $(2^{b+1} - 2)$ branches in a b unit of the code, this involves a $(2^{(b_t+1)-b_m} - 2)$ branch search. However, the $(b_t - b_m)$ branches belonging to the present tentatively decoded sequence have already been searched, and so the required number of branch searches is $(2^{(b_t+1)-b_m} - 2) - (b_t - b_m)$. Secondly, there are $2^{(b_t-b_m)}$ paths of length b_m stemming from the end of the $(b_t - b_m)$ unit, and each of these is searched by direct mapping. Neglecting the present tentatively decoded path, this requires a search of $2^{(b_t-b_m)} - 1$ b_m-units. Each b_m-unit search could require a maximum of b_m BBOs and $|t_{b_m}|_{max}$ DMs. Hence the maximum number of computations for this stage is $\{(2^{(b_t-b_m)} - 1) \times (b_m + |t_{b_m}|_{max})\}$. Finally, we add one computation for the orginal BBO that resulted in $t_1 = 1$. The maximum number of computations for a back-up search of $b_t > b_m$ is then

$$N \leq \{(2^{(b_t+1)-b_m}-2) - (b_t-b_m)\} + \{2^{(b_t-b_m)}-1) \times (b_m + |t_{b_m}|_{max})\} + 1 \quad (1)$$

Fig. 2 illustrates the above calculation for the case $(b_t - b_m) = 3$. In this case, there are 11 branch searches in the $(b_t - b_m)$ unit, and 7 b_m-unit searches stemming from the 7 branches at the end of the $(b_t - b_m)$ unit.

Let us now evaluate N for the decoding algorithm. We assume $b_m = 16$, that is, the direct mapping range is 16 segments. This choice is determined by the memory size allowable in the decoder. For example, in

reference 1 it is shown that when b_m = 10, we only need to store 11

permissible paths, and 30 tentative test-error sequences. Even if the

memory requirement grows exponentially with increasing b_m, the memory

size of a decoder with b_m = 16 is still feasible and relatively cheap to

implement. The actual value of b_m is therefore up to the individual

hardware designer, and does not affect the general nature of our

calculations.

Assuming b_m = 16; and that b_t = 25 and $|t_{16}|_{max}$ = 5, evaluation of

equation 1 shows that the maximum number of computations $N(b_t = 25)$ is

equal to 11,745. If b_t = 33, then $N(b_t = 33)$ = 3,014,617. If b_t = 50,

then $N(b_t = 50) \simeq 4 \times 10^{11}$.

Consider now a sequential decoder utilising the same coding parameters as

our decoding algorithm. When such a decoder enters a back-up search the

maximum back-up distance is b_t, and therefore a complete b_t-unit search

is required. Thus the maximum number of computations required for

sequential decoding, N_s, is equal to the total number of branches in a

b_t-unit, minus the number of branches of w already searched, plus the

original BBO. Hence $N_s = (2^{(b_t+1)} - 2) - b_t + 1$. For b_t = 25,

$N_s(b_t = 25) \simeq 2.6 \times 10^7$, and if b_t = 33, $N_s(b_t = 33) \simeq 1.7 \times 10^{10}$. If

b_t = 50, $N_s(b_t = 50) \simeq 2.3 \times 10^{15}$.

From the above calculation it can be seen that the ratio of N_s/N is 2213

for b_t = 25, and tends to a limit of

$$\frac{2^{b_m}}{\frac{1}{2}(b_m + |t_{b_m}|_{max}) + 1} \approx 5700 \text{ for large } b_t.$$ This represents a consider-

able improvement over sequential decoding.

4. Determination of the Maximum Number of Computations

In this section we tighten the bounds on the maximum number of
computations for our algorithm by allowing for the actual search procedure utilised in a back-up search. We will show that this results in
an even more marked decrease in decoding effort than that presented in
the last section, compared with sequential decoding. In order to
facilitate calculation of the bound we divide the analysis into four
sections based on four back-up distances b_t, and denote the new bound on
maximum computation to be N*. On the basis of b_m = 16, the four regions
are $b_t \leq$ 16, 25, 33, and 50, corresponding to the four test-error
weight conditions $|t| < 5$, = 6, = 7, and $\geq$ 8.

4.1 The Value of N* for $b_t \leq 16$

This case has been previously analysed, showing that at most one BBO and
one DM are needed if $b_t \leq$ 16. Hence N* = 2.

4.2 The Value of N* for b_t = 25

Let us assume that $|t_1|$ = 1 and $|t| = |t_{25}|$ = 6. We therefore have
b_t = 25 and want to search for a w'_{25} whose $|t'_{25}|$ = 5. We divide the
analysis into three cases based on the three possible values of the
test-error weight of the first segment of t_{25}, that is,

$(|t_{25}| - |t_{24}|)$. Figure 3 illustrates each case.

(i)   Fig. 3a. If $|t_{25}| - |t_{24}| = 0$, then its complement segment has

weight $|t'_{25}| - |t'_{24}| = 2$. Therefore, if there is a t'_{25} stemming from

$b^*_t = 25$ such that $|t'_{25}| = 5$, it will have weight,

$|t'_{24}| = |t'_{25}| - (|t'_{25}| - |t'_{24}|) = 5 - 2 = 3$ over the remaining segments.

This implies that the 24-unit can be searched by using direct mapping

only, as follows.

From the distance property of the code, we can see that when a back-up

search starts at $b^*_t > b_m$ and the t' is such that $|t'_i| - |t_i - b_m| \le$

$|t'| \le [d(b_m) - 1]/2$, where $b^*_t \ge i \ge b_m$, the t' can be searched by using

only b^*_t BBOs and $|t'|$ DMs. In this case $b_m = 16$ and $[d(b_m) - 1]/2 = 4$;

therefore $|t'_i| - |t'_{i-16}| \le 3 \le [d(16) - 1]/2 = 4$, and the 25 unit can be

searched with a maximum of 25 BBOs and $|t'_{24}| = 3$ DMs. Hence, when the

range of required back-up distance b^*_t is such that every compliment unit

between 17 and 25 segments back must be searched, that is, $25 \ge b^*_t \ge 17$,

the maximum number of computations is

$$N^* = \sum_{j=17}^{25} (j+3) + 1 = 217$$

(ii)   Fig. 3b. If $|t'_{25}| - |t'_{24}| = 1$, and $|t_{24}| = 5$ implying $b_t = b^*_t = 25$

only. Also $|t'| - |t'_{i-16}| \le 5 - 1 = 4$ for $24 \le i \le 17$, which is equal to

$[d(16) - 1]/2$, implying that the search at $b^*_t = 25$ can be carried out by

means of 25 BBOs and 4 DMs. Hence

$$N^* = 25 + 4 + 1 = 30.$$

(iii) Fig. 3c. If $|t_{25}| - |t_{24}| = 2$, its complement segment

$|t'_{25}| - |t'_{24}| = 0$, and $|t_{24}| = 4$ again implying $b_t = b^*_t = 25$ only. In

this case, $|t'_{25}| = 5$ which indicates that there is a possibility that

$|t'_i| - |t'_{i-16}| = |t'_{25}| = 5 > [d(16) - 1]/2 = 4$, for some i within

$25 \le i \le 17$, and so the search cannot be directly carried out with BBOs

and DMs only. The worst case situation is therefore one in which there

are $(25 - 16) = 9$ consecutive zero test-error weight segments stemming

from $b^*_t = 25$. In this case the b_m unit at the end of the path is search-

ed with direct mapping, and each of the 9 complement path segments having

double test-error weight are searched in a manner similar to case (i).

The zero test-error weight portion and the terminating b_m-unit can be

arranged with a maximum of 25 BBOs and 5 DMs, and the paths stemming from

the double error segments can be searched with $\sum\limits_{j=17}^{24} (j+3)$ computations.

Hence the maximum number of computations is

$$N^*(b_t = 25)_{max} = (25 + 5) + \sum_{j=17}^{24} (j+3) + 1 = 219.$$

From the above calculations, it can be seen that the maximum number of

computations for $b_t = 25$ will not exceed 219. Not only is this signifi-

cantly less than the value calculated for sequential decoding, but it is

also 53 times less then the bound $N(b_t = 25)$ calculated in the last

section.

4.3   The Value of N* for $b_t = 33$, and $b_t \ge 34$

By extending the analysis along similar lines to that presented above, we

can calculate[3] the maximum number of computations required at back-up

distances of 33 and more. For example, we can show that $N*(b_t = 33) \leq$
697, which is an extremely small amount when compared with sequential
decoding, and is 4325 times less than the value of $N(b_t = 33)$ presented
in section 3. Also, we can show $N*(b_t = 40) < 1800$, which is considerably less than that required by sequential decoding. However, let us at
this point say that we wish to restrict the number of computations in a
back-up search to under 1000 in order to have a small buffer. We must
therefore modify the algorithm to cope with searches at back-up distances
of $b_t \geq 34$. This is dealt with in the next section.

5.   Searches at $b_t \geq 34$ using Permissible Path Decoding

Consider that we have a v with test-error weight $|t|$, and we are search-
ing for a w' with test-error weight $|t'| < |t|$. In this case w' and t'
can be found from $w' = w \oplus P$, and $t' = t \oplus P$, where P is one of a set of
truncated patterns from the lower half initial code tree, and is denoted
a permissible path. Unfortunately, it is not possible to store all the
possible P of length ≥ 34, because of the large memory this would entail.
Fortunately, we are obtaining results which show that the number of
permissible paths can be reduced by simply limiting the maximum weight of
P, and that the effect of this path reduction on coding gain is extremely
small, even if the maximum weight of P is reduced to $|P|_{max} \leq d(L)$, where
$d(L)$ is the minimum distance of the code over L segments.

Let us therefore evaluate the approximate amount of storage needed to
store a reduced set of P by considering the weight structure of the code.

Minimum distance and weight spectrum as a function of constraint length

have been studied by using a sequential decoder simulator to analyse the

structure of different half rate systematic codes[4]. For the code used in

this paper it can be shown[3] that there are approximately 38,000 paths

which have length $34 \leq k \leq 50$, and odd weight $|x| < d(L=50) = 17$. Also,

the total number of odd and even minimum weight paths in this region is

124. We may now consider two ways of reducing the number of P stored for

$34 \leq b_t^* \leq 50$.

In the first case we apply the general rules for permissible path

selection, that is, $|P|$ is odd and $P_2 = 01$. In addition, we impose the

restriction $|P| \leq d(L = 50) = 17$. By knowing that roughly 1/16 of all

paths of a given length end in 01, we can estimate that the total number

of paths needed to be stored is about 2400. Hence, a maximum of several

thousand path comparison operations could be performed in searching for a

w' with $|t'| \leq |t|$, via $w' = w \oplus P$.

In the second case we restrict the selection of permissible paths in such

a way that (i) only minimum weight paths are stored, and (ii) if the

weight is odd $P_2 = 01$, or if the weight is even $P_1 = 0$. Approximately 40

of the 124 minimum weight paths satisfy the above two conditions,

indicating that an exceedingly small memory is sufficient to store the

permissible path in this case. The decoder would then proceed as

follows whenever a back-up search in the range $34 \leq b_t^* \leq 50$ is required.

(i)   If $d(b_t^*)_{min}$ is odd, Figure 4a, a search will be carried out at $b_t^* = b_t$

to find a t' with $|t'| = |t \oplus P| < |t|$, where the P are those stored permissible paths with length equal to b segments long. When such a t' is found, we will return to the BBO. Otherwise go to (iii).

(ii)   If $d(b_t^*)_{min} = d(b_t^* - 1)_{min}$ is even, Figure 4b, a back-up search at $b_t^* = b$ will be carried out as follows. We first denote t_{-1} as the portion of t without the last segment t_1, which therefore has length (b - 1) segments. The same applies to t'_{-1} and t'. We then search for a t'_{-1} with $|t'_{-1}| = |t'_{-1} \oplus P| < t_{-1}$ where the P are those stored permissible paths with length (b - 1) segments. When such a t'_{-1} is found, we extend it with the BBO to derive a t'_1. If the BBO in a $t'_1 = 0$, we accept t' as the minimum weight path. Otherwise go to (iii). For the case of $d(b_t^*)_{min}$ even, but $d(b_t^*)_{min}$ is odd, w is accepted as the minimum weight path without any search[1].

(iii) We go to the next value of b_t^*, or if this is $(b_t^*)_{max}$, we accept w as the best path and return to the BBO. In the latter case the oldest segment of w that is output as the corresponding segment of the transmitted sequence could be in error. If this happens, however, the decoder will eventually recover.

6.   Decoder Trade-Offs

By adopting different search techniques at different stages in the search procedure we can obtain an efficient trade-off between buffer size, coding gain, and decoder-memory requirement. We now discuss the various options available when implementing the algorithm by dividing the back-up distance into three regions, b_m, b_s, and b_p, where $0 \leq b_m \leq b_s \leq b_p \leq L$.

Firstly, we would utilise direct mapping for all back-up searches at

distance $b_t^* \leq b_m$, because the maximum number of computations

$N*(b_t \leq b_m)_{max}$ is only equal to 2. This is the direct mapping or b_m

region. The bigger the b_m region, the smaller the buffer requirements,

but the larger the decoder path storage requirement. For example, if

b_m = 10 only 30 test error patterns need to be recognised (about 100 3-

input gates) and at current memory prices operating directing mapping

over b_m = 16 segments is still cheap.

Secondly, the region of back-up distance which uses the minimum distance

search procedure is denoted the b_s region, where $b_s \geq b_m$. The bigger the

value of b_s, the bigger the buffer requirement, especially if $b_s \geq 40$,

and the better the performance in terms of coding gain.

Thirdly, we denote the long back-up distance region that requires a

larger buffer size, and that often causes buffer overflow in sequential

decoding, as the b_p region. In this region we use permissible path

decoding with path reduction on the total number of paths, and this

implies that the decoding is now sub-optimum. Two different path reduct-

ion techniques are used: one with $|P| \leq d(L)_{min}$, and another with

$|P| = d(k)_{min}$. The value of k used could be either $L \geq k > b_s$ or

$L \geq k > b_m$ depending on the trade-offs required. The $|P| = d(k)_{min}$

approach requires much smaller memory and much fewer computations then

the $|P| \leq d(L)_{min}$ approach, but will result in a slight loss of coding

gain in the lower signal-to-noise ratio region. Clearly a trade-off between decoder memory buffer size, and coding gain is involved here. For
example, the storage requirement is of the order of $\frac{1}{4}$ Mbit for the
$|P| \leq d(L)_{min}$ approach, and 4K bit for the $|P| = d(k)_{min}$ approach.
Alternatively, one may decide that in order to restrict the maximum number of computations to a value approximately equal to that derived for
the b_s region, the weight constraint on $|P|$ should be set slightly higher
than $d(k)_{min}$. This would also improve the coding gain.

We have shown that the computational and storage requirements for the
minimum distance algorithm compare very favourably with those of
sequential decoding. It is therefore entirely feasible to implement the
algorithm using fast microprocessor technology and achieve a hard
decision coding gain of 5dB at 10^{-5} output bit error rate.

7.   Sub-Optimum Decoders

In the last section we were concerned with the complexity of implementing
the full minimum distance decoding algorithm in order to achieve the
maximum of 5.1dB of coding gain, as in sequential decoding. We now
consider the complexity and performance of two decoders based on sub-
optimum forms of the algorithm.

Firstly, consider a very simple direct mapping only decoder which uses
the code out-lined in   paper. We have built such a decoder in hardware[5], and the block diagram is shown in Figure 5. The decoder operates
at 2.5 Mbits/sec with a decoding constraint length of 11 segments,

recognises 97 test-error patterns, and utilises 17 permissible paths.
Figure 6 shows the performance of the decoder in Gaussian noise,
normalised for rate, and indicates that even with such a simple realisation a coding gain of 2.1dB at 10^{-5} output bit error rate is achievable
(this is slightly more than that achievable with the Golay code).

The second sub-optimum decoder we consider[6] uses a one-third code and
soft decision decoding. The decoder does not use direct mapping but
utilises a set of permissible paths to search for a path with a smaller
test-error weight in the soft-decision sense. The decoder uses a decoding constraint length of 10 segments, 229 permissible paths, 8-level
soft-decision quantisation and has a complexity of only 200 standard TTL
SSI integrated circuits. Figure 6 also shows the performance of this
decoder, indicating that a coding gain of 4.1dB at 10^{-5} output bit error
is achievable.

8.   Conclusions

In this paper we have shown that practical low-complexity decoders may be
built by utilising our efficient minimum distance decoding algorithm. At
present we are working on the implementation of fast microprocessor-
controlled soft-decision decoders for $\frac{1}{2}$ rate codes, in order to achieve
the 7.2dB coding gain that is achievable by maximum-likelihood decoding
of a long constraint length convolutional code.

9. <u>References</u>

1.   NG, W.H., and GOODMAN, R.M.F.: 'An efficient minimum distance
     decoding algorithm for convolutional error-correcting codes',
     Proc. I.E.E., Vol. 125, No. 2, Feb. 1978.

2.   NG, W.H.: 'An upper bound on the back-up depth for maximum-likeli-
     hood decoding of convolutional codes', IEEE Trans., 1976, IT-22,
     pp 354-357.

3.   NG, W.H., and GOODMAN, R.M.F.: 'An analysis of the computational
     and storage requirements for the efficient minimum distance de-
     coding of convolutional codes', Proc. I.E.E. (to be published).

4.   FORNEY, D. Jr.: 'High-speed sequential decoder study', Contract
     No. DAA B07-68-C-0093, Codes Corp., 1968.

5.   WINFIELD, A.F.T.: 'Minimum distance decoding of convolutional
     error-correcting codes', Diploma Thesis, University of Hull,
     1978.

6.   NG, W.H., KIM, F.M.H., and TASHIRO, S.: 'Maximum likelihood de-
     coding of convolutional codes', I.T.C./U.S.A., 1976.

$|t|$	$d(b_t)$	b_t
1	2	1
2	3	2
3	5	6
4	7	11
5	9	16
6	11	25
7	13	33
8	15	40
9	17	48
≥ 10	17	50

Table 1 Maximum Back-Up Distance b_t for Different Values of $|t|$

b	d(b)	T*(b)	b	d(b)	T*(b)
1	2	2	26	11	7
2	3	2	27	11	7
3	3	3	28	11	7
4	4	3	29	12	7
5	4	3	30	12	7
6	5	3	31	12	7
7	5	4	32	12	7
8	5	4	33	13	7
9	6	4	34	13	8
10	6	4	35	13	8
11	7	4	36	14	8
12	7	5	37	14	8
13	7	5	38	14	8
14	8	5	39	14	8
15	8	5	40	15	8
16	9	5	41	15	9
17	9	6	42	15	9
18	9	6	43	15	9
19	9	6	44	16	9
20	9	6	45	16	9
21	10	6	46	16	9
22	10	6	47	16	9
23	10	6	48	17	9
24	10	6	49	17	10
25	11	6	50	17	10

Table 2   Distance Profile d(b), and Threshold Condition T*(b)
on Back-Up Distance $b_t^* = b$

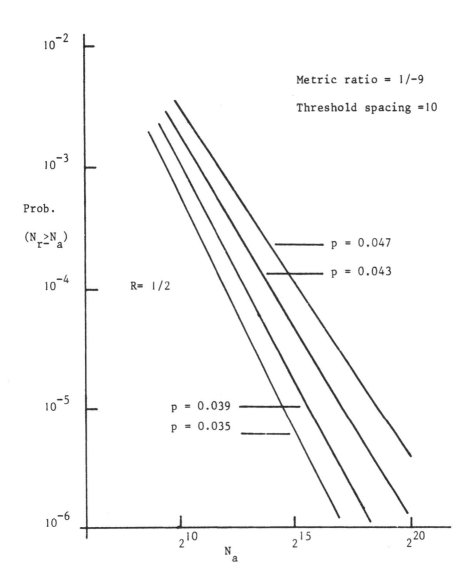

Figure 1. Distribution of computational effort for
a sequential decoder

$$N \leq [((2^{(b_t+1)-b_m}-2) - (b_t - b_m))$$

$$+ (2^{(b_t-b_m)}-1) \times (b_m + |t_{b_m}|_{max}) + 1]$$

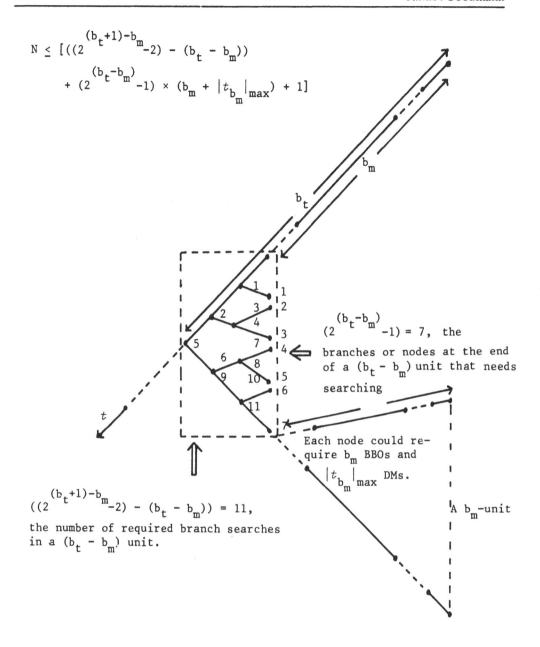

$(2^{(b_t-b_m)}-1) = 7$, the branches or nodes at the end of a $(b_t - b_m)$ unit that needs searching

Each node could require b_m BBOs and $|t_{b_m}|_{max}$ DMs.

A b_m-unit

$((2^{(b_t+1)-b_m}-2) - (b_t - b_m)) = 11$, the number of required branch searches in a $(b_t - b_m)$ unit.

Figure 2   Maximum number of decoding operations N for minimum distance decoding when $(b_t - b_m) = 3$.

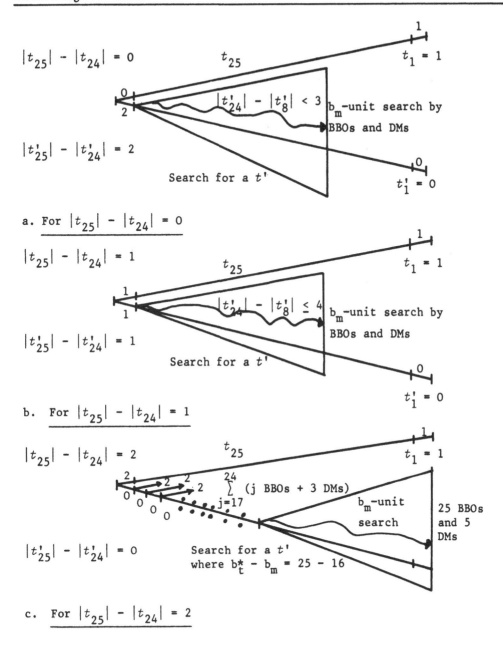

Figure 3   Calculation of N* for $b_t = 25$ and $|t_{25}| = 6$.

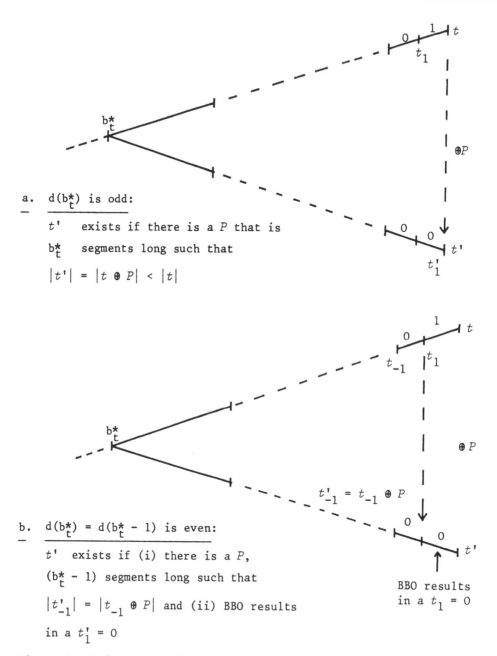

a. $d(b^*_t)$ is odd:

t' exists if there is a P that is

b^*_t segments long such that

$|t'| = |t \oplus P| < |t|$

b. $d(b^*_t) = d(b^*_t - 1)$ is even:

t' exists if (i) there is a P,

$(b^*_t - 1)$ segments long such that

$|t'_{-1}| = |t_{-1} \oplus P|$ and (ii) BBO results

in a $t'_1 = 0$

Figure 4   Using permissible path decoding to search for a t' with
            $|t'| < |t|$ at $34 \leq b^*_t \leq 50$

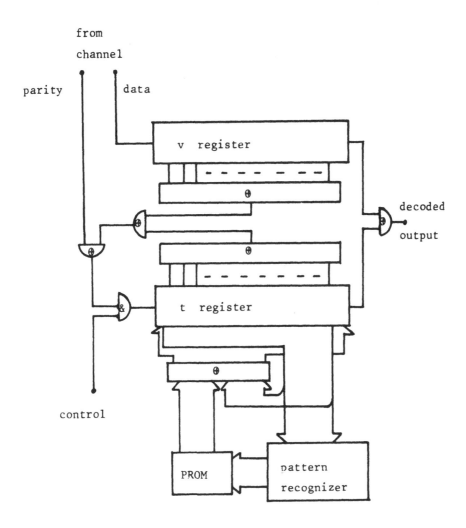

Figure 5. Decoder block diagram

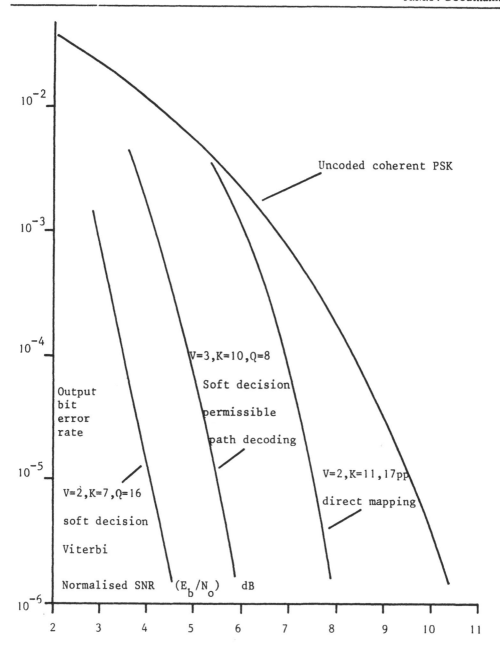

Figure 6. Performance curves

Soft-decision threshold decoders.

R.M.F. Goodman, B.Sc., Ph.D.,
University of Hull,
England.

Summary

Coding system designers are interested in threshold decoding for convolu-

tional codes because of the hardware simplicity of the decoder. Un-

fortunately, majority-decision threshold decodable codes are sub-optimum,

and this involves a loss in coding gain. In this paper a new method for

implementing soft-decision threshold decoding is introduced, enabling

some of the loss in coding gain to be recovered without too great a

sacrifice in hardware simplicity. Decoders for constraint length 2 and

12 segments are described, and their performance in Gaussian noise

evaluated. The soft-decision technique used can also be applied to block

codes with similar improvements in coding gain, and methods of imple-

menting this are discussed.

1. Introduction

Binary convolutional codes have been shown to exhibit extremely good
error-control properties under both Gaussian and burst noise conditions.
In the case of the additive white Gaussian channel, there are several
powerful convolutional decoding schemes (sequential decoding, Viterbi
decoding) that yield high coding gains (5dB at a sink bit error rate of
10^{-5}). Unfortunately, the hardware complexity of such schemes is high,
as the decoders are essentially large special-purpose computers. In
addition, the burst-noise performance of these powerful schemes tend to
be disappointing in comparison with convolutional code systems designed
specifically for burst-error correction.

The system designer is therefore often interested in convolutional decoding schemes that sacrifice a few dB of coding gain in order to
achieve low hardware complexity with reasonably good burst and random
error performance. Threshold decoding is one method of achieving this
aim. Majority-decision threshold decoding (ref. 1), is in terms of
hardware, one of the simplest convolutional decoding schemes possible,
and is applicable to a wide range of time-varying and fading channels.
Howeve , because the scheme is not optimum, some coding gain is lost.

In this paper we present a soft-decision majority threshold decoding
scheme (ref. 2) that improves on the performance achievable with
existing hard-decision decoders, thereby making up some of the lost
coding gain, whilst still retaining the inherent hardware simplicity of
threshold decoding. It has been shown (ref. 3) that the maximum increase

in coding gain that can be achieved by using soft-decision is about 2dB for infinite-level quantisation, and that the degradation involved in using equal-spacing 8-level quantisation (as assumed in this paper) is only 0.2dB. We therefore expect a maximum improvement of about 1.8dB for soft-decision majority threshold decoding when compared with existing hard-decision decoders.

In this paper we firstly outline hard-decision majority threshold decoding and then introduce our soft-decision scheme using a simple constraint length 2 code as an example. Next we describe our general method for soft-decision decoding of multiple error-correcting codes, using a constraint length 12 code as an example, and also present performance results. Finally, methods of applying the technique to majority-decodable block codes are discussed.

2. Hard-decision majority threshold decoding

A single-generator systematic convolutional code is one in which each information digit is encoded into V code digits (giving a message through-put rate of 1/V), the first of which is the unchanged information digit. In general, such a code is generated by a K segment generator sequence $g = g(1) \; g(2) \; g(4) \; \ldots \; g(2^{K-1})$, where K is the constraint length of the code in segments, and each segment contains V digits. For simplicity, we restrict our discussion in this paper to rate one-half codes.

Let us consider a rate one-half systematic code with constraint length K=2 segments, to review the basic hard-decision majority threshold decoding technique. The encoder for this simple code is shown in Fig. 1, and consists of only a single one-bit delay element and a single modulo-2

adder (exclusive-OR gate). Given a sequence of information digits

$x = x_{t-1} \, x_t \, x_{t+1} \, \cdots$, where t denotes the time unit of the information

digit x_t, each information digit is encoded into two code digits c_t' and

c_t'' . $c_t' = x_t$ is the unaltered information digit x_t, and $c_t'' = x_{t-1} \oplus x_t$

is a parity check sum based on the present information digit x_t and the

K-1 = 1 previous information digits. For serial transmission the coded

digits are sent to the channel in order $c_t' \, c_t''$ by appropriate action of

the switch. The encoder/decoder configuration for this code is shown in

Fig. 2. On the left of the diagram, the information digit x_t is encoded

into c_t' and c_t''; in the middle, two noise digits n_t' and n_t'' corrupt the

coded digits c_t' and c_t'' respectively; on the right is the decoder which

realises the (hard-decision) single-error-correction capability of the

code. The decoding action is explained with reference to the six points,

a, b, c, S_1, S_2, and n_{t-1}'. The six points are interpreted as follows:

$$a = x_t \oplus n_t'$$

$$b = x_{t-1} \oplus n_{t-1}'$$

$$c = x_t \oplus x_{t-1} \oplus n_t''$$

$$S_1 = a \oplus b \oplus c = (x_t \oplus n_t') \oplus (x_{t-1} \oplus n_{t-1}') \oplus x_t \oplus x_{t-1} \oplus n_t'')$$

$$S_2 = (x_{t-1} \oplus n_{t-1}') \oplus (x_{t-2} \oplus n_{t-2}') \oplus (x_{t-1} \oplus x_{t-2} \oplus n_{t-1}'')$$

$$\tilde{n}_{t-1}' = 1 \text{ if } S_1 = S_2 = 1$$

$$= \text{otherwise}$$

by cancelling information digits, S_1 and S_2 become:

$$S_1 = n_t' \oplus n_t'' \oplus n_{t-1}'$$

$$S_2 = \qquad\qquad n_{t-1}' \oplus n_{t-1}'' \oplus n_{t-2}' \qquad\qquad \cdots\cdots (1)$$

and it can be seen that the two parity check equations S_1, S_2 are ortho-gonal on the noise digit n'_{t-1}. Thus if a single error occurs anywhere in the 5 digit span covered by the orthogonal check sums, the only case when $S_1 = S_2 = 1$ is when $n'_{t-1} = 1$. In the decoder, the AND gate sends an estimate $\tilde{n}'_{t-1}$ to cancel the noise digit n'_{t-1} from the received digit $(x_{t-1} \oplus n'_{t-1})$, and thus produce an estimate $\tilde{x}_{t-1}$. From equation (1) it can be seen that if more than one error occurs in the 5 digit span covered by $\{S_1, S_2\}$, then the error correction capability of the code is exceeded and the decoded digit $\tilde{x}_{t-1}$ may be in error.

The decoder described above can be improved by the use of feedback. This is because if we are concerned with decoding x_{t-1} at the present moment, then x_{t-2} has already been decoded. We therefore have available an estimate of the noise digit n'_{t-2} before we decode x_{t-1}. Therefore S_2 can be simplified by feeding back $\tilde{n}'_{t-2}$ to cancel n'_{t-2} in equation (1). We may then replace S_2 with $\tilde{S}_2 = S_2 \oplus \tilde{n}'_{t-2} = n'_{t-1} \oplus n''_{t-1} \oplus n'_{t-2} \oplus \tilde{n}'_{t-2}$. If the estimate $\tilde{n}'_{t-2}$ is correct, that is $\tilde{n}'_{t-2} = n'_{t-2}$, then $S_2 = n'_{t-1} \oplus n''_{t-1}$. This means that provided the previously decoded digit was correct, the decoder check sums $\{S_1, S_2\}$ only span 4 digits, and can therefore correct a single error anywhere in 4 digits as opposed to 5 digits in the previous case. A decoder that makes use of past decisions to simpli-fy S_2 to $\tilde{S}_2$ is called a feedback decoder, whilst a decoder that does not use past decisions is called a definite decoder.

In general, if it is possible to form a set of 2e parity check equations which are orthogonal on a specified noise digit, then it is possible to

build a hard-decision majority threshold decoder which can correct any
combinations of e or fewer errors over one constraint span. Figure 3
shows the encoder/decoder arrangement for a triple error-correcting rate
one-half (24,12) majority decoder which has K=12, and an effective
constraint length of 24 digits within which 3 or fewer errors can be
corrected. This decoder can achieve a coding gain of 1.85dB at a sink
bit error rate of 10^{-5} on the binary symmetric channel (which is comparable to the (23,12) perfect Golay code), and can be built with only 16
standard integrated circuits (which is much less than that required to
decode the Golay code).

3.   Soft-decision majority threshold decoding

In this section we introduce our new method for soft-decision majority
threshold decoding. Our basic approach is to derive a modified set of
orthogonal check sums S_i^* which can be used to estimate each noise digit
in the soft-decision sense.

Firstly, let us assume that each received digit is quantised into Q = 8
levels, and can therefore be expressed as a 3 digit binary number, or the
BCD equivalent. For example, [000] = 0, [001] = 1, [010] = 2, ...
[111] = 7. The x_t are therefore expressed as [000] when x_t = 0, or [111]
when x_t = 1, in the soft-decision sense. The noise digits are expressed
in a similar manner but can take any intermediate value between 0 and 7,
that is, $0 = [000] \leq [n'_{t-j}] \leq [111] = 7$, where the square brackets
indicate a quantised or soft-decision noise digit. Note that the most
significant digit of a quantised digit is the hard decision digit itself.

For example, $[n'_{t-j}] = [010]$ implies $n'_{t-j} = 0$, and $[n'_{t-j}] = [110]$ implies

$n'_{t-j} = 1$. Similarly, received digits are given by $[r'_{t-j}] = [x_{t-j}] \oplus$

$[n'_{t-j}]$, and can take any value between 0 and 7. Let us define d_h to be

the hard-decision minimum distance between the two halves of the initial

code tree. The guaranteed error-correcting capability of the code over

K segments is then e_h digits where e_h is the largest integer satisfying

$e_h \leq (d_h - 1)/2$. The simple code used in section 2 has $d_h = 3$, and is

therefore a single error-correcting code. In the soft-decision sense,

the minimum distance of a code is given by $d_s = (Q-1) \times d_h$ levels, and

its error correction capability is e_s soft-decision levels, where e_s is

the largest integer satisfying $e_s \leq (d_s - 1)/2$. The simple example code

therefore has $d_s = (8-1) \times d_h = 21$, and $e_s = 10$. We can now estimate

the theoretical improvement to be gained by using soft-decision. In the

hard-decision sense an error occurs when sufficient noise is added to a

transmitted digit to form a received digit which lies on the opposite

side of the 0/1 decision boundary. For example, if we transmit [000]

(hard zero) and the noise is such that we   receive [101] an 'error' in

the hard-decision sense has occurred. Similarly, with transmitting

[111](hard one) and receiving [011]. Now, the minimum number of soft

level errors required to cause an error in the hard-decision sense is 4.

For example, transmit [000] receive [100]. As the simple code has a

level correcting power of 10 levels, this indicates that integer $[\frac{10}{4}]$

= 2 'hard' errors can now be corrected. Thus if two hard errors occur

and the total number of level errors amongst the 4 digits involved in

the decoding is ≤ 10, double error correction can be performed. Asymptotically, at high signal-to-noise ratios, soft-decision decoding therefore
doubles the effective 'hard' correcting power of a code.

We now outline the soft-decision technique. Consider the orthogonal
check sums for the example code (with feedback):

$$S_1 = n'_t \oplus n''_t \oplus n'_{t-1}$$

$$S_2 = \qquad\qquad n'_{t-1} \oplus n''_{t-1}$$

$$\text{..... (2)}$$

Our basic approach is to estimate, in the soft-decision sense, the value
of each noise digit that appears in the orthogonal check sums, for two
contradictory assumptions.

(a)   the data bit being decoded now (r'_{t-1}) is not in error, that is $\tilde{n}'_{t-1}$
$= 0$, and

(b)   the data bit is in error, $\tilde{n}'_{t-1} = 1$. For each assumption a sum of
the total number of level errors is formed. That is, $S^*_i = \Sigma_j [\tilde{n}_j]$ for all
j involved in the decoding (= 4 in this case), and i = 0 for the
assumption $\tilde{n}'_{t-1} = 0$, and i = 1 for $\tilde{n}'_{t-1} = 1$. The assumption which gives
the smallest sum of estimated errors is chosen to be the correct de-
coding decision.

Note that the noise digits cannot be directly found but have to be
derived from the received digits by a process of estimation as follows.
Firstly, let us make the assumption of no error in r'_{t-1}, that is,
$\tilde{n}'_{t-1} = 0$. Thus if the received digit at point b is
$[r'_{t-1}] = [x_{t-1} \oplus n'_{t-1}] \leq 3 = $ 'hard' zero, the estimate of $[n'_{t-1}]$, is

given by $[\tilde{n}'_{t-1}] = [x_{t-1} \oplus n'_{t-1}]$. If the received digit is $[x_{t-1} \oplus n'_{t-1}]$

≥ 4, then $[\tilde{n}'_{t-1}] = 7 - [x_{t-1} \oplus n'_{t-1}]$. Corresponding values for r'_{t-1} <u>in</u>

error are therefore $7 - [r'_{t-1}]$, and $[r'_{t-1}]$.

To estimate the remainder of the noise digits we need to know the result

of each orthogonal parity check sum in the hard-decision sense.

Consider first S_2. If $S_2 = 1$, that is, S_2 'fails' in the hard-decision

sense, then we must assume that $\tilde{n}''_{t-1} = 1$, because we have assumed $\tilde{n}'_{t-1}=0$

in the hard-decision sense. Hence the estimate of n''_{t-1} in the soft-

decision sense is $[\tilde{n}''_{t-1}] = [r''_{t-1}]$ if $[r''_{t-1}] \geq 4$, and $[\tilde{n}''_{t-1}] = 7 - [r''_{t-1}]$

if $[r''_{t-1}] \leq 3$. Conversely, if S_2 does not fail in the hard-decision

sense, then $\tilde{n}''_{t-1} = 0$ and $[\tilde{n}''_{t-1}] = 7 - [r''_{t-1}]$ if $[r''_{t-1}] \geq 4$, or

$[n''_{t-1}] = [r''_{t-1}]$ if $[r''_{t-1}] \leq 3$. Consider now S_1. If S_1 fails then

<u>either</u> n'_t or n''_t is in error. We choose the assumption which gives the

lowest number of level errors and then estimate the noise digits as

previously. If S_1 does not fail we assume no errors in n'_t and n''_t. S^*_o is

then formed by summing the noise estimates

$$S^*_o = [n'_t] + [n''_t] + [n''_{t-1}] + [n'_{t-1}].$$

The process is repeated for the assumption $\tilde{n}'_{t-1} = 1$ and S^*_1 is calculated.

If $S^*_o \leq S^*_1$, then $\tilde{n}'_{t-1} = 0$, and if $S^*_o > S^*_1$, $\tilde{n}'_{t-1} = 1$.

Consider the following example. Let us assume that $x_t = x_{t-1} = 0$, that

the noise digits are $[n'_{t-1}] = [101]$, $[n''_{t-1}] = [100]$, $[n'_t] = [001]$,

$[n''_t] = [000]$, and that the decoder has not made any previous decoding

errors. Note that as $n'_{t-1} = n''_{t-1} = 1$, a hard decision decoder would

decode $\tilde{x}_{t-1} = 1$, thus giving a decoding error. Using the above soft-decision procedure, however, x_{t-1} can be correctly decoded.

(1) Assume $\tilde{n}'_{t-1} = 0$. Hence the received digit $[r_{t-1}] = [x_{t-1} \oplus n'_{t-1}] =$
[101] is not in error and $[\tilde{n}'_{t-1}] = 7 - [101] = 2$ levels.

(2) $S_2 = 1 \oplus 1 = 0 =$ no fail. We therefore assume $\tilde{n}''_{t-1}$ is not in error.
Hence $[\tilde{n}''_{t-1}] = 7 - [r''_{t-1}] = 7 - 4 = 3$ levels.

(3) $S_1 = 0 \oplus 0 \oplus 1 = 1 =$ fail. Hence we assume either n'_t or n''_t is in
error. If we assume n'_t is in error than $[\tilde{n}_t] = 7 - [r'_t] = 7 - [001] = 6$
levels, as $[r'_t] \leq 1 \leq 3$. Also, n''_t is assumed not in error, giving
$[\tilde{n}''_t] = 0$ levels, and a total of 6 level errors. If we assume the converse, n''_t in error, then $[\tilde{n}'_t] = 1$ level, and $[\tilde{n}''_t] = 7$ levels, giving a
total of 8 level errors, we therefore assume that of the two $[\tilde{n}'_t]$ is
more likely to be in error.

(4) We now calculate $S^*_0 = 2 + 3 + (6+0) = 11$.

(5) Now assume that $\tilde{n}'_{t-1} = 1$, and that r'_{t-1} is in error. Hence $[\tilde{n}'_{t-1}] =$
$[r'_{t-1}] = 5$.

(6) S_2 does not fail. Therefore as $\tilde{n}'_{t-1} = 1$, $\tilde{n}''_{t-1} = 1$ to cause this.
Hence $[\tilde{n}''_{t-1}] = [r''_{t-1}] = 4$.

(7) S_1 fails. Therefore n'_t and n''_t must be assumed correct. Hence
$[\tilde{n}'_t] = 1$, and $[n''_t] = 0$.

(8) $S^*_1 = 5 + 4 (1+0) = 10$.

(9) Therefore $S^*_1 < S^*_0$ and we assume $\tilde{n}'_{t-1} = 1$, that is, $r'_{t-1} = 1$ is in
error, and x_{t-1} is correctly decoded as $\tilde{x}_{t-1} = 0$.

4. Soft-decision multiple error threshold decoding

In this section the approach used for the constraint length 2 code is generalised to deal with multiple-error correcting convolutional codes, using a constraint length 12 code as an example.

Figure 3 shows a triple-error-correcting hard-decision threshold decoding system. It is possible to form $2e = 6$ check sums orthogonal on the noise digit n'_{t-11} as follows.

$$S_{t-11} = n'_{t-11} \oplus n''_{t-11}$$

$$S_{t-5} = n'_{t-11} \oplus n'_{t-5} \oplus n''_{t-5}$$

$$S_{t-4} = n'_{t-11} \oplus n'_{t-10} \oplus n'_{t-4} \oplus n''_{t-4}$$

$$S_{t-2} = n'_{t-11} \oplus n'_{t-9} \oplus n'_{t-8} \oplus n'_{t-2} \oplus n''_{t-2}$$

$$S_t \oplus S_{t-3} \oplus S_{t-7} = n'_{t-11} \oplus n'_{t-6} \oplus n'_{t-3} \oplus n'_t \oplus n''_{t-3} \oplus n''_{t-7} \oplus n''_t$$

$$S_{t-1} \oplus S_{t-8} \oplus S_{t-10} = n'_{t-11} \oplus n'_{t-7} \oplus n'_{t-1} \oplus n''_{t-1} \oplus n''_{t-8} \oplus n''_{t-10}$$

Our basic approach is now to estimate the algebraic sum of a set of $2e+1$ soft-decision noise sums, one for each orthogonal check sum, and one for $[\tilde{n}'_{t-11}]$, and compare this to a fixed threshold value $T = (Q-1)(2e+1)/2$. Then if $S^*_o > T$ we decode $\tilde{n}'_{t-11} = 1$, and if $S^*_o \leq T$, $n'_{t-11} = 0$.

The method outlined here differs from the scheme detailed in the last section in that only one noise digit per orthogonal check sum is estimated in the soft-decision sense. This digit is always the 'worse' digit (that is the one nearest the 0/1 boundary) in each orthogonal sum, excluding the digit on which all sums are orthogonal. The reason for doing this can be seen with reference to the example given in the last section. In that example the estimated value of n''_t did not change for the two assumptions $\tilde{n}'_{t-1} = 0$, and $\tilde{n}'_{t-1} = 1$. The value $\tilde{n}''_t$ therefore

played no part in deciding which sum is the greater S^*_0 or S^*_1, and can

therefore be omitted. In general then, the only noise estimate which

will change for a given orthogonal check sum result is the 'worst' digit

in the check sum set.

Also, as a consequence of the above, and neglecting estimates which do

not change, it can be seen that the noise estimates for each orthogonal

check sum are complements of each other for the two assumptions $\tilde{n}'_{t-1} = 0$,

and $\tilde{n}'_{t-1} = 1$, that is, they add to $(Q-1) = 7$. For the triple-error

correcting code this means that the two sums S^*_0 and S^*_1 add to $(Q-1)(2e+1)$

$= 49$, and hence $T = 24$. It is therefore only necessary to compute S^*_0,

and compare its value to $(Q-1)(2e+1)/2$, because $S^*_1 = (Q-1)(2e+1) - S^*_0$.

Consider the following example for the constraint length 12 code. We

assume $x_t = x_{t-1} = \ldots = x_{t-11} = 0$ and that no previous decoding error

has been accepted. Also, $[n'_{t-11}] = [110]$, $[n'_{t-5}] = [101]$, $[n'_{t-10}] = [100]$,

$[n''_{t-4}] = [011]$, $[n'_{t-9}] = [100]$, $[n'_{t-8}] = [001]$, $[n'_{t-1}] = [010]$, and all

other noise digits are $[000]$. Note that this gives 4 hard decision

errors. The estimation of S^*_0 is performed as follows.

(1) $[\tilde{n}'_{t-11}] = 7 - [r'_{t-11}] = 7 - [110] = 1$, because we assume $\tilde{n}'_{t-11} = 0$.

(2) $S_{t-11} = 1 \oplus 0 = 1$. Hence $\tilde{n}''_{t-11} = 1$ and $[\tilde{n}''_{t-11}] = 7 - [r''_{t-11}] = 7 -$

$[000] = 7$.

(3) $S_{t-5} = 1 \oplus 1 \oplus 0 = 0$. Hence 'worst' not in error. That is,

$\tilde{n}'_{t-5} = 0$ and $[\tilde{n}'_{t-5}] = 7 - [r'_{t-5}] = 7 - [101] = 2$.

(4) $S_{t-4} = 1 \oplus 1 \oplus 0 = 0$. Hence 'worst' not in error. That is, $\tilde{n}''_{t-4} = 0$ and $[\tilde{n}''_{t-4}] = [r''_{t-4}] = [011] = 3$.

(5) $S_{t-2} = 1 \oplus 1 \oplus 0 \oplus 0 \oplus 0 = 0$. Hence, 'worst' not in error. That is, $\tilde{n}'_{t-9} = 1$ and $[n'_{t-9}] = 7 - [r'_{t-9}] = 7 - [100] = 3$.

(6) $S_t \oplus S_{t-3} \oplus S_{t-7} = 1 \oplus 0 \oplus 0 \oplus 0 \oplus 0 \oplus 0 \oplus 0 = 1$. Hence 'worst' is in error. That is, $\tilde{n}'_t = 1$ and $[\tilde{n}'_t] = 7 - \lfloor r'_t \rfloor = 7 - [000] = 7$.

(7) $S_{t-1} \oplus S_{t-8} \oplus S_{t-10} = 1 \oplus 0 \oplus 0 \oplus 0 \oplus 0 \oplus 0 \oplus 0 = 1$. Hence, 'worst' is in error. That is $\tilde{n}'_{t-1} = 1$ and $[\tilde{n}'_{t-1}] = 7 - [010] = 5$.

(8) Therefore, $S^*_o = 1 + 7 + 2 + 3 + 3 + 7 + 5 = 28 > T = 24$ and hence $\tilde{n}'_{t-11} \neq 0$ but $\tilde{n}'_{t-11} = 1$, giving a correct decoding $\hat{x}_{t-11} = 0$.

5. Decoder Design

The increase in complexity required to implement the soft-decision algorithm is not excessive. Essentially, the only complex items in the circuitry are a BCD adder capable of adding the (2e+1) noise estimates, BCD comparators for each orthogonal check sum, and a threshold comparator.

Figure 4 shows a soft-decision decoder for the simple K=2 code. The essential items in the design are the same for this code or a multiple error-correcting code, and are as follows.

Delay bistables (denoted D): are used to store both hard-decision and soft-decision digits.

Quantizers: these provide 8 level quantization of the received digits.

Basic Soft-Error Processors (BSEP): these devices output the number of

level errors in the received digit, assuming that the received digit is
not in error, in the hard-decision sense. This is therefore a simple
logic device with the following truth table.

INPUT			OUTPUT		
Quantized soft-decision digit			Binary		Levels
most significant (hard) bit		LSB	MSB	LSB	
0	0	0	0	0	0
0	0	1	0	1	1
0	1	0	1	0	2
0	1	1	1	1	3
1	0	0	1	1	3
1	0	1	1	0	2
1	1	0	0	1	1
1	1	1	0	0	0

Comparators: these operate on the outputs of the basic soft-error
processors in such a way that for any two BCD inputs, the greatest BCD
number is output. By this means the 'worst' digit in an orthogonal
check sum is identified. Note that in figure 4 only one such comparator
is required. In general, however, more than two noise digits are
involved in a check sum, and therefore a comparator with as many inputs
as there are digits in the orthogonal check sum, minus one, are required.
Such a device is easily constructed by simply iterating the basic 2-
input device as many times as required.

Compliment Processors (CP): these devices operate under control of a

hard-decision orthogonal check sum, and either allow a soft-decision
estimate [i] to be transmitted unaltered through them, or else compliment the estimate to 7-[i]. The device is again a simple logic element
with the following truth table.

INPUT			OUTPUT	
hard-decision control check sum input	soft-decision digits		binary levels	
	binary levels			
0	00	0	000	0
0	01	1	001	1
0	10	2	010	2
0	11	3	011	3
1	00	0	111	7
1	01	1	110	6
1	10	2	101	5
1	11	3	100	4

BCD Adder: In general, an adder with (2e+1) inputs that is capable of
adding input numbers in the range 0→7 is required. Finally, a threshold
device which outputs a 1 if the adder output is > T, and a 0 otherwise,
is required.

6.   Soft-decision threshold decoding of block codes

The soft-decision decoding algorithm outlined in the previous sections
can also be used to decode one-step or L-step majority-logic decodable
block codes, with very little modification. Consider as an example the
(15,7) cyclic double-error correcting one-step decodable code which has

a generator polynomial $g(x) = x^8 + x^7 + x^6 + x^4 + 1$. It is possible to form $2e=4$ parity check sums orthogonal on the noise digital n_{14} as follows:

$$A_1 = n_{14} \oplus n_{12} \oplus n_{11} \oplus n_3$$

$$A_2 = n_{14} \oplus n_{13} \oplus n_5 \oplus n_1$$

$$A_3 = n_{14} \oplus n_6 \oplus n_2 \oplus n_0$$

$$A_4 = n_{14} \oplus n_{10} \oplus n_8 \oplus n_7$$

Figure 5 shows a Type II decoder for this code, which operates as follows.

(1)   With gate 1 on and gate 2 off, the received block is read into the buffer register.

(2)   The 2e checksums orthogonal on n_{14} are formed and, the threshold gate outputs $\tilde{n}_{14} = 1$ if a clear majority of inputs are one.

(3)   The estimate $\tilde{n}_{14}$ is then added modulo-2 to the received digit to form the correct output digit $\hat{x}_{14}$.

(4)   The register is shifted once with gate 1 off, and gate 2 on. Hence the corrected digit $\hat{x}_{14}$ is fed back, thereby removing n_{14} from the equations, provided that a correct bit decoding has been made. The exclusive OR gates now form 4 check-sums orthogonal on n_{13}, which is now at the right-hand end of the buffer register, and decoding is again accomplished via the threshold gate.

(5)   Decoding continues on a bit-by-bit basis, until all the corrected information bits have been output.

It can be easily seen that the soft-decision algorithm can operate on this decoding scheme in exactly the same way as with convolutional codes. That is, for each information bit the sum S_o^* of $(2e+1)$ soft-decision noise estimates is computed: one for $[\tilde{n}_{14}]$ given the assumption $\tilde{n}_{14} = 0$, and one for each orthogonal check-sum based on the 'worst' digit in the checksum. The sum of estimates is then compared with the fixed threshold T, and n_{14} is decoded. Similarly, each information digit in the block is decoded on a bit-by-bit basis by simply shifting the quantized received block in the buffer register.

The above type of soft-decision decoding is again sub-optimum in that the full 2dB of soft-decision coding gain is not achieved. It is possible however to considerably improve the decoding performance, at the expense of more complex control circuitry, by modifying the scheme as follows.

The above block code soft-decision algorithm proceeds by decoding the information bits in their natural order, that is, we estimate the noise digits in the order n_{14}, n_{13}, ..., n_{n-k+1}, n_{n-k}. However, as decoding decisions are fed-back, thus affecting future decoding decisions, it would be wise to decode all the bits in the block in order of decreasing 'confidence'. We can form an estimate of the 'confidence' of each decoding decision by comparing the sum S_o^* with the threshold value T. The further the value of S_o^* is away from the value of T, that is, the greater $|T-S_o^*|$, the greater the confidence we have of a correct bit decoding decision. A decoder operating on this scheme would therefore calculate the sum $|T-S^*_o|$ for each bit in the block, and store a list of

the order in which bits are to be decoded, based on the increasing value

of $|T-S^*_o|$. The decoder then decodes the bits in the order indicated by

successively shifting them into the decoding position, that is, the

right-most end of the buffer register. In this way, a decoder which

realises most of the 2dB soft-decision coding gai available can be

built for a wide variety of majority-logic decodable codes.

7. Performance

Figure 6 shows the performance of various block and convolutional de-

coding schemes using the algorithm, under conditions of additive white

Gaussian noise. It can be seen that useful coding gains over that

achievable with hard-decision decoding are possible. Note that all

curves are corrected for rate, that is, plotted versus normalised signal-

to-noise ratio (energy per information bit E_b/N_o noise density), to

ensure a valid comparison between uncoded and coded transmission.

8. References

1. Massey, J.L.: Threshold Decoding, M.I.T. Press, Cambridge Mass.,
    1963.

2. Goodman, R.M.F., and Ng, W.H.: 'Soft-decision threshold decoding of
    convolutional codes', I.E.R.E. Conf. Proc. No. 37, 1977.

3. Wozencraft, J.M., and Jacobs, I.B.: Principles of Communication
    Engineering, Wiley, New York, 1965.

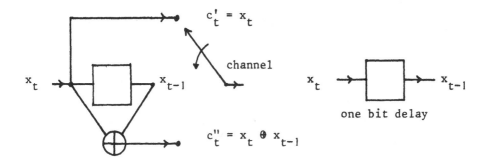

Figure 1.A simple convolutional encoder g = 11 01

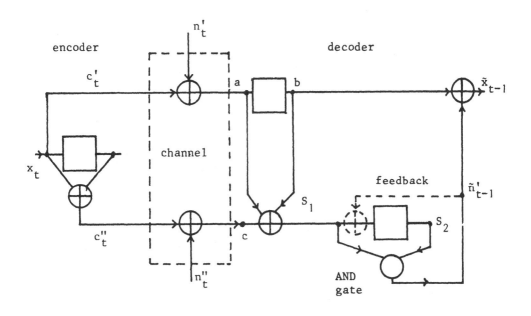

Figure 2. A K=2 convolutional coding system

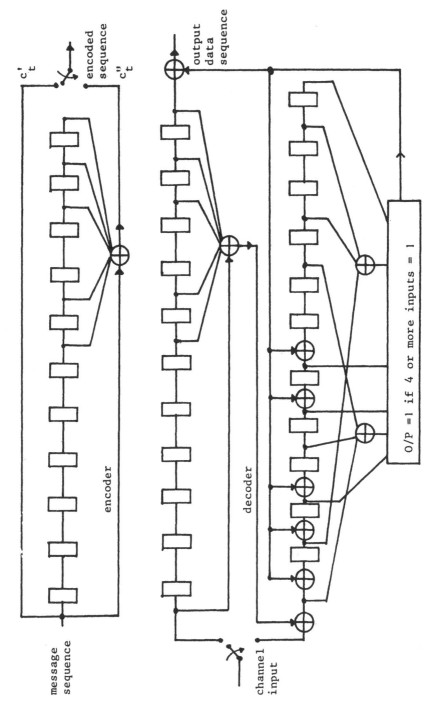

Figure 3 . A triple error correction threshold coding system

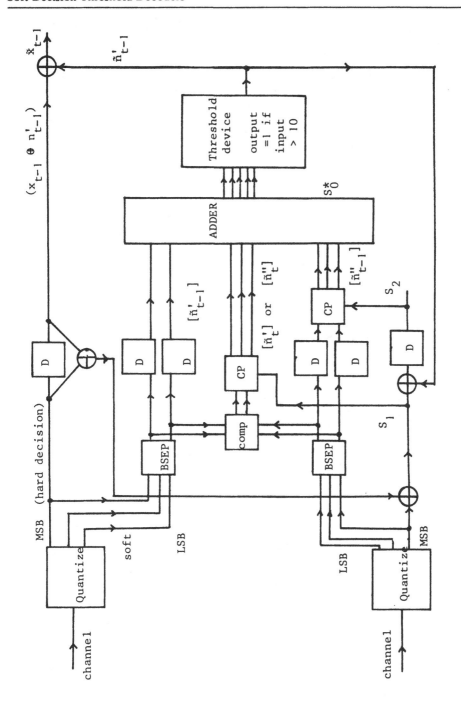

Figure 4. Soft-decision threshold decoder

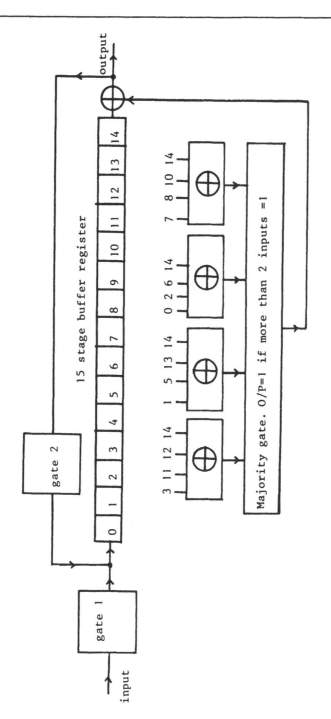

Figure 5. Type II one-step majority decoder for the (15,7) cyclic code

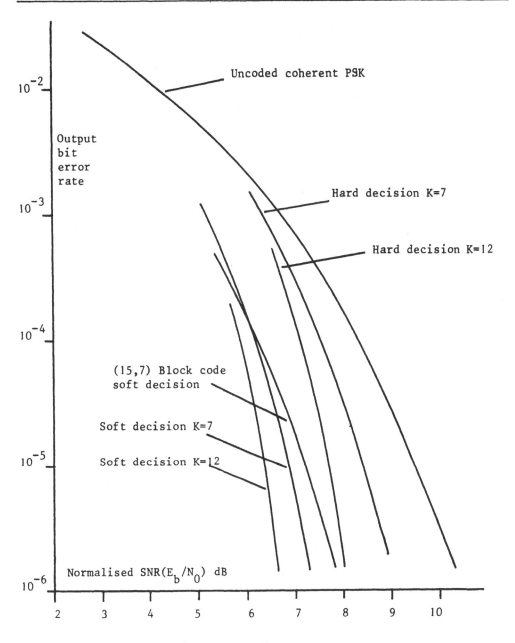

Figure 6. Performance curves

ALGEBRAIC CODES IN THE FREQUENCY DOMAIN

Richard E. Blahut
International Business Machines Corporation
Federal Systems Division
Owego, NY 13827

I. INTRODUCTION

Communication theory and signal processing are closely related
subjects that have been developed largely by engineers. Analysis and
synthesis problems in these fields depend heavily on reasoning in the
frequency domain. Thus, in the study of real- or complex-valued signals,
the Fourier transform plays a basic role. When the time variable is
discrete, the discrete Fourier transform plays a parallel role. Accordingly, Fourier transforms and discrete Fourier transforms are among the
major tools of engineers.

In contrast, the theory of error control codes has been developed
principally by algebraists; consequently, it picked up much algebraic
terminology as it evolved. And thus it tends to intimidate most engineers.
Actually, coding theory and signal processing are very similar.

It is possible to define Fourier transforms for functions of a discrete index that take values in a Galois field. These finite field
transforms are very useful in the study of error control codes, but they
are less well known than Fourier transforms over the complex field. To
draw the subjects of signal processing and error control codes more closely together, we shall study a frequency domain formulation for coding.

Finite field transforms were first introduced into the subject of
error control codes in the study of decoder complexity. These transforms, however, can be made to play a much more central role in the
subject. In retrospect, one can see that the early treatment of codes
using the Mattson-Solomon polynomial are really variations of a frequency domain analysis. By using the Fourier transform, known ideas of

coding theory can be described in a frequency domain setting that is much different from the familiar time domain setting.

Cyclic codes can be defined as codes whose codewords have certain specified spectral components equal to zero. Goppa codes and other alternant codes can be given a similar interpretation. Also, the decoding of many codes can be described spectrally.

The lectures recorded here cast much of the subject of error control codes into a transform setting. In this way we hope to stimulate interest in, and to accelerate, the development of a spectral view of coding. We believe the spectral formulation brings coding theory much closer to signal processing and makes error control coding more accessible to the nonspecialist. Most of the theory studied in these lectures is well-known, but approached along an unfamiliar axis. The list of references and the notes at the end show the principal sources for the theory on which the lectures are based.

II. FINITE FIELD TRANSFORMS

The discrete Fourier transform of $p = \{p_i \quad i=0,\ldots, n-1\}$, a vector of complex numbers, is given by

$$P_k = \sum_{i=0}^{N-1} e^{-j2\pi N^{-1}ik} p_i \qquad\qquad k=0,\ldots, N-1$$

where $j = \sqrt{-1}$. The Fourier kernal $e^{-j2\pi N^{-1}}$ is an N-th root of unity in the field of complex numbers. In the finite field, $GF(q^m)$, an element α of order n is an nth root of unity. Drawing on the analogy between $\exp(-j2\pi N^{-1})$ and α, we have the following definition.

<u>Definition 1</u> Let $e = \{e_i \quad i=0,\ldots, n-1\}$ be a vector over $GF(q)$, where n divides q^m-1 for some m, and let α be an element of $GF(q^m)$ of order n. The finite field Fourier transform of the vector e is the vector $E = \{E_j \quad j=0,\ldots, n-1\}$ given by

$$E_j = \sum_{i=0}^{n-1} \alpha^{ij} e_i \qquad\qquad j=0,\ldots, n-1$$

The most important values for n are those satisfying $n=q^m-1$. These values of n are called primitive blocklengths. Then α is a primitive element of $GF(q^m)$. It is natural to call the discrete index i "time" and to call e the time-domain function or the signal. Also, we call the discrete index j "frequency" and E the frequency-domain function or the spectrum.

In the case of the discrete Fourier transform, even though the time domain function p_i is real, the transform P_k is complex. Similarly, in the finite field Fourier transform, even though the time domain function e_i is over the field $GF(q)$, the spectrum E_j is over the extension field $GF(q^m)$. In error control applications, all the decoding action really takes place in the big field $GF(q^m)$; it is just that we happen to start with a vector in the small field $GF(q)$ that is consistent with the channel input.

<u>Theorem 1</u> Over GF(q), a field of characteristic p, a vector and its

spectrum are related by

$$E_j = \sum_{i=0}^{n-1} \alpha^{ij} e_i$$

$$e_i = \frac{1}{n \text{ modulo } p} \sum_{j=0}^{n-1} \alpha^{-ij} E_j$$

<u>Proof</u>

In any field,

$$x^n - 1 = (x-1)(x^{n-1} + x^{n-2} + \ldots + x + 1)$$

By the definition of α, α^r is a root of the left side for all r. Hence

for all $r \neq 0$ modulo n, α^r is a root of the last term. But this is

equivalent to

$$\sum_{j=0}^{n-1} \alpha^{rj} = 0 \qquad r \neq 0 \text{ modulo } n$$

while if r = 0,

$$\sum_{j=0}^{n-1} \alpha^{rj} = n \text{ modulo } p$$

which is not zero if n is not a multiple of the field characteristic p.

Combining these facts, we have

$$\sum_{j=0}^{n-1} \alpha^{-ij} \sum_{k=0}^{n-1} \alpha^{kj} e_k = \sum_{k=0}^{n-1} e_k \sum_{j=0}^{n-1} \alpha^{(k-i)j} = (n \bmod p) e_i$$

Finally, $q-1 = p^m-1$ is a multiple of n, and consequently n is not a

multiple of p. Hence n mod p $\neq$ 0. This proves the theorem.

The Fourier transform has many strong properties that carry over to the finite field case. An example is the convolution property. Suppose that

$$e_i = f_i g_i \qquad\qquad i=0, \ldots, n-1$$

Then

$$E_j = \frac{1}{n} \sum_{k=0}^{n-1} F_{j-k} G_k$$

with the understanding that all subscripts are interpreted modulo n (or equivalently that the spectra are defined for all j and are periodic with period n). This is proved as follows

$$E_j = \sum_{i=0}^{n-1} \alpha^{ij} f_i \left(\frac{1}{n} \sum_{k=0}^{n-1} \alpha^{-ik} G_k \right) = \frac{1}{n} \sum_{k=0}^{n-1} G_k \left(\sum_{i=0}^{n-1} \alpha^{i(j-k)} f_i \right) = \frac{1}{n} \sum_{k=0}^{n-1} G_k F_{j-k}$$

Note also that setting j=0 in the convolution formula

$$E_j = \sum_{i=0}^{n-1} \alpha^{ij} f_i g_i = \frac{1}{n} \sum_{k=0}^{n-1} F_{j-k} G_k$$

yields the Parseval-type formula

$$\sum_{i=0}^{n-1} f_i g_i = \frac{1}{n} \sum_{k=0}^{n-1} F_{n-k} G_k$$

Sometimes a space of vectors is associated with a space of polynomials. The polynomial

$$e(x) = e_{n-1} x^{n-1} + \ldots + e_1 x + e_0$$

can be transformed into a polynomial

$$E(x) = E_{n-1} x^{n-1} + \ldots + E_1 x + E_0$$

by means of the finite field Fourier transform. The latter polynomial is called the spectrum polynomial, the associated polynomial, or the

Mattson-Solomon polynomial, of e(x).

The roots of polynomials are closely related to the properties of

the spectrum as stated in the following theorem.

<u>Theorem 2</u> a) The polynomial e(x) has a root at α^j if and only if the

j-th frequency component, E_j, equals zero.

b) The polynomial E(x) has a root at α^{-i} if and only if the

i-th time component, e_i, equals zero.

<u>Proof</u> Part a) is immediate since

$$e(\alpha^j) = \sum_{i=0}^{n-1} e_i \, \alpha^{ij} = E_j$$

Part b) follows in the same way.

Thus, in finite fields, when one speaks of roots of polynomials or of

spectral components equal to zero, one really speaks of the same thing,

but the terminology and the insights are different. In the first

formulation, one draws on insight into the factoring of polynomials;

in the second, one draws on understanding of the Fourier transform.

III. CYCLIC CODES

A cyclic code over GF(q) is conventionally described in terms of a

generator polynomial g(x) over GF(q) of degree n-k. Every codeword then

is written as c(x) = i(x) g(x) where i(x) is a polynomial of degree k-1

and c(x) is a polynomial of degree n-1. This is the most familiar

description of a cyclic code. In this section, we give an alternative spectral description. Codewords are denoted by $c = \{c_i\ i=0, \ldots, n-1\}$ or more carelessly simply by c_i. We consider only n that divide q^m-1. The components of c are indexed by the integers $i=0, \ldots, n-1$, but sometimes it is convenient to index with the field elements $\alpha^i = \alpha^1, \ldots, \alpha^{n-1}$ instead.

<u>Definition 2</u> Let the frequency components $j_1, \ldots, j_{n-k}$, called the parity frequencies, be specified. A cyclic code is the set of words over GF(q) of length n whose spectrum is zero in components $j_1, \ldots, j_{n-k}$. Each such word is called a time domain codeword (or codeword). The transform of each such word is called a frequency domain codeword (or a codeword spectrum).

A cyclic code of primitive blocklength $(n = q^m-1)$ is called a primitive cyclic code. Notice that although each codeword in a cyclic code is a vector over GF(q), the codeword spectrum is a vector over $GF(q^m)$. Hence, we may think of a cyclic code as the inverse Fourier transforms of all spectral vectors that are constrained to zero in a prescribed set of components, provided that said Fourier transforms are GF(q)-valued. It is not possible to choose any spectrum that is zero in the prescribed components; some of these may have inverse transforms with components that are not in GF(q).

However, if m =1; that is, n = q-1; then every spectrum consistent with the constraints yields a codeword. One may encode by filling the unconstrained components of the spectrum with information symbols and then inverse transforming.

The most popular class of cyclic code is the class of BCH codes. From the spectral point of view, we have the following definition.

<u>Definition 3</u>   A primitive BCH code of designed distance 2t + 1 and blocklength $n = q^m - 1$ is the set of all words over GF(q) whose spectrum is zero in a specified block of 2t consecutive components. The BCH codes for which n = q-1 (or possibly a submultiple of q-1) are known as Reed-Solomon codes.

The adjective "consecutive" is the key one in specializing the definition of a cyclic code to that of a BCH code. It is well known that a BCH code of designed distance 2t + 1 corrects t errors. In section IV we give the proof couched in spectral terminology. The remainder of this section is concerned with encoding. Although we will speak mostly of BCH codes, the encoding techniques are applicable to any cyclic code.

Every BCH code of length $n = q^m - 1$ over GF(q) is contained in Reed-Solomon code over $GF(q^m)$. Thr Reed-Solomon code is the set of $GF(q^m)$-valued signals whose spectra are zero in the specified 2t consecutive places. The BCH code is the set of GF(q)-valued signals whose spectra are zero in the same places. Thus, since GF(q) is a subfield of $GF(q^m)$, the BCH code is actually a subset of the Reed-Solomon code. In this context, it is called a subfield-subcode.

The encoding of a Reed-Solomon code is straightforward. Some set of 2t consecutive frequencies (the first 2t for example) have been specified as the parity frequencies. The information symbols are loaded into the remaining n-2t symbols, and the result is inverse-Fourier-transformed to produce the time-domain codeword (in nonsystematic form).

Hence, k = n-2t.

In general, for a BCH code, n is larger, dividing q^m-1 but not q-1; and the encoding is more complex. Again, 2t consecutive locations are specified as the parity frequencies. The remaining frequencies must be chosen to represent the information only in those q^k possible ways that yield time domain codewords with components in GF(q). Therefore, we need to find conditions on the spectrum that will ensure a GF(q)-valued inverse transform.

Over the complex numbers, a function V(f) has a real-valued-transform if V*(-f) = V(f). The analogous condition for extensions of GF(2) is given by the following.

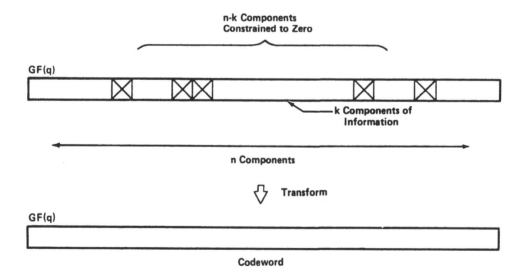

Figure 1. Encoding Via the Transform

__Theorem 3__ Let C_j $j = 0, \ldots,$ n-1 take elements in $GF(q^m)$ where n is

a divisor of q^m-1. The components of the inverse transform c_i i=0, $\ldots,$

n-1 are all elements of GF(q) if and only if the so-called conjugacy

constraints

$$c_j^q = C_{qj \bmod n} \qquad\qquad j = 0, \ldots, n-1$$

are satisfied.

__Proof__

For a field of characteristic p and any integer r, as is well known,

$(a + b)^{p^r} = a^{p^r} + b^{p^r}$. Further, if c_i is an element of GF(q) then

$c_i^q = c_i$. Using these two facts gives

$$C_j^q = \left(\sum_{i=0}^{n-1} \alpha^{ij} c_i \right)^q = \sum_{i=0}^{n-1} \alpha^{qij} c_i^q = \sum_{i=0}^{n-1} \alpha^{qji} c_i = C_{qj \bmod n}$$

Now suppose that $C_j^q = C_{qj}$ for all j. Then

$$\left(\sum_{i=0}^{n-1} \alpha^{ij} c_i \right)^q = \sum_{i=0}^{n-1} \alpha^{iqj} c_i \qquad\qquad j = 0, \ldots, n-1$$

Let k =qj in the exponent. Now, since q is relatively prime to $n=q^m-1$,

as j ranges over all values between 0 and n-1, so also k ranges over all

values between 0 and n-1. Hence

$$\sum_{i=0}^{n-1} \alpha^{ik} c_i^q = \sum_{i=0}^{n-1} \alpha^{ik} c_i \qquad\qquad k = 0, \ldots, n-1$$

By uniqueness of the Fourier transform, $c_i^q = c_i$. Thus, c_i is a root of

$x^q - x$ for all i, and all such roots are elements of GF(q).

Using Theorem 3, we can easily construct the Hamming (7,4) code in the frequency domain. This is shown in Figure 2. Since $t = 1$, selection of frequencies 1 and 2 as parity frequencies is sufficent ($C_1 = C_2 = 0$). Since Theorem 3 requires $C_0^2 = C_0$, C_0 can only be 0 or 1. This frequency can encode 1 bit of information. C_3 is an arbitrary octal character and so encodes 3 bits of information. The remaining frequencies are constrained by Theorem 3.

$$(C_4 = C_2^2 = 0, \ C_5 = C_6^2 = C_3^4)$$

Altogether, four bits are encoded, so $k = 4$.

To apply Theorem 3 in the general case, the integers modulo n are divided into conjugacy classes. These are

$$A_j = \{j, 2j, \ 4j, \ 8j, \ \ldots, \ \}$$

where the integers are modulo n, and the set enumeration ends just before the first entry j is repeated.

It is suggestive to use the term " chord" for the set of frequencies whose indices are in the same conjugacy class. If the spectral component C_j is specified, then every other spectral component whose index is in the conjugacy class of j must be a power of C_j. Hence only one member of a chord can be specified. The remainder are constrained by Theorem 3. Further, if the conjugacy class has r members, then we must have

$$C_j^{2^r} = C_j$$

Consequently, we are not free to choose any element of $GF(q^m)$ for C_j, but only those of order $2^r - 1$.

Frequency Domain Codewords							Time Domain Codewords						
c_0	c_1	c_2	c_3	c_4	c_5	c_6	c_0	c_1	c_2	c_3	c_4	c_5	c_6
0	0	0	0	0	0	0	0	0	0	0	0	0	0
0	0	0	α^0	0	α^0	α^0	1	1	1	0	1	0	0
0	0	0	α^1	0	α^4	α^2	0	0	1	1	1	0	1
0	0	0	α^2	0	α^1	α^4	0	1	0	0	1	1	1
0	0	0	α^3	0	α^5	α^6	1	1	0	1	0	0	1
0	0	0	α^4	0	α^2	α^1	0	1	1	1	0	1	0
0	0	0	α^5	0	α^6	α^3	1	0	0	1	1	1	0
0	0	0	α^6	0	α^3	α^5	1	0	1	0	0	1	1
1	0	0	0	0	0	0	1	1	1	1	1	1	1
1	0	0	α^0	0	α^0	α^0	0	0	0	1	0	1	1
1	0	0	α^1	0	α^4	α^2	1	1	0	0	0	1	0
1	0	0	α^2	0	α^1	α^4	1	0	1	1	0	0	0
1	0	0	α^3	0	α^5	α^6	0	0	1	0	1	1	0
1	0	0	α^4	0	α^2	α^1	1	0	0	0	1	0	1
1	0	0	α^5	0	α^6	α^3	0	1	1	0	0	0	1
1	0	0	α^6	0	α^3	α^5	0	1	0	1	1	0	0

Figure 2. Hamming (7,4) Code

Thus, to specify an encoder, we break the first 2^m-1 integers into conjugacy classes and select one integer to represent each class. These representatives specify the uniquely assignable frequencies. To form a BCH code, a block of 2t spectral components are chosen as parity frequencies and set to zero. The remaining assignable frequencies are information frequencies. All other frequencies in a chord are not free; they are obligatory frequencies.

Figure 3 shows the situation for GF(64). If we choose the first column as free frequencies and take C_1, C_2, C_3, C_4, C_5, and C_6 as parity frequencies, then we have a triple-error-correcting BCH code. The information frequencies are C_0, C_7, C_9, C_{11}, C_{13}, C_{15}, C_{21}, C_{23}, C_{27}, C_{31}. Of these, C_9 and C_{27} must be elements of order 2, C_{21} must be an element of order 3, and C_0 must be an element of order 1. All other symbols are arbitrary elements of GF(64). It requires a total of 45 information bits to specify these symbols. Hence, we have the triple-error-correcting (63, 45) BCH code.

After loading the free frequencies, the obligatory frequencies are padded with appropriate powers as required by Theorem 3. The completed spectrum is then inverse-Fourier-transformed into the codeword.

IV.   DECODING IN THE FREQUENCY DOMAIN

The weight of a vector is the number of nonzero components. In a BCH code, every nonzero codeword has weight at least 2t + 1. This BCH bound is proved very simply and intuitively in the frequency domain.

Free Frequencies	Obligatory Frequencies					Bit Content
{ c_0 }						1
{ c_1	c_2	c_4	c_8	c_{16}	c_{32} }	6
{ c_3	c_6	c_{12}	c_{24}	c_{48}	c_{33} }	6
{ c_5	c_{10}	c_{20}	c_{40}	c_{17}	c_{34} }	6
{ c_7	c_{14}	c_{28}	c_{56}	c_{49}	c_{35} }	6
{ c_9	c_{18}	c_{36} }				3
{ c_{11}	c_{22}	c_{44}	c_{25}	c_{50}	c_{37} }	6
{ c_{13}	c_{26}	c_{52}	c_{41}	c_{19}	c_{38} }	6
{ c_{15}	c_{30}	c_{60}	c_{57}	c_{51}	c_{39} }	6
—						—
—						—
{ c_{21}	c_{42} }					2
{ c_{23}	c_{46}	c_{29}	c_{58}	c_{53}	c_{43} }	6
—						—
{ c_{27}	c_{54}	c_{45} }				3
{ c_{31}	c_{62}	c_{61}	c_{59}	c_{55}	c_{47} }	6

Figure 3.   Structure of Spectrum Over GF(64)

Theorem 4 (BCH Bound)   The only vector in $GF(q)^n$ of weight $d-1$ or less that has $d-1$ sequential values of its spectrum equal to zero is the all-zero vector.

<u>Proof</u>   Let i_1, ..., i_ν denote the indices of the ν nonzero components

of the vector c, $\nu \leq d-1$. Define a frequency domain vector whose

inverse transform is zero whenever $c_i \neq 0$. One way to do this is by

defining the locator polynomial $\Lambda(x)$.

$$\Lambda(x) = \prod_{k=1}^{\nu} (1-x\alpha^{-i_k}) = \Lambda_\nu x^\nu + \Lambda_{\nu-1} x^{\nu-1} + \ldots + \Lambda_1 x + \Lambda_0$$

(But there are other choices that would also do.)

As a vector, Λ is a frequency spectrum that has been judiciously

defined so that its inverse transform $\lambda = \{\lambda_i\}$ equals zero at every

time i, at which $c_i \neq 0$. The product in the time domain is zero

($\lambda_i c_i = 0$ $i = 0,\ldots,n-1$); therefore, the convolution in the frequency

domain is zero.

$$\Lambda * C = 0$$

Since $\Lambda_0 = 1$, and $\Lambda_k = 0$ if $k > d-1$, this convolution can be written

$$C_j = - \sum_{k=1}^{d-1} \Lambda_k C_{j-k}$$

But C is zero in a block of length d-1. Consequently, the recursion

implies C is everywhere zero, and c must be the all-zero vector.

We now consider decoding of a BCH code. A received word

$r_i = c_i + e_i$ $i=0,\ldots,$ n-1 consists of a codeword and an error word.

The decoder must process the received word so as to remove the error

word e_i; the information is then recovered from c_i. Several arrange-

ments are shown in Figure 4: a conventional time-domain implementation

of a BCH decoder; a frequency-domain implementation; and several

hybrid implementations.

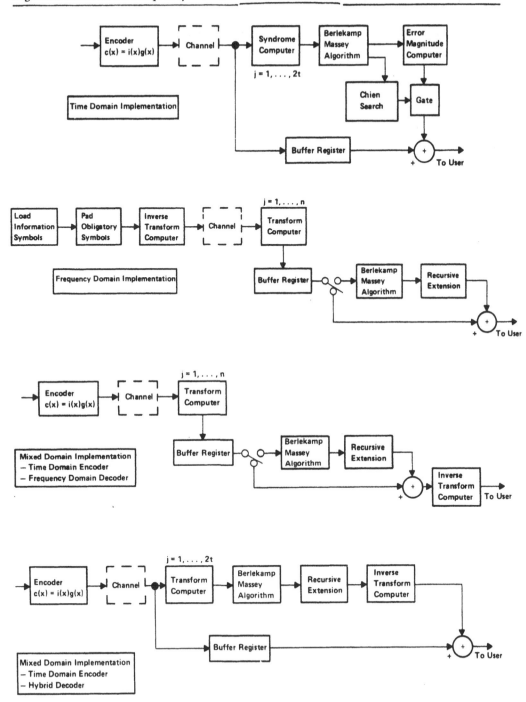

Figure 4.   Implementation of BCH Codes

In the frequency domain implementation, one first computes R, the transform of the received word r. The transform consists of the transform of the codeword and the transform of the error.

$$R_j = C_j + E_j \qquad j = 0, \ldots, n-1$$

Since codeword $\bar{C}_j$ is zero on a block of 2t components (say from 1 to 2t) we have 2t known values of E_j called the syndromes.

$$S_j = R_j = E_j \qquad j = 1, \ldots, 2t$$

Suppose there are $\nu \leq t$ errors. As in the proof of Theorem 4, define the error-locator polynomial $\Lambda(x)$

$$\Lambda(x) = \prod_{k=1}^{\nu} (1 - x\alpha^{-i_k})$$

(Actually any polynomial of degree at most t with these roots will do.) Since in the time domain, $\lambda_i = 0$ whenever $e_i \neq 0$, we have

$$\Lambda * E = 0$$

That is

$$\sum_{j=0}^{n-1} \Lambda_{k-j} E_j = 0 \qquad k = 0, \ldots, n-1$$

And, in this convolution, the first 2t components of E are known. All else is unknown. We find all terms in this equation in two steps: first finding the components of Λ from t equations involving only known components of E; then finding the unknown components of E using the remaining equations.

An efficient procedure for solving the convolution equation for the components of Λ is the Berlekamp algorithm which was put in a shift register formulation by Massey. This is a sequential procedure for solving the equation for Λ given the first 2t components of E. (Only slight changes are necessary if some other block of 2t components of E are the known syndromes: for example, cyclically shift E to place the known components at the front.) The algorithm processes the 2t known components of E in sequence and after 2t are processed, the computation of Λ is complete. It is worth mentioning (because it seems not to have been mentioned previously) that one can go in either direction by starting with either end of the 2t known values of E. Once Λ is known, the remaining components of E can be obtained by recursive extension; that is, sequentially computed from Λ using the above convolution equation in the form

$$E_j = - \sum_{k=1}^{t} \Lambda_k E_{j-k}$$

In this way E_j is computed for all j, and

$$C_j = R_j - E_j$$

An inverse Fourier transform completes the decoding.

Using this point of view, the Berlekamp-Massey algorithm can be thought of as a procedure for computing the complete spectrum of a vector from 2t successive known spectral components, given that the vector in the time domain has at most t nonzero components.

The encoding can be either in the time domain or the frequency domain. If the encoding is in the frequency domain, the information to be encoded is used to specify the values of the spectrum at information frequencies; the spectrum is then inverse-transformed into the time domain codeword. With this scheme, the corrected spectrum contains the information explicitly. The decoder does not have an inverse transform. The frequency domain encoder may be simpler than the time domain encoder if n is composite, because a fast Fourier transform may be simpler than a convolution (multiplication by g(x)). Another advantage of a frequency domain encoder is that it is easier to design. There is no need to find a generating polynomial g(x) and, hence, no need to search out minimal polynomials when designing the encoder/decoder.

The final circuit of Figure 4 shows a hybrid implementation. Here the transform of the error pattern is computed by recursive extension in the frequency domain, but the correction is done in the time domain. In many ways, the circuit is similar in appearance to the first circuit, but the development has been much different. The direct transform is the same as the syndrome generator. The inverse transform is quite similar to the Chien search. The final circuit has an advantage of a simpler structure than the first. It is especially attractive with nonbinary codes because it eliminates the error magnitude computer — a relatively cumbersome arithmetic computation. Of cource, the final choice of an approach depends on the specific parameters of a given application.

Notice that in each of the four circuits there are really two (one direct and one inverse) Fourier transforms, although they may be thinly disguised.   A syndrome generator is a Fourier transform that computes only 2t of the n spectral components.   A Chien search is an inverse transform that processes Λ to find the error locations, rather than processing E to find the error pattern.   It is a n $\times$ n transform with a $GF(q^m)$-valued output vector (the zero components specify the error locations), compared to an n $\times$ n transform with a $GF(q)$-valued output (the output vector is the error pattern).   The Chien search has an inherent inefficiency in that the computed nonzero components have no use after computation and are discarded.

V.   EXTENDED CODES

It is possible, in general, to add two extra components onto an alternant code; we will always place one at the beginning and one at the end of the codeword.   Codes obtained by adding one or both of the extra components are called extended codes (no relationship to extension fields).   If the symbol field $GF(q)$ and location field $GF(q^m)$ are the same; that is, if m = 1, then each of these extra components can be used either as information or as parity; that is, either to increase the rate or to increase the minimum distance.   If the symbol field is smaller, the code can be viewed as a subfield-subcode of a code over the larger symbol field $GF(q^m)$.   Because of constraints, over the subfield $GF(q)$ the extra components might not be useable as information places.   For example, binary BCH codes cannot be extended in information in this way.

The two new components must be identified and several notations are in use. If the original components are labeled by field elements, the zero field element can be used to identify one new component, and an additional symbol is needed to identify the other. Generally, ∞ is used. If the original components are labeled by exponents on a primitive element, then zero is not available to identify a new symbol, and two new symbols are needed. We will use $-$ and $+$ for these. Thus, an extended codeword is

$$(c_-, \ c_0, \ c_1, \ c_2, \ \ldots, \ c_{q^m-3}, \ c_{q^m-2}, \ c_+)$$

and $n = q^m+1$. The vector obtained by excluding c_- and c_+ will be called the interior. We shall study extended codes by means of Fourier transform properties of the interior together with additional properties of the extended vector space. When we speak of the spectrum of the codeword, we mean the spectrum of the interior.

<u>Definition 4</u> An extended cyclic code is the set of words of length $n = q^m+1$ with the properties that each word $(c_-, \ c_0, \ c_1, \ \ldots, \ c_{q^m-2}, \ c_+)$ has spectrum $(C_0, \ C_1, \ \ldots, \ C_{n-3})$ that is equal to zero in a set of components $j_1, \ \ldots, \ j_{n-k-2}$, and two other components satisfy

$$C_{j_{n-k-1}} = c_-, \ C_{j_{n-k}} = c_+.$$

(An extended cyclic code is generally not cyclic.)

<u>Definition 5</u> Let b and t be arbitrary integers. An extended Reed-Solomon code is a linear code over GF(q) of length $n = q +1$ whose codewords have spectra satisfying

i) $C_j = 0$ $j = b + 2, \ldots, b + 2t-1$

ii) $C_{b+1} = c_-$

iii) $C_{b+2t} = c_+$

The integer $2t + 1$ is called the designed distance of the extended
Reed-Solomon code. Figure 5 shows a frequency domain encoder for an
extended Reed-Solomon code.

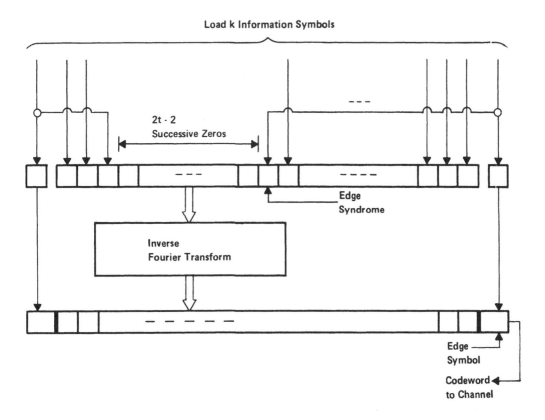

Figure 5. Encoding an Extended Reed-Solomon Code in the Frequency Domain

Compared to the original Reed–Solomon code, an extended Reed–
Solomon code always gives two extra information components without
changing the minimum distance. Later, we will examine this statement in
the frequency domain, but first we give a proof using properties of the
Vandermonde matrix.

Theorem 5   An extended Reed–Solomon code over $GF(q)$ is a $(q + 1, k)$ code
with minimum distance $2t + 1 = q-k + 2$.

Proof   The parity check matrix is

$$
H = \begin{vmatrix}
1 & 1 & 1 & \cdots & 1 & 1 & 0 \\
0 & \alpha & \alpha^2 & \cdots & \alpha^{q-2} & \alpha^{q-1} & 0 \\
0 & \alpha^2 & \alpha^4 & \cdots & \alpha^{2(q-2)} & \alpha^{2(q-1)} & 0 \\
 & \cdots & & & & & \\
0 & \alpha^{q-k-1} & \alpha^{2(q-k-1)} & \cdots & \alpha^{(q-k-1)(q-2)} & \alpha^{(q-k-1)(q-1)} & 0 \\
0 & \alpha^{q-k} & \alpha^{2(q-k)} & \cdots & \alpha^{(q-k)(q-2)} & \alpha^{(q-k)(q-1)} & 1
\end{vmatrix}
$$

As is well known, the code has minimum distance at least d if every set
of $d-1$ columns of the parity check matrix are linearly independent.
If the first and last columns are excluded, any set of $q-k + 1$ columns
is a Vandermonde matrix and so is nonsingular, so all the center columns
are linearly independent. But if we choose a set of $q-k + 1$ columns,
including the first column, the last column, or both, then the determinant can be computed by expanding about the one in the first column,
and then the one in the last column. This chops off the first row, or
the last row, or both rows of the Vandermonde matrix in the middle.

The result is a Vandermonde matrix that again has a nonzero determinant. Hence, any q-k + 1 columns are linearly independent, so the minimum distance is at least q-k + 2.

Any decoder for a Reed-Solomon code can be slightly modified to obtain a decoder for an extended Reed-Solomon code. One way is to simply guess in turn each of the q^2 possible error patterns in the two extended symbols, and then decode based on this guess. Only one trial guess can result in t or less corrected symbols.

A more direct procedure is to divide the possible error patterns into two cases: either an error occurs in an extended symbol, and less than t errors occur in the other symbols; or no error occurs in an extended symbol, and at most t errors occur in the other symbols. The message can be decoded twice; once for each of these hypotheses. Only one pattern with t or less corrected errors can result. For the first case, the 2t - 2 interior syndromes $S_{b+2}, \ldots, S_{b+2t-1}$ are sufficient to find the entire spectrum of the error pattern in the interior, because at most t-1 errors occurred in the interior. The remaining two syndromes give the errors in the edge symbols. For the second case, the 2t syndromes $S_{b+1}, \ldots, S_{b+2t}$ are sufficient to find the entire spectrum of the error pattern, because it is certain that all errors are in the n-1 interior symbols.

In practice, the two cases can be combined as follows. Start the Berlekamp-Massey algorithm at syndrome S_{b+2} and iterate out to syndrome S_{b+2t-1}. If the error locator polynomial has degree t-1 or less, than use the error locator polynomial to recursively extend the 2t-2 syn-

dromes and subtract from the spectrum of the received word, and use
the two extra syndromes to correct the extended symbols. If instead,
after 2t-2 iterations, the error locator polynomial has degree t, then
t errors occurred in the interior, and the error locator polynomial
must be revised to agree with the two edge syndromes. The Berlekamp-
Massey algorithm will do this revision with a slight refinement needed
to back-up to correct for the initial syndrome (or instead, one can
place both edge syndromes as the last two syndromes).

VI. ALTERNANT CODES

We have defined a BCH code over GF(q) of blocklength $n = q^m-1$ as a
subfield-subcode of a Reed-Solomon code over $GF(q^m)$. That is, the
BCH code consists of all those Reed-Solomon codewords that are GF(q)-
valued. As such, the BCH code has at least as large a minimum distance
as the Reed-Solomon code. Unfortunately, BCH codes of large blocklength and large minimum distance contain very few codewords. Stated
more precisely, in any sequence of BCH codes of increasing blocklength
either the rate k/n or the relative minimum distance d_{min}/n (or both)
approaches zero with increasing n. The original Reed-Solomon code has
a great many codewords, but the subfield-subcode uses very few of them,
or else has poor distance structure. Is it possible to twist the Reed-
Solomon code in some way so that the subfield-subcode has a larger
minimum distance?

Alternant codes are a class of linear codes that are a variation
of BCH codes defined so that large minimum distance can be obtained

(at least in principle). Choose h_i $i = 0, \ldots, n-1$, a fixed n-vector

of nonzero components over $GF(q^m)$, which will be called the (time

domain) template; and choose a Reed-Solomon code over $GF(q^m)$ with

designed distance $2t + 1$. The alternant code consists of all $GF(q)$-

valued vectors c_i $i = 0, \ldots, n-1$, such that $h_i c_i$ $i = 0, \ldots, n-1$ is

a codeword in the Reed-Solomon code. It is surprising, but true, that

if the template is selected properly, the code has a true minimum dis-

tance asymptotically close to the Gilbert bound; the best bound for

which codes are known to exist. Unfortunately, a practical rule for

choosing the template at large n is not known, although it is known

that good templates are plentiful.

Just as Reed-Solomon codes have been used as a starting point to

introduce BCH codes and alternant codes, so can one use extended Reed-

Solomon codes to introduce extended alternant codes. That is, an

extended alternant code over $GF(q)$ is a $GF(q)$ valued subfield-subcode

of the code obtained by multiplying each codeword in an extended Reed-

Solomon code over $GF(q^m)$ by a fixed vector over $GF(q^m)$. We will

include extended alternant codes in the discussion of Section

VIII.

The definition of the alternant codes is easily translated into

the frequency domain. Let H be the transform of h which will be called

the frequency domain template. Since h is everywhere nonzero, H is

invertible; that is, there is a G (the transform of the vector $g_i = h_i^{-1}$

$i = 0, \ldots, n-1$) such that $H*G$ is a delta function. (That is, if

$j = 0$, $(H*G)_j = 1$; otherwise $(H*G)_j = 0$.)

In the language of polynomials, this convolution becomes

$$H(x)G(x) = 1 \bmod (x^n-1)$$

From this it is easy to see that, if $H(x)$ is a polynomial over the

small field $GF(q)$, so is $G(x)$. The argument is as follows. $H(x)$ has

no zeros in $GF(q^m)$ because $H(\alpha^i) = h_i \neq 0$. Hence $H(x)$ is relatively

prime to $x^n - 1 = x^{q^{m-1}} -1$ and by the Euclidean algorithm there exist

$G(x)$, $F(x)$ over $GF(q)$ such that

$$H(x)G(x) + (x^n-1)F(x) = 1$$

That is

$$H(x)G(x) \quad \bmod (x^n-1) = 1$$

The alternant codes can be defined in the frequency domain as

follows.

Definition 6 Let H be a fixed n-vector in the frequency domain, and

let b and t be fixed integers. The alternant code $\mathscr{C}$ is the set of

vectors whose transforms C_j $j = 0, \ldots, n-1$ satisfy two conditions

i) $\quad \displaystyle\sum_{j=0}^{n-1} H_{k-j} C_j = 0 \quad k = b + 1, \ldots, b + 2t$

ii) $\quad C_j^2 = C_{2j}$

with indices interpreted modulo n in both conditions.

The first of these conditions is a convolution corresponding to

the time domain product mentioned earlier; the second condition ensures

that the time domain codewords are $GF(q)$-valued. The vector

$$T_k = \sum_{j=0}^{n-1} H_{k-j} C_j \quad k=0, \ldots, n-1$$

will be called the filtered spectrum of the codeword.

Because the alternant codes are so closely related to the Reed-Solomon codes, it is apparant that the minimum distance is at least as large as the designed distance $2t + 1$. The following theorem says also that the dimension satisfies $k \geq n - 2tm$.

Theorem 6   Let $\mathscr{C}$ be an (n,K,D) linear code over $GF(q^m)$ and let $\mathscr{C}$ ' be a (n,k,d) subfield-subcode of $\mathscr{C}$ over $GF(q)$.   Then

$0 \leq d \leq n$

$(n-K) \leq (n-k) \leq m(n-K)$

Proof   The only nontrivial inequality is the last one.   Each parity check equation for the code over $GF(q^m)$ yields at most m linearly independent parity check equations over $GF(q)$.   The last inequality follows from this.

We will see in the next section that some alternant codes have a minimum distance much larger than the designed distance, but the proof is nonconstructive.   It is worthwhile to also display a weaker, though direct, theorem that will lead into some decoder designs.   Therefore, we extend Theorem 4 to a frequency domain derivation of the distance structure of alternant codes.

Theorem 7   The only vector c_i i $=0$, ..., n-1 of weight d-1 or less, whose filtered spectrum T is zero on any d-1 successive components $(T_j=0$ j=b + 1, ..., b + d$) is the all-zero vector, where $T = H*C$ and H is an invertible filter.

<u>Proof</u> As in the proof of Theorem 6, define the error-locator poly-
nomial $\Lambda(x)$ so that its transform λ_i is zero whenever $c_i \neq 0$. Then
$\lambda_i c_i = 0$ which implies $\Lambda *C = 0$. Hence $H* (\Lambda *C) = \Lambda *T = 0$. But Λ is
nonzero only in a block of length at most $d + 1$, and T is zero in a
block of length d. Consequently, $T = H*C = 0$ in all components, and
in turn $C = 0$. Hence c is the all-zero vector.

Just as for the BCH codes, the alternant codes can be decoded
either in the frequency or time domains, and for both errors and
erasures. To recover the codewords, all that needs to be added to any
BCH decoder is a step to modify the syndromes by the inverse of the
template, either by multiplying in the time domain or convolving in the
frequency domain. To correct the received word, no other change is
necessary. The encoding and the recovery of the information from the
corrected codewords, however, may require new techniques.

A modified BCH decoder can decode alternant codes only out to the
designed distance $2t + 1$. However, the appeal of alternant codes lies
in their much larger minimum distance. It is not clear that an alternant
code used with a BCH decoder has any major advantage over a BCH code
used with a BCH decoder. (A minor advantage is the detection of unde-
codable errors.) Alternant codes will not have important practical
value until stronger decoding algorithms are developed so that their
large minimum distance is of some benefit to the user.

VII. PERFORMANCE OF ALTERNANT CODES

Alternant codes are attractive because, in this class, there are
codes of long blocklength that are good. By this, we mean that there
are sequences of increasingly long codes with rate k/n and relative
minimum distance d/n that remain bounded away from zero as n goes to
infinity. This we will now show. The technique used is to show that
there are not too many low weight words over GF(q) and each cannot
appear in too many codes. Hence, since there are very many alternant
codes by comparison, some alternant code has no low-weight word.
Hence, this code has large minimum distance.

In the proof of the theorem, we will not find k and d for any
code; instead we will find only lower bounds on them. For purposes
of this theorem, by an (n, k, d) code, we mean a code of blocklength n
whose dimension is <u>at least</u> k and whose minimum distance is <u>at least</u> d.

<u>Theorem 8</u>   For any GF(q) and m let $n = q^m - 1$ and let d and r be any
integers. Then there exists an (n, n-rm, d) alternant code, provided d
and r satisfy

$$\sum_{j=1}^{d-1} (q-1)^j \binom{n}{j} < (q^m - 1)^r$$

<u>Proof</u>   The idea of the proof given below is to count the number of
alternant codes of a certain type and then count the number of such codes
to which belongs a given vector v of weight j < d. There are not
enough such v to account for all of the codes, so some codes have no v
of weight j < d.

i) Let $\mathscr{C}$ be a Reed-Solomon Code over $GF(q^m)$ of minimum distance $d = r + 1$ and rate $K = n-d + 1 = n-r$. Let $\mathscr{C}(h)$ be the alternant code over $GF(q)$ generated from $\mathscr{C}$ by template h. That is h is a vector over $GF(q^m)$,

$$\mathscr{C}(h) = \{ c \in GF(q)^n : hc \in \mathscr{C} \},$$

and hc denotes the vector $\{h_i c_i \ i = 0, \ldots, n-1\}$. Since $h_i \neq 0$ for all i, there are at most $(q^m-1)^n$ such codes. Each such code is a subfield-subcode of the linear code $\{c \in GF(q^m)^n : hc \in \mathscr{C}\}$ and hence, by Theorem 6, for each such code

$$k \geq n-mr$$

ii) Choose a vector v over $GF(q)$ of weight $i < d$. There are $(q-1)^j \binom{r}{j}$ vectors of weight j and

$$\sum_{j=1}^{d-1} (q-1)^j \binom{n}{j}$$

vectors of weight less than d.

iii) A vector v of weight j appears in at most $(q^m-1)^{n-r}$ of the alternant codes defined in i). This is because any n-r places in a Reed-Solomon code are information places. If we fix v, then there are only n-r places in h that can be independently specified such that hv is in $\mathscr{C}$.

iv) Now combine i), ii), and iii), to compare the number of alternant codes defined in i) to the maximum number that can have a vector of weight less than d. Suppose

$$(q^m-1)^n > (q^m-1)^{n-r} \sum_{j=1}^{d-1} \binom{n}{j} (q-1)^j$$

then some code of rate n-mr has minimum distance at least as large as d.

This is equivalent to the statement of the theorem.

As it stands, the significance of the theorem is not readily appreciated without some background in the search for bounds on the rate and minimum distance of the best codes. For binary codes, aside from terms that are asymptotically negligible, as blocklength becomes large, the theorem is equivalent to a bound known as the Gilbert bound, which precedes the introduction of alternant codes by many years. The Gilbert bound asserted that codes this good exist, and alternant codes are one class of codes that fulfill the promise of the Gilbert bound. However, the alternant codes are a very large class, and without some constructive methods for isolating the good codes, the bound of Theorem 8 is another unfulfilled promise.

At the present time, there is no definite evidence that codes better than the Gilbert bound exist (aside from asymptotically negligible improvements). Hence, asymptotically optimum codes may very well be contained in the class of alternant codes. In fact, at the present time, there is no evidence that codes better than Theorem 8 (except for asymptotically negligible improvements) exist.

VIII. GOPPA CODES

Several subclasses of alternant codes were discovered earlier than the general case, and so have special names. The Goppa codes are a special case that are widely studied and remain worthy of individual attention. We define them in a way consistent with our spectral viewpoint, which is much different from the historical approach.

<u>Definition 5</u> A Goppa code of designed distance 2t + 1 is an alternant code of designed distance 2t + 1, with the additional property that the inverse frequency template G_j has width 2t + 1. That is, it can be described as a polynomial G(x) of degree 2t, called the Goppa polynomial.

This definition is slightly weaker than the usual definition, because it allows Goppa codes to have only primitive blocklengths (n = q^m-1) or a submultiple. We prefer to view all other blocklengths as shortened codes or extended codes. The techniques of Section V, in principle, give extended Goppa codes of blocklength q^m or q^m+1.

Just as for the general case of an alternant code, there is not much known about finding good Goppa codes, although it is known that good ones exist. Similarly, there are not yet good encoding algorithms, nor algorithms for decoding to the minimum distance.

The known Goppa codes are interesting primarily because they have an extra information symbol with no loss in minimum distance, as compared to a BCH code. In effect they give a way to extend a BCH code by one information symbol. This is worthwhile, because primitive BCH codes cannot be extended in information. That is, over GF(2^m), the subfield-subcode of any extended Reed-Solomon code has the same dimension as the subfield-subcode of the corresponding unextended Reed-Solomon code.

We will formulate frequency domain encoders and decoders for Goppa codes, relying on known facts about them. We can describe the Goppa codes in the frequency domain using the shift register circuit of Figure 6.

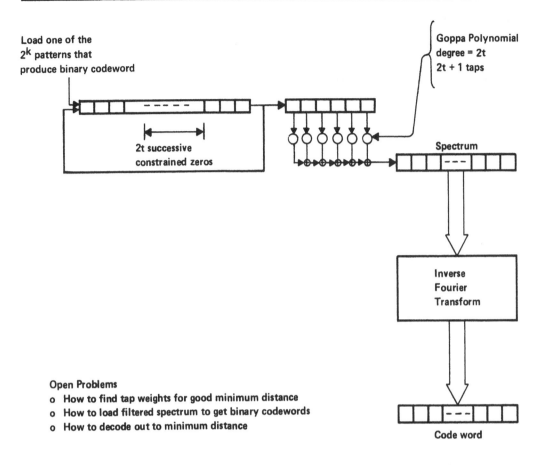

Figure 6.   Goppa Code – Frequency Domain Templating

Instead of inserting the information into the time domain codeword, it

is inserted in the frequency domain, either into the spectrum or into

the filtered spectrum, as shown in Figure 6, and in either case in such

a way that all constraints are satisfied. There is no general procedure

known for doing this, but in codes of modest size, it is possible to set up and solve algebraic equations that describe the constraints. We will give an example of this below. Once the filtered spectrum is loaded with the information, it is filtered by a finite impulse response filter whose tap weights are given by the Goppa polynomial. The filter operation is cyclic. That is, the input is treated as periodic. Finally, the spectrum is inverse-Fourier-transformed to produce a codeword.

The decoder reverses these steps, using the filter taps defined by $H(x)$ to pass from the spectrum to the filtered spectrum. Procedures discussed in Section IV will then recover the filtered spectrum of the codeword from the filtered spectrum of the received word. The information symbols can then be read out.

Although this gives the outline of a good decoder, there are several open problems that must be solved before the promise can be realized. These are: the problem of finding tap weights for good minimum distance; the problem of decoding out ot the miminum distance instead of only to the designed distance, and finally, the problem of encoding, in a simple way, the information into the filtered spectrum or the spectrum.

We will close this section with some remarks about binary Goppa codes and an example. It was proved by Goppa that for certain binary Goppa codes, the minimum distance is at least $2r + 1$, where r is the degree of $G(x)$. This is more striking than the more general bound $d_{min} \geq r + 1$. The key to the proof of this fact can be summarized by the following theorem.

<u>Theorem 9</u> Suppose that $G(x)$, a polynomial with no roots in $GF(2^m)$ is

a Goppa polynomial of a binary Goppa code. Then every codeword c has

locator polynomial $\Lambda_c(x)$ whose formal derivative $\Lambda_c'(x)$ is divisible

by $G(x)$ and conversely.

The proof of this theorem is rather lengthy when starting from our

frequency domain definition of a Goppa code, and so we omit it. A clear

description of this topic can be found in MacWilliams and Sloane.

To apply the theorem, notice that the formal derivative of any

polynomial over an extension of $GF(2)$ is a perfect square because the

coefficients of odd powers of x vanish. Therefore, if $G(x)$ has no

repeated roots in any extension field (called a separable Goppa poly-

nominal), not only does $G(x)$ divide $\Lambda_c(x)$ but so does $\overline{G}(x) = G(x)^2$. For

such a $G(x)$ we get the same code if we use $\overline{G}(x)$, instead, as the Goppa

polynomial. This has degree 2r and so $d_{min} \geq 2r + 1$.

The disadvantage of a separable Goppa code, as defined, is that

one produces only t syndromes rather than 2t, and the usual decoding

techniques do not apply directly. Patterson has developed a special

variation of the decoding algorithm for this case, but we prefer in-

stead to modify the description of the code. Use $\overline{G}(x)$ as the Goppa

polynomial. This gives the same code, but the performance bounds

become

$d_{min} \geq r + 1$

$k \geq n - \frac{1}{2} mr$

where r is now the degree of $\overline{G}(x)$. This is just as good as previously,

but now there are 2t parity frequencies, and all the familiar decoding techniques apply directly.

For an example of a binary Goppa code encoded and decoded in the frequency domain, we will choose the Goppa polynomial

$$G(x) = x^3 + x + 1$$

which has three distinct roots in GF(8) but none in GF(32). Then

$$\overline{G}(x) = x^6 + x^2 + 1$$

can be used as the Goppa polynomial for a (31, 16, 7) Goppa code or a (32, 17, 7) extended Goppa code. We will describe a frequency domain encoder and decoder. Depending on the needs of a particular application, this may or may not be preferrable to a time domain encoder and decoder. Even in cases where it is not practical, study of the frequency domain decoder gives a sharpened perspective.

The inverse Goppa polynomials are

$$H(x) = x^{30} + x^{27} + x^{25} + x^{24} + x^{23} + x^{20} + x^{18} + x^{17} + x^{16} + x^{13} + x^{11} + x^{10} + x^9 + x^6 + x^4$$
$$+ x^3 + x^2$$

$$\overline{H}(x) = x^{29} + x^{26} + x^{23} + x^{22} + x^{20} + x^{19} + x^{18} + x^{17} + x^{15} + x^{12} + x^9 + x^8 + x^6 + x^5 + x^4 + x^3 + x$$

At this point, there is a slight clash in conventions. We have given the Goppa polynomial in its conventional form, but it is an object in the frequency domain. The time domain values should be evaluated with an inverse Fourier transform $G(\alpha^{-i})$ rather than a direct Fourier transform $G(\alpha^i)$, which is commonly used in discussion of Goppa codes. So that we can use the inverse Fourier transform, we replace x^j by x^{31-j} in $\overline{G}(x)$ and $\overline{H}(x)$.

$$\overline{G}(x) = x^{31-6} + x^{31-2} + 1 = x^{29} + x^{25} + 1$$

$$\overline{H}(x) = x^{30}+x^{28}+x^{27}+x^{26}+x^{25}+x^{23}+x^{22}+x^{19}+x^{16}+x^{14}+x^{13}+x^{12}+x^{11}+x^{9}+x^{8}$$
$$+x^{5}+x^{2}$$

For the example we choose to insert the information directly into the spectrum. Then the filtered spectrum is given by

$$T_k = \sum_{j=0}^{n-1} H_{k-j}\, C_j \qquad\qquad k = 0, \ldots, n-1$$

and the parity frequencies are k = 0, ..., 5. We then have

$$c_\infty = C_1+C_3+C_4+C_5+C_6+C_8+C_9+C_{12}+C_{15}+C_{17}+C_{18}+C_{19}+C_{20}+C_{22}+C_{23}+C_{26}+C_{29}$$

$$0 = C_{1+k}+C_{3+k}+C_{4+k}+C_{5+k}+C_{6+k}+C_{8+k}+C_{9+k}+C_{12+k}+C_{15+k}+C_{17+k}+C_{18+k}$$
$$+C_{19+k}+C_{20+k}+C_{22+k}+C_{23+k}+C_{26+k}+C_{29+k}$$
$$k = 1, 2, 3, 4, 5$$

and the constraints

$$c_j^2 = c_{2j}$$

We can satisfy all of these equations by taking c_∞ and C_0 as arbitrary elements of GF(2), C_3, C_5, and C_{11} as arbitrary elements of GF(32), and C_1, C_7, C_{15} satisfying

$$C_1 = c_\infty + C_0 + (C_3+C_3^2+C_3^4+C_3^8) + (C_5+C_5^2) + (C_{11}+C_{11}^4+C_{11}^8)$$

$$C_7 = c_\infty + (C_3+C_3^2+C_3^4+C_3^{16}) + (C_5^2+C_5^8+C_5^{16}) + (C_{11}+C_{11}^2+C_{11}^4+C_{11}^{16})$$

$$C_{15} = c_\infty + (C_3+C_3^2+C_3^4+C_3^8) + (C_5^2+C_5^4+C_5^{16}) + C_{11}$$

All other C_j are determined by the conjugacy constraints. An inverse Fourier transform of $(C_0, \ldots, C_{30})$ completes the encoding.

The frequency domain decoder consists of a Fourier transform of the received word, followed by the filter $\overline{H}(x)$. The filtered spectrum is

Then corrected using the Berlekemp-Massey algorithm and the syndromes
$S_k = T_k$ $k = 0, \ldots, 5$. The spectrum is then recovered by filtering
with the inverse filter $G(x)$. Finally, the 17 bits of information are
recovered from c_∞, C_0, C_3, C_5, and C_{11}.

IX. MULTIDIMENSIONAL CODES

Just as codes can be defined in the frequency domain, so can codes
be defined in a multidimensional frequency domain. In fact, in the
guise of the Mattson-Solomon polynomial, multidimensional transforms
have played a significant role in the theory of error control codes.
We will introduce this topic, restricting the discussion to the two-
dimensional case.

Let $e_{ii'}$ be an n $\times$ n two-dimensional array over GF(q), which will
be called a two-dimensional time domain function, and suppose n divides
$q^m - 1$ for some m. Let α be an element of order n. The array

$$E_{jj'} = \sum_{i=0}^{n-1} \sum_{i'=0}^{n-1} \alpha^{ij} \alpha^{i'j'} e_{ii'}$$

will be called the two-dimensional spectrum, and the indices j and j'
are the frequency variables. It is obvious that

$$e_{ii'} = \frac{1}{n} \frac{1}{n} \sum_{j=0}^{n-1} \sum_{j'=0}^{n-1} \alpha^{-ij} \alpha^{-i'j'} E_{jj'}$$

by inspection of the one-dimensional inverse transform.

Figure 7 shows a two-dimensional spectrum over GF(8). Each square
in the grid contains an octal symbol. Select a set of N-K of these
components to be (two-dimensional) parity frequencies and define a code

by constraining these to be zero, as in Figure 7.   The remaining set

of K components are filled with K information symbols over GF(8), and the

result is inverse transformed (two-dimensionally).   The codeword is the

two-dimensional time function corresponding to the information symbols.

Clearly, this is a linear code, but in general it is not cyclic.   If the

desired code is in a subfield of GF(q) (in the example, GF(2) is the

only subfield of GF(8)), then one must restrict the set of codewords

to those that have only components in the subfield, and so one obtains

a two-dimensional subfield-subcode.   One could also obtain a two-di-

mensional alternant code by multiplying by a two-dimensional template

before extracting the subfield-subcode.

The two-dimensional spectrum need not be square, but if it is, and

$n + 1 = q^m$, then the largest field in the discussion is GF(n+1).   If

the spectrum is an $n \times n'$ array, $n' \neq n$, one must deal with the larger

field GF(Q), where $Q = \text{LCM } (n,n')$.   That is, let $e_{ii'}$ be an $n \times n'$,

two-dimensional time function where n and n' both divide $q^m - 1$ for some

m.   Let β and γ be elements of $GF(q^m)$ of order n and n', respectively.

Then

$$E_{jj'} = \sum_{i=0}^{n-1} \sum_{i'=0}^{n'-1} \beta^{ij} \gamma^{i'j'} e_{ii'}$$

Again, it is obvious that

$$e_{ii'} = \frac{1}{n} \frac{1}{n'} \sum_{j=0}^{n-1} \sum_{j'=0}^{n'-1} \beta^{-ij} \gamma^{-i'j'} E_{jj'}$$

by inspection of the one-dimensional inverse transform.

For an example, choose all of the elements in a set of vertical

stripes and a set of horizontal stripes to be parity ırequencies, as shown in Figure 9.   All the two-dimensional time domain functions

with these frequencies equal to zero are the codewords.   That is

$$\sum_{i=0}^{n-1} \sum_{i'=0}^{n'-1} \beta^{ij} \gamma^{i'j'} e_{ii'} = 0$$

for each parity frequency jj'. This can be interpreted in another way

by defining the two-dimensional polynomial

$$e(x,y) = \sum_{i=0}^{n-1} \sum_{i'=0}^{n'-1} e_{ii'} x^i y^{i'}$$

so that the code satisfies

$$e(\beta^j, \gamma^{j'}) = 0$$

for every j and every j' that are parity frequencies. Since the parity

frequencies were defined on vertical and horizontal stripes, we have

$$e(\beta^j, y) = 0$$

$$e(x, \gamma^{j'}) = 0$$

for every j and every j' that are parity frequencies. This says that

$e_{ii'}$ is a kind of code known as a product code.

A product code is a two-dimensional array of elements from GF(q)

such that every row is a codeword in a code $\mathscr{C}_1$ and every column is a

codeword in a code $\mathscr{C}_2$. A cyclic product code is a product code in

which the rows and columns are from cyclic codes $\mathscr{C}_1$ and $\mathscr{C}_2$. A cyclic

product code is not necessarily cyclic. To insure that a cyclic product

code is actually cyclic, one must impose the condition that n and n' are

relatively prime. We will show below that a cyclic product code can be

easily encoded in a two-dimensional frequency domain.

If we take the stripes of parity frequencies to be contiguous, we have a code that is the product of two Reed-Solomon codes. Figure 9

illustrates a (49,25,9) code over GF(8) defined spectrally. Each of

the 25 information symbols can be loaded with an octal information char-

acter. The result is transformed to the time domain to obtain the code-

word.

The same structure can be used to obtain a code over GF(2) by

selecting only binary codewords. In the frequency domain, only a set

of frequencies may be specified that yield a binary codeword. As in

Theorem 3, the conjugacy constraints are

$$c^2_{jj'} = c_{(2j \bmod n)(2j' \bmod n)}$$

We can construct the table shown in Figure 8 with this property. Each

set in the table shows a constrained set of frequencies. Any member of

a conjugacy set can be specified. The remaining symbols in a set are

not arbitrary. The frequency $c_{0,0}$ can be only 0 or 1 because it is

its own square. The remaining information symbols are octal. Altogether

49 bits specify the spectrum, but of course some of these are parity

and contain no information. Using this table, the code of Figure 9

is restricted to the binary subfield-subcode whose spectrum is shown in

Figure 9. There are only 16 open frequencies which, because of the

constraints, can encode 16 bits. This is a consequence of the fact

that row 1 and column 1 have their parity symbols scattered among

different rows of Figure 8. The code is an unimpressive (49,16,9)

code and, from the details of the construction, we can see that product

codes often will have poor performance. To get good product codes one

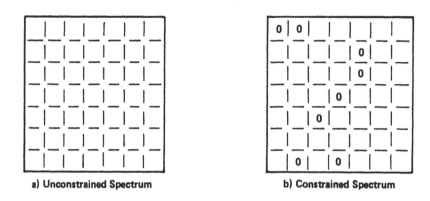

a) Unconstrained Spectrum   b) Constrained Spectrum

Figure 7.   Two Dimensional Spectrum Over GF(8)

must generally make the dimensions relatively prime, and hence the underlying field becomes large.

			Bit Content				Bit Content
{ $c_{1,1}$	$c_{2,2}$	$c_{4,4}$ }	3	{ $c_{3,3}$	$c_{6,6}$	$c_{5,5}$ }	3
{ $c_{1,2}$	$c_{2,4}$	$c_{4,1}$ }	3	{ $c_{3,5}$	$c_{6,3}$	$c_{5,6}$ }	3
{ $c_{2,1}$	$c_{4,2}$	$c_{1,4}$ }	3	{ $c_{5,3}$	$c_{3,6}$	$c_{6,5}$ }	3
{ $c_{1,3}$	$c_{2,6}$	$c_{4,5}$ }	3	{ $c_{0,1}$	$c_{0,2}$	$c_{0,4}$ }	3
{ $c_{3,1}$	$c_{6,2}$	$c_{5,4}$ }	3	{ $c_{1,0}$	$c_{2,0}$	$c_{4,0}$ }	3
{ $c_{1,5}$	$c_{2,3}$	$c_{4,6}$ }	3	{ $c_{0,3}$	$c_{0,6}$	$c_{0,5}$ }	3
{ $c_{5,1}$	$c_{3,2}$	$c_{6,4}$ }	3	{ $c_{3,0}$	$c_{6,0}$	$c_{5,0}$ }	3
{ $c_{1,6}$	$c_{2,5}$	$c_{4,3}$ }	3	{ $c_{0,0}$ }			1
{ $c_{6,1}$	$c_{5,2}$	$c_{3,4}$ }	3				

Figure 8.   Two Dimensional Conjugacy Sets

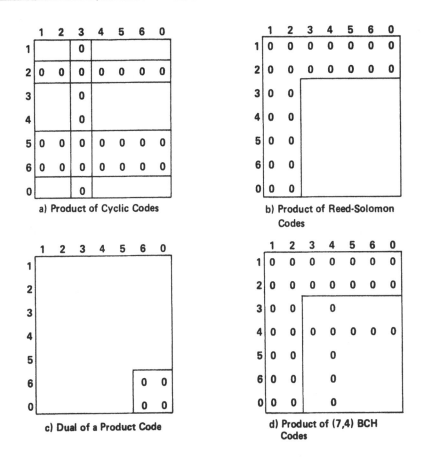

Figure 9. Spectra of Some Codes Over GF(8)

The second case, illustrated in Figure 9, is a dual to the idea of a product code. A rectangle, b frequencies wide and a frequencies high, is chosen for the parity frequencies. It is easily seen that the minimum distance satisfies

$$d \geq 1 + \min\ (a,b)$$

Hence, the example gives a (49,45,3) code over GF(8). The binary subfield-subcode is a (49,39) $d \geq 3$ code.

NOTES

Fourier transforms over a finite field were discussed in 1971 by
Pollard [1], and their use in error control codes was introduced by
Gore [2], and discussed further by Michelson [3], Lempel and Winograd
[4], and Chien and Choy [5]. Much earlier, in 1961, Mattson and
Solomon [6] used relationships that in retrospect are seen to be based
on the Fourier transform.

BCH codes are well known, and modern treatments may be found in
[7], [8], or [9]. Our proof of the BCH bound is based in part on a
proof of Chien [10] that we have transferred into the frequency domain.
The Berlekamp-Massey decoding algorithm for BCH codes may be found in
Massey [11] or Berlekamp [9]. The poor asymptotic behavior of BCH
codes is discussed by Berlekamp [12].

Alternant codes were introduced by Helgert [13] who named them
that because the parity check matrix can be put in a form known to math-
ematicians as an alternant matrix. The alternant codes subsumed the
earlier Goppa codes [14] and Srivastava codes [9]. Delsarte [15]
discussed the alternant codes as subfield-subcodes of modified Reed-
Solomon codes.

Product codes were introduced by Elias [16], and cyclic product
codes were studied in detail by Burton and Weldon [17]. The treatment
of multidimensional codes using Mattson-Solomon polynomials appears in
Lin and Weldon [18].

The idea of an extended code is widespread, but probably not yet
in the role it deserves. Extended Reed-Solomon codes are discussed by

Wolf [19]. A very readable discussion of extended Reed—Solomon codes and their relationship to other topics may be found in MacWilliams and Sloane [8].

REFERENCES

1. Pollard, J.M., " The Fast Fourier Transform in a Finite Field, "Mathematics of Computation, pp 365-374, Vol. 25, No. 114, April 1971.

2. Gore, W.C., "Transmitting Binary Symbols With Reed-Solomon Codes, "Proceedings of Princeton Conference on Information Sciences and Systems, Princeton, N.J., pp 495-497, 1973.

3. Michelson, A., "A Fast Transform in Some Galois Fields and an Application to Decoding Reed-Solomon Codes," IEEE Abstracts of Papers - IEEE International Symposium on Information Theory, Ronneby, Sweden, 1976.

4. Lempel, A. and Winograd, S., " A New Approach to Error Correcting Codes," IEEE Trans. Information Theory, Vol IT 23, pp 503-508, July 1977.

5. Chien, R.T., and Choy, D.M., "Algebraic Generalization of BCH-Goppa-Helgert Codes," IEEE Trans. Information Theory, Vol IT 21, pp 70-79, January 1975.

6. Mattson, H.F., and G, Solomon, " A New Treatment of Bose Chandhuri Codes," J. Soc Indus. Appl. Math., 9, 4, 654-699, 1961.

7. Peterson, W.W., amd Weldon, E.J. Jr., Error Correcting Codes 2nd Ed., MIT Press, 1972.

8. MacWilliams, F.J., and Sloane, N.J.A., The Theory of Error Correcting Codes, North Holland, Amsterdam, 1977.

9.   Berlekamp, E.R., <u>Algebraic Coding Theory</u>, Mc Graw Hill, New York,
     1968.

10. Chien, R.T., "A New Proof of the BCH Bound," IEEE Trans. Information
     Theory, Vol IT 18, p. 541, July, 1972.

11. Massey, J.L., "Shift-Register Synthesis and BCH Decoding," IEEE
     Trans. Information Theory, Vol IT 15, pp 122-127, 1969.

12. Berlekamp, E., "Long Primitive BCH Codes Have Distance $d \sim 2n \ln R^{-1}/$
     $\log n$, " IEEE Trans. Information Theory, Vol IT 18, pp 415-426,
     May 1972.

13. Helgert, H.H., "Alternant Codes," Information and Control, pp 369-
     381, 1974.

14. Goppa, V.C., "A New Class of Linear Error-Correcting Codes" Probl.
     Peredach. Inform., Vol. 6, pp 24-30, September, 1970.

15. Delsarte, P., "On Subfield Subcodes of Modified Reed-Solomon Codes,"
     IEEE Trans Information Theory, Vol IT 21, pp 575-576, September, 1975.

16. Elias, P., " Error Free Coding" IRE Trans. Information Theory, Vol
     IT 4, pp 29-37, 1954.

17. Burton, H.O., and E. Weldon, E.J. Jr., "Cyclic Product Codes" IEEE
     Trans. Information Theory, Vol IT 11, pp 433-439, 1965.

18. Lin, S. and Weldon, E.J. Jr., "Furthur Results on Cyclic Product
     Codes" IEEE Trans. Information Theory, Vol IT 16, pp 452-459, 1970.

19. Wolf, J.K., "Adding Two Information Symbols to Certain Nonbinary
     BCH Codes and Some Applications," Bell Syst. Tech. J., pp 2405-
     2424, 1969.

20. Patterson, N.J., "The Algebraic Decoding of Goppa Codes," IEEE
     Trans. Information Theory, Vol IT 21, pp 203-207, 1975.

APPENDIX

FUZZY CORRECTION CAPACITY

S.HARARI
Laboratoire de Probabilités
Université PARIS VI.

1. GENERAL ARRAY CODES : (3)

1.1. Introduction :

The combination of two single parity check detecting codes yield a single error correcting code through the usual construction. This is done by setting the information bits into a rectangular array and by taking a vertical and a horizontal parity check. A single error in the information bits has a consequence that the corresponding horizontal and vertical parity checks fail thereby localizing the error.

Figure 1.

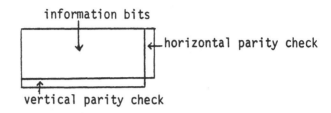

information bits

horizontal parity check

vertical parity check

Figure 1. Array of two error detecting codes.

1.2. <u>Single wing codes</u> : $\binom{3}{}$

In the preceding construction each information bit is checked by two parity check bits. Given r parity check bits, how many information bits can be checked by distinct couples of parity check bits ? The answer is $\binom{r}{2} = \frac{r(r-1)}{2}$ which gives rise to a $\left(\frac{r(r+1)}{2} , \frac{r(r-1)}{2}\right)$ single error correcting linear code named single wing code, and noted by A(r,1). A(r,1) can be represented by figure 2.

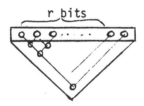

r bits

Figure 2 : A(r,1) single wing code with r redundancy bits.

Information bits are put in the lower triangle. The r parity checks are computed by taking the mod 2 sums of the information bits along the solid lines. Decoding is done by recomputing the parity check bits , of the received word. In the case where two of them fail, an error has occurred at the intersection of the solid lines passing by these two faulty parity checks.

Figure 3.

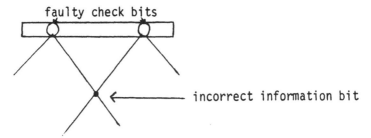

faulty check bits

incorrect information bit

Figure 3. Decoding of a single error for a wing code.

1.3. <u>Multiple wing codes</u> :

The parity check bits of a single wing codes, called parity check axis will be used to check many wings as we now show. Let $A_1(r,1)$, $A_2(r,1)$,..., $A_s(r,1)$ be s $\left(\frac{r(r+1)}{2}, \frac{r(r-1)}{2} \right)$ single wing code. Adding an extra parity check to each wing code and taking the mod 2 sum, componentwise of each of the s single wing code yields a $\left[\frac{1}{2} rs(r-1) +r+s, \frac{1}{2} rs(r-1) \right]$ linear single error correcting code. The extra parity check for each wing is taken as the sum of the information bits of the given wing.

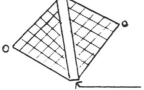

parity check axis.

Figure 4. A(r,2) a 2 wing code.

The parameters of the code must satisfy the equality

$$1 + \left(\begin{array}{c} \frac{r}{2} s(r-1) + r + s \\ 1 \end{array} \right) < 2^{r+s} < 1 + \left(\begin{array}{c} \frac{r}{2}(r-1)+r+s-1 \\ 1 \end{array} \right)$$

$$+ \left(\begin{array}{c} \frac{r}{2}(r-1)+r+s-1 \\ 2 \end{array} \right)$$

The preceding diophantine equations have only a finite number
of solutions listed in (3). We have the following further
result.

Theorem : Each (n,k) single error correcting code is representable
in at most two ways as a wing code.

Proof : The proof is based on the fact there are only two solutions
to the diophantine equation

$$sr(r-1) = s'r'(r'-1)$$

$$s + r = s' + r'$$

$$(s,r) \neq (s', r').$$

The preceding wing codes form a finite set of low rate easily
decodable codes. They are part of an infinite set of codes
which we now introduce.

2. CHECKERBOARD CODES (2) :

2.1. Some auxiliary material :

Let M(a,b) be the set of all (a,b) matrices with coefficients
in GF(2). Let A(a,b) be the subspace of M(a,b) generated by the
matrices (α_{ij}) having the property that there exists

$i_o \in \{1,\dots,a\}$ such that for all j, $\alpha_{i_o j} = 1$, for all i,

$i \neq i_o$ $\alpha_{ij} = 0$.

In other word $A(a,b)$ is the subspace of $M(a,b)$ of matrices

with "constant rows".

Let $B(a,b)$ be a subset of $M(a,b)$ made of matrices with

"constant columns" and of total weight $\frac{ab}{2}$. $B(a,b)$ is not a

linear subspace of $M(a,b)$.

However $|B| = 2^{b-1}$ and the distance between two matrices of

$B(a,b)$ is at least a.

2.2. <u>Definition of checkerboard codes</u> :

We have the following theorem defining checkerboard codes.

<u>Theorem</u> : The set $A(a,b) + B(a,b)$ is a linear subspace of $M(a,b)$

noted by $D(a,b)$. The sum $A(a,b) + B(a,b)$ is a direct sum

decomposition. $D(a,b)$ is a linear code whose parameters are

$(a\,b,\ a+b-1,\ \inf\ (a,b))$.

<u>Proof</u> : It is done in many steps. We will first show that

$D(a,b) = A(a,b) + B(a,b)$ is a linear subspace of $M(a,b)$.

Let $x + y$ and $x'+y'$ be two distinct elements in $D(a,b)$.

$x,x' \in A(a,b)$, y, $y' \in B(a,b)$. Let I denote the "all one"

matrix of $M(a,b)$. We then have :

$x+y+x'+y' = (x+x') + (y+y') = (I+x+x') + (I +y+y')$

$A(a,b)$ being a linear subspace $x + x'$ and $I+x+x'$ belong to

$A(a,b)$.

If y, y' ε B then either y + y' or I+y+y' belong to B.

D(a,b) is therefore a linear subspace.

Let us calculate its minimum weight.

Let x ε A have u non zero rows ; y ε B having v ($\leq \frac{b}{2}$) non

zero columns. The weight of x + y is u(b-v) + v(a-u).

We therefore have : w(x+y) $\geq$ inf (a,b).

D(a,b) includes words of weight a and b and therefore of

weight inf(a,b).

Finally let us show that D(a,b) = A(a,b) + B(a,b) is a direct

sum decomposition. This will prove that dimension of D(a,b) is

a + b - 1.

Consider x+y = x'+ y'   x,x' ε A(a,b), y,y' ε B(a,b)

set u = x + x' ; v = y + y'

we have x + y = (x + u) + (y + u).

If u $\neq$ o, u ε A then y + u $\notin$ B(a,b).

$$Q.E.D.$$

Remark : The name checkerboard code follows from the structure

of codewords of D(a,b).

Checkerboard codes are low rate codes. They are easily decoda-

ble using a version of correlation decoder.

2.3. Decoding of checkerboard codes :

Given a codeword matrix C of D(a,b) one notices that any

square (2,) submatrix of C is one among the following (2,2)

matrices.

$$\begin{pmatrix} 0 & 0 \\ 0 & 0 \end{pmatrix} , \begin{pmatrix} 1 & 1 \\ 1 & 1 \end{pmatrix} , \begin{pmatrix} 1 & 0 \\ 0 & 1 \end{pmatrix} , \begin{pmatrix} 0 & 1 \\ 1 & 0 \end{pmatrix} , \begin{pmatrix} 1 & 1 \\ 0 & 0 \end{pmatrix} , \begin{pmatrix} 0 & 0 \\ 1 & 1 \end{pmatrix} , \begin{pmatrix} 1 & 0 \\ 1 & 0 \end{pmatrix} , \begin{pmatrix} 0 & 1 \\ 0 & 1 \end{pmatrix}$$

These 8 matrices have the property that the mod 2 sum of their coefficients is zero. They are the only (2,2) GF(2) matrices having this property.

Decoding is done in the following manner. Given a received matrix, test the mod 2 sum of the coefficients of a sufficient set of submatrices. A single error has as a consequence that four (2,2) submatrices surrounding the error fail the test. These four failing matrices localize the error, allowing correction.

Such a decoding algorithm corrects all errors up to the minimum distance at least.

3. FUZZY MINIMUM DISTANCE :

The minimum distance of a code does not caracterize well the actual
performance of a code on a given channel. Two codes of same length
and same minimum distance have different residual error rate depending on the repartition of non zero coefficients of the weight
enumerator polynomial. This is why we introduce the fuzzy minimum
distance concept. For this we need more general definition of codes
and decoding algorithms.

3.1. Codes and decoding algorithms over an arbitrary field :

Let E be a finite dimensional vector space over a field K and
$d : E \times E \rightarrow K$ be a distance on E. Let C be a subset of E
C will be called a code. $d_C = \inf \{d(x,y)\ x \neq y, x,y \in C\}$ is
the minimum distance of the code C. We will be interested in
codes with positive minimum distance.

A decoding algorithm for the code C is a map A from a set F,
$C \subset F \subseteq E$, $A : F \rightarrow C$ such that $F_{|C} = id_C$.

A is complete if F = E ; trivial if F = C. A is a maximum
likelihood algorithm if

$d(x, A(x)) = \min \{(d(x,y))\ y \in C \}$

The set of vectors that are decoded into the same codeword are
called classes of A. For a given $c \in C$ the classes of c
$A^{-1}(c)$ will be denoted by $\bar{c}$. The classes of A need not be
spheres, or even connected components of E.

Definition : A decoding algorithm A : F → C of a code C is linear if the classes of A are spheres of equal radius.

3.2. Fuzzy correction capacity :

An algorithm that decodes beyond the minimum distance is caracterized by the relative density of strict decoding capacity spheres to the actual classes of the algorithm. We have the following definition.

Definition : The correction function of a code (C,A) is a mapping R^+ → (o,1) defined by

p (r) = min {dens ($\bar{v}$, B(v,r)), v ∈ C}

dens (A;B) is the density of the set A in the set B. If A and B are finite then dens(A,B) = $\dfrac{(A \cap B)}{|B|}$.

The correction function caracterizes the decoding algorithm. The correction function is equal to one for r less than the minimum distance of the code.

For a linear algorithm and for a distance on the underlying space E which is translation invariant we have the following property.

p (r) = dens ($\bar{v}$, B(v,r)), any v ∈ C.

Theorem : For a given code (C,A) if there exists r > o such that p(r) = 1, then the correction function is constant on (o,r).

Proof : Let A, B,C be three subsets of E. The following transitivity relation holds :

dens (C,B) $\geq$ dens (C,A). dens (A,B).

Let us compute p(s), s ε (o, r{.

From B(v,s)⊂ B(v,r) we have that dens(B(v,r), B(v,s)) = 1.

Q.E.D.

Remark - The correction function need not be non increasing. Its
variations are linked to the connectedness property of the
classes of the algorithm

 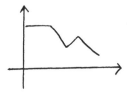

This leads us to the following definition.

Definition : A code (C,A) is regular if its correction function
is non increasing. A linear decoding algorithm is a regular
algorithm.

Definition : A code (C,A) has a (t,p) error correction capacity
if.f.   inf {p(r), p, r ≤ t } = p(t,p)   is the fuzzy error
correction capacity of the code C for the algorithm A.

- A (t,1) error correcting code is a t error correcting code
   in the usual sense.

- A regular code is (t, p(t)) error correcting.

3.3. Correction function and probability of correct decoding.

The correction function of a code is linked to the probability
of correct word decoding by the following. We have to distinguish two cases.

a) General case :

For a code (C,A) the probability on E that a vector x ε E

is decoded into a codeword v ε C, given a uniform distribution

on E knowing that the distance between x and v is at most t is :

$Pr(A(x) = v \mid d(x,v) \leq t) = Pr(x \in \bar{v} \mid x \in B(v,t)) =$

dens $(\bar{v}, B(v,t))$.

This probability is equal to the correction function p(t).

b) Let us suppose that E is a vector space over GF(q), C a code of

length n ; A an algorithm with decoding classes that are

isomorphic.

For such a code Pr $(A(x) = v \mid d(x,v) = t)$ depends only on t.

Let g(t) be this quantity.

<u>Theorem</u> : The probability g(t) and the correction function

p(t) of the code C are linked by

$$g(t) = p(t) + (p(t) - p(t-1)) \sum_{r=0}^{t-1} \binom{n}{r}\binom{n}{t}^{-1} (q-1)^{r-t}.$$

<u>Proof</u> : From the inclusion $B(v,t-1) \subset B(v,t)$ we deduce

$B(v,t-1) \cap \bar{v} \subset B(v,t) \cap \bar{v}$, therefore

$$g(t) = \frac{|(B(v,t) - B(v,t-1)) \cap \bar{v}|}{|B(v,t) - B(v,t-1)|} = \frac{|B(v,t) \cap \bar{v}| - |B(v,t-1) \cap \bar{v}|}{|B(v,t)| - |B(v,t-1)|}$$

$$= p(t) + (p(t) - p(t-1)) \frac{|B(v,t-1)|}{|B(v,t)| - |B(v,t-1)|}$$

For C under the given hypothesis $|B(v,t)| - |B(v,t-1)| = \binom{n}{t} (q-1)^t$

Therefore $\dfrac{|B(v,t-1)|}{|B(v,t) - B(v,t-1)|} = \displaystyle\sum_{r=0}^{t-1} \binom{n}{r}\binom{n}{t}^{-1}(q-1)^{r-t}.$

Q.E.D.

c) Same hypothesis, q = 2.

We will show how the probability of correct decoding after using this code on a binary symmetric channel can be obtained by the correcting function of this code. To this aim we need an auxiliary function f which now define

$$f : (o,1) \rightarrow (o,1)$$

for $k \in \{0,1,\ldots,n\}$, $f(\underline{k}) = g(k)$

$x \in (o,1)$ $f(x) = (g([nx]+1)-g([nx]))(nx-[nx])+g([nx])$

f(x) is a continuous and piecewise linear function on (o,1).

Let us recall that the continuity modulus of f(x) on (o,1) is given by

$w(u) = \max \{(|f(x) - f(y)|) \mid |x-y| \le u\} \; ; \; x, y, u \in (o,1).$

w is a monotonic non decreasing function such that w(o) = o

and $\dfrac{1 - f(1)}{2}$ $x < w(x) < x.$

For a binary symmetric memoryless channel, of crossover probability a the probability of correct decoding for the code is given by

$$P(a) = \sum_{k=0}^{n} \binom{n}{k} a^k (1-a)^{n-k} g(k). \qquad (*)$$

Theorem : For a given binary symmetric channel of crossover

probability a the performance of a code of length n is given

asymptotically by the correction function of this code :

$$|P(a) - f(a)| \leq w(\frac{1}{\sqrt{n}})$$

Proof : Consider the sequence of polynomials

$$P_n(x) = \sum_{k=0}^{n} x^k(1-x)^{n-k} \; h(\frac{k}{n})$$

$\{P_n(x)\}$ n ε N converges uniformly to f(x)   (1).

Q.E.D.

Corollary 1 : The probability of correct decoding P(a) of a

binary code (C,A) of correction function p(t) is given by

$$P(a) = \frac{1 - 2a}{1-a} \sum_{k=0}^{n} \sum_{i=0}^{n} \binom{n}{i} a^k (1-a)^{n-k} \; p(k) + (2a)^n \; p(n).$$

Proof : The result is obtained by replacing g(t) by its value
in the equation (*).

$$g(k) = p(k) + (p(k) - p(k-1)) \sum_{i=o}^{k} \binom{n}{i} \binom{n}{k}^{-1}$$

Remark : In the case of a t error correcting algorithm with no
decoding beyond error capacity the correction function has a
simple form.

$$p(k) = 1 \qquad o \leq k \leq t$$

$$p(k) = \sum_{i=o}^{t} \binom{n}{i} / \sum_{i=o}^{k} \binom{n}{i} \qquad t \leq k \leq n.$$

Therefore $g(t) = \begin{cases} o & k > t \\ 1 & k \leq t \end{cases}$

In this case we find the usual expression for P(a).

$$P(a) = \sum_{k=o}^{t} \binom{n}{k} a^{k} (1-a)^{n-k}$$

CONCLUSION :

Bad codes are good to use on very noisy channels. Corollary 1
shows that for a binary symmetric channel of probability of
error equal to a, the codes with biggest correct decoding probability are not those with the greatest minimum distance.

Example : Consider the $((2t + 1)^2, 2t + 1)$ binary checkerboard
codes, $t \geq 1$. These codes are (t,1) correcting but also (r,p)
correcting.

For $t < r < 2t$, $g(r) = 1 - (4t + 2)\left(\binom{2t+1}{r}^2\right)^{-1} \times$

$$\sum_{i=t+1}^{r} \binom{2t+1}{i} \binom{4t^2+t}{r-i}$$

The best binary (49,13) code C_1 has minimum distance 16. The corresponding checkerboard code C_2 has same parameters and minimum distance 7. $P_1(a) \leq P_2(a)$ for $a \geq 10^{-1}$, showing that the checkerboard code performs better than the code with largest minimum distance.

BIBLIOGRAPHY :

(1) Bernstein - Propriétés extrêmales des polynômes (en russe)1937.

(2) Harari-Montaron - Capacité floue de correction - Colloque
    Mathématiques discrètes - "Codes et hypergraphes".
    Université libre de Bruxelles. Avril 1978.

(3) Montaron - Codes à ailerons, codes à damiers et constructions
    combinatoires. Thèse 3ème Cycle - Université Paris VI. Mai 1978.

NONLINEAR FLOWER-CODES

by

ALAIN HUBERMAN
Faculté des Sciences, Yaoundé, Cameroun

I – INTRODUCTION

The problem is to find some codes with maximal cardinality for given length and minimum distance; some nonlinear codes will fill the space much more than linear codes do; for example, the nonlinear Preparata codes have twice as many words as the best linear code of the same length.

We describe the flower construction for nonlinear codes: we take a linear code, called kernel, and we complete it with some coset. We shall regard the Kerdock code built with the first order Reed-Muller code as a kernel and the cosets are bilinear forms.

II – REED-MULLER CODES

Definition: (cf. VAN LINT [8] p. 29 and MACWILLIAMS and SLOANE [5]).

The binary Reed-Muller code of order r and length $n = 2^m$ for $0 \leqslant r \leqslant m$ (denoted by RM(r, m)) is the set of all the vectors f, where $f(v_1, \ldots, v_m)$ is a Boolean polynomial of degree r; $v_1, \ldots, v_m$ are the rows of a matrix whose columns are the integers $1, 2, \ldots, 2^{m-1}$ in binary form.

Example :   RM(1, 3). (cf. VAN LINT [8] p. 29)

RM(1, 4). (cf. MACWILLIAMS and SLOANE [5] p. 374).

III – CODES DEFINED BY BILINEAR FORMS

(cf. J.-M. GOETHALS (2))

We will use alternate bilinear (symplectic) and quadratic forms to express the first- and second- order Reed-Muller codes. To a bilinear form over a vector space V, we associate a unique matrix of order $m : B = (b_{ij}) = B(e_i, e_j)$ in a basis $e_1, \ldots, e_m$ of V.

The matrix associated to the symplectic form is antisymmetric :

$$b_{ii} = 0$$

$$b_{ij} + b_{ji} = 0 \qquad 1 \leqslant i, j \leqslant m$$

We identify $\mathscr{B}$, the set of all bilinear alternate forms over V with the set of the antisymmetric matrices of order m over $GF(q)$.

Expression of R M(2, m).

Each word of R M(2, m) is a Boolean function S(v) of degree $\leqslant 2$.

$$S(v) = \sum_{1 \leqslant i \leqslant j \leqslant m} q_{ij} v_i v_j + \sum_{1 \leqslant i \leqslant m} l_i v_i + \varepsilon$$

We can write this as a matrix or a function:

$$S(v) = vQv^T + Lv^T + \varepsilon = Q(v) + L(v) + \varepsilon$$

where $Q(v) = vQv^T$; $Q = (q_{ij})$ is an upper triangular binary matrix, $L(v) = Lv^T$, $L = (l_1, \ldots, l_m)$, and $\varepsilon = 0$ or 1.

If Q(v) is fixed and the linear function $L(v) + \varepsilon$ runs over R M(1, m), then S(v) runs over one coset of R M(1, m) in R M(2, m); this coset is characterized by the matrix Q; we can associate to this coset the symmetric matrix $B = Q + Q^T$; this matrix is associated to the bilinear form $B(u, v) = uBv^T$.

Example 1 : The R M(1, 4) of length 16 is generated by the first 5 rows. The R M(2, 4) is generated by the first 11 rows. The R M(2, 4) is formed by $2^{11-5} = 64$ cosets of R M(1, 4), one of these cosets is R M(1, 4) and the quadratic and symplectic forms associated to this coset are zero.

Example 2 : Another coset consists of the 16 vectors

$$v_1 v_2 + v_3 v_4 + R(1, 4) .$$

If we take the 4 vectors

$$\begin{cases} v_1 v_2 + v_3 v_4 \\ v_1 v_2 + v_3 v_4 + v_0 \\ v_1 v_2 + v_3 v_4 + v_1 \\ v_1 v_2 + v_3 v_4 + v_0 + v_1 \end{cases}$$

then
$$Q(v) = v_1 v_2 + v_3 v_4 \\ = (v_1, v_2, v_3, v_4)Q \begin{pmatrix} v_1 \\ v_2 \\ v_3 \\ v_4 \end{pmatrix}$$

$$Q = \begin{pmatrix} 0 & 1 & 0 & 0 \\ 0 & 0 & 0 & 0 \\ 0 & 0 & 0 & 1 \\ 0 & 0 & 0 & 0 \end{pmatrix} \quad \text{and} \quad B = Q + Q^T = \begin{pmatrix} 0 & 1 & 0 & 0 \\ 1 & 0 & 0 & 0 \\ 0 & 0 & 0 & 1 \\ 0 & 0 & 1 & 0 \end{pmatrix}$$

The symplectic form corresponding to this coset is $B(u, v) = u\, B\, v^T = u_2 v_1 + u_1 v_2 + u_4 v_3 + u_3 v_4$.

There is a bijection between symplectic forms and cosets of R M(1, m) in R M(2, m). We denote the coset associated to the symplectic form B by C(B).

Example: $C(B_0) = R M(1, m)$.

We are interested in the binary codes built by making the union of cosets C(B) of R M(1, m) in R M(2, m).

If Y is a subset of B, we study the code $C(Y) = \underset{B \in Y}{\cup} C(B)$.

The distance distribution of the code C(Y) is obtained from the weight distribution of the coset $(B - B')$, $B, B' \in Y$.

The weight distribution of all the cosets C(B) depends only on the rank of B. When the rank of B is 2k, the coefficient A_i of $\Sigma A_i z^i$ is the weight enumerator of C(B).

Weight i	Number of words A_i
$2^{m-1} - 2^{m-k-1}$	2^{2k}
2^{m-1}	$2^{m+1} - 2^{2k+1}$
$2^{m-1} + 2^{m-k-1}$	2^{2k}

Example: $v_1 v_2 + v_3 v_4 + R M(1, 4)$

$$B = \begin{pmatrix} 0 & 1 & 0 & 0 \\ 1 & 0 & 0 & 0 \\ 0 & 0 & 0 & 1 \\ 0 & 0 & 1 & 0 \end{pmatrix}$$

rank$(B) = 4 \Rightarrow k = 2 \Rightarrow A_6 = A_{10} = 16$ is the weight enumerator of $R(2, m)$.

Maximal Set

The problem is to find the best code $C(Y)$, i.e. the code with the largest cardinality. This code has been studied by P. DELSARTE & J.M. GOETHALS [1].

The associated subset Y was called (m, k)-set of alternating bilinear forms and their number is bounded by $C^{\ell-k+1}$ with $\ell = (m/2)$ and $C = 2^{(m/2)/\ell}$; $|Y| \leqslant C^{1-k+1}$.
Definition : When the above inequality is an equality, we get the maximal (m, k)-set and the code $C(Y)$ is called k-optimal. These codes are denoted $D G(m, k)$ and are generalizations of Kerdock codes (DG stands for DELSARTE and GOETHALS).

IV – KERDOCK, PREPARATA AND OTHER FLOWER CODES

When $k = \frac{1}{2} m$, m even, we have the Kerdock codes of length 2^m, $K(m)$ ($m \geqslant 4$ even); $K(m)$ is the union of $2^{m-1} - 1$ cosets of $R M(1, m)$ in $R M(2, m)$ and $R M(1, m)$.

We have 2^m vectors of weight $2^{m-1} - 2^{1/2 m-1}$ and 2^m vectors of weight $2^{m-1} + 2^{1/2 m-1}$. $R(1, m)$ contains $2^{m+1} - 2$ vectors of weight 2^{m-1} and the words "0" and "1".

Weight (distance) distribution of the Kerdock codes K(m):

i	A_i
0	1
$2^{m-1} - 2^{(m-2)/2}$	$2^m(2^{m-1} - 1)$
2^{m-1}	$2^{m+1} - 2$
$2^{m-1} + 2^{(m-2)/2}$	$2^m(2^{m-1} - 1)$
2^m	1

These codes contain 2^m words, and their minimum distance is $d = 2^{m-1} - 2^{(m-1)/2}$.

For m = 4, we have the extended Nordstrom-Robinson code of length 16. One very interesting property is the "duality" existing between Kerdock codes and Preparata codes.

Preparata Codes: The Preparata code of length 2^m , m even $\geqslant 4$, denoted P(m), is the union of a linear code Π and $2^{m-1} - 1$ cosets of Π in the RM code of order m−2.

Recall that RM(m−2,m) is equivalent to the extended Hamming code and its dual is the RM(1, m) code. We have:

$$R(1, m) \subseteq \Pi^{\perp} \subseteq RM(2, m) .$$

K(4) = P(4) = NR_{16} extended Nordstrom-Robinson code [6].

Goethals Codes: J.M. Goethals has constructed a nonlinear triple-error-correcting code which is the "dual" of the DG(m, (m−2)/m) code. For m = 2t + 2 $\geqslant$ 6, this code, denoted G(m), has length 2^m, contains 2^s words, where s = $2^m - 3m + 1$, and its minimum distance is 8. The G(m) code contains four times as many codewords as the extended triple-error-correcting BCH code of the same length (cf. GOETHALS [2]).

BIBLIOGRAPHY

[1]   P. Delsarte, J.M. Goethals, "Alternating bilinear forms over G F(q)", J. Comb, Theory (A), 19, pp. 26-50 (1975).

[2]   J.M. Goethals, "Nonlinear codes defined by quadratic forms over G F(2)", Information and Control, 3, n.1, pp. 43-74 (1976).

[3]   A. Huberman, "Codes en pétales", Thèse 3ème cycle, Université Paris VII, (1977).

[4]   A Kerdock, "A class of low-rate nonlinear binary codes", Information and Control, 20, pp. 182-187 (1972).

[5]   J. MacWilliams, N. Sloane, "The theory of error-correcting codes", North-Holland (1977).

[6]   Nordstrom Robinson, "An optimum nonlinear code", Information and Control, 11, pp. 613-616 (1967).

[7]   F. Preparata, "A class of optimum nonlinear double-error-correcting codes", Information and Control, 13, pp. 378-400 (1968).

[8]   J. Van Lint, "Coding theory", Lecture notes in Mathematics, n. 201, Springer-Verlag (1971).

REALIZATION OF ERROR-FREE TRANSMISSION

USING MICROPROCESSORS

B.Furht, PhD.,dipl.ing.
S.Matić, dipl.ing.

Institute "Boris Kidrič"-Vinča
P.O.Box 522, 11001 Belgrade
Yugoslavia

1. INTRODUCTION

Some practical results, obtained during the realization of error-free transmission equipment, are described. Universal automatic error corrector based on 8-bit microprocessor INTEL 8080A has been designed. The error correction has been achieved using hybrid system, combining forward error correction (FEC) with error detection and re-transmission via a decision feedback line (ARQ-automatic request for repeat). Some error control codes based on BCH codes, combining with data interleaving, have been implemented and analyzed.

2. DESCRIPTION OF THE AUTOMATIC ERROR CORRECTOR

The system is designed as a universal error corrector, which enables the implementation of different error control codes by simple changing the corresponding PROM memory chips, that contain program for particular codes. The block scheme of the corrector is shown in Figure 1.

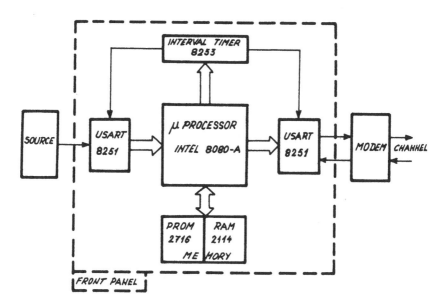

Figure 1. Block scheme of the automatic error corrector

The universal system has the following I/O and memory facilities:

  . 2 USART - universal synchronous/asynchronous receiver/transmitter

  . 6K-bytes EPROM (PROM) memory for program

  . 2K-bytes RAM memory for data

  . Programmable interval timer for automatic selection of data-rate of
    USART-s.

The memory can be extended very easy if necessary. The mode of operation
(encoder or decoder) can be choosen by a switch on the front panel.
The system provides the capability for full-duplex communication between
itself and an asynchronous interface to a computer or terminal over EIA
RS232C lines at speeds 50 to 2400 baud, with character format of 1 start
bit, 5 and 7/8 data bits, and 1, 1,5 or 2 stop bits. The choise of transmission rate, number of bits per character and the length of the stop
bit are selectable by the switches on the front panel.

3. APPLIED ERROR CONTROL CODES

The applied error control codes are based on the BCH codes[1,2,3], which have the possibility that for any positive integers m and t, there is a code that consists of blocks length $n=2^m-1$, that corrects t errors and requires no more than mt parity check bits. Taking into account that the
number of bits per character in our system is 5 or 7, the original BCH
codes are transformed into shortened BCH codes, which have the number of
information bits (k) as a multipl of 5 or 7. The table 1. shows the analyzed shortened BCH codes. The transmission rate R=k/n and error correction rate V=t/n are also given.

	n	k	t	r=mt	R	V	
	11	7	1	4	0.636	0.090	
*	15	7	2	8	0.467	0.134	"7 bits"
	29	14	3	15	0.482	0.103	character
	31	21	2	10	0.677	0.064	
	9	5	1	4	0.555	0.111	
	13	5	2	8	0.384	0.153	"5 bits"
	15	5	3	10	0.333	0.200	character
	30	15	3	15	0.500	0.100	
	30	20	2	10	0.667	0.067	

Table 1. Analyzed shortened BCH codes

The BCH codes are powerful for protecting against randomly distributed
bit errors. However, the nature of the channel is such that bursts of
errors can occur. For this reason the data are first grouped into packets
and then data randomizing is performed before transmission.

For example, the encoding procedure for the BCH code (15,7,2), denoted
with the asterisk in the table 1, is as follows:

1. The input data (7 bits) are converted into a BCH code, where each

each character to be transmitted is of 15 bits, where 7 bits are original input character and 8 bits are redudant check bits, which have been
added to give error correcting/detecting capabilities.

2. The 15 bits characters are grouped into packet of 15 words, where
each packet being preceded by a 15-bit synchronization character, as
shown in Figure 2. The total packet length in this case is 16x15=240bits.

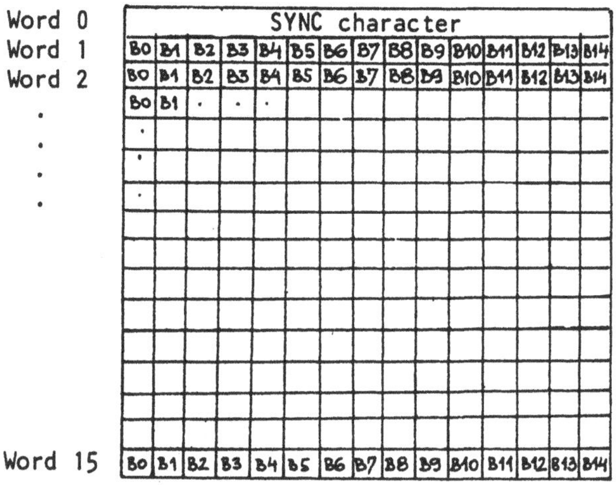

Figure 2. Transmitted packet of data for BCH code (15,7,2)
           B0-B6 original input character
           B7-B14 parity check bits

3. In order to protect data against burst errors tha data packet is not
transmitted serially, but data interleaved, sending bit B0 of word 1,
bit B0 of word 2,...bit B0 of word 15, bit 1 of word 1, bit B1 of word 2,
etc., until all bits have been sent.

4. Decoder first recognizes the start character (SYNC) and then reassem-
bles the transmitted data in reverse order.

5. Each 15-bit character is tested using decoding algorithm and error
correction/detection is applied if necessary.

6. The data packet is acklowledged positively or negatively. The negative
response is a request for retransmission of the packet, if the number of

detected errors was high (in this case greater than 2 and less than 5),
and the transmitter repeats the data packet.

Using described interleaving the data bursts of errors are transformed
to the random errors, that can be corrected by the BCH code.

4. ENCODING AND DECODING ALGORITHMS

The BCH codes are defined by parity check matrix

$$
M = \begin{bmatrix}
1 & 1 & \cdots\cdots & 1 \\
\alpha & \alpha^3 & \cdots\cdots & \alpha^{2t-1} \\
\alpha^2 & \alpha^6 & \cdots\cdots & \alpha^{2(2t-1)} \\
\cdot & & & \\
\alpha^{n-1} & \alpha^{3(n-1)} & \cdots & \alpha^{(n-1)(2t-1)}
\end{bmatrix}
\tag{1}
$$

where α is a primitive element of the finite field $GF(2^m)$. For the code
(15,7,2) the ireducible polynomial is $g(x)=x^4+x+1$ and the parity check
matrix may be written as

$$
M = \begin{bmatrix}
1000 & 1000 \\
0100 & 0001 \\
0010 & 0011 \\
0001 & 0101 \\
1100 & 1111 \\
0110 & 1000 \\
0011 & 0001 \\
1101 & 0011 \\
1010 & 0101 \\
0101 & 1111 \\
1110 & 1000 \\
0111 & 0001 \\
1111 & 0011 \\
1011 & 0101 \\
1001 & 1111
\end{bmatrix}
\tag{2}
$$

The generator matrix in reduced echalon form can be obtained from the
condition

$$
G \cdot M = 0
\tag{3}
$$

For the code (15,7,2) G becomes

$$
G = \begin{bmatrix} 1000000 \,|\, 10001011 \\ 0100000 \,|\, 11001110 \\ 0010000 \,|\, 01100111 \\ 0001000 \,|\, 10111000 \\ 0000100 \,|\, 01011100 \\ 0000010 \,|\, 00101110 \\ 0000001 \,|\, 00010111 \end{bmatrix} = \begin{bmatrix} I \,|\, G' \end{bmatrix} \tag{4}
$$

The parity check matrix M and generator matrix G are stored in the PROM memory for the corresponding BCH code. Then, the encoding algorithm is very simple and consists of receiving the 7-bit message word and, using the stored look-up table for generator matrix G, to construct the 8-bit check word. Adding the check word to the message word the full 15-bit character is formed. The 8-bit check word is constructed by the modulo-2 addition of the corresponding rows of matrix G'.

For example, if the message word is 1010100, the check word becomes:

   10001011 ⊕ 01100111 ⊕ 01011100 = 10110000

and the transmitted character is therefore: a= 101010010110000.

As the implemented BCH codes are single, double and triple error correcting codes, the simple decoding algorithms can be used. For the single error correcting codes the syndrome computation directly gives the error position. For the double and triple error correcting codes, Banerji[4] and Peterson[5] decoding algorithms have been implemented, respectively.

The decoding procedure for double error correcting BCH codes is as follows. First, from the received sequence r and the parity check matrix M syndroms s are computed

$$
s = \begin{bmatrix} S_1 \,|\, S_3 \end{bmatrix} = r \cdot M \tag{5}
$$

where the syndroms correspond to the bits in error α^r and α^s in the following way

$$
S_1 = \alpha^r + \alpha^s \tag{6}
$$

$$S_3 = \alpha^{3r} + \alpha^{3s} \tag{7}$$

Banerji has shown that

$$1 + \frac{S_3}{S_1^3} = \frac{\alpha^{s-r}}{1 + \alpha^{2(s-r)}} = f(s-r) \tag{8}$$

so it is possible to form the table which gives the correspondence between s-r and f(s-r). For the BCH code (15,7,2) this table is given as:

s-r	1	2	3	4	5	6	7
f(s-r)	α^8	α^5	α	α^2	1	α^{10}	α^4

From the eq. (6) it can be obtained

$$\alpha^r = \frac{S_1}{1 + \alpha^{s-r}} \tag{9}$$

Therefore, the implemented decoding algorithm consists of the following
steps:

   Step 1: Compute syndroms S_1 and S_3 from (5).
   Step 2: Compute $f(s-r) = 1 + S_3/S_1^3$.
   Step 3: From the stored look-up table f(s-r) find corresponding s-r.
   Step 4: Compute α^r from (9) and corresponding r.
   Step 5: Knowing r from s-r compute s.

Example. Assume that the transmitted sequence is a=101010010110000, and
the received sequence is r=101000010111000, so the errors are in 4th and
11th positions. The syndroms are:

$$s = r \cdot M = \left[1011 | 1110\right] = \left[\alpha^{13} | \alpha^{10}\right]$$

The function f(s-r) becomes:

$$f(s-r) = 1 + S_3/S_1^3 = 1 + \alpha^{10}/\alpha^{39} = 1 + \alpha^{10}/\alpha^9 = 1 + \alpha = \alpha^4$$

From the table the corresponding s-r=7. Now, from eq.(9) α^r can be computed:

$$\alpha^r = S_1/(1 + \alpha^{s-r}) = \alpha^{13}/(1 + \alpha^7) = \alpha^{13}/\alpha^9 = \alpha^4$$

so the error locations are r=4 and s=7+4=11.

For the triple error correcting codes Peterson algorithm[5] has been used, which contains the following steps:

1. Syndrom computation using (5).
2. Computation the elementary symetric functions σ_1, σ_2 and σ_3 solving the Newton's identities. The solutions are

$$\sigma_1 = S_1$$

$$\sigma_2 = \frac{S_1^2 S_3 + S_5}{S_1^3 + S_3}$$

(10)

$$\sigma_3 = \frac{S_3^2 + S_1 S_5}{S_1^3 + S_3} + S_1^3$$

3. Find the roots β_1, β_2 and β_3 of the polynomial

$$x^3 + \sigma_1 x^2 + \sigma_2 x + \sigma_3 = 0$$

(11)

which are the error locations.

5. CONCLUSION

The realized error corrector based on microprocessor enables the investigation and implementation of different error correcting codes. Some shortened BCH codes with data interleaving have been realized, however we intend to implemente the other effective codes as convolutional[6], Golay codes[7,8] etc. The comparative analysis of the codes will be performed in the near future by simulation and using the experiments on the real channels.

The implementation of more complex code, as concatenated codes[9] or BCH codes with more than 3-error correction[10], can be performed by multiprocessor microcomputer system, which has been also designed. The system consists of one master microprocessor and six slave microprocessors, where all microprocessors operate parallel at the same time. In this way it is possible to implemente very complex decoding algorithm dividing it in the particular sequences and distributing these sequences to the slave microprocessors for the handling.

References

1. Bose,R.C.,Ray-Chaudhuri,C.R., On a class of error-correcting binary group codes, Information and control, Vol.3,68,1960.

2. Hocquenghem,A., Codes correcteurs d'erreurs, Chiffres, Vol.2,147,1959.

3. Peterson,W.W.,Weldon,E.J., Error-correcting codes, MIT Press, 1972.

4. Banerji,R.B., A decoding procedure for double-error correcting Bose-Ray-Chaudhuri codes, Proc. IRE, Vol.49,1585,1961.

5. Peterson,W.W., Encoding and error correcting procedures for the Bose-Chaudhuri codes, IRE Trans. on information theory, Vol. IT-6,459,1960.

6. Viterbi,A.J., Convolutional codes and their performance in communication systems, IEEE Trans. communication technology, Vol. COM-19,751, 1971.

7. Golay,M.J.E., Binary coding, IRE Trans. on information theory, Vol.IT-4,23,1954.

8. Sloane,N.J.A., A short course on error correcting codes, Springer-Verlag, 1975.

9. Forney,G.D., Concatenated codes, MIT Res. Memo, No.37, 1966.

10. Berlekamp,E.R., Algebraic coding theory, McGraw-Hill, 1968.

11. Intel 8080 microcomputer systems user's manual, 1975.

LIST OF CONTRIBUTORS

Richard BLAHUT, Senior Engineer IBM, Owego, New York (USA).

Patrick G. FARRELL, Senior Lecturer, Electronics Laboratories, The University of Kent at Canterbury (England).

Borivoje FURHT, Research Engineer, Institute "Boris Kidrič", Vinča, Belgrade (Yugoslavia).

Jean-Marie GOETHALS, Professor, MBLE Research Laboratories, Brussels (Belgium).

Rodney GOODMAN, Lecturer, Electronic Engineer, The University of Hull (England).

Sami HARARI, Research Director, Paris (France).

Carlos HARTMANN, Professor, Syracuse University, 313 Link Hall (USA).

Alain HUBERMAN, Assistant Professor, Départment de Mathématique, Université de Yaoundé (Cameroun).

Spira MATIC, Research Engineer, Institute "Boris Kidrič", Vinča, Belgrade (Yugoslavia).

Robert McELIECE, Professor, Department of Mathematics, University of Illinois, Urbana (USA).

Jacobus VAN LINT, Professor, Department of Mathematics, Technological University of Eindhoven (Netherlands).

Coordinator of the course
Giuseppe LONGO, Istituto di Elettrotecnica ed Elettronica, Università di Trieste and CISM, Udine (Italy).

Printed in the United States
By Bookmasters